American
Freethinker

AMERICAN FREETHINKER

Elihu Palmer
and the Struggle for Religious Freedom
in the New Nation

Kirsten Fischer

PENN

UNIVERSITY OF PENNSYLVANIA PRESS

PHILADELPHIA

EARLY AMERICAN STUDIES

Series Editors
Daniel K. Richter, Kathleen M. Brown,
Max Cavitch, and David Waldstreicher

Exploring neglected aspects of our colonial, revolutionary, and early national history and culture, Early American Studies reinterprets familiar themes and events in fresh ways. Interdisciplinary in character, and with a special emphasis on the period from about 1600 to 1850, the series is published in partnership with the McNeil Center for Early American Studies.

A complete list of books in the series
is available from the publisher.

Copyright © 2021 University of Pennsylvania Press

All rights reserved.
Except for brief quotations used for purposes of review or scholarly citation, none of this book may be reproduced in any form by any means without written permission from the publisher.

Published by
University of Pennsylvania Press
Philadelphia, Pennsylvania 19104-4112
www.upenn.edu/pennpress

Printed in the United States of America
on acid-free paper
1 3 5 7 9 10 8 6 4 2

Library of Congress Cataloging-in-Publication Data

Names: Fischer, Kirsten, author.
Title: American freethinker : Elihu Palmer and the struggle for religious freedom in the new nation / Kirsten Fischer.
Other titles: Early American studies.
Description: 1st edition. | Philadelphia : University of Pennsylvania Press, [2021] | Series: Early American studies | Includes bibliographical references and index.
Identifiers: LCCN 2020015455 | ISBN 978-0-8122-5271-2 (hardcover)
Subjects: LCSH: Palmer, Elihu, 1764–1806. | Freethinkers—United States. | Deism—United States. | Freedom of religion—United States—History—18th century. | Freedom of religion—United States—History—19th century.
Classification: LCC BL2790.P28 F57 2021 | DDC 211/.5092 [B]—dc23
LC record available at https://lccn.loc.gov/2020015455

FRONTISPIECE. The engraved portrait of Elihu Palmer, which he considered a "good likeness" and that appeared as the frontispiece in the second edition of his book, *Principles of Nature; or, A Development of the Moral Causes of Happiness and Misery Among the Human Species* (1802). Courtesy of the American Antiquarian Society.

For Drew and Ava

CONTENTS

Prologue. "A Religious Tornado" — 1

PART I. EXPANSIVE CHRISTIANITY

Chapter 1. Steady Habits Upended — 13
Chapter 2. A Liberal Education — 34
Chapter 3. "All is Alive" — 55
Chapter 4. Freelance Universalist — 71

PART II. THE MAKING OF AN "INFIDEL"

Chapter 5. Palmer's Rubicon — 91
Chapter 6. Hard Fate — 113
Chapter 7. Fellowship — 132
Chapter 8. Sensitive Atoms — 150

PART III. LIGHTNING ROD

Chapter 9. Specter of Infidelity — 173
Chapter 10. Controversy Among Freethinkers — 190
Chapter 11. Weaponizing Freethought — 206
Chapter 12. The Best Kind of Revolution — 222

Epilogue. Into the Future — 242

Notes — 249
Index — 295
Acknowledgments — 303

NOTE ON STYLE

I have retained original spelling and punctuation when quoting from the primary sources with the exception of expanding archaic contractions. I have added small editorial changes in square brackets when it seemed necessary to clarify the text's meaning.

PROLOGUE

"A Religious Tornado"

THE NEWS SPREAD IN September 1802 that members of a secretive cult gathered regularly in New York City to mock Christianity and promote the irreligious and "wild philosophy" of the group's leader, a man named Elihu Palmer. According to a pamphlet then making the rounds, the "Columbian Illuminati" under "President Palmer" planned to remove Christians from leadership positions and "get all the public offices of the United States, filled with deists." The American republic would never survive such rule, the pamphlet implied. Freethinking deists revered a Creator-God, but they doubted or dismissed the saving sacrifice of a divine Jesus. Without a firm Christian foundation, morality must surely falter, jeopardizing the nation's political experiment in self-governance. Newspapers in several of the sixteen United States picked up the story and passed it along: Palmer the "infidel" posed a danger to the country.[1]

Maligned as a dangerous freethinker, Elihu Palmer might have reflected on how improbable such fame would have seemed just a decade ago. A simple newspaper advertisement ten years before had started him down his path toward unexpected infamy. In March 1792, the Philadelphia *National Gazette* had carried a brief notice of his upcoming lecture "against the divinity of Jesus Christ." Palmer, then twenty-seven, had given up his plan to become a minister, but he still loved to think and talk about theology. He considered himself an enlightened Christian with a rational faith that recognized Jesus as the fully human teacher of a sublime morality. This version of Christianity represented a vast improvement, he thought, over the gullible belief in a supernatural being who performed miracles and rose from the dead. Palmer had assumed his right to express his opinions freely, but ministers saw his open refutation of the Holy Trinity as the worst kind of blasphemy. Clergy from several Philadelphia churches conspired to shut him down, publishing anonymous attacks on his character. The verbal drubbing silenced Palmer for a while, but the humiliation also strengthened his resolve. He soon returned to public life determined to share his freethought—the skeptical and unorthodox ideas about religion he found so fascinating. In the years that followed, he came to reject Christianity outright and said as much in his lectures and publications. His religious convictions continued to evolve, but his passion for public speaking never waned. He traveled and lectured even after he lost his eyesight to yellow fever in 1793. Once an avid reader who explored the world by reading books, Palmer adjusted to blindness by relying on conversation partners. He created discussion groups everywhere he went and continued to lecture, aided by a strong memory and his fine speaking voice. Eventually, he dictated a book of some three hundred pages and edited a weekly newspaper that ran to sixty-five issues. Resilience and grit got him this far, as did the pursuit of meaningful work.[2]

Palmer was driven by the belief that he held the solution to the world's most tenacious problems of inequity and violence. His attacks on established religion were not his main point; they marked only the first step in a larger project. His ultimate aim was to share insights about the natural world that he thought could lead to human happiness everywhere. True morality, he insisted, did not rest on divine revelation but resided in the facts of nature. In speaking tours throughout the nation, from upstate New York to Augusta, Georgia, he explained that an accurate understanding of the physical makeup of the universe and of humanity's relationship to all living things would do more to develop ethical conduct than anything heard in houses of worship. These natural facts could be observed and agreed upon everywhere in the world, he said, and so end religious superstition and strife once and for all. His opponents called him an atheist, a description he firmly rejected. But what insights, exactly, did Palmer wish to share, and why is this once-famous freethinker virtually unknown to us today?

This book tells the story of Palmer's unusual path from his Calvinist upbringing in Connecticut, through his training as a minister, to his increasingly unconventional religious freethought—all in the context of a new nation brimming with ideas about how best to ensure its future. Everyone understood that a self-governing republic depended on the virtuous conduct of its people. Without an authoritarian ruler to strong-arm them into compliance, citizens of a representative democracy must *choose* to observe the law and norms of civility. To that end, the nation needed a revolution in social conscience. The Philadelphia physician Benjamin Rush expressed this clearly. "It remains yet to establish and perfect our new forms of government," Rush wrote in 1787, "and to prepare the principles, morals, and manners of our citizens, for these forms of government." Only a virtuous people would prioritize proper conduct over lawless striving for personal gain. As a newspaper put it in 1801, "Without morality no free government can long be sustained, and without religion there can be no security to morals." This much was clear: the health of the republic rested on the moral character of its constituents.[3]

But there was a catch. The nation was conducting an experiment in religious freedom. The Bill of Rights and several state constitutions articulated freedom of conscience as a right that merited protection, leaving many to wonder about the effects of such liberty. Would virtue weaken without the supporting brace of a required religion? Would public expressions of religious skepticism prove contagious, corroding citizens' faith and with it their rectitude? John Adams thought so. He saw selfishness as endemic to the human condition and a constant threat to morality. In 1805, the former president complained to Dr. Rush that self-serving ambition marked even those charged with governing the nation. "Is virtue the principle of our Government?" Adams asked Rush. "Is honor?" Or is it rather "ambition and avarice[,] adulation, baseness, covetousness, the thirst of riches, indifference concerning the means of rising and enriching, contempt of principle, [and] the Spirit of party and of faction" that govern in America? These were "serious and dangerous questions," Adams wrote. With immorality prevalent even among the nation's leaders, the rule of law was not guaranteed. On the contrary, it was under attack.[4]

Concerns about the social order were pressing in the 1790s, when the experiment of representative democracy faced threats to its very existence. Americans disagreed, however, about the greatest source of danger. Some feared most of all the anarchy of revolutionary violence. The Terror in France had taken tens of thousands of lives, and gory accounts of executions, massacres, rapes, and amputations filled American newspapers, sermons, public orations, plays, and broadsides. Meanwhile, news from the

West Indies described how former slaves on the French colony of Saint Domingue (renamed Haiti in 1804) had risen up in a bid for their freedom, struggling to end slavery's reign of terror in the face of slaveholder opposition that caused terrible bloodshed on all sides. Americans who feared that their republic might also experience social revolution on a grand scale viewed political stability as an imperative of the highest order. Others, however, saw a greater menace to American freedom in the slide toward repressive oligarchy. The mechanics of self-governance in the United States were decidedly partial, the promise of democracy not yet realized. Most states limited the vote to property-owning white men and required religious tests for public office, while the Constitution of 1787 protected the institution of slavery into the foreseeable future. Meanwhile, the wealthiest families consolidated their political influence. The real danger, many Americans believed, lay not in too much democracy but in a postwar retrenchment of elite power. The heated political partisanship of the 1790s, arguably the nation's first "culture war," reflected the high-stakes disagreement over whether the nation had gone too far or not yet far enough in establishing a democratic society.[5]

In the years between Rush's musings in 1787 about the need for a moral citizenry and Adams's complaint in 1805 about widespread corruption, Palmer developed his own understanding of the source of virtue. Ethical conduct, he said, grew from a better understanding of the natural world. More specifically, he believed everything in the universe is made of the same eternal substance. By "everything," Palmer meant not only human beings of whatever culture, religion, gender, or race, but other living organisms—animals and plants—as well as all matter, including rocks, water, and even light. A mysterious life force infuses this singular matter and keeps it eternally in motion, creating all things that exist. Nothing is inert, Palmer said. "All is alive, all is active and energetic."[6]

Not stopping there, Palmer believed that the smallest particles of matter—he used the word "atoms"—are *sensate*, meaning they experience and retain sensations like pleasure and pain. This idea changed everything, he thought, for accepting that all matter registers sensation means recognizing that one's own actions constantly impact the whole. All individuals exist in a vast web of life, and each individual action affects the substance of which all things are made. Pain inflicted on another being never disappears but persists in the endless reformulation of matter. Grasp the fact of a universal connection, Palmer told his audiences, and "sympathy or universal benevolence" will form the basis of all "subsequent conduct." A natural empathy for other beings will lead people to end wars, slavery, and oppression of all kinds. In this way, fundamental social change could occur without the violence that so often marked revolutions. Human society could be transformed for the better. Required was only clear-eyed, unprejudiced thinking about the facts of the eternal, sensate material world. Christianity could not help in this regard, because it concerned itself with things that do not exist: immaterial souls in an immaterial afterlife. For that reason, Palmer said, *true* morality, the kind a democracy requires, flourishes best alongside freedom of religion and even freedom *from* religion.[7]

Ministers and laypeople saw Palmer's ideas as a dangerous thought experiment. The majority of Americans assumed that morality rested on one kind of Protestantism or another. In their view, the belief in a judging God who sent souls to an eternal afterlife in either heaven or hell was the only thing that could reign in the human tendency toward selfishness and sin. If, as so many believed, the religious faith as taught in the churches formed a necessary foundation for moral conduct, then Palmer's irreverent speeches against organized religion threatened the republic and constituted a form of sedition. Palmer in turn accused his detractors of religious overreach and defended freedom of speech as essential to a free nation. With that, the battle lines were drawn, the only agreement being that the fate of the country hung in the balance.

Free speech had not yet been extensively legislated, and the First Amendment, which pertained only to the federal government and not to state legislatures, certainly could not guarantee it. Yet Americans who saw the First Amendment as aspirational in a broader sense expanded the bounds of public speech in everyday practice. In lectures, orations, and sociable conversation, as well as in the booming and relatively open print culture of inexpensive pamphlets, tracts, and newspapers, more and more people shared their opinions. Publishers even printed Thomas Paine's *Age of Reason* and other skeptical works without penalty. But full freedom of speech was not guaranteed either. Blasphemy laws remained on the books in many states and were sometimes put into practice. As late as 1811, a New Yorker named John Ruggles spent time behind bars for declaring in a tavern that Jesus was a bastard and his mother a whore. For those who dared openly to discredit Christian doctrine, charges of blasphemy hovered as a potential threat. Palmer was spared legal persecution; he suffered neither jail time nor fines for his open hostility toward Christianity. Yet these always lurked as a danger, making him one more test case in the nation's experiment in free speech.[8]

Although Palmer was not prohibited from preaching his unpopular ideas, his freethinking lectures came at the cost of his reputation. He wished to be regarded as a public intellectual among educated men, not seen as part of a lunatic fringe, and for that reason the road to freethought proved personally challenging. He had to choose between the social respectability he yearned for and the intellectual candor he also desired. His iconoclastic ideas displeased both the defenders of religious orthodoxy and the religious liberals who preferred milder versions of Protestant doctrine. His open condemnation of Christianity breached the etiquette of gentility that confined expressions of freethought to closed company.

Yet in another way he had plenty of conversation partners—the nation was full of freethinkers. Palmer's speaking tours introduced him to a whole range of freethinking people, some located within and others outside of Christian frameworks, who challenged received wisdom and tested the limits placed on freedom of speech. Telling Palmer's story brings to light new characters and unfamiliar contests in the struggle to define the moral foundations of the new United States. An intrepid bookseller in New York City; a skeptical steamboat inventor in Philadelphia; a freethinking physician on Long Island; an irreverent newspaper editor in Newburgh, New York; a frustrated minister in Augusta, Georgia; an eccentric world-traveling English philosopher; an Irish-born radical printer in Philadelphia; a mystic Swedenborgian minister in Baltimore—these are just some of the people Palmer encountered, engaged, and sometimes enraged. In describing Palmer's conversation partners, those sympathetic to him and not, the terms "conservative" and "radical" are seldom useful. Individuals might promote continuity in some things and fundamental change in others. In general, the intellectual landscape of the early republic resembled more an unruly collage of overlapping ideas than a neat spectrum with conservative on one end and radical on the other. Palmer encountered complex positions rather than blocs of opinion. What comes into focus through Palmer's conversations is a field of public debate more expansive than we knew yet heatedly contested nonetheless, even among freethinkers.

Palmer's career as a public freethinker unfolded in the tension created by divergent impulses in the new United States: the growth of religious pluralism alongside immense anxiety about the public expression of that diversity. In the concern over whether the national experiment in self-governance would endure, freedom of religion and of speech became stakes in the nation's first culture war, which was waged between Federalists and Democratic-Republicans who cherished different visions for the country's future. In this volatile context, Palmer's lectures and publications took on a symbolic valence. His orations, first spoken and then printed, had the effect of expanding the public tolerance for religious freethought, because every time he expressed his ideas without incurring punishment, his supporters took heart, and his opponents gained practice in enduring speech they deplored. Yet it was not without friction, and Palmer produced a whirlwind of opposition. A friend of his once put it this way: a "religious tornado," he said, "has shaken the country, on account of Mr. Palmer."[9]

Prolific in the printed and spoken word and infamous in his own day, Elihu Palmer did not survive in public memory. His book, *Principles of Nature; or, A Development of the Moral Causes of Happiness and Misery Among the Human Species*, which appeared in 1801 and was published in an expanded second edition in 1802 and 1806, was reprinted a few more times after that, then remained out of print for more than a century. In the 1930s, when historians rediscovered his writings, Palmer's ideas about the vital matter that comprised all the universe's creations had been forgotten. That crucial aspect of Palmer's thought, the one he cherished most, had disappeared from view. If historians noticed him at all, they described him as a popularizer of deism, the Enlightenment-era belief in a Creator-God who does not intervene in the world with miracles or revelations. In a common description, the deist's "watchmaker God" abides at a great distance from the universe that operates according to the immutable laws of nature. Deism had a profound impact in certain educated circles in America, influencing several political leaders, notably Benjamin Franklin and Thomas Jefferson. Palmer certainly supported deism as a rational improvement on Christianity, yet it served as a platform from which to pursue an idea he cared about even more: the notion of a divine life force residing within shared, sensate matter. This was the concept he thought capable of evoking a truly transformative compassion for other beings.[10]

The view of Palmer as primarily invested in popularizing deism, narrowly defined and without reference to vital matter, carried over from the 1930s. In 1976, the historian Henry May described Palmer as "a deist of the militant, post-French Revolution variety." In his history of American deists, Kerry S. Walters noted in 1992 the "sad obscurity into which Palmer has fallen" and suggested that a "full-length treatment of Palmer's thought and his pivotal role in the deist movement is sorely needed." Even most recent work on religious freethought in the early United States portrays Palmer as the main force behind an effort to institutionalize deism, a movement that supposedly flared up briefly then disappeared.[11]

Palmer was not simply or only a deist, at least not as conventionally understood. To be sure, my initial assessment of him followed those of previous historians in assuming that his advocacy of deism both exemplified and exhausted his religious beliefs. But parts of Palmer's writings remained baffling, even incoherent, until I read the works of obscure authors he quoted at length. Texts by the New York physician Isaac Ledyard and the enigmatic English traveler John "Walking" Stewart revealed the universe of eternal, sensate matter in which Palmer so firmly believed. Palmer appreciated deism's stance of religious skepticism, and he supported it as the next, best replacement for revealed religion. More important to him, however, was the vital cosmology that dispensed altogether with a divine judge of immortal human souls. What set Palmer apart from so many of his freethinking peers was his belief in sensate matter and the immediate and constant exchange of atoms among all of Earth's creations. How to label this set of ideas did not seem to matter to him at all. He simply considered them the true "principles of nature."[12]

Like his ideas, Palmer's life has been shrouded in mystery. He left behind a handful of printed speeches, a book, and a newspaper but no cache of personal documents and only a few letters scattered in other people's collected papers. Without much information about Palmer's upbringing, his education, and his encounters with a wide variety of freethought, first within Christianity and eventually outside it, historians have known him only as he appeared later in print: as a strident, hostile, outspoken critic of Christianity in the way of Thomas Paine. In these histories, Palmer appears invested only in deism. But buried in disparate manuscript collections, newspapers, church records, and old town chronicles are the archival discoveries that have enabled this reconstruction of Palmer's more surprising, halting, even inadvertent journey toward a life of freethinking infamy. Perusing runs of newspapers for his advertised lectures helped me track Palmer's movements across state lines. Reading widely in the personal letters and diaries of people who *might* have known Palmer brought the occasional and invaluable find. Old town chronicles told of Palmer's influence in various cities, while works authored by his (now) obscure friends opened up the world of conversation that inspired Palmer. A list of names on headstones in Connecticut graveyards led me to his hometown, after which church and property records, family genealogies, and—what extraordinary luck—a diary from his hometown minister helped reconstruct the world of Palmer's childhood.

Putting all these pieces together, what emerges is Palmer's gradual evolution as a freethinker, first within and then eventually beyond a Christian framework. His opposition to Christianity developed only in fits and starts, and it wasn't deism he was after so much as a new understanding of the natural wellspring of morality. Palmer combined his vital universe with a lenient Christianity until the churches closed their doors to him. Only when clergy rejected his version of the faith while insisting that Protestantism, patriotism, and morality required one another, did Palmer find himself pushed out of even the most permissive Christian fold and in need of a new platform from which to speak. He eventually embraced his role as a lightning rod for his critics; the negative attention affirmed the unsettling impact of his message. His main interest was not scandal, however, but the path to a better future. He trusted that full freedom of religion and of speech would enable people to reexamine supernatural religion and replace it with the insight that true morality can be found in the interconnected system of all life.

Palmer was a man of his era, a strong proponent of eighteenth-century convictions about the potential for human progress and even future perfectibility. Yet his ideas still have resonance. The ongoing challenge of establishing shared ethical guidelines in a religiously and culturally diverse world, the difficulty of creating social and economic justice on scales both local and global, and the question of how to preserve the interconnected system of life on planet Earth are problems that call for creative solutions. Palmer engaged with these questions deeply and on his own terms, and his unconventional answers can still spark our imagination.

PART I

Expansive Christianity

CHAPTER 1

Steady Habits Upended

REVEREND JAMES COGSWELL adjusted his powdered wig then straightened the twin white preaching bands that hung from his clerical collar over the front of his black suit. A glance in a looking glass would have shown his alert brown eyes and ruddy cheeks in a clean-shaven face. He was sixty-two years of age and in good health, praise God. But the upcoming memorial service made him uneasy. A young man, full of promise, had hanged himself. The dreadful event had shaken Cogswell. "My mind feels anxious what to say with propriety on such an uncommon Occasion," he wrote in his diary in April 1782. He hoped to find the right words, especially for the village youth gathered to commemorate their lost friend. Their conduct of late troubled him greatly. As the war for independence dragged on, bringing scarcity, inflation, and the grim news of compatriots wounded or killed, the young people in Connecticut's sparsely populated eastern hill country exhibited strangely frivolous, even callous, behavior. Cogswell had observed "unseasonable" wartime "gaity," also cursing, intemperance, and "merriment and revelling," together with an "absence of seriousness" and a kind of "criminality of insensibility." Had wickedness and then remorse contributed to the young man's premature death? The minister planned an urgent appeal to the youth of Scotland village. Their eternal souls were in imminent danger, he would warn them. They must acknowledge their depravity, repent their sins, and seek the healing balm of divine mercy. Yet Cogswell fretted that he had not found the right tone for this sensitive occasion.[1]

We can imagine seventeen-year-old Elihu Palmer sitting in the Congregational meetinghouse as Cogswell arranged his notes and prepared to deliver the funeral oration. In this town of a few hundred people, Palmer would have known the young man, close to him in age, whose life had ended in tragedy. The village youth had built a pew for themselves in the new clapboard-sided church; maybe Palmer joined them on the bench. He and his seven siblings had been baptized in the old meetinghouse, which was no longer in use. His mother, Lois, before her untimely death, had for years participated in the holy sacrament of communion, and his father, Elihu Palmer Sr., served for many years as a member of the ecclesiastical society that oversaw church governance in Scotland Parish. For over a decade now, Cogswell had preached the Sunday sermons. Palmer was probably even then studying with Cogswell, whose ministerial duties included religious education for the youth in town, along with preparing eligible young men for college.[2]

Two momentous upheavals shaped the society in which Palmer came of age: the Protestant religious revivals, later dubbed the First Great Awakening, that had begun when his parents and Reverend Cogswell were young themselves; and the American Revolution, which had been waged during Palmer's youth. Both events raised questions of lasting import: Which sources of moral and political authority were legitimate and trustworthy? What was the proper mix of reason and emotion in religious faith and political fealty? Which forms of religious devotion most pleased God and encouraged moral conduct? These questions were not merely academic, as those who gathered for the memorial service understood. The answers either helped or hindered as one tried to find moral ballast in turbulent times. In Cogswell's view, only a rational and earnest faith could ward off the most dangerous impulses, be they religious or political. As he prepared the funeral oration, he could look back on decades of religious tumult and try to distill life's lessons in ways that might persuade and protect the youth of Scotland village.

Since Elihu Palmer wrote nothing about his family or his childhood and no personal papers from his parents have survived, Cogswell's diary offers a singular glimpse into the world of Palmer's youth. Cogswell's ideas about religion and politics must have influenced this churchgoing boy, who would study for the ministry and ever after concern himself with theology. Elihu Palmer came of age knowing that his parents and minister chose traditional church authority over emotionally charged religious revivalism. From Cogswell the boy would have heard about the dangers of piety gone awry, the hazards of relinquishing one's reasoning powers to an emotional experience of the Holy, and the importance of keeping one's critical faculties intact when others seemed to be losing their wits. Immorality could come under the guise of a holy possession, as Cogswell knew firsthand. Palmer was probably raised on tales of the revivals that flamed up before he was born, searing souls and scorching friendships and family ties. The outlandish behavior of the born-again made for shocking stories that conveyed just how thin the barrier of reason was when religious emotions took hold. The adults closest to young Palmer held convictions of faith forged in an era of religious turmoil and stark choices. For them, the crucial role for reason in religion was no abstraction; it was an urgent lesson they passed on to the bright, young boy.

Cogswell remembered well how the religious revivals began. In October 1740, when he was twenty, news spread by word of mouth that the traveling English minister, George Whitefield, was preaching in Middletown, Connecticut. People left their farming tools in the field and their tasks unfinished and rushed to hear the charismatic speaker. Whitefield's vivid, emotive, and extemporaneous preaching, which was marked by dramatic gestures and strong feeling, gripped his audiences. He reminded those gathered that all humans are born into a state of moral depravity. Sinners cannot save themselves from the punishment they so richly deserve, he said, and an "Eternity of Misery awaits the Wicked in a future state." One's only recourse was to repent and humbly pray that the Holy Spirit will "re-instamp the Divine Image upon our Hearts, and make us capable of living with and enjoying God." As the crowd witnessed Whitefield's impassioned exhortations, some felt the inner working of a saving grace. One Connecticut farmer said that hearing Whitefield preach "gave me a heart wound." It was an emotional devastation of the best kind, people later said, with the power to change their lives.[3]

Not everyone appreciated Whitefield's message or method. A physician in Middletown reported to a friend that the "Famous Enthusiast Mr. Whitefield was along here, making a great Stir and noise." Doctor Osborn disparaged Whitefield's extemporaneous and emotional preaching style as a "heap of confusion, Railing, Bombast, Fawning, and Nonsense" marked by "distorted motions, Grimaces, and Squeeking voices." The emotional appeal was precisely the problem, Osborn thought. For without one's

FIGURE 1. A portrait of Reverend James Cogswell, ca. 1795–1799. Reverend Cogswell served as a minister in Scotland, Connecticut, from the time Elihu Palmer was seven until he left home for college. Cogswell's piety and sociability shaped how Palmer viewed a career in ministry. Courtesy of Historic New England. Gift of Bertram K. and Nina Fletcher Little, 1991.1445.

reasoning faculties in play, how was one to know that it was the voice of God in one's head and not satanic delusion?[4]

What, indeed, constituted authentic religious experience? Did it suffice to use finite human reason to study the revealed word of God in the Bible? Or did direct, emotional experiences of the Holy Spirit more reliably convey a sense of God? Did reasoned exegesis from a theologically trained minister best convey God's will, or the powerful experience of the indwelling presence of the Holy Spirit? These pressing questions continued to preoccupy people well after Whitefield had moved on.[5]

In eastern Connecticut, as elsewhere, local preachers took up the new form of preaching, referring to a few notes rather than reading aloud their sermons. As the delivery became more direct, the message gained in emotional impact. Twelve miles west of Scotland in Lebanon Crank parish, Reverend Eleazar Wheelock exhorted his congregants about the utter depravity of humankind and the need for the redemptive power of being born again in Jesus Christ. Wheelock counted himself among the New Lights, and within a year, nearly three hundred members of his own "dear flock" had also been born again. Wheelock and other New Light preachers especially targeted church members in good standing, the pious folk who regularly attended church service, took part in the Lord's Supper, and did their best to follow the example of Christ. None of this was any good, New Light revivalists warned, unless one felt overcome by the Holy Spirit. Without the transformative experience of being "regenerated," or born again, all Christian rituals were worse than useless; they obscured a sinner's depravity and encouraged a smug pride that ended in everlasting damnation. Even upstanding members of the church were not true Christians unless they had experienced the living spirit of Jesus. The same was true of ministers who had not experienced a saving grace powerful enough to take their breath away. Outward piety and knowledge of the Scriptures were nothing. Love of God must be written directly on the heart.[6]

Other ministers displayed more physical manifestations of the divine power at work. Wheelock's brother-in-law, James Davenport, was an ordained Congregational minister when he encountered George Whitefield and the Irish Presbyterian revivalist Gilbert Tennent. On fire for God, Davenport took to the road and preached to large audiences, often outdoors and without the consent of local ministers. His speeches came to him as immediate revelations of the Holy Spirit and lasted for hours on end. He repeated words and phrases as a chant or a shout, riffed on excerpts from the Bible, and offered graphic accounts of torments in hell. At his meetings, Davenport encouraged his listeners to engage in extemporaneous prayer and exhortation, resulting in a cacophony of sound: singing, laughing, shrieking, and weeping. His gift of spiritual discernment showed him who among the settled ministers was saved and who was the *"Devil incarnate."* When he ordered a public book burning in New London in 1743, a hundred men and women threw their volumes into the flames, especially the "heretical" ones penned by ordained but unregenerate ministers.[7]

As the revivals took hold in eastern Connecticut, familiar hierarchies frayed. People with no theological training and marginal social status spoke with new authority in matters of the spirit. Native American converts arrived to preach and sing with the congregants in Lebanon. A black man sermonized at an outdoor meeting of the Colchester congregation, eighteen miles from Scotland. In Canterbury, an enslaved man named Pompey stood up during a meeting and exhorted his owner's son in the matter of conversion. Women described extraordinary religious experiences and men believed them. Children fell into trances and revived after days of stupor to tell astonished adults about their visions. In these unsettled times, spiritual authority shifted in new ways, inverting the customary relations of respect. For many, it was a moment of much promise when spiritual power could, at least for a while, override social norms.[8]

All of this the Palmers and their neighbors in Scotland village heard about with amazement, while the ministers they knew best, Reverend Ebenezer Devotion in Scotland and Reverend James Cogswell, who was then still in the neighboring town of Canterbury, became personally entangled in the struggle. As Old Light ministers, who required that church members display upright behavior rather than evidence of a personal experience of divine grace, Devotion and Cogswell could hardly avoid sparring with the revivalists. Connecticut had an established Congregational church, which meant its governing structure was codified in a law (the Saybrook Platform) passed by the colonial legislature in 1708. The church could draw on civil power to enforce ecclesiastical rules. Dissenters who defied official church injunctions about who could preach or take communion could be fined or jailed by state authorities. Called Separates or Separatists because they wished to leave existing congregations to create independent ones, the dissenters objected that legal might did not make moral right. They resented the compulsory church taxes that paid the salaries of settled ministers. They also thought that ministers should be chosen by the individual congregations, not by a regional association of clergy. Their independence from the law stemmed, revivalists said, from having covenanted directly with God, while the settled ministers and their congregations had merely come together under "the *Saybrook* Platform, which we think to be disagreeable to the word of GOD, and therefore reject it." The Separates harkened to a power above the law of mortals.[9]

When Cogswell arrived in Canterbury in 1744, he was a twenty-four-year-old graduate from Yale College, an institution founded for the purpose of educating Congregational ministers. Cogswell had not been born again and did not require that would-be church members testify to a personal conversion experience. Canterbury had been without a minister for three years, during which time laypeople preached to the congregation. Two of these, Elisha and Solomon Paine, were well-connected townsmen who had converted during the revivals. Soon after Cogswell's arrival, Elisha Paine, a lawyer, approached Cogswell after a lecture and said "with a grave Countenance" in a room full of people that he would rather be "burnt at the Stake than to have heard such a Sermon." The whole thing had been "Trifling," he complained, an exercise in proving something obvious, "like a young Attorney at the Bar." Paine also objected to Cogswell's claim that "we must have recourse only to the Word of GOD, to prove that CHRIST suffered and died for Sinners." In Paine's view, conversion to faith in Jesus the Redeemer could come about in other ways too, not only through reading the Bible but also and more powerfully through the direct "Influences of the Spirit of God" on an individual.[10]

Paine and Cogswell conversed at length. They discussed whether any sin is unforgiveable, whether all souls will eventually be saved (Paine thought not), and what constitutes a saving faith. To the last point, Paine said God had disclosed that "CHRIST died for me." What could be clearer evidence of his salvation than this direct message? Cogswell argued against that certainty in favor of a hopeful faith absent any divine confirmation. Paine remained firm in his conviction, claiming that "the old Puritan doctrine" of an immediate and personal conversion experience was "much safer to hold" than the notion "that a Person might be Converted, and not know it." Both men brandished their arguments, and Cogswell's recounting of the exchange suggests he enjoyed the theological discussion in a room full of witnesses. He took seriously his duty to instruct in matters of theology, and he gladly parried the revivalist message that theological training was of no consequence if one had personal experience of the Holy Spirit.[11]

The revivalists remained unmoved, however, and Paine persisted in his opposition to Cogswell. He defied the General Assembly's prohibition of unauthorized itinerant preachers and became a lay preacher himself in the raucous style of James Davenport. The revivalist tumult in Canterbury grew so heated that it made news elsewhere. The *Boston Gazette* reported in December that "Canterbury is in worse confusion than ever." Without a settled minister, "they grow more noisy and boisterous so that they can get no minister to preach to them yet." Lawyer Paine "has set up for a preacher," the *Gazette* continued, and he goes "from house to house and town to town to gain proselytes to the new religion. Consequences are much to be feared."[12]

Throughout that year and into the next, tensions in Canterbury flared over who had the authority to choose the town's new minister. A minority in town supported Cogswell, while the revivalist faction refused to hear him and met illegally in private homes, risking the consequences. Elisha Paine spent a month in the Windham County jail for his unauthorized sermons, preaching from his prison cell in the "Spirit of the Lord." When Cogswell was installed as pastor, the revivalists refused to acknowledge both his ordination and the authorities behind it. They soon found themselves out of doors and effectively without a church at all. Undaunted, these fifty-seven townspeople, many from wealthy families and related to one another, formed the Canterbury Separate Church, with Solomon Paine as its minister.[13]

As Cogswell settled into his position as Canterbury's minister, the revivals continued to challenge traditional norms. One of the most troubling manifestations of this spiritual revolution was the idea of perfectionism. Some converts believed the experience of salvation through divine grace meant they could commit no sin, even when they aggressively flouted entrenched norms. In 1748, just two years after Reverend Devotion banished Mary Wilkinson from the Scotland meetinghouse for calling it a

"Church of Antichrist," she shocked the townspeople of Canterbury when she shouted at a young man named Thomas Bates. "I am Jesus Christ and You are the Divel," she exclaimed, "git you behind me Satan." Then she offered Bates another solution. "If you Will Come and lie in my Crotch I will Bless you, and you Shall be Saved, But if you Will Not I Will Curse you and you Shall be Damned." To demonstrate she was in earnest, Wilkinson hoisted her skirts and exposed her "Naked Thighs, in a very Obsean manner," all the while "offering to Expose her nakedness forther to him." To Reverend Cogswell and other townspeople, Wilkenson's claims to holiness and her disregard for norms of female chastity offered proof enough of the anarchic disorder that flowed from perfectionist pretensions.[14]

As if to make this very point, another woman felt spiritually called to more than one adulterous relationship, with disastrous results. In the newly formed Separate Church in nearby Newent parish, a married man named Bliss Willoughby brought Mary Smith to live in his household as his "spiritual wife." The legal Mrs. Willoughby endured this arrangement for a number of months until her husband recognized he had been tricked by Satan. By 1749 Mary Smith had moved on to Canterbury, where John Smith, no relation to her, claimed she was his spiritual wife. More ominously, Smith announced that his legal spouse and the mother of their four children, Mehetabel Smith, would soon make way for his new and divinely ordained union. After a few months, Mary served her rival a pancake laced with arsenic, and Mehetabel went into convulsions and died. Cogswell and the other villagers saw with horror that the social fabric was at risk when salvation placed people above the law. Surely, this was the Devil's work.[15]

In these tumultuous times, everyone could at least agree that the legitimacy of a spiritual experience, or its counterfeit, involved the highest possible stakes. To be wrong, to be mistaken about God's will, dashed all hope of salvation and invited misery and ruin. But certainty lay in the eye of the beholder, and what Cogswell denounced as devilish chaos appeared to others as the unpredictable and mysterious working of divine power.

Generally of a pleasant disposition, Cogswell weathered the opposition to his ministry. He settled in for the long haul in Canterbury, married Alice Fitch, the daughter of a local lawyer, and started a family. He preached as persuasively as he could. Ministers should use "a rational, plain, easy, natural Method in composing their Sermons," he said. They should organize their talks with "suitable, distinct" subheadings, "keep close to their Subject," and reason "with Plainness and Perspicuity, and at the same Time with Pungency." This method may indeed have reminded lawyer Paine of an attorney at the bar, but Cogswell saw the careful parsing and explication of the Bible as far superior to the spontaneous exhorting of charismatic revivalists. Those who offer only unstructured "Harrangues" and "crude, indigested, and unstudied Discourses," Cogswell said, "may gain the Applause of the injudicious, and inconsiderate Persons," but they are not "rightly dividing the Word of Truth."[16]

The most important task of a minister, Cogswell knew, was to explain the foundational doctrines of the faith and "confute Gainsayers, and how can he do this without a very thorough Understanding of the Word of God?" To "divide," or parse, the teachings in the Bible meant drawing on "Connection or Analogy" to explain the "harmony and Connection of Scripture." This complex intellectual labor required that ministers know the "learned Languages, so that they need not take all on Trust but may be able to trace these divine Streams of Knowledge up to the Fountain Head." In the serious matter of biblical interpretation, "great Care should be taken that no Others be introduced into, or encouraged in performing this Work." With revivalist lay preachers all around him, Cogswell pushed hard on the dangers of untrained ministers. When "wicked ungodly Men pretend to officiate in the sacred Office," he said, they "do the most of any Men to destroy the Interest of the Redeemer." People should not listen to those "altogether unqualified for, as well as unauthorized to this Work," and they ought not to encourage "so daring an Invasion on the Sacerdotal Office."[17]

In addition to his ministry, Cogswell ran a school for boys out of his home and tutored them in Greek, Latin, mathematics, and public speaking. He was not an authoritarian presence, and some boys took advantage of his leniency. An unruly youth named Benedict Arnold came to the school in 1752 and stayed for three years. Arnold's mother, who was related to Cogswell, requested that her kinsman use a firm hand with her son. "Pray don't spare ye rod and spoil ye child," she wrote from Norwich, fifteen miles away. The boy was indeed a challenge, Cogswell reported. Young Arnold was smart but too "full of pranks and plays," some of them dangerous. When a barn caught on fire, Arnold climbed to the top of the building and walked the ridge pole from end to end. For Cogswell, such defiance was familiar. Challenges to his ministerial authority extended from men to boys, never abating as long as he lived in the village. Resistance to established authority was part of Canterbury's way of life.[18]

In nearby Scotland village, Reverend Ebenezer Devotion also faced a revivalist uprising in the 1740s, but he responded more aggressively than Cogswell. A Yale graduate known for his extensive reading and Old Light convictions, Devotion favored sober study of the Bible over inspections of one's soul for signs of a divine and saving grace. He was well connected in the intertwined institutions of church and state, having served on the General Assembly as well as in the Ecclesiastical Society for Windham, Connecticut. He expected his parishioners to attend meeting twice on the Sabbath and spend the remainder of the day in Bible reading, meditation, and prayer. When lay revivalists began to preach in town, Devotion pursued them with vigor. He denounced their preaching as the work of enthusiasm, initiated punitive action against lay preachers, and barred Separatists from communion and from participation in church governance until they repented. The dissenters complained bitterly that Devotion "did not preach Christ according to their understanding," and they sought out revivalist preachers, like Solomon Paine, "whose preaching fed their souls."[19]

Devotion dug in for the fight and published a pamphlet against his detractors. If the dissenters meant by "the present work of God in the land" the ignorant exhortations of lay preachers; if they meant "judging, censuring, and in words *Damning* men whom they dis-esteem;" if they meant "boisterous treatment of their fellow creatures," such as "Bellowing after them" in the streets, which had become "common with many Separates," then, no, Devotion wrote, "we are so far from calling it a work of God's Spirit, that we esteem it highly dishonoring to God, and even blasphemous, to impute such folly and wickedness to his Holy Spirit." He criticized the dissenters for their holier-than-thou pretentions and described the "horrid Outcries" of revivalist meetings as the result of delusion, not the Holy Spirit. He never accepted the Separatists, and when he could not defeat them, he harassed them. Every Sunday morning for years, he sent his slave, Peter, to deliver to the Separate Church a written notice forbidding their minister to preach there that day.[20]

As the Scotland congregation split, so too did the Palmer family. Elihu Palmer Sr. was second cousin to the Separatist minister. Reverend John Palmer was "deficient in education and somewhat rough in speech and manner," some thought, but he showed an "estimable character and sound piety," and he once spent four months in the Hartford jail for his unauthorized preaching. Elihu Palmer Sr. preferred traditional, orderly religion over unpredictable personal experiences of the Holy Spirit. In the Separatist conflict, he sided with the established church and remained a member of the Third Ecclesiastical Society of Windham, which owned the meetinghouse in Scotland and conducted matters of church business. Palmer Sr. valued social order and stability, and the established church was good for that.[21]

His wife, Lois Foster Palmer, agreed. She was among the female communicants of the Scotland meetinghouse since at least 1753, the year after she married. She was four generations descended from Myles Standish, the aggressive military man the Pilgrims hired to travel with them on the *Mayflower* to what they called New England. As the military commander for Plymouth colony, Standish had ordered preemptive and brutal attacks on American Indian communities. He was a hero by most Anglo-Americans' sights, and the Palmer children grew up knowing about the family connection to him. Elihu's younger brother, Nathan, boasted about this lineage into old age. The only glimmer we have of the personality of their mother, Lois, aside from her church attendance, is that she must have spoken to her children with pride about her family tree.[22]

The Palmers were not showy people, but they enjoyed their share of self-respect. The paternal side of the family traced its line back to Walter Palmer, an English Puritan who arrived in Salem, Massachusetts, in 1629. Around 1700, one of Walter's grandsons, Jonas Palmer, moved with his family to the densely forested and steeply rolling hills of what was then Mohegan land. Jonas Palmer's youngest son, Elihu, married Abigail Robinson, herself the great-granddaughter of the Puritan minister John Robinson, who led the Pilgrims from England to Holland before they sailed, without him, on the *Mayflower*. Elihu and Abigail had seven children, one of whom, also named Elihu, would become the father of the future freethinker. These long-standing Puritan lineages must have shaped the youngest Elihu Palmer's sense of self. He came from a family that was serious about religion.[23]

Elihu Palmer Sr. gradually acquired over one hundred acres of land that lay just south of the road—still called Palmer Road today—that runs east-west through town. He would have planted what his neighbors did: wheat, rye, flax, barley, and corn. Perhaps he also kept sheep, cattle, and swine. Other Palmer men held a high proportion of the minor offices in Scotland village, but Palmer Sr. was modest in his civic contributions. In the 1750s, he served as brander and poundkeeper, impounding and feeding loose livestock until their owners reclaimed them. Then his younger brother was elected to these posts, and after 1761, Palmer Sr. does not appear to have served in any official role at all. This fact is suggestive of his personality. Only the Huntington and Robinson families held more offices in Scotland than did men named Palmer, and Palmer Sr. certainly could have availed himself of such positions. He was not inclined to assume official leadership roles.[24]

Hardship and loss came early. In autumn 1754, Lois and Elihu Palmer Sr. buried their first two children in the Scotland village cemetery. One-year-old Eunice and her infant brother died within weeks of one another, perhaps carried off by the same illness. After this double loss, it was Lois's fate to give birth every two years between 1755 and 1771. Reverend Devotion baptized the Palmer babies in Scotland's meetinghouse, and eight of them survived their infancy. The fifth of these surviving children, the second boy, was named Elihu after his father and his recently deceased grandfather.[25]

The year 1771 brought significant changes to the Devotion, Cogswell, and Palmer families. After decades of trying, the Separatists of Canterbury finally ousted Cogswell from his pulpit, and he moved with his wife, Alice, to an interim position in another Connecticut town. In July, Reverend Devotion died unexpectedly at the age of fifty-seven, leaving his wife Martha to grieve her sudden loss. After some time, the Scotland meetinghouse gave Cogswell the call to serve as preacher, and he was pleased to be installed as minister in January. Tragedy struck the Palmer household that winter when Lois died at the age of forty, a few months after giving birth once more. When Palmer Sr. and his children gathered at the top of the steeply sloping cemetery in Scotland, close by the headstones of the children who had predeceased Lois, it was probably the recently arrived Reverend Cogswell who conducted the service. In February, Cogswell's own wife of many decades died, leaving him to settle into his new church community without the aid of a helpmeet. After a year of mourning, Cogswell married his predecessor's widow and moved into Martha Devotion's home.[26]

Palmer Sr., by contrast, did not remarry. He continued in his ways, focusing on farm work and avoiding any high-profile civic involvement, even at the local level. His teenaged daughters must have stepped up their domestic responsibilities, helping each other with the cooking, cleaning, gardening, and tending of animals. His three sons, Thaddeus, Elihu, and Nathan, participated in the predictable cycles of planting, cultivating, and harvesting crops and in the endless need to milk cows, herd sheep, repair farm tools, maintain fences and walls, and cut and haul firewood.

The Palmer children would have received religious instruction from Reverend Cogswell, who was not inclined toward severity. He sometimes wondered if he was ministerial enough for his post. "I fear I was not grave enough," he admitted after one "very friendly" church service. During a visit to a sick woman, Cogswell engaged the convalescent in a long conversation but later wished he had offered a prayer as well. The family "did not ask me to pray," he wrote, but "I did not do right that I did not offer it of my own Accord." He did not want to be remiss in his ministerial duties, but neither did he wish to impose them. Cogswell readily admitted that "politics or something of a Temporal Nature too often diverts me," and that "one Chore or other takes up a great part of my Time—& leaves me not enough to employ in Study, prayer & Meditation." A good-natured, comfortable man—"I do not Love being in Hurry," he noted in his diary—Cogswell enjoyed an active social life. He often wished his faith were stronger and the Lord's presence clearer. One Sunday he "had little sense of Divine Things To Day," and on another he "had some sense of Religion To Day tho not so affectionate & zealous as at some other Times." Still, Cogswell found it "pleasant to pray & preach," and most mornings he woke up with Jesus on his mind. The most influential minister in Palmer's youth, Cogswell was orthodox but not humorless; dedicated but not dogmatic. He nurtured an earnest, hopeful Calvinist faith. Sincere repentance for his sinful nature, along with heartfelt entreaties to a merciful God, filled him with gratitude and lightened his sense of inadequacy.[27]

Passion might be dangerous when it came in the form of religious enthusiasm, but it had a proper place in politics. Cogswell ardently supported the war for independence, and he would have encouraged this sentiment in his pupils. Young Palmer was nine years old when patriots disguised as Indians jimmied open boxes of imported tea and dumped the leaves over the sides of the ships anchored in Boston harbor. The English Parliament responded with the Coercive Acts, one of which closed the harbor until the colonists paid for the ruined tea and its tax. Throughout New England, feelings of solidarity with Bostonians ran deep. In June 1774, townspeople from Scotland joined others in nearby Windham to denounce the Coercive Acts as "the Violent Deprivation of private property and Liberty." Maybe Palmer gathered some of the two hundred and fifty-eight sheep the locals sent to relieve the blockaded inhabitants of Boston, eighty miles away.[28]

Most of the adults around Palmer were fired up for the patriot cause. Tories lay low—less than a handful in the region were willing to call themselves Loyalists. News spread in July 1774 that the Boston Tory, Francis Green, had come to Windham to collect his debts and was encouraged to leave town by the cannon aimed at the door of the tavern where he stayed. Seventeen miles west of Scotland, the townspeople of Hebron forced Reverend Samuel Peters, an Anglican minister and a well-known Loyalist, to ride a horse to the town green and read aloud a scripted apology for his opposition to non-importation agreements. When word spread on September 10 that the British general Thomas Gage had attacked Boston, some twenty thousand men from eastern Connecticut gathered within hours and began the trek to Boston before the rumor could be exposed as false. Elihu would have heard the talk of war and seen men muster for militia drills. Meanwhile, local committees of observation made sure the townspeople complied with the nonconsumption resolutions, and Elihu's sisters cleaned and mended only homespun clothes.[29]

In April 1775, news of the shots fired on Lexington Green took only a day to travel the seventy-five miles to Windham County, prompting scores of young men to gather their gear, say farewell to their families, and head toward Boston to fight the British. The following year, Scotland's own Samuel Huntington, born and raised in the village and married to Reverend Devotion's oldest daughter, put his signature to the Declaration of Independence in Philadelphia. Elihu was too young to fight, but his brother Thaddeus, at seventeen, would have had militia duty, as would have their father, Palmer Sr., since Congress in 1774 asked the colonies to form militia companies from all able-bodied men between the ages of sixteen and fifty. (In 1776, Palmer Sr. was forty-eight.) Some local boys enlisted early, but if Elihu Palmer even considered this option, his father probably quashed it. Did his older brother Thaddeus fight in the war? In a motherless family of eight children, his father could have made the case to keep Thaddeus at home. Plenty of others in Windham preferred to pay the £5 fine rather than show up for militia duty. Or maybe Thaddeus did go; the local enlistment records are incomplete. Palmer Sr. apparently stayed home with his children, the youngest of whom was only three.[30]

As children during wartime, Elihu and his siblings knew scarcity. The hard winter of 1777–78 brought shortages of grain, meat, and salt. Governor Jonathan Trumbull, working out of his home in nearby Lebanon, responded to General Washington's calls for help by ordering cattle rounded up from eastern Connecticut and driven 250 miles to Valley Forge in Pennsylvania, where the animals were devoured within days. Inflation ravaged any savings people had, and increased poll taxes on land and livestock helped pay the bounties of enlisted men. Palmer's wartime childhood was one of hardship and deprivation, made more difficult, one imagines, by the absence of his mother. Tension and grief appeared on the faces of neighbors as news trickled in of local men who had died in the fighting. The home front was not glorious, Palmer understood, even when calls for the nonconsumption of British goods came in the most triumphalist language.[31]

Moments of heartening excitement occurred, too. In June of 1781, the townspeople of Scotland gathered to watch as French soldiers under Lieutenant General Jean-Baptiste Rochambeau marched in from Rhode Island, up the steep and narrow road from the east and past the Scotland green on their way west to meet up with Washington's army along the Hudson. From there they would move on to Virginia. Three regiments of a thousand men marched through town. Infantry soldiers passed by, each clad in a regimental coat, breeches, black gaiters buttoned over the shins, and a tricorn hat adorned with a white, red, and black cockade. The men bore sixty pounds of equipment on their backs. Mounted scouts rode past, looking down at the townspeople. Horses hauled field artillery. Musicians played marching songs to the beat of young drummers. Black servants, some free, some enslaved, walked behind the troops, as did some local white women hired on as cooks, craftsmen ready to repair faulty equipment, and local townsmen driving supply wagons. Reverend Cogswell was impressed by the scene. The French soldiers were "a fine Body of Troops, & under the best Discipline," he wrote, and "not the least Disorder is committed or Damage done by them." One French soldier, in turn, described Scotland village as "a small emerging place where nature is still quite wild." The regiments stayed in a camp outside of Windham, the soldiers in tents and the officers in inns and private homes. As at every camp, the local people came to listen to music, dance, and bring food and other items to sell to the French soldiers. It was a social occasion that people in Scotland would have talked about for many weeks.[32]

A more frightening event occurred a few months later. In September 1781, residents of Scotland could see an ominous red glow to the south. They would later learn that Benedict Arnold, the very same whom Cogswell had tutored, led the forces that torched New London on the coast, and that he had threatened to march inland and do the same to Norwich, his own home town. Reverend Cogswell heard the news from his stepson, who had walked through New London in the aftermath of the attack and reported that most of the town—all but three houses—had been "consumed in the Flames & laid in ashes." The "Misery of ye people is great beyond Description," Cogswell wrote. The minister was appalled to learn that his kinsman had turned traitor and murderer. The reckless prank Arnold had once played in Canterbury—walking the ridgeline of a burning barn—now seemed prophetic. Arnold himself had destroyed much of New London, and he gloried in the carnage. Cogswell lingered on the horror of the deaths. The "Cruelty" shown to the men within the garrison was "shocking to Humanity," Cogswell wrote. Seventy men were found "mangled from Head to Foot." They had been "butchered in cold Blood, begging for Quarter." Arnold seemed bereft of all human feeling and committed "to all Evil." The minister struggled to comprehend the vicious nature of the assault.[33]

What did it mean for the teenaged Palmer to hear that an American turncoat could murder his former neighbors? What message lay encrypted in the terrible scene? Did Cogswell preach about Cain and Abel? Of original sin, which was always latent and ready to strike? Certainly one could see here emotions gone wrong, twisted into a demented brutality. Cogswell felt a profound weariness and dismay. In November 1782, as in the year before, he watched French troops march through town on their way to help the Continental Army. The soldiers impressed him once again, but he was in no mood to celebrate. The destruction of New London by his kinsman had brought the war home to Cogswell. War was a horror, and the soldiers were here to wage it by "Destroying their Fellow men." Armed combat meant brutality, chaos, and death. Cogswell wished only that "a speedy End may be put To the american and all other wars." Peace could not come soon enough.[34]

That same dreary year, Cogswell had the challenge of delivering the funeral sermon for the local man who so unexpectedly killed himself. The message Cogswell struggled over said much about his own faith. He addressed with compassion the self-loathing that follows sin, the abhorrence for one's own wickedness that he believed had led to the man's untimely death. The only solution to this anguish was a repentance born of the sinner's "wish to return to God with his whole heart." When we "feel our hearts broken within us for our sin," Cogswell said, the choice "to repent and turn to God, is the most reasonable thing which can be conceived." To the mourners in the pews, Cogswell offered consolation and hope in "the great mercy of God, and his readiness to forgive all, who truly repent." With warmth he spoke to the relatives of the deceased man. "Your case is so singularly pitiable and distressed," he said, "that I know not how to address you.—My heart bleeds for you." He especially hoped the dead man's elderly, widowed mother would find true comfort in the Lord.[35]

Then Cogswell addressed the stunned friends of the deceased man, the seventeen-year-old Palmer possibly among them. Cogswell had seen the inexplicable wartime "gaity of some, and the unreasonable and unaccountable stupidity" of others, "especially among those to whom God has been most loudly speaking"—the born again—"for months and years past." He had noticed drinking and swearing, "merriment and revelling, chambering" (sexual impurity) and "frolicking," together with an "absence of seriousness" and a callous "criminality of insensibility." He found this shallow self-indulgence especially egregious in the face of the war that dragged on. Your countrymen have been "slaughtered and imprisoned in great numbers," he told the youth sitting before him. "How many of your dear friends and neighbors have fallen in battle, or perished by inhuman cruelty in captivity? Have not many others returned enfeebled, half dead." Given this tragedy, "where is that sobriety and apparent concern" that these distressful occurrences demanded? And now this dreadful suicide. The young people assembled would do well to see in it a warning to themselves, and Cogswell entreated them to reject their sinful ways and turn to God.[36]

A local man who attended the funeral service, Daniel Waldo, found Cogswell's sermon "impressive," its admonitions "pertinent and solemn." The minister was not an "eminent" speaker, Waldo freely admitted. According to Waldo, Cogswell read his sermons in a style "usually not very animated." He viewed things "very much in detail" and could be "tediously minute." Every spring he elicited small smiles when he instructed the youth on proper church behavior and told the young men to stop ogling the ladies. But in casual conversation Cogswell was "free and communicative," Waldo recalled, and full of anecdotes, some of them "very humorous." Cogswell was courteous and "exceedingly modest," a "polished, well-informed, and amiable man" who was oddly terrified of thunderstorms. Waldo's father, a Separatist minister, "was always on familiar terms with Cogswell, and esteemed him highly as a neighbor and a minister." This, then, was the minister who formed young Palmer's understanding of what it meant to be a man of the cloth. Earnest and compassionate, warm but not overly solicitous, Cogswell modeled a humble belief in pervasive sin and the need for redemption through sincere faith in Christ.[37]

From his elders, young Palmer learned to value reason in both religion and politics. Revivalist Christianity was a dangerous form of enthusiasm that could lead to anarchy, adultery, even murder. Ardent patriotism was appropriate, but even here lurked the danger of twisted attachments, as Benedict Arnold showed with such murderous hate. Of all the errors to which human beings were prone, fanaticism was perhaps the greatest, most lethal danger of all. Palmer's father taught moderation by example, preferring predictable order in religion as in the rest of his life. He would have appreciated the nickname the state of Connecticut acquired in the early nineteenth century: "the land of steady habits." That notion represented his own preferred way of being in the world. Palmer Sr. comes across as a responsible father, intent on achieving economic stability and without ambition for political influence. He was possibly reclusive but not freakishly so, serving as a pillar of his ecclesiastical society, after all. Steady habits, indeed.[38]

Reverend Cogswell would have liked the moniker as well, but he might have considered it aspirational more than established fact. He recalled too well the tumult in Canterbury when the New Lights fled his church to start their own and claimed to know whose soul had been saved. Cogswell himself was less adamant in his proselytizing. He preferred to be asked for a prayer than to impose one. He deplored apostasy and godless frivolity, but he had learned to coexist with people of unlike mind.

Between the influences of his father and his minister, Palmer found the intellectual freedom to explore ideas. The physical labor his father required did not come with strong demands of strict theological conformity, as far as we know, and the affable Cogswell would not have discouraged the curiosity of a younger student. Palmer *was* curious, certainly also about options that might lead to a life beyond farming since, as the second son, he was not in line to inherit his father's farm. When peace finally came in 1783, he considered his options. At nineteen, he knew what life in Scotland village had to offer. The third of three Elihu Palmers in a row, descended from storied forebears, he was related by blood and marriage to many in the village. Although his father kept a low public profile, the Palmers were one of the prominent families in the small town. He could easily imagine how his life would unfold if he stayed. He did not share his father's preference for a life of reclusive privacy. He may have explored the fine library Cogswell had inherited from his predecessor, and perhaps Palmer was already alive to the rhythm of words and the theatrical performance of speeches. Given the life of public speaking Palmer eventually chose, it seems possible that already as a youth he itched for something other than rounding up sheep and following the plough through rocky ground. But how was he to make the leap?[39]

College offered a path to other occupations. The ministry or law were options for the younger sons of rural families who would not inherit the family farm. The problem was money. About half of all college students received scholarships, which they supplemented by teaching during their vacations. Even so, higher education in those days was an unusual path for anyone. Only about 1 percent of eligible men in New England attended college. In the 1780s, all the colleges combined had only about one hundred graduates each year. Palmer could see that higher education held out the promise of a professional life, but the way to a college degree was fraught with financial uncertainty. Fortunately, Reverend Cogswell had a proven ability to prepare young men for college, and Palmer landed a scholarship to Dartmouth. The college had been founded by Reverend Wheelock, the New Light minister from Palmer's corner of Connecticut, who raised funds on the promise of educating and converting American Indians. When few Native students appeared, that money went instead to students like Palmer whose families could not afford a college education. The funds may have been earmarked for the training of future ministers, setting Palmer on that career path.[40]

Hanover, in the woods of New Hampshire, lay 150 miles away. Far enough, Palmer might have thought, to spell his freedom. The war was finally over, and the country was just beginning a new chapter as an independent nation. Palmer was ready for a fresh start too. A strong student, he would devote himself to a life of the mind. He would have known what kind of minister he wanted to be: learned, rational, and persuasive. Certainly not searingly emotional in the way of his revivalist kinsman, Reverend John Palmer. And always with room for more questions. Palmer arrived at Dartmouth ready to see what the college had to offer. He would learn there more than he expected, and more than his professors ever intended.

CHAPTER 2

A Liberal Education

Elihu Palmer stepped to the front of the room, chin up and eyes flashing, armed with incisive arguments and zest for debate. In September 1787, he was twenty-three and self-possessed. He wore his straight, brown hair in a low ponytail at his neck. Long eyebrows arched over deep-set eyes, and his prominent nose curved downward. He had round cheeks and a small mouth over a decisive chin. His boyish appearance was unremarkable overall, but everyone noticed his voice. His "pulmonary apparatus gave force to a deep, sonorous and emphatic utterance," one man later recalled. He had a "strong, musical voice," said another, was "eloquent and solemn in his address," and displayed "much ardor and sincerity." In his final student debate at Dartmouth College, Palmer showed himself to be intelligent and loquacious, an extrovert skilled in the art of persuasive argumentation.[1]

Palmer later complained that much of what passed as education involved only the mechanical memorizing of texts. Genius "does not consist in servile imitation, or in mechanically reading over a huge collection of authors," he wrote in a newspaper column. What one really needed, what every human being deserved, was the invitation into deep, original thought. True knowledge comes from sustained and open-minded "*thinking*," by which he meant "independent reflection" with "a strong mind and a persevering investigation." That was not the educational ideal when he attended college.[2]

Even so, he had acquired practice and poise as a speaker. Self-confidence came with success, or perhaps it seemed the birthright of his generation. College students in the newly minted nation believed the future was theirs to make. They belonged to the tiny elite of college-educated men, only about a hundred graduates every year nationwide. Palmer embraced the privilege. He would write sermons for a living, tending souls not beasts and planting ideas rather than crops. As he prepared for a clerical career, he could envision himself as an intellectual, a philosopher theologian bearing a rational religion in service to the new nation. He could look forward to the intellectual rigors of biblical exegesis and the pleasures of educated sociability. Centuries of theological contestation had, by the eighteenth century, expanded the field of debate to include more lenient or "liberal" versions of Protestantism that both challenged and coexisted with stricter forms of Calvinism. Doctrinal disputes were at a lively pitch, denominations outside of the established Congregational and Anglican Churches were growing, and many theological options were on the table. As Palmer honed his analytical abilities and trained his speaking skills, nothing suggested that down the road there might be a conflict between intellectual independence, freethinking forms of religiosity, and social respectability—or that he would ever have to choose among them. For the moment, his world seemed expansive enough for even the most freethinking Christian.[3]

The professors at Dartmouth were not inhumane, whatever Palmer might have thought. They followed the best educational practices of their day. The founder of Dartmouth, Reverend Eleazar Wheelock, copied the curriculum of Yale, his alma mater. After Wheelock's death in 1779, his son and successor, John, continued in the same vein, emphasizing the translation and absorption of time-honored texts, rather than a critical engagement with them. Two-thirds of the coursework focused on learning Latin, Greek, and Hebrew and on reading the ancients. Unfortunately, the school's linguist, John Smith, was timid, formal, and mind-numbingly dull. John Wheelock and his two brothers-in-law taught the remaining courses: rhetoric, English grammar, geography, logic, and moral philosophy in the second year; physics, arithmetic, and astronomy, in the third. Seniors studied metaphysics, theology, and "political law" with Wheelock, who was known for his officious posturing and stilted, florid prose. Students practiced their own ornate prose in weekly speaking exercises and in three additional orations each year. Attendance at the Congregational Church service on Sundays was required, and Wheelock sat in on the students' early morning and evening prayers. To shield Dartmouth students from immoral distractions, "tragedies, plays, and all irreligious expressions and sentiments are sacredly prohibited."[4]

Fortunately for Palmer, intellectual stimulation flourished in students' literary and debating societies. At Dartmouth, as at Yale, Harvard, and the other colleges, students organized extracurricular societies that encouraged reading and debate as part of their social entertainment, along with the usual pranks and excesses of young male sociability. The Society of Social Friends began at Dartmouth in 1783, possibly Palmer's first year on campus. Members paid into a fund to purchase books, and they donated their volumes to "the Socials" when they graduated. Students practiced their skills of forensic disputation and held regular debates on a wide range of subjects, especially those of contemporary public and political concern. In 1786, some of the Socials left to form a rival group, the United Fraternity. (A hint that the new group disliked the conservative bent of the Socials comes from a United Fraternity member, Daniel Webster, who wrote in 1802 about a classmate: "I think him a worthy fellow, and almost the only Social Friend who possesses any liberality of mind, though those pious folks would be very angry with me at saying so.") Palmer joined the United Fraternity in its first year and may have taken part in its founding; he later started or joined groups of sociable freethought wherever he went.[5]

Students found exciting material to discuss. A surviving library catalog from the Social Friends lists some of the books that could have been on hand in the 1780s when Palmer was on campus. "Locke's Essays" probably included the English philosopher John Locke's *Essay Concerning Human Understanding*, which asserted that any accurate perception of reality relies on what one can know through one's senses and experiences. Locke insisted on the veracity of Christian truths, but some readers found that the essay left room for doubt about divine revelation and the mind-boggling miracles recounted in the Bible. "Hume's Essays" also raised questions about biblical claims. David Hume's *Enquiry Concerning Human Understanding* included the skeptical account "Of Miracles," and his *Enquiry Concerning the Principles of Morals* described a system of morality based solely on its utility for human beings and without recourse to divine commands. "Rousseau on Education" was probably the English translation of French philosopher Jean-Jacques Rousseau's *Emile, ou Sur l'Education*, which includes the "Profession of the Savoyard Vicar," a discussion of natural religion that required no Christian foundation. Meanwhile, Thomas Jefferson's *Notes on the State of Virginia*, published in 1785, advocated full freedom of conscience and an end to the legal prosecution of blasphemy. "The legitimate powers of government extend to such acts only as are injurious to others," Jefferson wrote. "But it does me no injury for my neighbour to say there are twenty gods, or no god. It neither picks my pocket nor breaks my leg." Such works encouraged readers to rely on their own powers of observation and to reconsider claims of divine revelation.[6]

Not listed in the catalog but circulating on college campuses since the colonial period were the works of religious dissenters in England who belonged to Protestant denominations that had broken with the Church of England. Many dissenters challenged a central tenet of Calvinism: that salvation was limited to an already determined group of the "elect" and that no human effort could alter the fate of one's soul in the afterlife. Some dissenters questioned the Trinitarian doctrine of a divine Jesus who was one with God and part of a triune deity composed of Father, Son, and Holy Spirit. Others raised doubts about the supernatural aspects of Christianity, miracles in particular.[7]

Some of the skeptical works circulating on college campuses disputed Christian beliefs even more overtly. Their critics called the creators of these works deists, a label the authors often rejected. Men like Lord Shaftesbury, Lord Bolingbroke, Charles Blount, Anthony Collins, John Toland, Thomas Chubb, and Matthew Tindal differed in their opinions about religious doctrine, but they claimed to have an interest in retrieving an authentic, original Christianity from beneath the layers of mystical obfuscation. These writers maintained that the straightforward moral teachings of Jesus had been veiled by metaphysical absurdities added after Jesus's lifetime. The Holy Trinity with Jesus-as-God was one such example; another was the notion that Christ's sacrifice could atone for the sins of others and bring about reconciliation with God. These heterodox writers claimed to promote a truer version of Christianity, leaving in place the central ideas of a Christian God who merited worship, the immortality of souls, the importance of virtuous conduct, and sometimes even the redemptive sacrifice of a partially divine or fully human Jesus. A skeptical state of mind did not necessarily result in disbelief, nor did it produce a single system of faith. No uniform deist doctrine appeared, and people who identified as deist held very different views about the nature and activity of what they variously called the Supreme Being, the First Cause, the Creator of the Universe,

Nature's God, the God of Nature, Divine Providence, the Great Principle, or the Grand Architect. A person need not reject Christianity to interrogate inherited beliefs, weigh anew the claims of divine revelation, and question ecclesiastical authority. To be a Christian deist in this era was not a contradiction in terms for those who identified as such, and plenty of them left the biblical mysteries and miracles intact.[8]

Some writers of deistical bent did openly contest supernatural beliefs. John Toland, an Irish philosopher Palmer later admired, wrote in *Christianity Not Mysterious* (1696) that all phenomena have only natural causes. The so-called miracles, Toland said, were simply events that had not yet been properly understood. Any true religious doctrine must be accessible to human reason because God "has no Interest to delude his Creatures, nor wants [lacks] Ability to inform them rightly." Toland advised against believing what the mind cannot fathom. Believing the incomprehensible was not an admirable act of faith, Toland said; it was "a rash Presumption, and an obstinate Prejudice" more suited for "Enthusiasts or Impostors." According to Toland, the mysterious doctrines of Christianity were invented by clergy and "purposefully made downright unintelligible, or very perplex'd," and "plac'd above the Reach of all Sense and Reason." The obfuscation needed to be undone, Toland said. He knew some would counter that faith is then "no longer *Faith* but *Knowledg*," to which Toland affirmed that "if by *Knowledg* be meant understanding what is believ'd, then I stand by it that *Faith* is *Knowledg*."[9]

More dramatically still, in his *Letters to Serena* (1704) and the *Pantheisticon* (1720), Toland argued for a single-substance universe that was at the same time entirely materialist *and* theist. He had translated the writings of the sixteenth-century Italian philosopher Giordano Bruno, who imagined an endless universe of matter in motion and worlds beyond count with life on other planets. Toland had also read the work of the seventeenth-century Dutch philosopher Benedict de Spinoza, who denied any dualism between God and the world, between spirit and matter. Spinoza identified God as all that exists, which is endless and eternal substance, or what Spinoza called nature. Nature, then, as God, was sacred. Following Spinoza and Bruno, Toland portrayed God as effectively the same thing as infinite matter in eternal motion. Nothing existed beyond the reality of the material universe, Toland wrote; no immaterial souls, angels, or a transcendent deity. Importantly, he did not imagine a universe without God but rather envisioned a divine power infused in and inseparable from everything, everywhere. What was one to call the identification of God with the physical universe? Toland coined the term "pantheist," but it was not widely used, and he did not employ the noun "pantheism" for his ideas. The term "deist," broadly conceived, would have to suffice as a moniker for Toland's mind-bending conception of the universe.[10]

Whether Palmer read Toland in college or only afterward is unclear; he did express his admiration for Toland in the book he published in 1801. More obvious in the 1780s was Palmer's overt admiration for the dissenting Christianity of Reverend Richard Price in London. Price described "a rational and liberal religion" whose God "regards equally every sincere worshipper" who acts according "to the light they enjoy." Price revered Christianity as the true faith, certain that Jesus had been sent by God on a divine mission and had "*tasted death for every man*," giving hope for an eternal afterlife. Even so, Price believed that God favored the devout and virtuous of *all* religions. God "willeth all men to be saved, and will punish nothing but wickedness," Price wrote. Given God's generosity, by what right did human authorities make punitive distinctions among religions? Price urged civil governments to get out of the business of enforcing particular religious institutions and beliefs. Mere toleration was not enough either; he wanted full liberty of conscience for all faiths and an end to established religion. Would not "perfect neutrality" on the part of civil powers toward religious matters "be the greatest blessing?" he asked.[11]

It was easy for Palmer to love Price, as so many American patriots did. The minister had befriended leading American figures like Benjamin Franklin, and his popular pamphlets supported the American cause. With independence won, Price expressed his optimistic wish that the new nation would become "an empire which may be the seat of liberty, science and virtue." He hoped that from the United States "these sacred blessings will spread, till they become universal." Eventually, "kings and priests shall have no more power to oppress, and that ignominious slavery which has hitherto debased the world is exterminated." Price went so far as to say that, second only to the introduction of Christianity, "the American revolution may prove the most important step in the progressive course of human improvement." The new nation might be able to "free mankind from the shackles of superstition and tyranny," and for that reason, Price said, he could not resist the idea that American independence was "ordained by Providence." These heady words and ardent hopes assigned worldwide importance to the fledgling nation.[12]

Some American ministers joined English dissenters like Price in challenging the Calvinist doctrines that had long troubled theologians and lay people alike. Irremediable human sinfulness, the complete dependence on divine mercy for salvation, and preordained and eternal damnation for all but the saved elect—these were difficult lessons about depravity and helplessness. The Puritans had built their "city on a hill" on these Calvinist foundations, and religious revivalists like Elisha Paine in Canterbury had returned to this bedrock in the mid-eighteenth century. But other theologians saw greater leniency in a God who must be as benevolent as he was just. Arminianism, a reformist tendency named after the sixteenth-century Dutch Reformed theologian Jacobus Arminius, posited that people could, with God's help, choose to avoid sin. Though convinced that all human beings lean toward sin and require divine assistance to choose virtue instead, Arminians rejected the notion that only the predetermined elect would be saved.[13]

Within some Congregational churches, especially in eastern Massachusetts, the idea grew that a merciful God would eventually save all souls. The idea of Universal Salvation, or Universalism, posed another strong contrast to the Calvinist doctrine of predestination and eternal damnation of all but the elect. Charles Chauncy, the longtime pastor of the First Church in Boston, pondered Universalist ideas for decades before he published his support for them in 1784. A merciful God would limit the torments of hell, he decided, and a scourging repentance would purify sinners' souls until they too could enter heaven's gates. Even if it took a thousand years of suffering, Chauncy thought, the most inveterate sinners would eventually be reconciled with God. By the time Palmer was in college, proponents of Arminianism and Universalism had begun to proclaim openly their heterodox ideas. Yet even the most liberal theology remained within the capacious tent of Protestant Christianity. Palmer could join the lively and long-standing conversations on how to improve understandings of God's word, just as Protestants had done since the Reformation. He could scrutinize doctrines from within an expanding Christian faith.[14]

Defenders of orthodox Calvinism, meanwhile, viewed both liberal Christianity and deist skepticism as corrosive influences that ate away at the faith of believers. Reverend Timothy Dwight in Connecticut responded to freethought in 1788 with a satirical poem, *The Triumph of Infidelity*. Dwight denounced not only deistic writers like Shaftesbury, Bolingbroke, and Hume but also Satan's lesser "subs, / His Tolands, Tindals, Collinses, and Chubbs." Deism was infidelity, Dwight said, but he was no less exercised about the Universalism of ministers such as Boston's Charles Chauncy. Their misguided leniency, Dwight said, would make room in heaven for the worst of sinners, and even for the Devil himself. What all infidels had in common, in Dwight's view, was the seductive deception that there was an easy way out for sinners. This idea invited immoral self-indulgence from humans who by their very constitution are drawn to sin. The false promise of universal salvation was a complete travesty, an abandonment of any responsible ministry.[15]

Just as ordained theologians disagreed about these matters, so too did students training to become ministers. On college campuses, divisions over freethought played out within the student body. At Yale, a young Jedidiah Morse described the "Universal Depravity" of his college peers. Morse and Palmer would one day openly provoke and oppose one another in matters of faith, and perhaps they already sensed their diverging religious inclinations. They could have known one another growing up, because Morse, older by three years, grew up in Woodstock, Connecticut, which was twenty miles north of Scotland village. Both men came from landed but not extravagantly wealthy farming families. In college, if not before, they parted ways on religion. While Palmer read liberal theology and possibly skeptical philosophy, Morse at Yale doubled down on his faith's commitments. In 1781 he joined the college church, one of only 13 students out of 160 who took communion that year. When he decided to become a minister, he found himself "exposed to the ridicule of the ungodly multitude." He complained about the routine cursing he heard on campus and approved when President Ezra Stiles expelled forty students who broke windows during a ruckus. "This I am glad to see," said Morse, who valued strong authority figures and "severe discipline." When Morse graduated in 1783, he expressed "gloomy" and "dreadful" feelings regarding the "degenerate, the melancholy State of Mankind." In particular, he had trouble with religious doubters. In his opinion, freethinkers wildly overestimated the powers of human reason by conveniently forgetting the abject nature of humankind after Adam's fall from grace. They mocked the Bible as revelation and Jesus as the Savior, Morse complained. He did not know it then, but over time he would see that Palmer did the same.[16]

Their discord, however, lay in the future as Palmer finished his studies at Dartmouth. His spirits must have soared during the graduation ceremonies in September 1787. In the small town of Hanover, "the most respectable inhabitants of this and the neighboring towns" gathered on campus to witness the formal spectacle. In the morning and then again in the afternoon, the twenty-nine graduates, wearing black "uniforms" for the first time since war's end, proceeded from the president's house to Dartmouth Hall. The building was still under construction, but the ceremonies took place on the first floor, with a makeshift stage erected for the purpose. After President Wheelock's opening prayer, the graduates held orations in Latin, Greek, Hebrew, and English. Then they teamed up to debate predetermined questions in disputations that displayed their skills of logical argumentation. The debates showcased the graduates' readiness to participate in public life as educated and articulate men, the next generation of leaders skilled in the civil contention that a democratic republic required. All went according to plan until mid-afternoon, when the platform holding up the seated dignitaries suddenly collapsed. The tumbling of the wigged authority figures no doubt added to the excitement of the day. Some of the graduates may have seen the plummeting professors as symbolic of an older generation of authority figures giving way to their own time on the public stage.[17]

Palmer's turn to perform came during or just after the platform collapse. He and two fellow students debated a team of three others on the question "*ought a man to be excluded from holding any civil office on account of his religious sentiments?*" The proper relationship between freedom of conscience and political officeholding had occupied the constitutional convention in Philadelphia, which had just recently disbanded. The graduates assigned to argue against the religious discrimination of public servants could draw on the year-old Virginia Statute for Religious Freedom, which asserted that "civil rights have no dependence on our religious opinions, any more than our opinions in physics or geometry." Barring a citizen from public office "unless he profess or renounce this or that religious opinion, is depriving him injuriously" of his natural rights, the statute said, and no one should "suffer on account of his religious opinions or belief." Whichever side of the debate he argued that day, Palmer had considered the issue deeply and could shine.[18]

A highlight of the graduation ceremony for Palmer was his nomination to the newly established Dartmouth chapter of Phi Beta Kappa, an academic honor society that recognized scholastic achievement. With his induction, Palmer joined a select group of high achievers among the already small minority of college graduates in the country. The society's secret initiation rituals and handshakes added to the sense of its exclusivity and distinction. Palmer had made the leap: he had joined the educated classes and was on track for a life in the ministry. That evening, the graduates celebrated, perhaps joking about the stage collapse and undeterred by a severe nor'easter that blew in and toppled elms and oaks. Palmer had his own reason to feel festive: he had left behind a life of farming and was headed for a career of ideas and conversation.[19]

Degree in hand, Palmer set off to become a minister. Clerical training required that a college graduate spend some time apprenticed to a clergyman before becoming a probationary candidate with an interested congregation. Students had to find such a mentor, and Palmer probably availed himself of his college connections to make contact with Dartmouth alumnus John Foster, class of '83, only a year older than Palmer. A native of Massachusetts, Foster was minister of the First Parish Church of Brighton, six miles west of Boston. He had married Hannah Webster of Boston, and they lived in an old farmhouse in the center of town. Brighton was quite isolated in the winter, especially when the Charles River froze, but during the warmer season, farmers from all over brought their cattle to market, making Brighton the largest, most bustling place Palmer had ever lived.[20]

The Fosters' liberal faith made the town even more welcoming for Palmer. Reverend Foster was a mild-mannered man who enjoyed books and literary discussions and who would, in over four decades as the minister in Brighton, lead his congregation toward Unitarianism, the idea of a singular God rather than a holy Trinity. In the 1780s, when Palmer studied with Foster, Unitarianism was not yet an official or separate Protestant denomination. Instead, doubts about the Trinity spread quietly within Congregational churches. The Massachusetts ministers Ebenezer Gay and

Jonathan Mayhew had been preaching the unity of God to their congregations since the 1750s, reserving judgment about how best to describe Jesus. For these proto-Unitarians, Jesus was not part of the Holy Trinity, a doctrine that had been in place since the fourth-century Council of Nicaea declared it orthodoxy. But neither did Unitarians view Jesus as an ordinary human being, because he had clearly been sent on a divine mission to redeem humankind. He was sinless and infallible, possibly partially divine, maybe an angel of sorts. This was the Arian view of Jesus (named after the fourth-century priest, Arius, who had been denounced as a heretic). Still, the Arian position in the early United States continued to hold that faith in Jesus as the Redeemer remained the only path to salvation and that the Bible was divine revelation. The change to orthodoxy lay in the demotion of Jesus from an equal part of the divine Trinity to a position somewhere between God and humans. The advocates of this position, later designated Unitarians for their belief in a singular God, saw themselves as Christians who believed that Christ was just as he had described himself: the separate son of the divine Father.[21]

Other theologians went even further in reassessing the status of Jesus. In England, the ministers Theophilus Lindsey and Joseph Priestley adopted the Socinian view (named after the sixteenth-century Italian theologian Socinus) that Jesus was fully human. Socinians saw the worship of Jesus *as God* as a form of idolatry. By the 1780s, the American ministers James Freeman in Boston and William Bentley in Salem were openly discussing such views. These ministers still identified as fully Christian, embracing what they considered a more authentic, original version of Christianity. In the nineteenth century, both Arian and Socinian views of Jesus would find a home in Unitarian churches. In Palmer's day, however, the ongoing discussion about Jesus as separate from God took place within already-existing denominations. Ministers of such persuasion remained within their Congregational and Episcopal Churches and continued to preach that the crucifixion and resurrection of Jesus made possible humanity's atonement with God. Doubt about the divine Trinity would spread in Massachusetts and eventually become the dominant view in the Congregational churches, leading outnumbered Trinitarians to depart and found their own churches.[22]

These denominational rifts still lay in the future when Palmer arrived in Brighton, but the issues that underlay them shaped the conversations he had with Foster. Foster revered a God whose expansive love was a model for Christian philanthropy. The poet Oliver Wendell Holmes later remembered the "mild-eyed" Foster with "the lambent aurora of a smile about his pleasant mouth which not even the Sabbath could subdue to the true Levitical aspect." Foster was "a well-read scholar," Holmes said, and "of most kindly disposition, fond of anecdote, a good talker, and dwelt more on the practical than on the theological side of religion." Palmer had landed well in Brighton.[23]

Mrs. Hannah Foster offered welcome companionship too. She had enjoyed a good education and before her marriage had published political articles in newspapers. In between caring for six children, she wrote an epistolary novel based loosely on the true story of a middle-class woman who died in nearby Danvers in 1788 after the stillborn birth of an illegitimate child. Published anonymously in 1797 as *The Coquette*, Foster's best-selling novel offered a sympathetic and nuanced account of the unwed protagonist and the constraints she faced as a woman. Foster's second novel, *The Boarding School*, commented on women's education in the United States. Hannah and her daughters were themselves "diligent readers of the best books," according to a relative who witnessed the "spirited discussion of free, independent, and active minds." The Fosters frequently read aloud as many families did. One person could read while others did handiwork, and the practice saved candles and spared those with impaired vision. When Palmer lived in Brighton in 1787–88, Hannah Foster had not yet written her books, but her interests were richly political, sociological, and literary. Five years older than her husband, Mrs. Foster may have been the first woman with whom Palmer had extended intellectual conversations. She certainly demonstrated that a wife could be a conversational peer and not just a helpmeet in the household.[24]

After half a year with the Fosters, Palmer continued his internship in Pittsfield, Massachusetts, a river town of almost two thousand people just eight miles from the state's western border with New York. There Reverend Thomas Allen at Christ Church preached the redemptive power of the Savior's love. At Harvard, Allen had learned to question central Calvinist tenets such as the predestination of every soul and that atonement with God was limited to the elect few. Allen had come to believe that people's moral choices *could* make a difference in the fate of their souls. He also held that human happiness in this life, not only the next, was a worthy goal. Like Reverend Cogswell in Scotland, Connecticut, Allen reached toward a faith that was humane and practical rather than rigidly austere or abstract. His sermons nurtured an optimistic belief in God's mercy alongside the Calvinist conviction of unavoidable human sin.[25]

A slender, vigorous man, Allen had energy for political work alongside his ministerial duties. During the war for independence, he had served as a chaplain in three military campaigns, preaching fiery sermons to soldiers who called him the "fighting parson." After the war, when armed Regulators in Shays's Rebellion closed the courts that had ordered land foreclosures for farmers who couldn't pay their taxes, Allen objected. The desperate farmers whose petitions for tax relief had been ignored were not freedom fighters in the way of revolutionary-era rebels, Allen thought, but were outlaws in a working system. Allen held another controversial position when he opposed the Constitution, which Massachusetts ratified in February of 1788. Not one to mince words, Allen wove his political opinions into his sermons, offending those in the pews who thought differently and who had not come to church to receive his political counsel. In April 1788, a committee investigated the recent "disunion in the town" and identified Allen's political sermons as one source of the tension. In his "official character" as minister, the report said, Allen had "repeatedly interested himself in the political affairs of the country, and publicly interposed therein in an undue and improper manner."[26]

That very spring, Palmer arrived in Pittsfield and made his presence known by publishing his opinions in the local newspaper. In the first issue of the *Berkshire Chronicle* in May, an essay of his appeared on the front page. He wrote under the pseudonym "Alfred," a name associated with the ninth-century English ruler who expanded boys' education to include those of common birth. In seven essays under the heading The Moral Observer, Palmer, as Alfred, shared his views about human nature, education, virtue, vice, and the best way to worship God. These first writings from Palmer show his optimism about the human condition. He rejected the idea that humans are born into a condition of moral depravity following the original sin of Adam and Eve's disobedience to God in the Garden of Eden. Vice was *learned*, he said, hypothesizing that a person raised alone on an island in complete isolation would not know sin at all. The "source of all vice and injustice" lay in society, he wrote. He noted that immorality proliferated especially when "men frequently collect together for the purpose of contracting ruinous habits, and gratifying irregular appetites." (Maybe he experienced this in college.) Palmer warned his readers in the tone of a preacher: "Beware then, O man! of the snares which are hid for thee in the vulgar throng." A "vicious inclination" could and "must be corrected."[27]

Original sin was on the chopping block for Palmer, but much else of what Cogswell had taught him remained in place. The "Creator and Governor of the Universe; who holds all worlds in his hands," was a demanding and judging God. He "is strictly just, and will punish thine offences," Palmer wrote. Simply love and worship the Creator, "live justly, be generous to thy fellow-men, practice virtue, and thou shalt not fear to die; nay, thy death shall be happy." This first published credo from Palmer posits an omnipotent God, an immaterial soul with an eternal fate determined by one's behavior in this life, and the absolute necessity of virtue for happiness in this life and the next. It says nothing about Jesus or the Bible. The most important mandate is virtue, an idea Palmer returned to again and again. The "noble principles of generosity, gratitude, and benevolence" should guide one's actions, he wrote. One's true "business in life" is to make one's "own existence a sacrifice to the greatest happiness of rational beings." This act honors the Creator, raises one's own dignity "to the highest perfection," and secures "eternal happiness." A virtuous life should begin right away, Palmer advised, for one cannot know "how far the Ruler of Nature may be pleased to accept of a patch'd-up piece of virtue, made in the decline of life, and composed of those miserable ingredients, *necessity* and *fear*."[28]

Along with virtue, Palmer prized stoic fortitude. The man who suffers pain with patience "sheweth a noble soul" and "declareth to his Creator, that he can bear the part assigned to him." Greatness lies in resilience, he said, the ability to endure adversity and the "firmness of mind" that can "support a man, when the powers of the earth are all united against him." Such strength of mind "is one of the highest blessings of nature, it is the richest possession below the skies." Mental fortitude "does not exclude the finest sensibility, and the tenderest feelings of compassion." Inner strength and sensitive compassion for others "are highly compatible," Palmer said, and they "ought ever to go together." In matters of education, he preferred lenience. "Youth is the age of innocence and purity; and it is also likewise the age of levity and inattention. Let it be so; for it is impossible, as well as improper, to alter it." Teachers should not give the youthful mind any "instruction which it cannot digest."[29]

By putting his opinions into print so soon after his arrival in Pittsfield, Palmer created a public persona for himself in his new locale. Like other aspiring young men, he wished to demonstrate that he had something of value to share with the community. As the Moral Observer, he introduced himself as a public intellectual endowed with the mental prowess and moral gravitas expected of a minister. When one reader printed a rebuttal to Palmer's claim that vice was learned in society rather than innate, Palmer had the satisfaction of seeing that his work mattered enough to merit a refutation. The call and response between writers and their readers were bids to shape public opinion, and Palmer had joined a public conversation over how best to understand the human condition.[30]

Another opportunity for Palmer to build his public profile came on July 4, 1788. Throughout the country, townspeople gathered in meetinghouses, taverns, and parks to remember the revolutionary struggle and celebrate the new political order. Orators paid homage to virtuous patriotism, and in so doing they presented themselves as part of the natural aristocracy that would uphold the new political order. New in 1788 were comments about the Constitution. Ratification had been highly contentious, and citizens were asked to leave partisan politics aside to commemorate Independence Day with decorum. Not everyone felt so moved. In Albany, New York, thirty-five miles from Pittsfield, a street fight was underway: Federalists fired guns, anti-Federalists burned the Constitution, one person was killed, and twelve others wounded. The holiday celebrated a successful war and a united nation, but the moment was sensitive and symbolically fraught. In Pittsfield, Reverend Allen, who had openly opposed the Constitution, may have been too divisive a figure to give a unifying speech on the day of national celebration. The orator that year would be the minister in training.[31]

When Palmer stepped onto the elevated chancel in the Pittsfield meetinghouse and looked at the people sitting on benches before him and in the pew boxes lining the room, he faced a community under some strain. Some townspeople revered their "fighting parson," whereas others resented

Allen's political sermons. What did Palmer do, aged twenty-three and giving his first public speech on the Fourth of July? He did what he had learned at Dartmouth: he borrowed from authors he most admired to craft his position then argued for it as if in a college disputation.[32]

Orators openly copied lines from one another's speeches, and Palmer's oration shared similarities with others delivered on that holiday. Speakers frequently began by placing the American Revolution in the context of world history, and Palmer, too, opened with a reference to the rise and fall of empires over the centuries. But while some orators discussed ancient Greece and Rome before turning to the British Empire, Palmer skipped ahead to European settlement in America. Not long ago, he said, America was home "only to the voracious beast, or the no less hideous savage of the wilderness." He partook of a discourse dear to colonials who imagined that Native American communities no longer existed in New England, or at least not as polities that should matter to white people. Having evoked an ugly caricature of American Indians, Palmer quickly moved on to the cause of the day's celebration. Here, too, his historical narrative was cursory. He found it "unnecessary, at this time, to trace the steps by which AMERICA has risen to her present height of honour and importance" because, as he said, "they are within the reach of every man's memory." This was not really the case, since Palmer himself was too young to remember the beginnings of the colonial conflict, but he preferred to gloss over the details of the past and dwell instead on how the American Revolution would shape the future.[33]

That future looked very good, he said, because the "sacred flame of liberty" that burned bright in America would surely make its way around the world and spark movements for emancipation everywhere. The "heroic sons of France" who had fought in the American Revolution had returned home bearing the republican sentiments that would soon bring liberty to that oppressed people. From Europe, the "sacred flame" would move to Asia and beyond, liberating countries "debased and depress'd by the iron chains of slavery." Like other orators, Palmer expressed the fond hope that America's form of self-governance would spread to other countries. He shared the opinion that a narrow concern with only one's own nation was a provincial position and that the proper ambition for Americans was the liberation of all people around the globe.[34]

Not all Americans were free, of course. The recently ratified Constitution protected the institution of slavery, ensuring that Congress could not end the Atlantic slave trade for at least another twenty years and mandating the return of runaway slaves to their owners. When Palmer used the term "slavery," he meant religious and political oppression, not the hereditary slavery of African-descended people in the United States. In fact, Palmer overlooked those held in physical bondage when he described America as divinely preferred, "a country peculiarly favoured by Heaven, and which shall be the parent of innumerable blessings to the human race." He did not remark upon people held as chattel in virtually every state in the union.[35]

His omission contrasts with the open condemnation of slavery in the writing of Richard Price, whom Palmer greatly admired. "The NEGRO TRADE cannot be censured in language too severe," Price wrote. It is "shocking to humanity, cruel, wicked, and diabolical." Price even ventured to say that as long as slavery exists in the United States, "it will not appear they deserve the liberty for which they have been contending." Palmer knew of this critique, yet when he said "Americans" he meant European immigrants and their descendants. Of them he could say that "never did the hand of Heaven more richly bestow his benefits upon a country." He hoped the nation's future generations, and again he meant white people, would "ever be free from civil and religious slavery," so that the country may "finally become the seat of science, the land of virtue, and the glory of the whole earth." Palmer would one day take a stand against racial slavery, but in this speech he elided the subject altogether.[36]

The most important freedom bar none, in Palmer's opinion, was mental liberation from false religion: "The slavery of men's consciences (the worst of all kinds of slavery) must sooner or later be abolished." Superstition continued to hoodwink people who were legally free but intellectually blinkered, and Palmer hoped for the ruin of every "institution formed for the abominable purpose of enslaving men's minds and consciences." His larger point was that freedom of conscience was the prerequisite for any lasting political, social, or economic improvement. Once relieved of religious prejudice, liberated human reason could lead the way to a better future. The "Sons of Science" would explore the world unimpeded, he effused, making possible "the most illustrious display of genius, and the profoundest investigations of the human mind."[37]

Those seated in the Pittsfield meetinghouse may have been glad when Palmer turned to the American situation in particular, the reason for their gathering. He lingered first on the unsung heroes of the American Revolution, the "multitude of heroes and soldiers" whose names are recorded "in the *celestial archives above*," for they had fought for "universal liberty and the happiness of the human race." The soldier's ultimate sacrifice helped form the "foundation for the happiness of millions, yet unborn, and establish an *asylum* for the oppressed in every part of the earth." All too quickly, however, Palmer moved from this shared ground of reverence for patriotic martyrdom to partisan politics. Like most New Englanders at the time (but not Reverend Allen), Palmer had Federalist sympathies. He celebrated the framers of the Constitution as the "wisest and best of men" who drafted it "with a noble zeal for the liberties of their country, and the happiness of the human race." The framers' motivations were pure, Palmer believed, and the "sole end of their intentions was the public good." He perceived no self-interest behind a stronger federal government that ensured the nation's creditors would receive interest payments on their loans; he saw no threat in a standing arming ready to quell any domestic insurrections that might arise. Certainly he showed no sympathy for the recent armed protest of the Regulators in Massachusetts, and he thought it proper to quash all "broils and commotions."[38]

If anyone in the meetinghouse felt uncomfortable with Palmer's political judgments, he made things worse by belittling their concerns. Compared to the unfreedom that existed elsewhere, America was a "free and happy country," he said, "if we had but wisdom enough to think so." Those who complain of "civil oppressions" should look at the systemic injustice in other parts of the globe and then "wonder at the patience of Heaven, that we are not destroyed for our ingratitude and wickedness." Millions of people in Asia and Africa are "bound in the chains of ignorance, slavery, and wretchedness." Compare this suffering to the situation in the United States, and it will appear "astounding" that we should be "restless and uneasy with our condition, murmuring at our civil oppressions, and disposed to throw every thing into a state of anarchy and confusion." Was Palmer referencing disagreements over the ratification of the Constitution? The ongoing grievances of the Regulators or their sympathizers? Or even local complaints about Thomas Allen? He did not care to specify, but regardless, he was not sympathetic. Some infringement on personal liberty was necessary, Palmer said, as we cannot "live in civil society, without giving up a part of our natural liberty." Americans should be grateful "that we live in a land where the rights and privileges essential to the dignity and happiness of human nature are not taken from us; and where science and virtue may prevail and flourish." The political battle had been won, freedom of religion and of scientific inquiry would do the rest. The glorious future he predicted was, he thought, a foregone conclusion.[39]

As Palmer stepped away from the chancel, secure in his opinions and confident about his eloquence, he might have recalled the education that had brought him this far. His exposure in college to the works of Richard Price and other liberal Christians, along with his conversations with the proto-Unitarian Fosters in Brighton, had persuaded Palmer that a new and better day was dawning in America and that it rested on a generous, tolerant, freethinking version of Christianity. Palmer included himself among the "Friends of liberal Sentiments," as he would later put it, with which he meant an open-minded faith that supported unfettered scientific inquiry and that presumed a nearly unlimited human capacity for learning and moral improvement. As Palmer looked to the future—his own, the nation's, the world's—he saw himself as an educator in the pulpit, weaning people from Calvinist creeds that stood in the way of intellectual independence. In the meantime, he would affirm his standing as a man of education and influence by publishing his speech and making it available for sale.[40]

Not everyone took him seriously. The local newspaper published a spoof of the day's events and referenced Palmer's youth: "*Palmer* told mighty things might be—/ A little boy, was Adam free? / Did *Adam* know a little thing, / *Palmer*, a big boy, may begin." Such ridicule did not give Palmer pause. He performed an exhibition, or verbal disquisition, in the meetinghouse the following month. He also expanded his repertoire of the subjects he discussed in print. In October, again under the pseudonym Alfred, he published three articles on politics in the *Massachusetts Spy*, a Worcester newspaper with wider circulation than the *Berkshire Chronicle*. The first essay explained the benefits of a stronger federal government, the second argued in favor of amendments to the Constitution, and the third advocated for trial by jury. These longer essays showed him to be well-read and articulate, not only about religion but also about politics and the law.

Eager to enter public conversations about matters of national concern, Palmer considered his thoughts worth sharing. His chosen career suited him well, because as a cleric he would continue to shape popular opinion.[41]

The last phase in Palmer's ministerial education began when a Presbyterian church in Newtown on Long Island invited him to come for the usual probation period. Palmer's "good reputation for integrity and literary proficiency" had impressed the search committee. If, after three months or maybe six, the congregation appreciated Palmer's talents, they would offer him a "call" to be their minister, with the expectation that he would hold that position for life.[42]

Traveling south from Pittsfield on his way to Long Island, Palmer passed through the small town of Sheffield, Massachusetts. The village was between settled ministers, and visiting preachers were welcome to take the pulpit. On a designated day of prayer and thanksgiving, Palmer stood in the spacious whitewashed church, with the light coming in from the large windows, and told the villagers that the best way to show gratitude for the Creator's bounty was to take conscious delight in it. As Palmer's friend, a Sheffield native named John Fellows, later told the story, "Instead of expatiating upon the horrid and awful condition of mankind in consequence of the lapse of Adam and his wife, he exhorted his hearers to spend the day joyfully in innocent festivity, and to render themselves as happy as possible." Palmer's sermon did not go over well with those who expected a Calvinist sermon about the innate depravity of human beings and the importance of repenting one's sins in hope of receiving divine mercy. One parishioner chided Palmer in no uncertain terms for his inadequate sermon. The man, a *"sound believer,"* lectured Palmer "for giving such liberal advice." Palmer was not deterred by the criticism, and when he preached in New York City soon afterward, he was reprimanded once more. Reverend John Rodgers, a senior minister of the United Presbyterian Churches of New York City and a prominent New Light minister, "reproved" Palmer "for the liberality of his sentiments." Whatever Palmer was preaching, it emphasized happiness and gratitude over sin and repentance.[43]

By the time Palmer arrived at his probationary pulpit in Newtown, he may have already considered himself a Universalist. He almost certainly rejected the doctrine of the Trinity. (Two years later he claimed that he had only ever preached the Socinian view of Jesus as fully human.) No further evidence reveals what Palmer thought about Jesus or his teachings, but that is the point: Palmer did not discuss, reference, or even gesture toward Jesus in the writings he published in the 1780s. Palmer wrote nothing about atonement, redemption, miracles, or salvation through faith alone. He spoke frequently of an omnipotent "Creator," a "Ruler of Nature," and "the hand of Heaven." He described the deity as present, active, interventionist, pro-American, and male, but Palmer offered no clue about which religious doctrines mattered the most. Virtue certainly mattered, and Palmer assumed an eternal afterlife, the quality of which depended on one's behavior in the here and now. He issued warnings about vice and about harmful religious superstition. He also urged emancipation from an unthinking faith. Most of all, he insisted that human beings had the ability to improve the human condition and achieve a better world. They could do it with reason, virtue, and science. Jesus need not have anything to do with it.[44]

Palmer had received a far-ranging education since he left behind the calm, earnest Calvinism of his hometown minister, Reverend Cogswell. Liberal versions of Protestantism, and possibly also religious skepticism, had widened his horizons, yet he could still envision a life in the ministry. He did not fear heterodoxy, nor did he seem to mind being reprimanded for his "liberal" sermons. In his view, theological friction was not a problem to be avoided but rather an opportunity to delve deeper into one's thinking about religion. He had a compelling reason to work it out, since he desired a life of the mind. A ministerial career could sponsor his passion for theology and employ his talents as a public speaker. He had plenty of opinions and the authority, as a college graduate and minister-in-training, to share them. As he set out for his post on Long Island, Palmer foresaw no impediments to his career as a freethinking minister.

CHAPTER 3

"All is Alive"

DOCTOR JOHN RIKER and the other trustees of the Presbyterian Church welcomed Elihu Palmer to their small but thriving village in late 1788. Newtown, the seat of Queens County on Long Island, featured a town hall, a jail, a tax office, and the town clerk's office, along with the St. James Protestant Episcopal Church and the octagonal meeting house of the Dutch Reformed Church. The Presbyterian meeting house was still under construction, Palmer learned. British soldiers had destroyed the building during the American Revolution, and for the time being the Presbyterian congregation met every other week in the Reformed church. For the last three years, they had heard the Calvinist sermons of Reverend Peter Fish who had been smitten at the age of thirteen by the preaching of George Whitefield. Fish had studied theology under the New Light ministers at the College of New Jersey (later renamed Princeton University), and his parishioners in Newtown had come to expect his warnings about the inherent depravity of all humans born in sin, and their utter dependence on a divine and saving grace to preserve them from the eternal hell they fully deserved. Palmer, now twenty-four, brought a different message. He would tell his congregants that virtuous conduct could make a difference in the fate of their souls and that the best way to worship the divine Creator was to treat others with generosity and compassion. Whether that message would pass muster in Newtown remained to be seen.[1]

A physician from the congregation named Isaac Ledyard, who was a decade older than Palmer, soon invited him into private conversation. Initially, Ledyard pressed the recently arrived minister on Christian doctrine. Maybe he asked Palmer to explain how Jesus's sacrifice could atone for the sins of others, or maybe he asked about the miraculous resurrection.

Whatever the questions, the younger man found the doctor's inquiry about the tenets of Christianity "very irksome," a friend later recalled, because Palmer "could not conscientiously defend them." On probation to become the Presbyterian minister in Newtown, Palmer initially withheld from Ledyard his skepticism about the supernatural parts of the Christian faith. But once Palmer decided Ledyard "was trust-worthy" and would keep their exchange confidential, he "begged a truce with him, stating, that there was no disagreement in their opinion." Both men discounted the divine status of Jesus, his redemptive sacrifice on the cross, and other miracles recounted in the Bible. Both also rejected the doctrine of predestination for every soul and the notion of eternal damnation. That much could be quickly established. Ledyard, however, had more to say than that, if he could count on the younger man's discretion.[2]

Palmer would have been flattered by the attention from his new friend. The established Ledyard family lived in Groton, Connecticut, thirty miles south of Palmer's village of Scotland, and Ledyard's well-known cousin, John Ledyard, had accompanied Captain Cook on his third voyage to the Pacific in the 1770s. Palmer readily perceived the differences of age and social status: Ledyard was an established physician, whereas Palmer was just embarking on his ministerial career. Then again, both men hailed from eastern Connecticut, had attended college, and rejected Calvinist ideas about sin and damnation. Once they recognized their common ground, Ledyard decided to confide in Palmer.[3]

Or maybe he simply handed the minister *An Essay on Matter*, the twenty-six page pamphlet Ledyard had published anonymously in Philadelphia five years before. Did he watch Palmer read it, scanning his face for a reaction? The ideas in the pamphlet were the ones Ledyard wanted to discuss, especially the notion that only matter exists. Eternal matter in endless reformulation makes up all things that ever existed or ever will, the pamphlet explained. Nothing, not even God, transcends matter, nor are there immaterial objects of any kind, such as angels or souls. This matter is not inert, for it is infused with a life force and remains eternally in motion, creating everything in the universe. The notion of vibrant, self-activating matter, itself an ancient idea, would in the early nineteenth century come to be called vitalism. Ledyard did not use that term in his pamphlet, and neither would Palmer when he wrote about the concept in 1801. But lively matter was a natural fact, they agreed, and this "important information to mankind," Ledyard's *Essay* declared, was based on the insights of natural philosophy, "Chymistry" in particular.[4]

Where had Ledyard encountered the idea of endless matter in eternal motion? If Palmer had asked about its provenance, Ledyard might have repeated the pamphlet's claim that only his own logic, and no outside reading, had led him to grasp the truth of vibrant matter. But that was not the full story. The medical education of Ledyard's day participated in a transatlantic conversation about the healing powers of an immanent life force. That larger discussion, and Ledyard's particular adaptation of it, shaped Palmer's own view of the universe. Once seen, the lively material universe could not be unseen. Yet the idea of a vital force within matter did not initially replace Christianity, in Palmer's thinking, but mixed with his existing doubts about certain Christian teachings and sharpened his critique. It also jeopardized his career. Within six months of his arrival in Newtown, Palmer found himself out of a job and looking for a new line of work. If, in retrospect, vibrant matter proved to be a kind of milestone in Palmer's development as a freethinker, what, exactly, was it? And why, if it was such "important information to humankind," should it remain a carefully guarded secret?[5]

Ledyard almost certainly came to vitalism through his medical education in New York City's first, and for a long time only, medical school. In the mid-1770s, Ledyard studied at King's College (later renamed Columbia University) with John Bard, the quarantine physician for New York City who tried to protect the public from contagious diseases. The medical school was a recent innovation and an improvement on the long-standing colonial practice for training physicians. Before the revolution, students studied with a doctor for a year or two, observing their mentor's work with patients, then started practicing themselves. The colonies had no medical clinics, schools, clubs, journals, or libraries, and no license or certificate was required to practice medicine. Patients who complained of poorly trained physicians were often right. In the 1740s, Bard and his Scottish-educated colleague Peter Middleton made a first attempt at formalized medical teaching when they offered a private course in human anatomy in New York City. In 1768, Bard's son, Samuel, just back from his medical studies in Edinburgh, helped found the medical school at

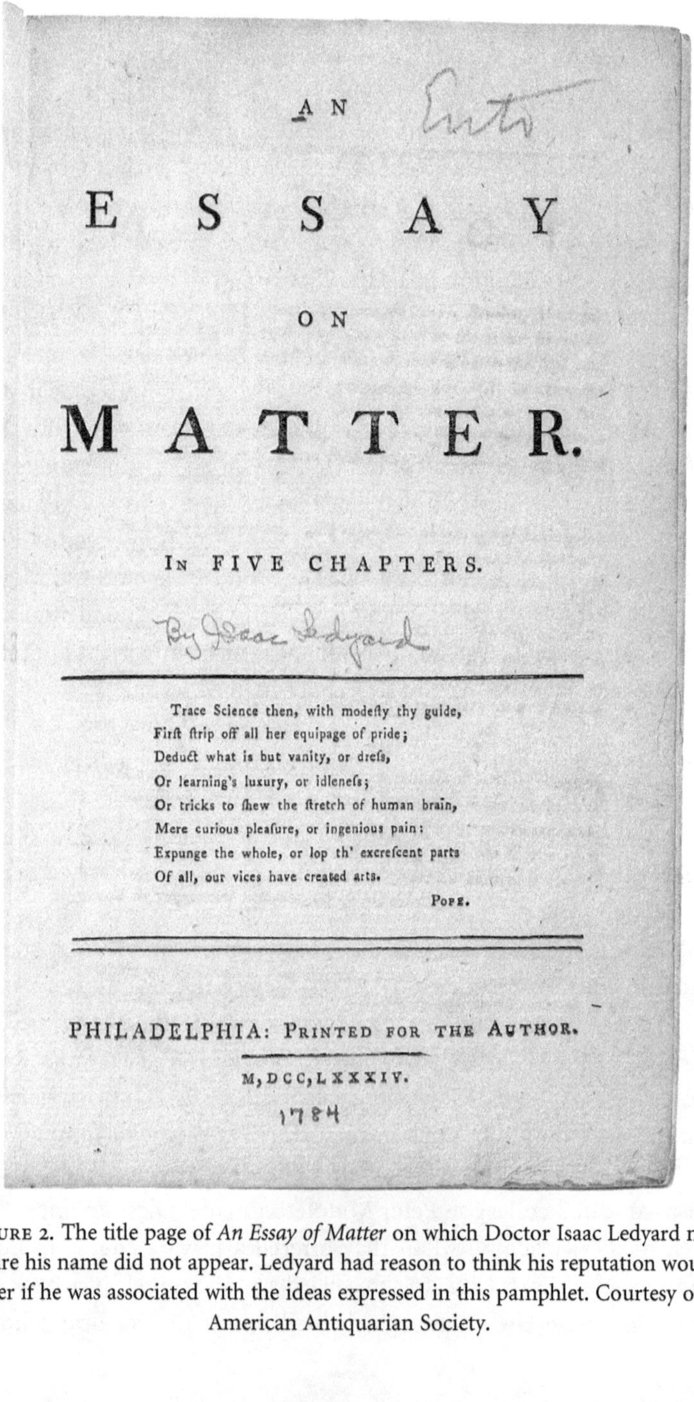
AN

ESSAY

ON

MATTER.

IN FIVE CHAPTERS.

By Isaac Ledyard

Trace Science then, with modesty thy guide,
First strip off all her equipage of pride;
Deduct what is but vanity, or dress,
Or learning's luxury, or idleness;
Or tricks to shew the stretch of human brain,
Mere curious pleasure, or ingenious pain:
Expunge the whole, or lop th' excrescent parts
Of all, our vices have created arts.

POPE.

PHILADELPHIA: PRINTED FOR THE AUTHOR.

M,DCC,LXXXIV.

1784

FIGURE 2. The title page of *An Essay of Matter* on which Doctor Isaac Ledyard made sure his name did not appear. Ledyard had reason to think his reputation would suffer if he was associated with the ideas expressed in this pamphlet. Courtesy of the American Antiquarian Society.

King's College. After a year of hearing lectures on anatomy, physiology, pathology, surgery, obstetrics, chemistry, and materia medica (pharmacology), students received a bachelor of medicine degree. One or two additional years of study gained them the degree of doctor. Physicians were called "doctor" in either case, and it is unclear which degree Ledyard received.[6]

What is clear is that Ledyard found physiology particularly fascinating. Since the mid-eighteenth century, natural philosophers in Edinburgh, London, Paris, Montpellier, Halle, Göttingen, and elsewhere had pondered the healing powers within the human body. What was it, precisely, that caused a return from sickness to health? Empirically inclined natural philosophers peered through newly improved microscopes at tiny organisms and sensitive nerve endings, hoping to identify what caused cells to replicate and nerves to twitch. Others speculated more theoretically about the properties of the "vital principle." Was it an ethereal fluid, they wondered, or more like electricity? How best to imagine the invisible and yet effective power that moved an organism through its many changes?[7]

When Ledyard considered the self-healing properties of the human body, he may well have leaned on the work of William Cullen, the influential Scottish physician and chemist. Cullen and his colleague Robert Whytt had developed a human physiology that posited a quasi-autonomous life force within the physical body. Their model diverged from the well-established mechanistic account of the human body as a kind of marvelous machine with a hydraulic system of blood circulation and a network of nerves. Cullen and Whytt preferred to see the body as a self-regulating entity, a life system with internal forces naturally inclined toward self-preservation. Whytt spoke of a "sentient principle" that communicated through the body's nervous system, making possible the spontaneous, involuntary, unconscious responses to stimuli in ways that supported the body's health. The principle of self-preservation was ubiquitous and self-activating, he said, and it infused *all* living organisms. Cullen held that the physician's role was largely to get out of the way of the vital principle, what he called the *vis medicatrix naturæ*, and let it do its healing work. The vital force required no dramatic medical interventions—such as the enemas and emetics favored by eighteenth-century physicians—to produce the processes of healing. As an admiring Benjamin Rush put it, Cullen sought "to explode useless remedies" and emphasize instead the "influence of diet, dress, air, exercise, and the actions of the mind."[8]

Cullen's popular lectures had a strong influence on American medical training. Aspiring physicians who could afford the trip studied in Edinburgh and brought their learning back to the colonies. By 1775, some four hundred physicians in America held medical degrees, only about fifty of which had been granted by American colleges; the rest had come from European institutions. Americans who studied in Edinburgh returned home with books, lecture notes, and often a great deal of enthusiasm for Doctor Cullen's theories. Benjamin Rush, for example, spent two years in Edinburgh in the 1760s and returned to Philadelphia inspired. Cullen taught his students "the art of teaching others the most successful methods of curing diseases," Rush said, and in that way Cullen "conveyed the benefits of his discoveries into every part of the United States."[9]

Rush could confirm that the concept of vital matter melded easily enough with Christian beliefs. Others had found the same. Jonathan Edwards, the famous New Light minister in Massachusetts, had described a Calvinist God who worked within, and communicated himself through, the processes of nature. With God present in the natural world, Edwards thought, nature itself became a site of divine revelation. The pious Quaker botanists in Philadelphia, John Bartram and his son William, observed in natural processes the "immediate finger of God" (John) and the "secret divine influence" (William) that showed God to be both immanent in nature and the transcendent Creator of it. In other words, medical and philosophical conceptions of a life force within matter folded readily into a larger theism that saw God's hand in nature.[10]

This vitalism meshed just as well with religious doubt, and Benjamin Rush noted that the Scottish physician "professes himself to be a skeptic." Cullen had no "regular system for himself" in matters of religion, Rush acknowledged, as his "habit of thinking for himself & of doubting the truth of every principle of science until it is proved" had carried over into a "spirit of free inquiry" regarding religious matters. Rush decided differently for himself, separating the requirements of good medicine from those of a strong faith. The "truths of religion are objects of faith & not of reason," he wrote. The limitations of the human mind meant for Rush that some aspects of Christianity must remain mysterious and require belief without proof. "We ought to believe them although we cannot comprehend them," Rush thought. A leap of faith was necessary, because without religion "there can be no virtue, and without virtue there can be no liberty, and liberty is the object and life of all republican governments." Rush combined vitalist physiology with his Christian faith, declaring in his eulogy of Cullen that "Revelation enables us to say, with certainty and confidence, that he [Cullen] still LIVES."[11]

When theories of vitalist physiology circulated at King's College in New York City, Ledyard's professor of chemistry, Peter Middleton, refuted them outright. Middleton adhered to a mechanical view of the human body as a "most complicated Machine" with its "*Powers* of MECHANICS" and "*Laws* of HYDRAULICS." God was the divine Maker and Mover behind nature's mechanics, assuring that every "*Atom* is formed, and placed" in its proper spot. Physiology took two forms, Middleton said, and he approved of only one of them, namely the hands-on empirical study that aided the actual practice of medicine. The branch of physiology that Middleton found suspect was the kind of "Natural Philosophy" that was "pleasing and instructive to Men of *Speculation* and *Letters*" who researched "no farther than the immediate Objects of their Senses." In other words, Middleton disparaged those who engaged in physiology as a creative thought problem, or "*Speculation*," without the benefit of researching beyond what they could see with their own bare eyes—exactly the kind of theorizing that Ledyard enjoyed.[12]

Plenty of people in Ledyard's day, medically trained and not, valued such speculative theorizing about a lively material universe. In Paris, Denis Diderot was among those taken by the image of a mysterious vital force that infused the material world with unpredictable, even whimsical, power. He gave the idea strong representation in the *Encyclopédie* he edited for two decades, and he explored a vitalist cosmos in his posthumously published *D'Alembert's Dream*. Erasmus Darwin, Alexander Pope, and Mary Wollstonecraft in England and Johann Goethe in Germany wrote poetry and novels about a life force within matter. Vitalism gained recognition well beyond medical circles in Europe as the multivocal articulation of the idea of the universe as a single, living system, an evocative way to reconsider nature, the cosmos, and the divine. All of this would have irritated Middleton, but not Ledyard, who believed the foot soldiers of empiricism would eventually catch up to the theorists of vitalism and prove their theories right. By the time he left King's College, Ledyard had heard arguments for and against an animating, healing power within matter, and he had chosen Cullen's *vis medicatrix* over Middleton's "complicated Machine."[13]

When war broke out with England, twenty-one-year-old Ledyard decided to put his medical training to good use. In March 1776, he entered the medical department of the army and became surgeon's mate to the First New York Regiment and then assistant purveyor of the Hospital Department. He continued to ponder vital matter and in 1782 shared some of his ideas in a letter to his close cousin, John. That letter has apparently not survived, but John responded to it with concern. "I lament my separation from thee," John wrote to Isaac. "O thou companion from my youth shall I loose thee? Is it an affection of being thought a clever fellow that you have thus thought? Or did you mask yourself and act the fool for follies sake? Or did you read Voltaire and Bolinbroke & suffer—." The rest of the sentence was carefully cut out, presumably by Isaac. Tantalizingly incomplete, John's letter suggests that Isaac had shared his thoughts about eternal, vibrant matter, and maybe religious skepticism as well, and that John strongly disapproved. The letter brought home to Ledyard the adverse reaction he could expect if he went public with his freethinking ideas.[14]

Ledyard had no desire to jeopardize his reputation or his medical career with notions that would mark him as a freethinker. In the early 1780s, readers circulated skeptical works with discretion. The term "deist," easily flung about, implied libertinism and a slippery slope toward irreligion. At the ragged end of a long and violent war for independence, moral rectitude was in high demand. By general consensus, religion offered moral guidelines and helped instill virtue, placing critics of religion on shaky ethical ground. With this in mind, when Ledyard published his *Essay on Matter* in 1784, he chose to remain anonymous.

He did so for good reason, because his essay conflicted with prevailing Christian tenets. Ledyard described a universe in which human beings are comprised of the same material as everything else, not made separately in God's image, as the Bible had said. Ledyard explained that the singular substance of the universe engaged in a perpetual "exchange of matter" among *all* forms. The "animal creation, for instance, is constantly exchanging parts with the earth," its "atmosphere," and with plant life, too. Ledyard rejected the traditional belief in a hierarchy of ontologically distinct creations, with humans holding a uniquely special place. That model grew out of misguided human chauvinism, Ledyard thought. "The Ignorant and Proud may exclaim—are we nothing more than finely-qualified matter!" To this Ledyard answered yes, precisely. "Notwithstanding the envied place of distinction man supposes himself to hold in this world, compared to other matter in it," humankind is, in fact, "no more than the first order of animals." It was "hateful to our pride" but no less true that humans are "actuated by the same principle that actuates the animal creation and other matter."[15]

Ledyard perceived the Earth as equally dependent on all its parts. The "animal, vegetable, and mineral kingdoms" are all necessary to life on the planet, he wrote, and are perhaps to the Earth "what excretatory organs, the organs of perspiration, are to us." Just as the parts of the human body function in concert, so too did the Earth appear to him as a living system, like a breathing, sweating body. His description moved from micro systems to the macro and back again, seeing in analogies of scale a satisfying logic that signaled their own facticity. As the human body is an organism within the larger living system of the Earth, so too was the planet a living system within the galaxy. As he put it, "the stars, &c. must be sister parts" within the universe. The "harmony and [mutual] dependence which we observe in things that we can see" can reasonably be projected into infinity. "Creation then, as far as we can trace it, would appear to be one INFINITE MASS OF MATTER."[16]

What kept this living system in motion? This was the most exciting idea of all, Ledyard said—that a singular and eternal life force infuses everything. Every single object "is possessed of the same living principle," which causes motion "in every form of matter." The power that "actuates" a person does the same for "a vegetable, an oyster, or a stone." He also believed the living principle could not be separated from matter. The life force and matter are "co-existent"—"the one as durable as the other, and both from everlasting to everlasting." Considered in this way, there is no such thing as death, he said, although people commonly misunderstand this. When a person's body ceases to function, we call that person dead and imagine an immaterial soul with an eternal afterlife. But the particles that made up the body do not ever die; they live eternally, always forming themselves into something new. Matter can change its form, but it cannot "waste," and "as life is co-existent with matter, life cannot cease." According to Ledyard, we should do away with the confusing word "death" and more accurately call it "CHANGE: for death, in the sense which it is used, cannot happen any more than eternity can end."[17]

Ledyard's materialism did not lead him to atheism. On the contrary, he had no doubt that God exists. "That there is a God we believe from this, THAT THINGS ARE, AND THAT THEY MOVE." Things cannot move without a cause, and the cause is God. This was not the personal God of the Bible, in Ledyard's view, but a deity impossible to describe. Language, which afforded only "the most imperfect signs of thoughts," could not produce conceptual clarity or linguistic precision in the face of such overwhelming mystery. "Whenever I impiously attempt to identify God,—to give him a likeness to any thing which I can conceive of,—to shape him to my comprehension, and fashion him after the frailty of my senses, I cannot feel that satisfaction, love, reverence and devotion; because, in this prophane way of reasoning, I do not find Truth, I do not feel my God." No person had the ability to communicate what God was, a subject best left in thoughts only, as "words only tend to lead us on from error to error." Ledyard used synonyms for God, most often Universal Agent and Universal Cause (with a male pronoun), but he considered these insufficient ciphers, for no word "will ever give us an idea of God as a BEING."[18]

Where language ends, however, emotions can still convey the divine. "The best idea that my mind can have of God," Ledyard wrote, "is from the idea it has of TRUTH; wherever I find this, I feel in myself an instantaneous glow of ineffable love, reverence, and adoration, which tell me, this must belong to the UNIVERSAL CAUSE, this must be God. These sensations I cannot convey to others, because words cannot be made to have relation to them." Divine power exceeded the grasp of human intellect and language. Ledyard decided that God "is a subject that will scarcely apply to words at all, but belongs entirely to the thoughts." Intellectual modesty was required; any dogma based on human conceptions of the divine was hubris. "Here then REASON art thou bounded!" he exclaimed.[19]

When Ledyard shared his ideas with Palmer, he could tell the younger man that his *Essay* had been denounced. Published critiques pointed out that *An Essay on Matter* did not allow for immortal souls abiding in an eternal afterlife, making moot the need for a Judgment Day. Absent a

Supreme Judge apportioning eternal rewards and punishments, why would any mortal choose acts of virtue over selfish sin? A fellow physician published *"Answer to an anonymous pamphlet just published in Philadelphia, entitled An Essay on Matter: Wherein the Author's Design is supposed to be an attack on the Christian Religion."* The author's answer was simple enough, namely to insist that immortal souls did indeed exist and that God had created all of them during the six days of Genesis some six thousand years ago. As soon as a human body is born and begins to breathe, "a rational soul instantly enters, and takes its turn of action" for "as long as that body lasts." Where souls abide when not embodied remains a mystery that is "best known to the Creator."[20]

A leading figure in the Episcopal Church, Charles Henry Wharton, similarly rejected *Essay on Matter*'s "doctrine of materialism" because it did not allow for "the immortality of the soul" or for "a future state of punishments and rewards, two principle bases of the christian system." Matter in eternal motion seemed to Wharton an utterly *"melancholy and hateful"* prospect. After all, cycling "through the various changes in the animal, vegetable and mineral worlds without a consciousness of past or present or future existence" was no better than annihilation, in Wharton's opinion. "We are made for immortality," Wharton objected, "and thither we shall arrive." *An Essay on Matter* was an "absurdity," and he hoped its "gloomy" author would "cease to dogmatize."[21]

Reverend Timothy Dwight learned that Ledyard was the author of *An Essay on Matter* and mocked him in his 1788 poem, *Triumph of Infidelity*. "Even plodding L****** did but little good, / Who taught, the soul of man was made of mud: / Cold mud was virtue; warmer mud was sin; / And thoughts the angle-worms, that crawl'd within: / Nor taught alone; but wise, to precept join'd / A fair example, in his creeping mind." Ledyard's muddy mind was crawling with wormy ideas, Dwight suggested, because he denied the eternal life of immaterial souls.[22]

For the most part, however, Ledyard's authorship of *An Essay on Matter* remained unrecognized, and his reputation and career rose unimpeded by his freethought. The year after the pamphlet's publication, he married in the First Presbyterian Church in New York City. The pious Doctor John Bard probably helped Ledyard land the position as health commissioner for the Health Office of New York City. Eventually, Ledyard bought a large farm in Newtown on which he ran a successful dairy. He had learned his lesson and exercised caution in sharing his vitalist ideas.[23]

But what a secret to keep! If Ledyard did not wish to expose himself as the author of *An Essay on Matter*, he nonetheless wished for a conversation partner. He was pleased to find Palmer open-minded, intelligent, and willing to discuss unconventional ideas. Palmer had tested his theological assumptions in and after college and had rejected the doctrines of original sin and predestination. He thought highly of science, and just six months before, in his July Fourth speech, had positioned truth-seeking "Sons of Science" against false and tyrannical religion. Ledyard's talk of chemists and physiologists investigating the vital force probably made a deep impression. Palmer would later pronounce that only "those who have made some progress in science" can have "any clear and correct ideas of Theology." That Ledyard's revelatory conversations had a lasting influence can be seen in Palmer's book *Principles of Nature*, published more than a dozen years later. In a chapter he added to the second edition of 1802, Palmer wrote: "To corroborate the ideas which have already been suggested upon this subject [of animated matter], the following strong and philosophic reflections are taken from an anonymous pamphlet, entitled, 'An Essay on Matter.'" Thirty-three sentences from Ledyard's essay follow about the "living principle" that animates all matter. Palmer's debt was real: his own thinking built on the ideas Ledyard had shared with him on Long Island.[24]

Yet Palmer's enthusiasm for vital matter did not lead him to reject Christianity outright. Two years after his encounter with Ledyard, he wrote in a private letter that he had recently "openly avowed the universal & Socinian doctrines." Not only that, Palmer said, but "I believe them both & think I can maintain them by conclusive arguments." Universal salvation pertained to immaterial souls, and the Socinian talk of a fully human Jesus left open the possibility that he had been sent on, and had fulfilled, a divine mission. That these ideas remained part of Palmer's vocabulary, and that he argued for and believed them both, suggests that he did not, in Newtown, reject Christianity and replace it with a vitalist cosmology. Nor did he claim to be a deist at this time—and why would he? He knew from his Dartmouth days that the term was often one of opprobrium and was closely associated with "infidel" and "atheist," of which he was neither. Paine had not yet published *The Age of Reason* with his proud self-identification as a deist, and there were few if any public expressions of support for deism among men of high social standing. Jefferson's call for full freedom of conscience, claiming "it does me no injury for my neighbour to say there are twenty gods, or no god. It neither picks my pocket nor breaks my leg," had made him the subject of vituperative attacks. Even putting aside Palmer's concern for his reputation, no evidence suggests that he identified with deism at this time. Instead, he seems to have combined a liberal—meaning nontraditional and Universalist—version of Christianity with his ideas about the vital principle. In other words, he spoke as a freethinking Christian.[25]

Just how to understand God in a vitalist universe remained an ongoing challenge for Palmer, as it did for Ledyard. Even years later in his book, *Principles of Nature*, Palmer struggled with ways to express his ideas about God. Sometimes he spoke of the deity as the intelligence behind the cosmos. "The laws of nature are immutable," he wrote, "and God, their author, is free from every species of imperfection." Never would God breach the laws of nature with a miracle, because "truth, immortality, and eternal uniformity of action, are essential to his character and existence." Palmer recognized the limited human ability to perceive the deity, because the "essence of such a being is inconceivable." We can have only faint glimmerings of it, and for now, in our ignorance, "it is sufficient that we refer the universe, its laws, and order, to the divinity of thought emanating from the most perfect of all beings." The finite human mind was at the edge of its capacity and unable to fathom or describe the qualities of divine power. But Palmer was sure about one thing: matter was not inert, waiting to be acted upon by external forces. "There is not a single particle of dead matter in the universe," he proclaimed. Everything is active to varying degrees "according to circumstances, locality, and combination." Even "thinking is only the finer action of matter," Palmer said, as is light: the rays of sunlight display their "essential power and activity." He rejoiced that "all is alive, all is active and energetic." The universe shimmered and hummed with a vital force that coursed through it and connected it all.[26]

When people later called Palmer an atheist, he rejected the moniker outright, even as he denied the existence of a personal God. No human being could grasp "the shape or form" of the "mighty power by which the universe is sustained," Palmer said, but certainly the deity would be nothing like a human being. Even so, the concept of vibrant matter did not conflict with theism. He and Ledyard held to an unconventional *theology*, not to a form of irreligion. Theirs was a numinous cosmology that inspired them with feelings of gratitude, wonder, and awe. Sometimes they were transported by it, overjoyed by the feeling of connection with everything in the universe. In his mind's eye, Palmer saw the universe as "a vast assemblage of living creatures, whose relations are reciprocal and reciprocated under a thousand different forms, and supported by a thousand different ligaments of an imperceptible nature." All was connected, and "nothing is foreign or irrelative in the vast fabric to which we belong. Union is most intimate." The recognition of humanity's "true connection with Nature" was the source of "highest happiness."[27]

The ministry still appealed to Palmer. He loved thinking about theology, enjoyed public speaking, and believed he held important information for the future happiness of humankind. But could he contain himself in the ways Ledyard had modeled? Yes, he avoided discussing the doctrines of depravity and the predestined fate of all souls, and no, he did not reference Jesus much, preferring to speak of a benevolent "Ruler of Nature" who expected humans to bring about their own happiness in this earthly life. But the Universalist belief in the salvation of all souls was generous enough to keep him within an expansive Christian fold. To stay on track for a clerical appointment required only that Palmer emulate Ledyard and refrain from discussing his unconventional ideas in public.

In the face of his convictions, such self-restraint proved difficult. While staying with Dr. Riker's family for a few days during an inoculation, possibly for smallpox, Palmer "was engaged one evening in study, when he repeated the lines of Dr. Watts which begin with 'Lord I am vile, conceived in sin, / And born unholy and unclean;' setting forth the doctrine of original sin." Turning to the doctor's wife, Palmer "declared that he did not believe a word of it, no, not one word, he repeated with emphasis." Perhaps Palmer hoped Mrs. Riker would respond in the way of Mrs. Hannah Foster in Brighton, a woman of independent mind open to seeing something familiar in a new light. Instead, the surprised Mrs. Riker "advised him not to give utterance to such sentiments in public, for the people would not hear him."[28]

Palmer did not take her advice, or perhaps it was already too late. Not that he lacked talent for the ministry. He had "displayed good qualifications for the sacred office," James Riker, a relative of the church trustee, later recounted. Palmer had a sonorous voice and fine speaking skills, and he showed "much ardor and sincerity." But he avoided mention of "the peculiar and mysterious doctrines of the Christian religion, confining himself to its moral precepts." The Newtown congregants noticed and, upon further investigation, "soon discovered that his views were far from orthodox." His preaching "gave dissatisfaction, and after a stay of six months he not only left the congregation, but renounced the Presbyterian ministry."[29]

James Riker, the town chronicler, was at pains to absolve the people of Newtown of any responsibility for Palmer's slide away from Christian orthodoxy. Riker made a point of adding that the "assertion formerly made that Palmer was converted to Deism while in Newtown, by Dr. Ledyard, is said to be incorrect." Ledyard had been suspected of harboring freethought, but if his reputation suffered from his conversations with Palmer, the damage did not linger. While Ledyard's medical colleagues later remembered him as an "intellectual" man, none indicated that he had entertained unusual religious ideas or had ever published an essay on the vibrant matter that makes up everything in the universe.[30]

When the Newtown congregation ended Palmer's probationary period, he was without a job and in need of a new beginning. He could not ask the local Presbyterians to attest to his credentials as a minister, even if he loved preaching and could imagine reforming Protestantism by downplaying supernatural doctrines and emphasizing the values of gratitude and generosity. Who would have him on those terms? He cast about for another career option. For a man of his eloquence, the legal profession seemed an obvious choice. He would need to find a source of income while he studied law and then apprenticed with a practicing lawyer. Palmer had taught school during his vacations at Dartmouth, and teaching could tide him over once more, so he turned his sights to Richmond Academy in Augusta, Georgia. Maybe a published advertisement told him of an opening there, or perhaps he had heard by word of mouth. He could have written to the academy in advance, presenting himself as a Dartmouth-pedigreed minister-in-training with teaching experience. As he packed his bags for the journey south, he may have had mixed ideas about how to proceed. On the one hand, he could better appreciate Ledyard's concern for protecting his reputation from scandalous association with freethought. Fascinating but unconventional ideas should not jeopardize the social standing Palmer had only so recently, as a college graduate, achieved. He wished for upward mobility and respectability, not fringe status as a heretic. On the other hand, he was a natural proselytizer, a good public speaker with passion for his ideas. Would he really remain silent, in the way of Ledyard, about these most exciting opinions? Must he choose between respectability and candor? Perhaps in Augusta he could find a way to navigate between freethought and social respectability, cultivating and enjoying both.

CHAPTER 4

Freelance Universalist

PRESIDENT WASHINGTON HAD proclaimed November 26, 1789, a national day of prayer and thanksgiving, and the townspeople of Augusta, the state capital of Georgia, gathered to watch the spectacle as it unfolded there. Advance messengers ceremoniously called out for people to make way for the high-ranking men of government who paraded from Richmond Academy, which doubled as the state house, to St. Paul's Episcopal Church. At the head of the festive procession strode twenty-five-year-old Elihu Palmer. The secretary of state walked beside him. Behind them came the secretaries of Governor Telfair, followed by the secretaries of the senate, the clerk of the house of representatives, various public officers, then the governor himself, flanked by the president of the senate and the speaker of the house, and finally a long row of house representatives, lined up in pairs. When the entire who's who of the state government had entered the church and found their seats, those gathered heard "a sermon, well adapted to the occasion," delivered by none other than Palmer himself. The general assembly had asked "the Rev. Mr. Palmer" to speak, and the whole event took place, a reporter noted, "with greatest religious decorum."[1]

Just six months after losing his position as probationary minister in Newtown on Long Island, Palmer stood in the pulpit of St. Paul's Church and addressed the political leaders of the state of Georgia. Fair to say, he had landed on his feet. Even as he began the study of law, he continued to speak as a minister, indulging his passion for theological discussion. He also pursued respectability in this new place by presenting himself as having already achieved it. In Augusta, until recently a trading post but now a boomtown of some two hundred houses, Palmer would start fresh, joining other upwardly mobile white men in pursuit of social recognition. He could not expect to join the landed elite, foreseeing instead a place among the middling rank of people who supported themselves with nonmanual labor: retail shopkeepers, clerks, schoolteachers, doctors and lawyers with small practices, ministers of small congregations. But while legal work could procure a living, he might also authorize himself as a man of education and refinement who could parlay his speaking ability into a position of respect. The key to his success as a lecturer and public orator, he might have told himself, would be to say just enough, but not too much, about his liberal theology.[2]

Palmer personified a footloose quality that irritated men like Jedidiah Morse, the Calvinist minister in Charlestown, Massachusetts, who hailed from Palmer's northeastern corner of Connecticut. The letters Palmer sent Morse from Augusta showed a man on the move, both in terms of geographic mobility as well as in his emboldened liberal theology. And who could stop him? In the new nation, dissenting opinions proliferated. The restraining lid of established churches had come off, and other denominations grew apace. Church and state still intermingled, both symbolically, as in the presidential call for a national day of prayerful thanksgiving, and structurally, in state mandated religious establishments like the one in Massachusetts that required taxpayers to support a religious institution of their choice. But within and around the mainstream Calvinism that Morse preferred, other forms of Christianity also took hold: dissenters like the Baptists, Methodists, Presbyterians, Quakers, and Shakers, as well as the increasingly bold Universalists and proto-Unitarians, who challenged the doctrine of damnation and the divinity of Jesus, respectively. Who could vet all the probationary preachers or quiz recent arrivals to the chancel? In Morse's considered opinion, men like Palmer took advantage of the unsettled situation to pass as Christian, only to lead true believers astray. For the moment, however, Palmer could not be stopped.

By June 1789, Palmer had settled into new living quarters and begun his employment at Richmond Academy as chaplain and instructor in Latin and rhetoric. In this upper-level school for mostly boys and a few girls, students took college-level courses, and upon graduating they could enter college as sophomores or juniors. Examinations were a public affair, and in July, in front of an audience that included the governor, his executive council, and the academy's board of trustees, Palmer's students acquitted themselves beautifully. The young scholars delivered speeches in Latin and performed sketches in rhetoric to the "very general applause" from the impressed audience. That same day, the enthusiastic trustees "Resolved, That the Rev. Mr. Palmer be appointed Professor of Rhetoric and Oratory in the Academy."[3]

Teachers at the academy received modest pay, and Palmer's decision to pursue a legal career made sense for practical reasons. Still, the law likely seemed to him a lesser occupation than the ministry. For one thing, his true passion involved thinking and speaking about theological matters, especially from a critical and reformist perspective. For another, the public generally granted ministers greater respect than it did attorneys. Lawyers collected debts and recovered property, litigated civil disputes, and drafted deeds, titles, wills, and contracts. Given the often unpleasant encounters people had with sheriffs, courts, and their fees, many treated the legal profession with suspicion. But Palmer needed work, opportunities in law abounded, and the training for a legal career was not particularly difficult. Each state had its own rules for admittance to the bar. Most required two or three years of "reading law" with an experienced lawyer, more if the lawyer-in-training had not attended college. Georgia required five years "as an Articled Clerk, to some Sworn Barrister, Attorney, Solicitor or Proctor," followed by an examination conducted by the state's chief justice. Palmer began studying law even as he established himself in Augusta as a talented teacher.[4]

Not only that, Palmer somehow installed himself as a part-time preacher at St. Paul's Episcopal Church, the only house of worship in town. The sitting minister, Reverend Adam Boyd, resented the intruder, and for good reason. Palmer had no Episcopalian credentials and had never been ordained in any denomination. He simply brimmed with religious opinions and had an engaging manner of sharing them. Boyd was a relative newcomer himself. Originally from Pennsylvania, he had moved to Wilmington, North Carolina, where he edited the patriotic *Cape Fear Mercury*, then served as chaplain of the Fifth North Carolina Regiment during the war. After armistice, he preached in Wilmington for several years before coming to Augusta as rector in 1786. Two years later he traveled to Connecticut for his ordination as an Episcopalian minister. Now fifty years old and tending toward corpulence and ill health, Boyd prepared to serve out his ministry in Augusta's only church. He was a mild-mannered person, "an honest good sort of man," as Palmer himself later said. But the sermons Boyd read from the page did not excite, and he found himself nudged aside by an unexpected rival half his age who spoke freely and with passionate eloquence.[5]

Boyd complained to the vestrymen about Palmer's encroachment, and the vestry "*Resolved*, That the Rev. Mr. Boyd, and the Rev. Mr. Palmer, do perform morning service alternately in the church," and that whoever did not preach in the morning could preach in the afternoon. Alternately! Only strong support from the vestrymen could have landed Palmer equal time in the pulpit on Sundays. Apparently, enough influential congregants preferred his sermons to Boyd's. Recognizing the awkward situation, the vestry resolved "also, That no itinerant preacher shall in future be suffered to preach in the said Church, unless permission for that purpose has been previously obtained" from the vestry chairman or a churchwarden. For Boyd, however, the damage was done. The brazen young interloper had established himself as a de facto minister on equal footing with Boyd. Adding to the injury, Palmer became the preferred speaker at public events. Whereas Boyd still preached the public sermon on the Fourth of July that year, by November Palmer was chosen over Boyd to deliver the thanksgiving sermon to the assembled members of the state government.[6]

Not content with expressing himself in sermons and public orations, Palmer began publishing essays in the local newspaper. Using the pen name "Alfred," as he had in Pittsfield the year before, Palmer's Observations in the *Augusta Chronicle* demonstrated to readers that he had a mind of his own and ideas on offer. His essays expressed his disregard for the traditional educational practice of learning by rote, as well as his impatience with norms of propriety that foreclosed conversations about unconventional ideas. He described "mechanically reading over a huge collection of authors" as a form of stuffing one's brain to enable "servile imitation." The ability to think independently required the development of "a strong mind and a persevering investigation." To that end, he wrote, proper education should nurture open-minded curiosity and an "invincible love of truth," and "prevent prejudice" against unfamiliar ideas. Furthermore, a real education would "assist nature in her operations, and exhibit to the view of the world, effects different from what we have hitherto seen." What natural operations did he mean, and what different effects? Did he mean the eternal motion of lively matter? He was not yet prepared to say, at least not in print—just that an open mind could perceive natural truths that had been there all along.[7]

The longest essay held up a most cherished idea that Palmer had touted in Pittsfield as well, namely the "Perfection of Human Improvement." Humans have a natural tendency, he wrote, to "advance in knowledge and, by progressive steps, to rise gradually toward the pinnacle of perfection." Progress was neither linear nor quick, but he agreed with the "celebrated Dr. *Price*" that a perfect God must have planned for eventual human happiness, for how could a benevolent deity allow "ignorance, vice and prejudice, to ravage, to lay waste and destroy the beauty and harmony of creation?" The very idea was absurd. Humanity just needed to find the key to unlock its potential, and that key was knowledge. The "Deity hath so constructed us, that, in the acquisition of science, we find nothing within our reach but *progressive advances.*" Palmer saw no limits to what could be investigated: an active mind "will not be bounded in its researches." Nothing less than "the universe is the theatre of its action, and infinite space opens to its rapid movements."[8]

Granted, human improvement would take time. Perhaps only in the distant future would science, truth, and philanthropy banish ignorance and vice to let "the kingdoms of the earth become peaceable and happy." But was it not reasonable, he asked rhetorically, to think that the "perfection of human improvement" might "one day, be the state of the world, nay of the whole universe itself?" Reverend Price had said that "there may be a secret yet remaining to be discovered in education, which will cause future generations to grow up virtuous and happy." Perhaps Palmer believed he had glimpsed that secret in the vitalist universe he had discussed with Isaac Ledyard on Long Island. If so, he certainly would not say so on the pages of a newspaper; the consternation his unorthodox ideas had incurred in Newtown had taught him that much. But in a bid to continue the conversation, he planned to establish a "Philosophical Society" in town, a forum for open-minded discussion. This proposal and his newspaper articles demonstrated Palmer's sense of his own worth, his confidence in the value of his contributions as a thinker, speaker, and teacher. They show him to be sociable, extroverted, and eager for conversation, maybe as a way to work out and share his ideas, and certainly as a means to develop his public profile as an intellectual—the cultural capital available to him.⁹

Augusta offered many opportunities for well-read sociability, and Palmer probably investigated all of them and instigated others. In December, the *Augusta Chronicle* announced that subscribers of a library society would hold their first meeting at the Richmond Academy the following month. (Maybe this was the philosophical society Palmer had proposed.) In many cities and towns, library societies created spaces that combined intellectual liberality with social exclusivity. Members, mostly men who donated money or books, met not only for reading and private discussion but also for lectures, debates, and dining. Palmer had enjoyed just such sociability at Dartmouth when he belonged to the United Fraternity. No subscription records or meeting minutes survive to show whether Palmer helped found or joined the Augusta group, but he felt at home in literary company, discussing unconventional ideas with all the self-confidence and reassurance of belonging to an elite club.¹⁰

The local Masonic lodge provided Palmer with another forum for respectable male sociability. Freemasons understood themselves to be part of a long genealogy of enlightened, scientific men, and they promoted science, education, and virtue for the good of the American republic and ultimately for all of humanity. Palmer joined the local lodge Columbia and established himself as a prized speaker. On December 27, 1789, at the annual festival of St. John the Evangelist, the freemasons processed from Richmond Academy to St. Paul's Church, where they (and possibly Reverend Boyd, also a member) heard an "excellent discourse" from "Rev. Brother Palmer." The following June, at the festival of St. John the Baptist, the freemasons repeated the parade to St. Paul's and once more heard "an excellent and well adapted discourse . . . delivered by our Rev. Brother Palmer." That evening the lodge members "dined together with the utmost harmony and friendship," demonstrating "great joy and rational festivity," along with a "spirit of accommodation and benevolence, which is the boast of Masons and of all good men." As the day's featured speaker, Palmer enjoyed a central role in the pomp and circumstance of the Masonic celebration.¹¹

Eager for additional work, Palmer collected information for Jedidiah Morse's *American Geography*. Compiled initially as a textbook and then published in revised form as the *American Universal Geography*, Morse's book came out in many updated editions, each one featuring information sent to him by writers in different parts of the country. Palmer researched and wrote sections on South America and the Caribbean, and he would have been the source of the details on the town of Augusta for the third edition, including that the academy in 1791 taught "between 80 and 90 students."[12]

Their business relationship proceeded despite their religious differences. Doctrinally orthodox and a self-described "moderate Calvinist," Morse deplored the emotional display and certainty of salvation that came with religious revivalism on the one hand and the diluted piety and moral laxity he saw in liberal forms of theology on the other. He walked the narrow path between these erroneous options, seeking to protect his parishioners from the danger on all sides. In 1789, the year Palmer lost his position in Newtown, Morse became the minister in Charlestown, just six miles from Brighton, where Palmer had studied in 1788 with the liberal Reverend Foster. The region had strong and growing congregations of proto-Unitarians, and not by accident did Morse's first sermon defend the Trinity as incontestable, "the very foundation of the Christian System." Morse would spend his long career denouncing "liberal" and "Arminian" (and later "Unitarian") encroachments on the traditional Calvinism of New England's Congregational churches. So why work with Palmer? Because as much as Morse was committed to proper Calvinism, he was invested in his success as an author of the *Geography*. In fact, Morse focused so much on the income and renown his publications garnered that his parishioners eventually charged him with neglecting his duties as minister. Palmer had access to valuable information in Augusta, and he could write well. The relationship was mutually beneficial, as reports for the *Geography* provided Palmer with some income as well as another way to establish himself as a man of education and learning.[13]

In his first year in Augusta, Palmer succeeded beyond all reasonable hope, becoming the go-to minister for some of the region's wealthier families. When one Mrs. Mildred Spencer died in January 1790, for example, a large procession of "ladies and gentlemen of the first distinction" accompanied the mourning family to the cemetery. The crowd was so large and the procession took so long that Palmer postponed his funeral oratory until the following Sunday. In April, he preached the funeral sermon for Bertha Stallings, the wife of Colonel James Stallings. On July 4, his sermon was followed by thirteen cannon balls fired in celebration of the nation's birthday. Palmer had knit himself into the town's social fabric, establishing himself as a person noteworthy for his education and his oratorical ability.[14]

Success brought with it a moral dilemma, however, because the wealthiest parishioners owned slaves. Palmer saw more slaves in Augusta than he had ever seen before. Over eleven thousand people lived in Richmond County, and enslaved men, women, and children made up more than a third of these. Enslaved workers drove carts filled with tobacco leaves into town, unloaded the crop into warehouses, and floated full barrels on pole boats down the Savannah River to the harbor near the Atlantic coast. Slaves hauled firewood and wares to the workshops that lined Broad Street. They tended to the luggage and horses of merchants and government officials who came to do business in the state capital. Palmer had seen enslaved people all his life, beginning in his Connecticut hometown, where the ministers Ebenezer Devotion and James Cogswell had owned people. In New York City, Philadelphia, and elsewhere, Palmer had observed slaves working on the docks and delivering merchandise in town. But in Augusta the institution existed on a different scale. Reverend Richard Price, the English minister whom Palmer so greatly admired, had openly denounced slavery. Maybe Palmer thought to do the same, but he hesitated. His critique of slavery conflicted with his desire to be accepted by local elites, whose educated company, library groups, and Masonic ceremonies he wished to enjoy.[15]

Yet the suffering of people in bondage was obvious to anyone who cared to notice. Reading the newspaper made that clear, since ads for runaways inadvertently evoked their wretched condition. The same issue of the *Augusta Chronicle* that explained how Boyd and Palmer would share the pulpit also carried an evocative advertisement for two runaways. Eighteen-year-old Peter was likely heading for Charleston, the ad said. He had fled to Charleston once before and lived in freedom for two years before being recaptured and returned to Augusta. This time, Peter had persuaded a younger boy to join him. Fourteen-year-old Jem, bearing on his thigh a scar "occasioned by a burn," had put his trust in Peter, who had tasted freedom for two whole years.[16]

And so it went. The following week, just below the announcement that Palmer was appointed professor of rhetoric and oratory at Richmond Academy, a note in large font announced a "GANG of 14 Prime seasoned Negroes, Ten of whom are workers," to be had for money or produce. The four who were not workers were likely very young children, and the "GANG" might well have included a family, to be sold off individually, if need be. In August, a lone seven-year-old boy was for sale. The next week's newspaper featured a "small negro fellow named John," about forty years old, who said his Antiguan master had left him behind in Charleston when the British occupied the city during the war. More likely, John had hid until his master left without him. Since then John had been "in the possession of divers persons," which sounded vague enough, but his bid for freedom had come to end now that one James Lewis was prepared to deliver John to anyone who would claim ownership and pay "charges."[17]

Palmer had a choice to make. He could be complicit with the slave system that enriched the educated men he sought to impress, or he could take a stand that risked their reproval. He discussed the matter with a fellow teacher at the academy, Isaac Briggs, a Quaker from Haverford, Pennsylvania. A year older than Palmer, Briggs had a master's degree in engineering from the College of Pennsylvania. Together with William Longstreet, Briggs had invented an early version of the steam engine, for which the state of Georgia issued a patent in 1788. The young engineer had served as secretary at the Georgia state ratifying convention, and he was considered an eloquent speaker on the merits of democracy. Briggs grew hot discussing the evils of slavery and the imperative of its abolition, and he must have pushed Palmer on this matter.[18]

Moral courage was a muscle that needed flexing, and Briggs helped Palmer do it. In September 1790, while Palmer was out of town, Briggs took pen in hand to request that they both be admitted to the Philadelphia Abolition Society. In his letter, Briggs vouched for Palmer as "a young man of firm integrity, shining abilities, extensive knowledge, universal benevolence and powerful eloquence." The two were admitted to the society. A decade later, Palmer would denounce in print "the immoral opinion, that the whites have a right to enslave the blacks." He called slavery the "complete abandonment of the principle of reciprocal justice, and a violation of the fundamental laws of Nature." He may well have held that opinion in

1790, but it is not clear how loudly, if at all, he articulated his antislavery position to Augusta's slaveholding elite. Perhaps he was experimenting with ways to express unpopular or unfamiliar ideas without being dismissed out of hand. To be sought out by wealthy patrons in Augusta meant veiling his criticism of the beliefs and institutions he most rejected, whether they be religious doctrines or the system of slavery. At this moment in time, his effort to achieve social respectability while expressing liberal religious ideas may have come at the cost of speaking openly about slavery.[19]

Palmer was not present when Briggs wrote his letter to the abolition society, because he had left Augusta to visit family and friends in Connecticut. In his hometown of Scotland, Reverend James Cogswell was the same man, still combining his pious devotion to God with his natural sociability. "When in Company," Cogswell admitted to himself, "I am so much taken up with Friends that in a Measure I forget God and am apt to let Cheerfulness degenerate into Levity." Religious revivalism had never disappeared, and when a traveling Anabaptist preacher was "highly extolled by ye New Lights," Cogswell "pray[ed] to God to hinder the spread of Enthusiasm & Anabaptist principles." But possibly a greater threat came now from liberal versions of Protestantism, with their Universalist ideas of the eventual salvation of all souls and the heretical Socinian disavowal of the Trinity in favor of a human Jesus. Cogswell was sorry to learn that Palmer was among those who preached this erroneous message. In August 1790, Reverend Morgan in Canterbury told Cogswell he was "dissatisfied with Mr Palmers preaching" which "give Ground of Suspicion that he is . . . a Socinian & almost a Deist." To be a Christian who denied the divinity of Jesus—the Socinian view—was bad enough, Morgan implied. Even worse was deism, which Morgan seemed to think entailed a complete rejection of Christian belief. A few days later, Cogswell heard over dinner that one General Gordon did "not like Mr Palmer at all for a preacher," because he was "a freethinker[,] a Universalist &c."[20]

Cogswell had the opportunity to form his own opinion when Palmer offered to preach in the Scotland meeting house. What did it feel like for Palmer to take the pulpit and look out over the benches where he had sat as a youth? Certainly he would have felt that he had a better message on offer than his former tutor, regardless of what Palmer thought of Cogswell personally. Cogswell, meanwhile, came with low expectations but found

Palmer to be "a very good speaker" who "preached with out Notes altogether." Palmer "prayed short but fluently," Cogswell remarked, his "language is good and elegant," and his "sentiments were good in the Main." Some of Palmer's comments "savored of Universalism but other ones were very opposite hereto." Cogswell thought Palmer said too little about the "Doctrine of special & supernatural Influences," by which knowledge of God comes from divine revelation and other miracles in the Scriptures. But on the whole, Cogswell decided, Palmer was "an ingenious likely Man & preached more agreeable to my sentiments than I expected." Palmer may have soft-pedaled his message to appeal to the local congregants. He clearly did not wish to offend, for when a neighbor relayed to Palmer some of the "Exceptions" Cogswell "took at some Expressions in his Sermon," Palmer replied that these expressions "were inadvertent & did not justifie" Cogswell's critique.[21]

Palmer had reason to temper his message: he was courting that summer. At twenty-six, the time was right to marry, an important milestone in becoming an independent man. He could assume that his teaching and preaching, with a legal career in the making, would support a family. The woman he married that year—her name remains a mystery—may have come from Canterbury. Supporting that inference is the fact that when her health declined the following year, the Palmers traveled to Canterbury, not to Palmer's home village of Scotland, where his father still lived. Did Mrs. Palmer wish to convalesce in the circle of her family? Both of Palmer's brothers married women from Canterbury. The eldest brother, Thaddeus, married a Canterbury native in 1782 and settled there. Nathan, who had moved to Wilkes-Barre, Pennsylvania, returned home briefly in 1794 to marry a woman from that village. In between, in the summer of 1790, Elihu Palmer visited Connecticut and—this remains conjecture—married after a courtship of a month or two. If he married a local woman, his bride's family would have considered his good standing guaranteed in absentia by the well-known Palmer family. His college education and status as a minister and professor in Augusta boded well. There is no indication that Palmer's betrothed shared his liberal religious views. Maybe he assumed that he would, in time, persuade her. The only certainty is that by September he was a married man and that on Sunday, September 26, 1790, in auspiciously fair weather, the packet *Juno* left New York City, "in whom went passenger, the Rev. Mr. Palmer and Lady for Georgia."[22]

Back in Augusta, Palmer resumed his public lectures and his teaching. His stature as an instructor received a thrilling boost in spring 1791, when President Washington came to Augusta for a few days during his southern tour. On May 19, at "an elegant dinner," the president "dined with a large number of citizens" and the governor. After the meal, the president "attended a ball in the large room at the Richmond Academy." Given Palmer's prominence in the academy, Masonic lodge, and St. Paul's Church, he was surely present at these occasions. The next day Washington "honored the examination of the students with his presence, and was pleased to express himself handsomely of their performances." Palmer as professor of oratory would have played a supervisory role in the "declamation contest." Washington personally awarded the prizes to the winners, and Palmer, as their tutor, could be proud of coming to the president's attention in such a favorable way.[23]

Augusta suited Palmer, but his wife suffered poor health there. The "climate of Georgia would not by any means agree with Mrs Palmer," he reported to Jedidiah Morse. In the spring of 1791, she was in all likelihood either pregnant with or nursing her first child, and perhaps there had been complications. With some reluctance, Palmer felt obliged to leave behind the social network he had built up over two years, along with the social regard he enjoyed in Augusta. "Health is preferably to every thing else," he wrote to Morse, "whereupon I resolved to move, tho' very *detrimental* to me." The couple's departure in late May was "very unexpected," Palmer said, and they returned to Canterbury, Connecticut, to consider their next step.[24]

This time, Palmer's reputation as a freethinker preceded him. Reverend Cogswell had heard in March that "Palmer the Georgia preacher is a Deist." Cogswell did not specify what the term meant to him, remarking only on "the folly & absurdity of the skeptical philosophy." Once back in Connecticut, Palmer may have avoided conversations with his former minister (whose diary made no mention of a social visit), but Mrs. Palmer, who was on the mend in Canterbury, felt comfortable speaking with Reverend Cogswell even about scandalous gossip. One day in June when "Elihu Palmers & Josiah Smiths wives" dropped by, Mrs. Palmer told Cogswell "that the same Spalding girl" who "years ago" had given birth to an illegitimate child and identified the father as the lawyer Jones "has had Twins lately &

lays Them to" Jones again. Mrs. Palmer's familiarity with older stories, and her chattiness with Cogswell about the latest news, strongly suggests that she was a local woman.[25]

Palmer preferred conversations with the Universalists in Canterbury, who preached that every soul would eventually be saved. Cogswell's friend and successor, Reverend Morgan of Canterbury, preached as best he could "against the Doctr[ine] of ye Universalists," fearing as Cogswell did that the assurance of eventual heaven for everyone would wreak havoc on morality. Without the threat of eternal damnation, how would any sinner have the strength to resist temptation? The Universalists "prevail in Canterbury & despise Mr. Morgan & treat him ill," Cogswell noted in July. He feared "they will do much damage" by enticing believers with an easier but erroneous faith. In August, Cogswell recorded, Palmer "preached at Canterbury on the Sabbath, by Dint of the Importunity of the Universalists." To the idea of universal salvation, Palmer may have added that Jesus was human rather than divine. Neither of these ideas made Palmer any less Christian, in his own view. His was a rational and true Christianity, he thought, not the "deism" referenced by his Calvinist colleagues, if by this they meant a rejection of the Christian faith.[26]

While in Canterbury, Palmer wrote to Morse in Charlestown to explain his delay in submitting material for the next edition of the *Geography*. The "misfortune of my wife's being sick," he wrote, "greatly impeded me in the Geographical business." Palmer had finished the section on South America and part of the West Indies, but most of his material on the United States had been lost the previous year on his trip from Georgia to New York. In transition now while his wife recovered her health, Palmer was weighing whether to move to New York or Philadelphia. He reassured Morse that "as soon as I can get a little settled shall pursue the work" for the *Geography*.[27]

When Palmer wrote to Morse again in September, he had moved with his family to Philadelphia. The nation's capital, he thought, would offer "a more extensive field for the display of his talents." Morse was more concerned about the twenty-five copies of the *Geography* he had sent to Augusta for Palmer to sell. Palmer had received the copies only a few days before his departure from Augusta, he explained. He had sold a few and left the rest with a friend to sell, but "I will be accountable, & send the money to you as soon as possible." Morse wondered if Palmer could advance the money, essentially his own paycheck, to continue his work on the *Geography*. To this Palmer responded that he would "gladly do it" if he had the funds, but that "the numerous expences of moving & the sickness in my family have reduced me pretty low." By now, the Palmers had a baby boy.[28]

Perhaps the pressure from Morse over money prompted Palmer to let fly his theological opinions, or maybe Palmer enjoyed verbal sparring with a theological opponent. Certainly, the two men knew well how to rankle one another. Aware that Palmer preached against the divinity of Jesus, Morse had challenged Palmer to defend his views. Palmer gladly complied, and his reply—one of the few personal letters from Palmer that has survived—reveals much about Palmer's religious thought at this time.

Palmer repeated the challenge Morse had posed in his previous letter: "I see not how you can deny Christ's deity & maintain the universal salvation of all men." Morse assumed that only Christ as the divine Savior could bring about a reconciliation of sinning humanity with God. Palmer did not believe that Jesus was part of a Holy Trinity, or that he died for the sins of all humanity, or that salvation was made possible by his sacrifice on the cross. The very idea that a divine being could suffer pain and death seemed nonsensical, even sacrilegious, to Palmer. As he put it to Morse: "In answer, let me ask you, whether you believe your Christ-God suffered in his eternal or human nature? I presume you will say that the eternal God of the universe was not hung on a tree by infamous Jews, or at least that his divine nature could not suffer." If God was omnipotent, then how could he suffer and die at the hands of—Palmer trucked in commonplace anti-Semitism—Jewish criminals? The notion of a God killed by humans was absurd. But more to Palmer's point, the sacrifice of Jesus had achieved only partial success, since Christians agreed that not all were saved through the sacrifice of Jesus. "After all," he told Morse, "you get only a finite atonement." The atonement did not apply to *all* sinners, in Morse's view; it was finite, not universal, in its reach. A partial salvation was flawed, Palmer scoffed, and not anything a perfect "God of the Universe" would allow. "Besides," Palmer continued, the belief in a divine Jesus "is making God resemble ourselves to put him into a body of clay." Palmer rejected the idea of God walking the Earth in human form. "I would as soon believe there was no God at all, as to believe he was such a childish being."[29]

Morse had heard this kind of thing from Palmer before and had already told him to stop. "Again you advise me to leave off preaching," Palmer wrote to Morse. But Morse was the one who should quit, Palmer said, because Morse's own theological presumptions made his preaching a useless endeavor. Morse believed in predestination, the Calvinist notion that God had already and irrevocably determined the fate of each human soul in the afterlife. According to followers of Calvin, only the tiny "elect" of true believers would be saved, and the rest, regardless of their behavior during their lifetimes, would suffer eternal hellfire. "I therefore advise you to leave off preaching," Palmer taunted Morse, "for the elect will be saved at any rate, & you cant save any of the rest, if you should preach to all eternity." Why bother with sermons that Morse himself must admit were futile? Palmer must have found his logic irrefutable, and perhaps he imagined Morse stymied by his arguments. But Morse could ward off the rationalist assault easily enough by turning to the foundational mysteries of the Calvinist tradition and to an inscrutable God. Palmer's attack on the apparent contradictions of Calvinism seemed to Morse only a sinner's attempt to deny his own abject depravity and utter dependence on a merciful God. There could be no reconciliation of their views.[30]

Palmer's own sermons focused on universal salvation and an entirely human Jesus. "I have openly avowed the universal & Socinian doctrines," he wrote to Morse. "I believe them both, & think I can maintain them by conclusive arguments." Palmer's beliefs could be conclusively argued, he thought, because they were *reasonable* and therefore persuasive. Rational preaching could change minds as well as hearts, and while Palmer was making headway, Morse's preaching was, by his own Calvinist logic, useless. Palmer disavowed the rumor that he left Georgia because the townspeople rejected his preaching: "The report, that I left Augusta because I had embraced these [Universalist and Socinian] sentiments is positively false,—the offspring of calumny & ill-nature." His lectures had been well received in Augusta. "There are four universalists to one damnationist in the town of Augusta," Palmer crowed.[31]

Palmer was not finished. Morse had decried Universalism as "prejudicial to society" on the grounds that only the threat of eternal hellfire kept sinful humans within any moral restraints at all. Palmer assumed a different psychological dynamic. Tell a man either "that he shall be punished according to his crimes" or that "he shall be damned to all eternity" regardless of his actions. Which of these prospects is most conducive to good behavior? Palmer considered the question rhetorical. He found it obvious that people who believe their salvation depends on good behavior will contribute more to a peaceful and just society than those who think their behavior has no effect on the fate of their souls.[32]

Morse had written that Palmer "shall have the prayers of all praying people against [his] success." This metaphysical threat deterred Palmer least of all. "Let them pray on then," he wrote. The "God of the Universe is more immutable than to listen to their contradictory petitions. Light and liberality are gaining ground rapidly, and it must be something more than the prayers of superstitious mortals that will stop the progress of information." Palmer believed humanity stood poised on the edge of a better future. Perhaps he thought of the startling events occurring in France, where revolutionaries were dismantling the authoritarian structures of the ancien régime. It was an exciting time of new beginnings, and Morse's traditional religion held no sway with him. They could be business partners, but Morse should not flatter himself that he held any moral influence over Palmer. "On the whole, my friend, I will observe, that I can pursue the business of science," which included collecting facts for the *Geography*, "with men of *any* religion," Palmer wrote. "But as to my own religion, I presume, that if I ever change, it will be to a greater degree of *heresy*." The emphasis was Palmer's own. He was happy, for the moment, to use the language of Unitarian and Universalist Christianity to combat Calvinist doctrines, but he might someday go beyond these into even greater freethought. His letter to Morse was a warning shot over the orthodox bow.[33]

Even so, he signed off as "your friend E. Palmer." In a polite postscript he offered "Mrs Palmer's and my compliments to Mrs Morse," who had given birth to a son in April. Such assertions of friendship did not assuage Morse. Their theological differences ran too deep. Whereas Morse advocated the sin-focused humility of orthodox Calvinism, Palmer promoted Universalism and anti-Trinitarian freethought. Whereas Morse warned that time "not employed in study or useful labour . . . is generally spent in hurtful or innocent exercise," Palmer told his listeners to celebrate a day of thanksgiving "joyfully in innocent festivity, and to render themselves as happy as possible." Morse and Palmer were at odds in their religious views, and they competed for conversions. Each told the other to quit preaching. Each insisted the other was ineffective.[34]

Flush with his success in Augusta, Palmer disregarded the lessons about discretion he had learned on Long Island. In Newtown, his unorthodox language had cost him his ministerial post. In Augusta, however, Palmer enjoyed success with his preaching and was welcomed into the circles of academy professors, freemasons, and well-read men, gaining the respect of government officials, local elites, and even church vestrymen. He could imagine that a new era of religious freedom had begun. From within a Christian framework, capaciously defined, Palmer prompted believers to question all orthodoxy and shed any religious superstition. The main thing was to authorize oneself to examine one's beliefs and to resist any unthinking obedience to authority. Piqued by Morse's needling questions, Palmer could not resist the challenge. Morse personified the judgmental Calvinism that Palmer opposed, and Palmer spoke his mind directly. The future belonged not to "damnationists" like Morse but to Universalists like Palmer. He was enthusiastic about his message and certain of its logic. This made him brash. Unwittingly or maybe recklessly, Palmer sowed the seeds of future conflict, arming his theological opponent by revealing his heterodox opinions and exacerbating Morse's enmity with insults and provocation. Living now in Philadelphia, the nation's metropolis and the birthplace of the Constitution, Palmer felt a spirit of religious liberalism in the air, a space for freer religious expression. A new day was dawning, he might have thought, and old restrictions on religious speech must fade away. He could not guess that Morse's Calvinist friends and colleagues would soon make him eat humble pie.

PART II

The Making of an "Infidel"

CHAPTER 5

Palmer's Rubicon

On the ides of March in 1792, the owner of the Long Room in Philadelphia's Church Alley went looking for Elihu Palmer. Palmer had recently rented the Long Room for the span of two months, with the intention of giving lectures there. An advertisement had appeared in that morning's *National Gazette*: "Mr. Palmer desires the Public to take notice, that at half past ten o'clock, A.M. on Sunday next, he will deliver a Discourse at the Long Room in Church-Alley against the divinity of Jesus Christ." Palmer had given this kind of lecture many times before in Augusta and also to the members of Philadelphia's Universalist congregation. But on the day the advertisement appeared, the unhappy landlord hurried to find Palmer. The problem was not that the landlord objected to the proposed speech; he belonged to the Universalists and had heard Palmer speak numerous times. Palmer had been clear about his reasons for renting the room, and based on the "tenor of the agreement," he believed he had an "unquestionable right" to "deliver freely his own religious opinions." The objection to Palmer's speech had another source. Bishop William White, the Episcopalian minister of Christ Church, which abutted Church Alley, had read the advertisement and would have none of it. Either White or an emissary sought out the landlord and "frightned" him with consequences should he allow Palmer to speak in the Long Room. The anxious landlord could not know that rescinding the rental agreement would mark a turning point in Palmer's career as a freethinker.[1]

In the days and weeks that followed, Philadelphia church leaders of different denominations joined forces against Palmer. In their view, the "rights of conscience" as referenced in the Pennsylvania constitution of 1790 never entailed blasphemy. Religious liberty properly ended where licentiousness and vice began. When Palmer complained in the newspapers about the infringement of his freedom of speech, his critics responded with ridicule. They implied that his form of irreligion merited neither respect nor protection from public shaming. He had outed himself as an infidel and deserved the character assassination he got in the press.[2]

Palmer had not anticipated such forceful opposition to his advertised lecture. In fact, he had not intended to cause a ruckus at all, since his desire for respectability and the need for an income exerted a powerful pull. He had assumed that Philadelphia, the nation's capital after all, could accommodate at least as broad a range of ideas about God as he had discussed in Augusta's Episcopal Church. But having stepped, quite inadvertently, across the line of what could be said in public without repercussions, Palmer arrived at a new position in his opposition to revealed religion. He came to see the contest as a matter of principle—as a fight for freedom of conscience and of speech. Whether he had allies in the struggle or would have to go it alone, remained an open question.

When the Palmer family moved to Philadelphia in the autumn of 1791, they encountered the nation's largest city. Some forty-five thousand people lived in Philadelphia, including large numbers of German, Irish, and Scots-Irish immigrants, all of whom had arrived before the Revolution. By the 1790s, newcomers hailed from Ireland, France, Africa, and the West Indies. The gradual emancipation law of 1780 had reduced the number of slaves in the city to about three hundred by the time Palmer arrived, and he witnessed a thriving free black community of over two thousand participating in the economic life of the city. African American women marketed their wares and sat by tubs of hearty soup, crying, "Pepperpot, smoking hot!" Black men called out their "fine, fat, salt oysters!" freshly harvested from Delaware Bay. White and black girls sold fruit from baskets they bore on their heads or over an arm, as well as hot corn boiled in their husks and baked pears carried in earthen pots. Street vendors each had their own specific call: the "unpleasant and unnecessary bawling" of the chimney sweeps yelling "Sweep-O-O-O-O," the men with flat trays on their heads hollering the long cry of "Hot Muf-fins" in competition with boys shouting out "R-U-S-K, Fine, light rusk" for teatime. All day long one could hear songs about beautiful melons, fine sand clams, and fresh milk.

The city attracted all kinds of people. Government officials from the fourteen states (Vermont had joined the Union that year) explored the neat grid of streets and the five large city parks. Every year, hundreds of ships sailed up the Delaware River to Philadelphia's docks, where muscled stevedores unloaded European manufactures and Caribbean sugar and fruit before refilling the ships with American-grown wheat and flour. Philadelphia's merchants, shopkeepers, and artisans kept up a lively trade on Market Street, while town watchmen and constables struggled to curtail the gambling, brawls, illegal trade, petty theft, and prostitution that went on near the docks. Religious denominations flourished, including Quakers, Baptists, Congregationalists, Presbyterians, German Reformed, Lutherans, Methodist, Anglicans, and Catholics. The meeting house of the Universalists attracted a variety of laboring people, and the first African Episcopal Church in Philadelphia would open in 1794. In this diverse and growing city, Palmer could surely find an audience for his liberal religion.[3]

Philadelphia neighborhoods were not segregated by class or ethnicity, but laboring families tended to cluster in the northern, southern, and western edges of the city. There the rutted streets remained unpaved and the garbage rotted in place. The Palmers probably rented rooms in a narrow two- or three-story row house made of wood or brick. They shared the outdoor privy in the back with other neighbors and dumped their trash into the street. These were modest circumstances, but Palmer was still studying law, and starting over in his career meant accepting such living arrangements.[4]

Happy to preach as a guest minister, Palmer initially found a good reception at the Universalist church. The Churches Believing in the Salvation of All Men went by a shorter name, the Society of Universal Baptists or, even shorter, the Universalists. Palmer hoped the Philadelphia Universalists would accept him as a regular preacher, as St. Paul's Episcopal Church in Augusta had done. He knew the Universalists revered the Bible as divine revelation and believed in Jesus as the divine savior—and he disagreed with them about these crucial matters. But he shared their rejection of the idea of eternal damnation, and he claimed for himself a universalist message. On those grounds the lay leaders initially granted him permission to preach. Many in the pews enjoyed Palmer's lively and thought-provoking sermons, and he preached to "great applause among all ranks of people."

FIGURE 3. William Birch, *Arch Street Ferry*, Philadelphia. Elihu Palmer and his family moved to the nation's capital in 1791 and lived within a few blocks of the wharves. Public domain, courtesy of Library Company, Philadelphia.

This lasted only until one of the church leaders, a well-established tavern keeper (and future state senator) named Israel Israel, developed "some Suspicion" about Palmer's "orthodoxy & thought [it] his Duty to enquire something about his Faith." When the two men met, Israel told Palmer "that as he proposed joining them, & probably preaching among them," the Universalists should know if he had "the same Sentiments in Religion." Did Palmer believe the Old and New Testaments to be the word of God, Israel asked, and that "Jesus Christ, the Saviour of Mankind, is the Son of God?" Palmer replied "that he must candidly confess he could not go so far." Israel had suspected as much.[5]

The Universalists had reason for caution with Palmer because they were already under suspicion of harboring doctrinal laxity and therefore, critics thought, moral complacency. The idea that all sinners would eventually be saved, regardless of the severity of their transgression, seemed to Calvinists a free pass that could only produce moral indifference and sinful self-indulgence. Universalists guarded against such aspersions by seeking to exclude from their ranks any and all libertines. Their own preaching centered on the sacrifice of Jesus as a sign of God's love and on the necessity of repenting one's sins to be granted entry into the kingdom of heaven. In terms of doctrine, the Universalists changed one admittedly significant aspect of Calvinist teaching when they imagined salvation extending from Calvin's small group of the predestined "elect" to all of humanity. They continued to believe in original sin, the need for redemption through faith in Jesus Christ, and the supernatural miracles of the Bible. Palmer's notion of a human Jesus was anathema to the Universalist faith. When Ebenezer Hazard, an influential elder at Philadelphia's Second Presbyterian Church, heard from Israel about his conversation with Palmer, Hazard mocked Palmer's fantasy that the Universalists would tolerate his views of a human Jesus. After all, Universalists believed the salvation of all souls rested entirely on the sacrificial blood of the divine Savior. Hazard found it "stupid" of Palmer, "after denying the Divinity of Christ, & teaching men so, to apply for admission among the universalists, who allow more Efficacy to his Blood than any other Sect!"[6]

Palmer knew of his difference of opinion with the Universalists, but he hoped for toleration nonetheless. They were, despite their ardent faith, the most liberal religious group in town. (Palmer would have found a haven among the Unitarians, but he was too early; they organized the first Philadelphia meeting in 1796.) When Palmer learned on February 14, 1792, that he was no longer welcome to preach in the Universalist meetinghouse, he was "angry" with Israel for "preventing his admission into their Church." Given that Palmer did not share fundamental Universalist beliefs and was heading for a legal career anyway, Israel might have wondered why Palmer was so upset. But for Palmer the reason lay near at hand. When the Universalists revoked their hospitality, he was without a church home altogether. His days of speaking within any church were over. Palmer had all the passion of a missionary, and he loved to share his Universalist and proto-Unitarian faith in a magnanimous Creator-God who intended human happiness and even eventual earthly perfection. A legal career might pay the bills, but Palmer remained, at heart, a preacher. Where could he find an audience, if not with the Universalists?[7]

Less than a week after the Universalists disinvited Palmer from their pulpit, he received a visit from a small and homely man. That very day, John Fitch had learned from a friend that the Universalists had "shut their doors on Mr. Palmer and refused him leave to speak at their House any more altho he had gained great applause amongst all ranks of people while he spoke there." Fitch came to Palmer with an invitation to join forces with Philadelphia's Society of Deist Natural Philosophers (also called the Universal Society, not to be confused with the Universalist Church), a club of some thirty members that Fitch had started two years before.[8]

An emotionally complex man, Fitch was in turn self-deprecating, quarrelsome, generous, easily slighted, loyal, and chronically resentful. Forty-eight years old and from Connecticut (Windsor, north of Hartford), Fitch had grown up in a laboring family of modest means. As a young boy, Fitch had a thirst for knowledge that his widowed father, a strict Presbyterian task master, did not respect. At the age of nine and "exceeding small of my age," Fitch could cut and thrash only a small amount of flax per day. Nonetheless, he was put to "that pitiful trifling labour" and "prevented from going to school any more than one month in winter," even though his father could "see that I was nearly crazey after learning." Fitch never forgave his father for this "piece of injustice" and thought "heaven dealt very hard by me to give me such a mean niggardly wretch for a father."[9]

He did indeed have his share of hard luck. Fitch survived the challenges of captivity among the Indians in the Northwest Territory in 1782. In the mid-1780s, he worked on his invention of a steamboat with Henry Voigt, a watchmaker from Germany, then spent years feuding with another steamboat inventor over the patent rights—and lost. When both Henry Voigt and Fitch applied for a position at the United States Mint, Voigt got the job. The two men became close friends with a widowed tavern keeper, Mary Krafft, and when the married Voigt got Krafft pregnant, Fitch offered to protect them both by marrying her and pretending to be the father of her baby while pledging "on his word of honor never to bed with her." Krafft declined his offer. Even so, Fitch moved into her boardinghouse and tended her during her pregnancy. In August 1789, he even became "the Midwifes assistant" and handed over the swaddled infant to the wet nurse. When

Krafft got pregnant a second time by Voigt, she left town and told her relatives, without first consulting Fitch, that she and Fitch had married and the baby was his. When Krafft returned to Philadelphia and summoned Fitch *as her husband*, he was shocked. He was also in a bind, for he knew that if he neglected her now, "the world would suppose that I was the father and that I had been the ruin and destruction of a valuable Family and of the most deserving woman." He chose to go along with the deception. He even had his autobiography sealed for thirty years after his death, assuming that by then the children of Krafft and Voigt would be grown and married, their reputations beyond harm from their parents' illicit liaison.[10]

Misused by even his closest friends, Fitch hardly expected better. "My despicable appearance, my uncouth way of speaking and holding up extravagant ideas, and so bad in address, must ever make me unpopular," he wrote. In other ways, though, Fitch thought very highly of himself. He prized his intellect and his inventions, and he considered himself a man of honor. Fitch's biographer concurred with this mixed assessment of his character. Writing in 1857, Thompson Westcott wrote that Fitch "possessed sterling qualities. He was perfectly honest" and upheld "a high code of integrity." But he also had his weaknesses: a "quick and passionate" temper, spiteful pride on the frequent occasions when he felt wronged, an overbearing demeanor, and the "haughtiness" that came from his certainty of being entirely in the right.[11]

The Deist Society in Philadelphia came about after Fitch and his friend Voigt, "both Deists by Profession," Fitch said, spoke openly about religion. Many curious people came to see their steamboat, he wrote, "and we frequently getting mildly glad in Liquor, spoke our sentiments perhaps more freely than was prudent for us to do." Their loose-lipped conversation about "an unpopular sentiment" led Fitch to realize that many people "were of our belieff altho too delicate to confess it." Having encountered many for whom "Christian Creeds had no weight," it occurred to Fitch "to forme a society out of that class of people." He imagined an honorable society of freethinkers whose behavior must offer no easy target for critics. To that end, any "improper conduct either to the society or others" would result in expulsion and having one's transgression published in the newspaper. (Voigt was warned.) Fitch envisioned more than just private conversation among wealthy freethinkers. He planned to "invite all Ranks of people to join us that we might not be looked upon as a Deistical Society only" but that it might be a place for open debate among believers of different faiths. Inspired by the Freemasons and by the Quakers' founder, George Fox, Fitch envisioned a "friendly Society" in which "all questions should be freely discoursed even to the denial of the divinity of Moses Jesus Christ or Mahomet." He wondered if members might be persuaded to wear colored ribbons to mark their religious allegiances. Fitch wanted to throw "open our doors for all classes of people to hear our debates." Two members objected to this open-door policy, and Fitch may not have prevailed on this point, but his intention was clear. He sought an open exchange of ideas among religiously unlike-minded people. Such a society would practice learning from others and tolerating differences of opinion, both indispensable habits in a democratic republic.[12]

If Fitch's primary motive for founding the Deist Society was to support "Civil Government," his second motive bore no such altruism. He admitted in his diary that he felt a spiteful need to prove himself to the world. He was "stimulated by Pride," he wrote, "and determined to let the world know as contemptable as I was and despised by all ranks of People from the first Officers of Government down to the Blacburry garls that I would call in all the world into my doctrines." Fitch imagined nothing less than a one-world religion of his own devising that would bring in "the Jews" as well as "the Gentile Nations and establish one Area throughout the World." He combined considerable self-loathing with the grandiose ambition to prove wrong all who underestimated him. Laughed at even by female street vendors (the blackberry girls), he puffed up with confidence when he imagined his ability to change public discourse and religious sentiments on a global scale.[13]

Fitch's Society of Deist Natural Philosophers first convened in February 1790 and soon had some forty members. Henry Voigt attended, as did a clerk at the mint, an engraver, a cabinetmaker, and other artisans. Wealthy members came too, leading Fitch to claim that "more than half the wealth in Philadelphia is possessed by real Deists." By "real Deist," Fitch did not invoke a creed but rather an open and questioning state of mind that feared neither honest conflict nor intellectual taboos. Fitch and the other members proposed questions for debate at the weekly meetings, for example: whether "a Plurality of Wives" is immoral (Voigt's issue); whether the conscience is innate or arises solely from education; whether and how religion can be made socially useful; whether suicide can ever be a noble act (perhaps even then a pressing question for Fitch, who would end his life within the decade); why the passion of envy was given to man and whether it can be made socially useful (Fitch suffered terribly from that emotion); whether life's greatest lessons come from one's friends or one's enemies; whether children owe their parents gratitude (Fitch had his doubts); and whether life is a chemical "Eliment" or not. The question about the chemistry of living things referenced the medical vitalism that had inspired Palmer, and suggested that the idea circulated among well-read people.[14]

The Deistical Society did not aim to forge a consensus on any of these issues; rather, it sought an open-minded investigation of them. This point merits emphasis, because scholars often define deism narrowly as a particular understanding of God: the noninterventionist "watchmaker" Creator-God. The Philadelphia deists did not seek to replace one set of beliefs with another, but rather to question all creeds and to test their own thinking. No assent to any particular theological proposition was required for membership in this group except, perhaps, that there is a divine power at all. Tolerance for other views was a paramount virtue among these freethinkers, and members of the Deist Society agreed not to insult common beliefs. Like many freethinkers of the era, most prominently Thomas Jefferson and the elderly Benjamin Franklin, the members of the Deist Society saw no need to antagonize their pious neighbors. Most Americans subscribed to Protestantism of one sect or another, and many state constitutions had religious tests for public office. In this context, the freethinkers chose to be tactful and avoid social strife.

Despite their desire to avoid antagonizing anyone, freethinkers drew the unwanted attention of high-ranking ministers in town who worried that the public expression of religious doubt was becoming socially acceptable. Clergy had noticed that when Congress convened in town, Secretary of State Thomas Jefferson patronized a local newspaper "in which infidel publications occasionally appeared." Reverend Ashbel Green, the assistant minister of Philadelphia's Second Presbyterian Church, decided to take action against the advancing infidelity. In January 1792, he met with four other churchmen to create "a plan for preventing the spread of infidel principles, through the medium of the newspapers." Green's colleagues in this endeavor included Reverend Robert Annan, the minister at the Scotch Seceding Church, and Robert Aitkin, one of the elders in Annan's congregation. Reverend John Blair Smith, the pastor of the Third Presbyterian Church on Pine Street, joined them, as did Ebenezer Hazard, a well-connected elder in Green's church. The churchmen began by publishing anonymous letters that objected to newspapers "cramming impiety down our throats."[15]

Press releases against freethought had a chilling effect on the Deistical Society, and by February, when Fitch went to see Palmer, the Deist Society was "dwindling to nothing." It needed a boost, an infusion of new energy. Palmer's ouster from the Universalists was therefore "great news" to Fitch, and he "immediately resolved to make a great nois in the World and do the greatest good." As the two men spoke, Fitch found Palmer "as well established in my belieffs as I was myself." Excited about meeting an opinionated and articulate freethinker who was amply blessed with speaking skills and charisma, Fitch told Palmer that he "had been preparing the Way in the Wilderness for him thro' unbeaten Paths." Palmer would be an evangelist for religious skepticism, and Fitch had already gathered the Philadelphia flock. Fitch could "bring in 40 generous clever fellows into his Society in a lump and mentioned near 20 More whome I had great confidence in if he [Palmer] would take the Helm." Fitch lacked the social presence and speaking power of the younger minister-turned-freethinker, but Fitch had organized a society, and Palmer, who had speaking talent and ideas in abundance, needed an audience. They agreed to combine their efforts. Fitch's deists would attend, and Palmer would bring with him those Universalists who enjoyed hearing him speak and who tolerated, and maybe secretly endorsed, his iconoclastic message. One of those Universalists was the owner of the Long Room in Church Alley.[16]

The landlord of the Long Room did not anticipate a problem when he arranged a two-month rental with Palmer. Palmer still advertised himself as a preacher of the Universalist message that God would save all souls. On March 3, an announcement in *Dunlap's American Daily Advertiser* informed "the friends of liberal Sentiments" that "Mr. Palmer," a "Preacher of Universal Salvation, will Preach in the Long-Room in Church alley, near Christ church, at half past 10 o'clock To-Morrow Morning, and at 7 in the evening." The event went off without a hitch. Fitch recorded that "Mr. Palmer Preached yesterday from the 6th Chapter of Malachi and 8th verse to love mercy deal justly and Walk humbly with our God." Palmer did more than that, however. He also "publicly denied the divinity of Jesus Christ before a Crowded audience and fixed on tomorrow evening for those possessed of liberal sentiments to meet him."[17]

After that successful lecture, Fitch had reason to "hope that we by that means shall form a very respectible Society." It remained only to find a way of sponsoring Palmer somehow, making him economically independent enough to speak freely. Fitch fancied himself the man behind the curtain, orchestrating it all. Did Fitch enjoy provoking a public quarrel, and was he more a troublemaker than a missionary for a cause? He recorded in his diary and then crossed out: "I have set all Christendom at war to stand as spectator and see the sport as soon as I can render Mr. Palmer independent of the world and that his lips shall not be locked for the want of a pecuniary Living." Fitch decided that "if I can amuse myself better in the contest I shall step forward further."[18]

But then things took a turn when Palmer advertised a lecture that caught the attention of one of the nation's preeminent churchmen. On March 15, readers of the *National Gazette* learned that Palmer planned to speak against the divinity of Jesus Christ in a meeting room just across a narrow alley from Christ Church. This public show of infidelity, so brazenly announced in the newspapers, prompted Reverend White to take action. It marked the beginning of a contest that would not end well for Palmer. In retrospect, Fitch thought, the excitement about Palmer's first public lecture had encouraged Palmer "to do more than perhaps otherwise he would."[19]

Christ Church in Philadelphia had a steeple that made it the tallest building in America, and its minister enjoyed the social clout to match. Reverend William White had served as chaplain to the Continental Congress. In 1787, he traveled to London to be consecrated by the Archbishop of Canterbury as the first presiding bishop of the Episcopal Church of the United States. At the time Palmer advertised his speech, White ministered to the United States Senate, and many of the nation's leading political figures warmed the pews of Christ Church on Sundays. Distinguished visitors, including the nation's first three presidents, enjoyed hospitality at White's large home on Walnut Street. In 1795, White would again become the denomination's chief pastor and hold that position for forty years.

White's opposition to Palmer's speech stemmed not from a rigid dogmatism. A liberally minded man of ecumenical bent, White supported many causes for the public good. He gave substantial aid to the Society for the Alleviation of Miseries of Public Prisons, the African Methodist Episcopal Church, a school for African American and Native American children, and the Magdalen Society of Philadelphia for unwed mothers, the first such institution in the country. During yellow fever outbreaks, when many townspeople fled the pestilence, White stayed behind and cared for the afflicted. Later in life he helped found and lead the Pennsylvania Institution for the Deaf and Dumb. All this is to say that the bishop was no narrow-minded parson, yet Palmer's advertised lecture against the divinity of Jesus went beyond what White would tolerate. In White's considered opinion, the Socinian view of Jesus was anti-Trinitarian heresy, and Palmer's public show of it constituted a disrespect for the Savior that was not only blasphemous but also dangerous in its very brazenness. It was one thing to speak in closed company about such matters, but Palmer was bringing it to anyone who opened the newspaper, and he planned to expound on his blasphemy only a few steps from the doors of Christ Church.[20]

As soon as White read Palmer's advertisement on March 15, he set about contacting the owner of the Long Room. In the next day's *General Advertiser*, Palmer reported that the landlord feared financial reprisal, or what Palmer poetically called "temporal injury" to his business, if he let Palmer proceed with his "Discourse" in the Long Room. Other landlords got the message too, because Palmer could find no space in which to deliver his lecture. Fitch chided Palmer for folding to pressure and canceling the talk, which Palmer effectively did when he announced in the newspaper that he had been barred from the Long Room. Palmer should speak anyway, Fitch thought, even in a public space, because the world was "Ripe for a revolution in Religion." Fitch displayed some of his contradictory nature. Members of the Deist Society should not offend one another, he had insisted, yet now he hoped Palmer would start a religious brawl so Fitch could "see the sport." He expressed disappointment that Palmer "was conquered on the first repulse and I may say by the advance guards only of the Broken Christians." But Palmer wanted no such showdown, whether it be a forced entry into the Long Room or an ad hoc venue out of doors. He envisioned a respectable indoor gathering, not open-field proselytizing in the style of itinerant revivalists. With his rented room closed to him, he had a choice to make. He could retreat once more into the private spaces of freethinking conversation or press forward into the public sphere, taking his grievance to the newspapers.[21]

It took Palmer only a few hours, if that, to decide to go public and make it a matter of principle: at stake in the contest were freedom of conscience and freedom of expression. Granted, the recently ratified Bill of Rights prevented only Congress from making laws "respecting an establishment of religion, or prohibiting the free exercise thereof; or abridging the freedom of speech, or of the press." The First Amendment did not pertain to state legislatures, which could continue to regulate religious matters as they saw fit. But many Americans took the First Amendment as aspirational, an ideal worth working toward at all levels of government, and some state constitutions did offer qualified protections of free religion and speech. Pennsylvania's constitution of 1790 declared the right of all people "to worship Almighty god according to the dictates of their own consciences." Public office in the state, however, was reserved for those willing to attest to their belief in a God and an afterlife. Speech also had limits, although where these lay remained unclear. The "free communication of thoughts and opinions is one of the invaluable rights of man," the constitution declared, "and every citizen may freely speak, write and print on any subject, being responsible for the abuse of that liberty." What constituted "abuse of that liberty" had not been determined at the time Palmer posted his advertisement.[22]

In his view, however, the matter was clear as day: the abuse lay on the side of those who infringed on his freedom of conscience and of speech by curtailing his access to a lecture venue. He rather quickly penned a message "TO THE PUBLIC" and sent it to Benjamin Franklin Bache's *General Advertiser*. He was "extremely sorry to inform the Public," he wrote, "that the Gentleman from whom he engaged the house, has taken an alarm at the novelty of his sentiment, and fearing a temporal injury, has forbid his entrance into the house." Here Palmer fudged a bit, perhaps to protect the owner of the Long Room. The landlord may have been surprised by the public *announcement* of Palmer's intended speech against the divinity of Jesus, but not by the idea itself, which the landlord had most certainly heard Palmer express before. The part about "fearing a temporal injury" shifted the blame elsewhere—to unnamed persons who would harm the landlord's business if he allowed Palmer to speak in his establishment. Then Palmer made his main point: religious prejudice drove the effort to silence him. Despite the "legal and nominal freedom that obtains in this country," Palmer said, the "spirit of persecution, bear hard upon the rights of conscience." With hyperbole he described himself as persecuted for his freedom-loving principles nigh unto death. "But he does not yet despair," he wrote about himself, in the third person. For "if his life is spared, he is determined to exert his feeble abilities to demolish the ancient fabric of superstition." Once Christianity had fallen, Palmer would "erect on its ruins an immortal building, guarded by the engines of truth, and on its front engraved in letters of gold—'Virtue is the dignity of man.'" He signed his name, this time without the prefix of "Rev." or even "Mr.," as ELIHU PALMER.[23]

His complaint of persecution fired up the opposition. Already engaged in using the press to combat infidelity, Reverend Ashbel Green and his colleagues now had a new target, a particular person to pillory as an infidel. The same day Palmer's complaint appeared, Reverend John Blair Smith wrote a response. Smith was "a warm, animated, zealous, calvinistical Preacher," his friend Ebenezer Hazard said. Smith was also well connected. He and his older brother, Samuel Stanhope Smith, had attended the College of New Jersey under the leadership of the celebrated John Witherspoon. There they combined devout Presbyterian faith with the Enlightenment learning coming out of Witherspoon's native Scotland. John Smith, at thirty-five, had already served ten years as president of Hampden-Sydney College in Virginia, and now he ministered to the Presbyterian Pine Street Church. He drafted a response to Palmer's complaint that the rescinded rental agreement represented a trampling of his right to free speech. As Ashbel Green recorded in his diary, "A certain Mr. Palmer, an Universalist and Socinian preacher, made a considerable stir in the city. Dr. Smith then issued a publication in a newspaper, to which he affixed the signature of A. B."[24]

Smith, as "A. B.," used sarcasm to mock Palmer's lament. "A certain Mr. P——has published in the General Advertiser of this morning a sorrowful notice, that he is disappointed in obtaining a proper theatre for the display of his talents in disproving the Divinity of Jesus Christ. The gentleman is certainly much to be pitied," Smith wrote disingenuously. Too bad "so glorious an avenue to fame and emolument has been shut, on the present occasion." Smith had heard that Palmer studied law in Georgia. Given that career choice, Palmer could have showcased "his ambidextrous abilities in taking either side of a question." Palmer should be adept at this, Smith went on, because his proposed speech "was directly to oppose a cause of which he has professed to be an advocate for a number of years." As a sometime minister who argued now against the divinity of Christ, Palmer was either a recent turncoat or a longtime hypocrite.[25]

A defense of the landlord came next. Perhaps the "proprietor of the room" had not fully understood "the extent of his [Palmer's] project." (The nervous landlord may have said exactly this to the vexed Reverend White or his emissary.) One cannot blame a landlord for protecting his property from "a man, who was about to throw 'firebrands, arrows, and death' in direct hostility against an 'ancient fabric,' the fall of which, if Mr. P—— should effect it, would excite no small combustion in the country." The landlord's instinct for self-preservation made perfect sense. What did not make sense, Smith continued, was Palmer's claim to offer startling new ideas. The "landlord certainly could not have been alarmed at the '*novelty*' of the sentiments which Mr. P——proposed to vent, because they are as old as the days of the apostle Paul, who tells us, about 1700 years ago, that there were even at that time 'men of CORRUPT minds, reprobate concerning the faith.' 2 Tim. iii. 8." Palmer was simply one more hardened sinner eager to corrupt others. The apostle Peter had warned of the likes of Palmer, those "'false teachers, who would bring in DAMNABLE heresies, even DENYING the Lord who brought them.' 2 Pet. ii. I." Here it was, the nub of the matter. Palmer's Socinian view of a human Jesus constituted damnable heresy because it denied the doctrine that Jesus was the Lord God, part of the holy Trinity. Smith recognized Palmer as an enemy to the faith but denied any alarming novelty. As for freedom of religion, Palmer would be wise to "avoid saying much about the rights of conscience," because "that phrase has been of late pretty much used to signify no conscience at all."[26]

Smith wound up for the finish. Palmer had summoned the pathos of a heroic figure saving humanity from religion. Hardly, Smith replied, evoking instead a pathological antihero from ancient Greece who had sought eternal fame through senseless destruction. Palmer's supporters "are cheered at finding him still *bold* and *daring*," Smith wrote, but they are also "afraid that he will be called the modern Herostratus," a reference to the arsonist who burned a glorious Greek temple simply to achieve notoriety. Palmer's friends "wish him not to be too rash nor sanguine in his expectations of overturning ancient systems, or of erecting an immortal monument of praise to himself." They worried, Smith said, that only vast ignorance could explain why Palmer "is not deterred from his undertaking by the many unsuccessful attempts which have already been made in the same way, by men of stronger heads and more extended influence than he can pretend to be." In Smith's savvy telling in the *Federal Gazette*, Palmer was vainglorious, ignorant, corrupt, and destructive. Even his friends were worried about him.[27]

Palmer reacted promptly and point by point. Why didn't the anonymous writer "come forward in the way of fair argumentation, instead of making use of personal invective and scurrilous abuse?" Palmer reiterated the important principle at stake. The "constitution of this state, and of the United States, protects every man in the free exercise of his religious sentiments." If A. B. wanted to know what Palmer meant by "the law of opinion and the internal spirit of persecution," he need only "refer to his own feelings, and the bitterness of his own heart, at the time he was writing." The piece showed "the overflowings of a heart filled with envy, and the ebullitions of a revengeful mind." To the charge of hypocrisy, namely that Palmer's "design was to oppose a cause, of which I had professed to be an advocate for several years," Palmer responded with a denial. "This is not true—I never professed to be an advocate for the divinity of Jesus Christ—I have spoken publicly against it, both in Georgia and Connecticut, long before I ever preached in this city. And if any one here supposed I believed it, it is because he has not given attention to the public discourses which I have delivered." Palmer said his only weapon was "fair argumentation," and if "the '*old fabric*'" of religion "cannot stand this test, it ought to fall to the ground." Censorship of ideas was never appropriate, Palmer continued, and "no power on earth" has the "right to determine what heresy is." As long as a man's actions remain within the law, "he has a right to propogate his own opinions."[28]

To the charge of being a modern Herostratus, Palmer responded that the snub would backfire. The government of ancient Greece decreed that the arsonist's name should never be mentioned, with the result that he became as immortally famous as he had hoped. Similarly, although A. B. was "unwilling that I should have credit, even if I should promote the cause of truth," he had now inadvertently promoted "that, which he represents to be my main object, that is—the acquisition of fame." Palmer said he would take the moral high ground and disregard personal invectives (although he had just called his opponent bitter, envious, and vengeful). He assured his "fellow citizens that I wish to propagate my sentiments, guided by a spirit of benevolence towards all sects and parties—let truth therefore have fair play, and let strength of argument decide the contest." He ended with a postscript: "He will not hereafter answer any one, whose object is mere cavil and personal abuse."[29]

Reverend Ashbel Green took it from there. As he remembered later in his diary, Palmer had "rather broadly asserted that A. B. and all his other opposers were influenced by the odious spirit of persecution. To this I replied in a letter of irony, addressed to 'The preacher of liberal sentiments, and containing a liberal man's creed or confession of faith.'" Green published his response as a separate twenty-three-page pamphlet using the satirical pseudonym, "Eliphaz Liberalissimus." He began by responding directly to Palmer's last press release: "My object in writing is far different from those who address you for the sake of 'mere cavil and personal abuse.'" With the pretended tone of being solicitous of Palmer, an ally of shared liberal sentiments, the pamphlet's author defended the landlord who acted in accord with his *own* freedom of conscience. Surely Palmer could not object to that? As to Palmer's claim that A. B. had "a heart filled with envy," Liberalissimus responded with mockery: "As to envy, it does not appear to me that you are, at present, in a situation calculated in the least degree to produce it." In fact, Liberalissimus would "as soon think of envying a toad under a harrow, as of envying you in your present unfortunate circumstances." To Palmer's claim that A. B. wrote in a spirit of bitterness, Liberalissimus replied that Palmer's own publication teemed with "virulence," while A. B. "was & is still quite in a laughing humour, and only disposed to make a little diversion for himself and others at your expence, while at the same time he holds you in utter contempt." Palmer's serious response to the satirical lambasting made it look "as if you were desirous of representing yourself of more consequence, by a great deal, than this laughing scoundrel had any intention of making you." None of Palmer's critics took him seriously, Liberalissimus implied.[30]

But if Palmer's response was mostly ludicrous, Liberalissimus went on, the claim that he had never professed the divinity of Christ was evidence of terrible hypocrisy. Palmer had been "sent into the ministry" by sincere Christians who "would sooner have recommended you to the halter than to the pulpit, if they had not taken it for granted, that you would be an advocate for it. You were received, countenanced, and recommended by others, with the same ideas. Nay, you have in your public prayers, if not in your preaching, ascribed divine honours to Christ. And after all this, you have never been an advocate for his divinity!" If Palmer had never accepted Jesus as divine, then he was guilty of despicable deceit, namely "having joined yourself to a party, which at the very time you did so, you deliberately abhorred." Given Palmer's constant cry against "hypocrisy, deceit, and craft," this was a most serious admission. Where were your "wits gone a wandering when you intrapped yourself in this disastrous manner?" Liberalissimus understood that Palmer "had for a long time carried false colours: and been taken for what you have been wise enough to declare that you were not. A plague on the whole affair."[31]

No further response from Palmer appeared in print. Green noted that his "piece of irony and ridicule," which had circulated among his colleagues and received the "approbation" of Dr. Witherspoon and the Reverend Charles Nisbet, president of Dickenson College, "put an end to the controversy." By May, Jedidiah Morse in Massachusetts had heard the news from Ebenezer Hazard, who was also the uncle of Morse's wife. "Do you know Elihu Palmer?" Hazard asked Morse. In response to the "ludicrous attack on him" in the newspaper, the foolish Palmer had "explained seriously" his grievance. This produced another attack that "seems to have silenced him—& after that the enclosed pamphlet [by Green] made its appearance." The publicity had brought Palmer to the unfavorable attention of well-placed Philadelphians. He had outed himself as not believing in the divinity of Jesus, and his opponents roundly attacked him as a hypocritical heretic who passed as a minister but was in fact an enemy to Christianity.[32]

That Palmer raised the issue in the nation's capital, no less, would not have helped his cause. People were quick to say that irreligion endangered

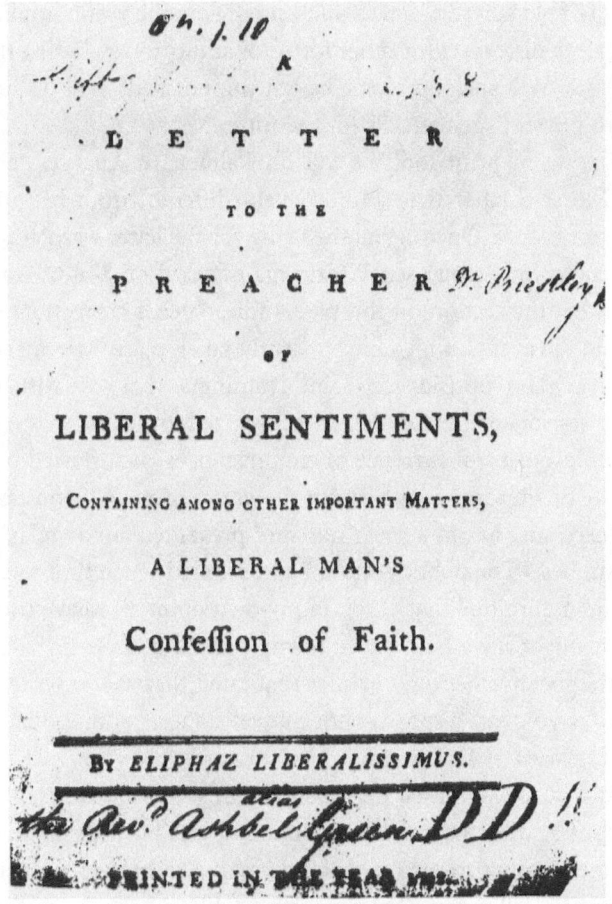

FIGURE 4. Ashbel Green's pamphlet, with its mocking pseudonym (Philadelphia, 1792). Green later claimed the work as his own in the autobiography he published in 1849. The pamphlet contributed to the public ridiculing of Palmer. Courtesy of Houghton Library, Harvard University.

both the moral health of the nation and the proper functioning of its political institutions. One critic in South Carolina wondered, "What shall we think of the editor of the National Gazette, printed in Philadelphia," who published Palmer's advertisement for a lecture against the divinity of Jesus Christ? The newspaper might as well have advertised "that the Christian religion is but a fairy tale, and the members of congress are a set of fairies, or a parcel of blockheads." An assault on religion, the writer implied, might quickly lead to disrespect for other forms of authority, including the federal government. "Will such an attack be left unpunished? Will no method be adopted to prevent such attacks for the future?"[33]

The flaying in print took its toll on Palmer. In August, Palmer sent Jedidiah Morse a letter that sounded very different from his pugnacious note the year before. Once again, the cause for the letter was Palmer's work for the *Geography*. Palmer sent Morse his material on South America and explained that the section on the West Indies "needs correction, especially considering the events, which have recently taken place." He meant to discuss the 1791 slave uprising on Saint Domingue that was turning into a longer war for independence. Palmer apologized for taking so long but said that "an unforeseen concurrence of circumstances" had slowed him down. "That scene of altercation with which the *heresy* of my religious sentiments has perplexed me, has in a great measure prevented any regular attention to other studies." The public contest had occupied much time and peace of mind. Palmer admitted that "tho', in my own opinion, I have truth on my side, yet it might have been more to my private interest to have avoided some of the inconveniences." Palmer requested that Morse write back and say "how far you can dispense with my assistance," adding that if "absolutely necessary I shall press hard to forward the work." Then Palmer shifted from business to their personal relationship. "I am sensible, Sir, that our religious sentiments are widely different; but notwithstanding that, It will give me pleasure to pursue with any man a science of this kind, so far as my situation will permit. Your real friend, Elihu Palmer." In this time of trouble, Palmer saw his longtime combatant with a different eye, perhaps as someone who knew Palmer to be honorable, despite their strong differences of opinion. It was quite the olive branch, but Morse had other allegiances. Twelve days after he received Palmer's letter, Morse wrote to "My Brother" Ashbel Green to congratulate him on his parody of Palmer. Morse had read "with great pleasure that keen instrument which so happily put to death, the *Preacher of Liberal Sentiments*." Morse wished "it may do execution wherever it meets with proper subjects, of which we have many this way."[34]

Palmer's reputation among historians for being a firebrand deist stems from this incident in Philadelphia, but a more accurate portrayal shows a man with proto-Unitarian beliefs who unexpectedly stepped into a hornet's nest. Overly confident that he could publish without much ado his opinion that Jesus was not divine, Palmer had miscalculated. When the clergy took action to hinder his lecture and smear his reputation, Palmer found himself alone. Fitch upbraided Palmer first for overreach and then for cowardice, but neither Fitch nor anyone else backed up Palmer in the press. Palmer was dismayed by the public attacks on his character, admitting to Morse that the altercation had been troublesome. Philadelphia's religious establishment had delivered a bruising experience. His friend, John Fellows, later considered Palmer's advertised lecture against the divinity of Jesus "an act of impudence, at that time, that nothing but his inexperience and impetuous zeal in the cause of truth can palliate or account for." What was he thinking, Fellows wondered? "Universalism itself was then hardly tolerated in this country." Palmer had gone too far, too soon.[35]

In fact, Palmer was on the cusp of a change that would not come quite soon enough for him. Just two years later, Joseph Priestley, the famous English chemist and Unitarian, moved to Pennsylvania after crowds smashed his laboratory and looted his home in England. Bishop White became acquainted with Priestley, enjoyed their conversations, and came to acknowledge Unitarianism as a legitimate, if misguided, form of Christianity. A small number of Unitarians in Philadelphia organized their first meeting in 1796, and in May of that year a Scottish-born Unitarian named James Taylor asked Bishop White to vouch for the group in their request to hold worship services in a building of the University of Pennsylvania. By then White was prepared to say that "if you are nearer the truth than we are, & can set us right, we ought to be obliged; but if we hold the truth, & we think we do, we shall keep our ground; for the truth must prevail. You may do us good, but you cannot do us harm." But White's confidence that Unitarianism was harmless lay in the future when Palmer posted his lecture notice. For Palmer, it was the same lesson twice, first in Newtown, now in Philadelphia; in the early 1790s there were limits to what could be openly said about Christian doctrine, as well as real social costs for expressing disbelief. Palmer had been forced to recognize that a group of forty people willing to listen to him speak in closed company against the Trinity did not mean that such ideas could be uttered in public with impunity. That was true even when he presented himself as a Christian.[36]

The fight in Philadelphia in 1792 was not about deism per se, but about the freethought that bloomed within the bounds of Protestantism. The Episcopalian William White, the Presbyterian Ashbel Green, and the Congregationalists Jedidiah Morse and Timothy Dwight all agreed that Socinian and Universalist beliefs had strayed beyond the edge of Christianity into infidelity. Christian freethinkers had abandoned the crucial orthodoxy of a divine Savior whose sacrifice was indispensable in the face of innate and unavoidable human depravity. Ministers policed their sectarian boundaries, and for good reason. If one accepted Universalism, what about the doctrine of predestination? If Socinian views could be openly proclaimed, what happened to Trinitarian orthodoxy as it had been since the Council of Nicaea? These were not trifling matters, as men like Bishop White, Ashbel Green, John Blair Smith, Ebenezer Hazard, and Jedidiah Morse knew. Certain aspects of the Christian faith were indispensable, they believed, and without these core tenets, the religion became a counterfeit version of itself. Palmer might claim to be a Christian of the most liberal sort, but his clerical opponents saw him as an infidel. As far as they were concerned, Palmer could tread his path to hell on his own, his freedom of conscience unimpaired, but they would not stand by as he tried to convert members of their own flocks. Tolerance of different Christian sects who worshipped in private did not protect outspoken individuals from being rebuked or even prosecuted for blasphemy when they made their religious views known. That fact might explain why Palmer's freethinking companions declined to publish their support. Sticking their necks out could incur real costs.

Palmer was vexed, distracted, and perhaps disheartened by the conflict in Philadelphia. His reputation had taken a beating, and he defended himself alone, while Fitch and the other freethinkers lay low. After a few months, Palmer decided to move with his family from Philadelphia to Wilkes-Barre, a hundred miles to the north. There he could get some emotional backup from his younger brother, Nathan. During a winter in Wilkes-Barre, Palmer would rebuild his self-confidence and practice resilience in the face of an uncertain future.

CHAPTER 6

Hard Fate

Mrs. Palmer had worries of her own that summer of 1792. Perhaps she was even then, during the weeks of her husband's humiliation in Philadelphia, pregnant with or nursing her second son while caring for his toddling brother. Money was scarce. The public trouncing had tainted her husband's reputation, a situation she never anticipated when they wed two years earlier. He had presented himself as a legitimate minister, even if he did prefer the company of the Universalists. When they lived in Augusta, Georgia, he had garnered respect for his teaching and preaching. Now he was a student of law without a steady income, a proselytizer without a pulpit, and a social pariah among God-fearing Philadelphians. Did Mrs. Palmer stand by her husband and offer emotional support during the public debacle that summer? Did she express disappointment at the betrayal of her marital expectations? No records remain to tell us anything about her, not even her name. Whatever her response to the challenges they faced, Mrs. Palmer's options were limited, her fate tied to that of her husband.

For the moment, Elihu Palmer's path remained unclear. He stayed in town into the fall but did not advertise any lectures. Then in September he traveled with his family to Wilkes-Barre. Ashbel Green took perhaps too much credit for their departure when he gloated that "soon after" his mocking pamphlet appeared, Palmer "left the city." Palmer had other reasons to leave Philadelphia. Rents had risen steeply, and he could not earn money by giving lectures. His brother Nathan lived in Wilkes-Barre; perhaps he could get Elihu some work. Still, when the Palmer family departed the nation's capital, it may well have felt like a retreat, so different in mood and outlook from their optimistic arrival in Philadelphia one year before. The feeling of persecution carried over into the version of events that Palmer's friend, John

Fellows, later recounted. Palmer had been driven from town under the threat of violence, Fellows said, "somewhat in the stile of ancient apostles upon similar occasions." Either Palmer exaggerated when he told Fellows the story a few years later, or Fellows embellished the tale when he wrote it down decades after that, but the image of an apostle in flight suggests that Palmer felt attacked. A speaker of truth, by his own lights, he had been slandered and mocked into silence by a cabal of Christian adversaries.[1]

How should he respond to adversity? As a younger man, Palmer had extolled an uncomplaining stoicism during hard times. He had praised the ability to endure difficulty without complaint, commending a "firmness of mind" that can "support a man, when the powers of the earth are all united against him." Such strength of mind had seemed to him "the richest possession below the skies." Perhaps he summoned such fortitude on the long road to Wilkes-Barre. The matter was not theoretical; soon enough, his resilience would be put to a far greater test.[2]

For the moment, however, Palmer concerned himself with the logistics of finding a living arrangement in Wilkes-Barre and work with a local attorney. Aspiring lawyers in Pennsylvania had to study law in-state for two years under the direction of an attorney and then pass an examination. Nathan, who would pass the bar himself in 1794, knew someone in Wilkes-Barre who could help Elihu clear that professional hurdle.[3]

Nathan may have done more than that for his brother. Five years younger than Elihu and still a bachelor, Nathan at twenty-three was probably already a man of considerable self-regard. He boasted of his descent from Myles Standish, the military strongman of the early Puritan settlers, and maybe he fancied himself an adventurer of the same stock. Nathan had followed the lure of the Susquehanna Company, a Connecticut enterprise that encouraged New Englanders to fight for the contested lands in the Wyoming Valley in northeastern Pennsylvania. He would go on to hold various positions in local government, wage extended print battles with Federalist opponents, and eventually serve as a Pennsylvania state senator before moving to New Jersey to found a newspaper. All this lay in the future when Elihu Palmer and his family arrived in the autumn of 1792, but Nathan's taste for verbal sparring, and his show of confidence laced with arrogance, may have been well along. The Philadelphia smear campaign against his older brother would have raised Nathan's ire. Ambitious, bold, and pugilant, Nathan could have fortified his older brother and helped him prepare for his eventual return to Philadelphia.[4]

Elihu Palmer, meanwhile, did what he always did: he set out to find a community of men who would grant him an audience for his favorite ideas. Wilkes-Barre was tiny compared to Philadelphia, but it was the seat of Luzerne County, and its one hundred families took pride in their courthouse, meetinghouse, academy, jail, Episcopal church, and several stores and mechanics' shops. Enough people lived in town for Palmer to rustle up a group who would gather for conversation and hear his arguments against the Holy Trinity and eternal damnation. Palmer lived in Wilkes-Barre only half a year, but he had a lasting effect. The freethinkers continued to meet after he returned to Philadelphia, and even four years later, "several of the leading spirits in the town were disciples of Elihu Palmer." By then Nathan Palmer had become "a lawyer and a man of influence, and took a leading part in the infidelity circle."[5]

When Palmer and his family returned to Philadelphia in March 1793, he was a changed man, and not just because he had passed the bar and now presented himself as an attorney. He came back ready to reassert his position as a freethinker in the public sphere of Philadelphia. The previous year he had accidentally exposed himself to public attack in a way he could not undo, but by the next spring he had accepted and maybe even embraced this position as a truth-speaking outsider. The public print scuffle the year before had clarified his position, pushing him to cast aside his clerical persona for good and leaving him free to speak out on the subject of religion, this time with more audacity than before.

"Citizen," the letter began. Writing from Philadelphia in March 1793, Palmer could imagine its recipient, Jedidiah Morse, bristling at the address. French revolutionaries had abolished aristocratic titles and required that people greet one another as Citizen rather than Madame or Monsieur. In the United States, supporters of the French Revolution adopted the custom to show their allegiance with the political and social transformation that was underway in France. Democratic-Republicans, who were just then organizing themselves into societies, embraced the address. Palmer could guess that Morse as a strong Federalist did not support the French Revolution and would not appreciate being called Citizen. Then again, offending Morse may have been partly the point. Hailing Morse as Citizen announced Palmer's political allegiance and also said something about his state of mind: he had returned to Philadelphia unrepentant and unbowed, ready to go toe to toe once more with Morse over religion and politics.[6]

The reason for the short note was not friendship, but instead Morse's *Geography*. Palmer had not received a response from Morse to his last message, which Palmer sent in August just before departing for Wilkes-Barre. At the time, under the assault of public ridicule, a smarting Palmer had chosen words of unusual warmth for his longtime nemesis, calling himself Morse's "real friend," despite their theological differences. Now it was March, and Palmer still had heard nothing from Morse. Palmer did not plea for the paid work he badly needed but wrote instead that he had "now more leisure" and could "assist" with the *Geography*, "if necessary." If Morse needed help, Palmer suggested, he could oblige him. This time, no assertion of friendship appeared in the letter, and Palmer signed off with a formal, "I am with respect etc[,] E Palmer."[7]

No matter how cool his tone, Palmer urgently needed work. The Palmers had moved into 400 Front Street, most likely a row house that stood between Coates and Brown streets in the Northern Liberties neighborhood of Philadelphia, just a few blocks from the Delaware River. Their second son had been born, or would be soon. Two children made for a busy, noisy household in what was presumably a rather small space. Palmer put out the word that he was an attorney looking for legal work. He also pursued other jobs. He sought out Mathew Carey, the Irish-born printer and bookseller who had fled to America in 1784 to elude British prosecution for publishing nationalist newspapers in Ireland. Carey and Palmer disagreed about religion and American politics, as Carey was Catholic and, at the time, still a Federalist, but Palmer was glad to do some work for Carey, possibly related to the project of the *General Atlas*, a collection of maps Carey would publish in 1795. Palmer's contributions to Jedidiah Morse's *Geography* had given him relevant experience.[8]

The relationship with Mathew Carey helped with cash-flow troubles. In June, for example, Palmer had a note delivered to "Citizen" Carey with the request to "send me, by the bearer, five dollars & charge the same to your Friend[,] E. Palmer." When Nathan Palmer came to visit in July, Palmer asked Carey, in rather grandiose fashion, to "let my Brother have such articles out of your store as he wants & charge the same to my account." Later that month Palmer wrote to Carey once more, saying "I should be extremely glad of a little more cash to relieve me of my present little embarrassments." As important for Palmer as the cash was the fact that Carey considered his word good and his reputation honorable.[9]

Palmer still had supporters in town, even if they had ducked the ink fight the year before. Fitch's Deist Society had fizzled, but plenty of people still wanted to hear what Palmer had to say. How else could he have landed a prized spot as a public orator at that year's Fourth of July celebration? Palmer had backers in part because public political expressions were changing in response to events in France. The French king, Louis XVI, had been executed in January, the Committee on Public Safety was in control of the French government, and by June the radicals had seized power in the National Convention and were arresting their more moderate colleagues. This was drastic enough, but the Reign of Terror had not yet begun, and Democratic-Republicans in America believed France would follow the United States in creating a representative democracy. They saw the French struggle as an extension of America's own ongoing quest for liberty and greater equality. Federalists, meanwhile, deplored the excesses of a revolution already too far gone, in their view. They pointed to the slave-led rebellion in Saint Domingue as a warning of what lay ahead if the revolutionary momentum was not halted. The interpretation of events in France as either salutary or dangerous deepened the partisan divide in the United States and led to separate celebrations of the national holiday.[10]

In this apprehensive moment, Democratic-Republicans took issue with Washington's stance of neutrality in the European conflict. They rejected the idea that President Washington stood above partisanship or that only bipartisan efforts were honorable. They also began to criticize the administration in newspapers, printed letters, and resolutions. Newspaper editors supported unrestricted political speech, and the new Democratic-Republican societies affirmed it too. But it was one thing to pronounce upon the principle and another thing to enact it. Palmer's willingness to speak boldly made him valuable beyond his actual message. He tested the principle of free speech before it had been legally secured. It may therefore have been for his daring, as well as for his gifts as a speaker, that

Democratic-Republicans granted him a place as an orator on the nation's birthday. Regardless of the reason, Palmer was ready to make his comeback speech and reclaim his place as a public speaker. Not for nothing had his brother Nathan traveled one hundred miles to hear it. Perhaps they discussed how Elihu would speak out after the shaming he had experienced the previous summer and what, in particular, he would he say about Christianity and its ministers.[11]

Numerous people gathered on the Fourth of July at Federal Point, a park of "pleasing situation" on the Delaware River. The assembled company sat "under a bower erected for the purpose, to partake of an elegant entertainment" that included a speech by "Elihu Palmer, *citizen* of Pennsylvania." Palmer, who had joined the Democratic Society of Pennsylvania, gave his occupation as lawyer. He no longer used the title "Reverend," but he also dispensed in this case with "Mr." The term "citizen" had become an honorific in its own right. "Friends and Fellow Citizens!" Palmer began. "The age of reason and philosophy has at length arrived, and begins to illuminate the world!" As in his July Fourth speech in Pittsfield five years before, Palmer emphasized the all-important project of intellectual liberation, which he placed once more within a global frame. A "veil of darkness" created by the collusion of church and state had hung "over all nations," he said, but "enlightened men" had exposed the conspiracy. "King-craft and priest-craft, those mighty enemies to reason and liberty," received a death blow from the "genius of 1776" and would soon belong to "the dark abodes of oblivion."[12]

Palmer had said as much five years before, but the words held a different meaning for him now. Back then, Palmer had praised high-profile revolutionaries, including Washington and John Adams. Now he noted that some political leaders had backslid after they signed the Declaration of Independence. "Beware, ye American aristocrats!" he warned. His audience understood what Palmer meant to say. The Federalists had turned against the principles of liberty and equality for which they had once contended, and now in their reach for power they sidled up to monarchical England. Palmer issued them a warning: if they did not cease in their attempts to impose "Civil and religious oppression," he said, the "just resentment and indignation of an injured people will hurl you into eternal infamy." Palmer felt he had personally experienced such oppression the year before, when anonymous pamphleteers joined forces to ridicule and silence him. It had been a lonely experience. But now, with an appreciative audience seated before him on this holiday, Palmer's trials from the previous year appeared to him within a larger, even heroic, frame. Intellectual liberation from religious superstition was of utmost importance for political freedom, Palmer told his audience, for without ecclesiastical power "over the minds of men, the civil oppressions of the world would long since have tumbled into ruin." The clergy feigned "superior sanctity and virtue," but they gladly supported the "civil tyrant, and prepared every living creature for the completest slavery." He had experienced their evil intentions himself.[13]

Palmer used his moment on stage to pillory his personal antagonists. No American cleric should ever have "assumed the mysterious carriage and imaginary dignity of an European bishop," he said. The dig referred to Reverend William White, the first bishop of the Episcopal Church in Philadelphia, who had pressured the owner of the meeting hall to shut down Palmer's lecture the year before. Palmer also targeted Morse. The printed version of Palmer's speech carried a footnote to show that the Charlestown minister had "*deviated from the revolutionary principles of 1776.*" Palmer quoted Morse's *Geography* as reporting that the Connecticut clergy had "*preserved a kind of aristocratical balance in the very democratical government of the state; which has happily operated as a check upon the overbearing spirit of republicanism.*" Palmer's oration implied that White and Morse belonged to the "American aristocrats" who undermined the democratic republic.[14]

Utterly absent from Palmer's speech was the idea that a republic required a shared religious faith. He said nothing about civil religion or the importance of faith to a democracy. What mattered to a republic was not shared religion but rather the guarantee of religious freedom. Only freedom of thought and of speech made possible an "empire of reason," a society based on rational discoveries of the world. One could see such a society developing, Palmer said with excitement. The revolutions in America and France had "awakened in the intellectual world a new energy of thought, and turned the pursuit of man upon scientific principle." As "fanaticism and oppression are vanishing away," those who study "the philosophy of the human mind" are engaged in "deep researches, to develope the nature of those principles, which will afford a permanent hope to the wretched in every part of the world." This was the path to human happiness.[15]

Although the terminology was still in the making, Palmer was referring to the eighteenth-century moral sciences that combined the study of nature with observations about human psychology and society (the precursors of what we now call the social sciences). Palmer expressed his enthusiasm for a rational and universal science of morality. He spoke of the need to "investigate the principles of nature" so that "a lasting source of felicity may be established for the great family of mankind." Contemporary philosophy "teaches the most pure and unadulterated morality," he said, one entirely devoid of the "mysteries and external trappings" of revealed religion. That was his major point, and he would repeat it for the rest of his life: observations of the natural world provided a code of conduct far superior to any advanced by divine revelation. A moral philosophy based on science will ultimately "ameliorate the condition of the human race." The importance of the work could not be overstated, in his view. Nothing less than the future of humanity was at stake.[16]

Taking his bow, Palmer could feel he had resumed his place in the public life of Philadelphia. His published speech signaled his reentry into the public conversation. He no longer feared losing face among Federalists, for he had stalwart supporters among his "fellow citizens." The recent establishment of Democratic-Republican societies had changed the political scene, splitting the public audience in two. A new day was dawning for freedom of religion and freedom of speech, and Palmer had the mettle to put these liberties into practice. He would be despised by Federalists and Calvinists (Jedidiah Morse was both), but he found collegiality and respect in other circles. Democratic-Republicans valued his willingness to speak out publicly against Federalists, even if they demurred on some aspects of his message. When social respectability, like political opinion, divided along partisan lines, it proved liberating for Palmer. Enmity from Federalists was hardly a strike against him now—among Democratic-Republicans it was almost a badge of honor. Palmer could feel exuberant on that July Fourth, for he had rebounded from adversity and proclaimed his personal independence from his critics. He had absorbed the knocks to his reputation and returned to Philadelphia to receive recognition and applause as a speaker. Flushed with success, he had no hint of the far greater challenge that lay in store.

Only a month later, in August 1793, Doctor Benjamin Rush sat down at his writing desk "at a late hour, and much fatigued," to inform his wife that "a malignant fever has broken out in Water Street." He believed its source to be the "putrefied" coffee beans unloaded on one of the wharves. The sickness was "violent & of short duration," he reported. It could strike and kill in the space of only twelve hours; the longest time between first onset of illness and death was four days. The cases were "acute & alarming," Rush noted. Already twelve of his patients had died. A few days later, Rush wrote again to say the fever had spread through the city; he was reminded "of the histories I had read of the plague." Rush described the course of the disease. "Sometimes it comes on with a chilly fitt, and a high fever, but more frequently it steals on with headache, languor & sick stomach. These symptoms are followed by stupor—delirium—vomiting," cold hands and feet, a feeble pulse. "The eyes are at first suffused with blood," he wrote, then they become yellow. The skin turns yellow too. Most patients died on the second or third day of showing symptoms, and few survived the fifth. Rush tried to heal patients by bleeding them to reduce the amount of toxins in the body, but mostly his remedies failed to stop the jaundice, the hemorrhaging of blood from all orifices, and the violent vomiting of black matter. In some cases, he wrote, "the patients possess their reason to the last."[17]

Mathew Carey and Israel Israel were on the committee charged with the awful task of tracking the deaths street by street. The fever moved "northwardly up Water street to Vine Street," the committee reported. "Front street," where the Palmers lived, "was next attacked, whence it spread into parallel streets." By the first week of October, 126 of the residents on Front Street, north of Market Street, had died of the fever, and 80 more perished in the following weeks. The Palmers watched their neighbors pack up and leave. On their street alone, four hundred white and ten black residents fled the sickness, leaving about seven hundred white and some fifty black inhabitants behind. Philadelphians with the means to travel fled at all hours of the day and night in carts, wagons, and coaches, heading for the countryside. Those who remained tried to ward off the fever with any remedy. The College of Physicians recommended vinegar and camphor as disinfectants. The townspeople lit bonfires, burned tar, sprinkled vinegar on their clothes, smoked cigars, or carried garlic in their pockets and shoes. Business came to a standstill, Carey reported, "and the streets wore the appearance of gloom and melancholy." The city stopped tolling bells for the dead, as the doleful sound "had been constantly ringing the whole day."[18]

Fear warped all social interaction, and Carey called it a "Frightful view of human nature." Spouses fled without their feverish partners, and parents left sick children behind to die. These horrors were "daily exhibited in every quarter of our city," Carey wrote. The panic exposed a primal and shameless survival instinct, and people showed less concern at "the loss of a parent, a husband, a wife, or an only child" than they would, under normal circumstances, show for "a favourite lap-dog." What occurred within families pertained also to friends, who "avoided each other in the streets," Carey noted, "and only signified their regard by a cold nod." A person wearing any signs of mourning "was shunned like a viper." Fear of contagion destroyed all common courtesy. Even the most "respectable citizens" were sent to their burials on horse-drawn carts, "unattended by a friend or relation, and without any sort of ceremony." Ebenezer Hazard wrote to Jedidiah Morse and described a city under siege. A "friend dares not visit a friend who is sick, lest he should be infected, & carry the Disorder to his own family. No friends attend at Funerals except perhaps two or three who keep at a Distance from the Body, which is carried in an hearse, accompanied by three or four Negroes who bury it." No clergyman attends, Hazard continued, and no proper ceremony occurs before "the putrid Corpse is committed to its kindred Earth, & covered up as expeditiously as possible."[19]

Hazard reported to Ashbel Green that black nurses "are in such Demand that they cannot be had," while "white people are afraid to undertake the Task." During the epidemic, many black Philadelphians worked as nurses and undertakers, in part because whites believed African Americans were immune to yellow fever and should be pressed into service. The African American church leaders, Absalom Jones and Richard Allen, knew that black people were just as vulnerable to the deadly disease. They also recognized that the nurses who tended white patients received pay only begrudgingly or were suspected of stealing from the sick and the dead. When Hazard's family contracted the fever, "seven down at once, or nearly so," Hazard reported that "no friends visited us in our Sickness, & we had to hire Negroes for Nurses." He objected that "they charged *four Dollars per Day* for nursing, & were but poor hands after all." Hazard's family survived, courtesy of the African Americans who came to their aid when no white people would, but Hazard showed the nurses little gratitude.[20]

In this time of panic, the fever became a proving ground for religious faith. Doctor Benjamin Rush, although acutely distressed by the deaths of so many patients, felt strangely calm about his own fate. "I enjoy good health and uncommon tranquility of mind," he wrote to his wife. "While I depend upon divine protection and feel that at present I live, move, and have my being in a more especial manner in God alone, I do not neglect to use every precaution" to prevent infection. He was willing to trust in the Lord and stay in the center of the epidemic, even if it should cost him his life.[21]

Others felt less certain about what God called them to do. Reverend Ashbel Green, who had removed to Princeton, New Jersey, corresponded with Ebenezer Hazard about whether Green should return to his congregation in this moment of crisis. Their letters discussed the optics of Green's absence during the plague, and the opinions of religious skeptics loomed large in their minds. Should Green return to Philadelphia to avoid the charge of cowardice? Hazard thought not. He described to Green the horrible scene of "open Graves," the "Hearses, with Coffins & dead Bodies in them, continually passing every Street," and the "hourly Information of the Death of Friends or Acquaintances." He urged Green to stay put, because divine Providence had obviously "called you to a place of safety." Of course the "Enemies of Religion" would criticize Green for staying away, for "it is *their Business*, & they will do it:—how can you hinder them?" But it was a no-win situation with religious scoffers. If Green remained safely in the countryside, the critics would say he was "as much afraid of death as other men;—you leave your Flock when they most need your Services;—& your Conduct shews that Religion is all a name." If he returned to the city, caught the fever, and died, they would say he was a "mad Enthusiast, that was wonderfully religious, & came into the midst of Disease to shew us that a Faith will keep a man from Infection; but we see he has died as well as other Folks; he might as well have been without his Religion for all the good it did him." The dilemma could not be avoided, but why care? Hazard told Green to recall "whose Reproaches are we considering? Those of the *Enemies* of Religion:—they are not worth minding:—God will take care of his Cause in spite of them." But Green did worry about what religious skeptics would make of his absence, and the question preoccupied him perhaps more than what action, as a matter of principle, he ought to take as a leader in his religious community.[22]

The most notorious skeptic in Philadelphia, Elihu Palmer, had entirely other concerns than accusing clergy of saving their skins. In their home on Front Street, Mrs. Palmer took to bed with the tell-tale symptoms of a headache and fatigue. As with so many other victims of yellow fever, she may have declined so rapidly that she hardly had time to realize she would not recover. Did the twenty-something woman say farewell to her husband and sons? Did she pray to Jesus as her Savior, or had she adopted her husband's view of a human Jesus? Did Elihu try to offer some comfort, or was he already too sick himself? As both parents shivered with fever, maybe a kindly neighbor tended to their two young boys. Did Elihu witness his wife's dying moments, or was he too delirious himself? Once she had died, where did her body find a resting place? The Palmers had no money to speak of, and he belonged to no church. Philadelphians tasked with removing the dead from their homes piled the bodies onto carts and dumped them in an open grave. Mrs. Palmer's corpse probably landed in the communal grave reserved for paupers in a potter's field. The grave was left open for many weeks—for as long as the fever raged.[23]

No account of the Palmers' experience during the fever remains, except for one small, suggestive fragment. Doctor Benjamin Rush later told John Fellows that Palmer refused to undergo the bleeding treatment. Rush shook his head at the stubborn man, apparently a freethinker in matters of medicine as well as religion. The doctor had Universalist sympathies, and although he did not join their church, he would have known Palmer as the lecturer who had been disinvited from the Universalist pulpit, had sparked a public ruckus the previous summer, and had left town for a while only to reappear in the spring, more brazen than ever. Even with the daily death toll rising at a shocking rate and doctors doing what they could to ease patients' symptoms, Palmer thought he knew best and "was opposed to being bled." What a strangely certain, even conceited man, Rush might have thought, as Palmer lay sick in bed, his fate in the balance. This was no time for conversation, but under completely different circumstances Palmer might have told Rush his ideas about the immanent vital power that could restore a body back to health, and possibly better with the blood inside the body rather than drained from it. Isaac Ledyard on Long Island had impressed upon Palmer the power of the vital principle, just as Rush's onetime teacher, the Edinburgh professor William Cullen, had described the ability of the *vis medicatrix* to heal a sick body. Rush himself had admired Cullen's effort to reduce invasive treatments that got in the way of healing, but in the dire, urgent chaos of the epidemic, Rush thought it advisable to take drastic measures. Perhaps it was too difficult not to take action in the face of such desperate tragedy. He could not have known that Palmer's refusal to be bled might have stemmed from an idea that Rush also shared, namely that marvelous self-healing properties reside in the body.[24]

Palmer recovered from the fever only to experience the full impact of the loss of his wife mingled with profound relief that his young sons had survived. There was something else: the fever had blinded him. Yellow fever causes the hemorrhaging of blood from ruptured vessels, and when this occurs within the eye, the fluid puts pressure on the optic nerve, leading to blindness. To what extent his sight was impaired is difficult to assess, since blindness affects everyone differently. Perhaps he could, like many blind people, make out colors or differences in light and shade. A friend, however, said Palmer experienced complete loss of vision. He had to "grope his way in darkness," John Fellows recounted. Years later, Palmer ran a book advertisement that claimed he had suffered a "total loss of sight." Whatever the extent of his impairment, Palmer could no longer *read*, and this was a devastating discovery. He lived for ideas; he read avidly and then discussed what he had read. What would sustain his voracious appetite for philosophical ideas if he could not read? Who would he even *be*?[25]

On a more immediate level, the question arose how Palmer would provide for his children. He could hear his boys, both under three years of age, but he had to feel his way toward them. Did he hold them close and take comfort in their embraces? Did they cry together about the loss of their mother? Palmer had lost his own mother when he was seven, and he knew about a motherless upbringing. Did he despair about his ability to care for his children? Perhaps a concerned neighbor helped feed, clean, and dress the young boys. Palmer had no income with which to hire help. The weather in November was turning colder, and he could not light or tend a fire. The shock of his multiple losses—his wife, his eyesight, and his ability to care for his sons—was staggering. He struggled to adapt to the cataclysmic changes that had occurred in such a short time.

Not all of his neighbors were sympathetic. While Rush thought Palmer's blindness had a physical cause, namely the refusal to be bled, others attributed Palmer's blighted vision to supernatural intervention. Blindness had a long and potent symbolic history of being associated with punishment for sin, as many examples in the Bible attest. Just as old was the association of blindness with seers and prophets, but Palmer's Christian neighbors did not perceive his loss of vision in those terms. Some of them, at least, believed that God's displeasure with Palmer's infidelity had produced this terrible affliction, and they told him so. John Fellows recalled that Palmer received "little sympathy or disposition in the sectarians of any denomination to lend a helping hand to soothe his misfortune. Indeed, some did not scruple to pronounce it a judgment of God for his unbelief." To his critics, Palmer's blindness seemed a perfect, if painful, metaphor for the fact that he had lost his spiritual way. He had not kept his eyes on the prize of eternal life, and a judging God had punished him for his blasphemy and pride. If those who judged Palmer wondered how to explain the other four thousand, presumably God-fearing, Philadelphians who had succumbed to the mysterious disease before a late autumn frost slowed its terrible progress—well, that was God's mystery. Government officials also saw the hand of God in the epidemic, and Governor Mifflin designated December 12 as a "day of general humiliation, thanksgiving, and prayer." He exhorted his fellow citizens to abstain from work and "to unite in confessing, with contrite hearts, their manifold sins and transgressions." The clergy weighed in too, suggesting that the designated day be "kept holy to the Lord, not merely as a day of thanksgiving" but also "as a day of solemn humiliation and prayer, joined with the confession of our manifold sins" and a renewed commitment to "obedience to his holy will and laws."[26]

In responding to Palmer's fever-induced blindness, Philadelphians drew upon ideas about disability that were in transition and marked by contradiction. They recognized that some forms of impairment simply came with the aging process—for example, the loss of hearing, sight, teeth, and mobility. These gradual losses need not signal more than physical deterioration. But other forms of deformity (the commonly used word) might signal an inner moral twistedness that corresponded to the missing eye or misshapen limb. Some people saw in physical deformity a marring of the otherwise harmonious and orderly workings of nature. If the ideal human figure made the argument for heavenly design, then the deformed body appeared as a botched exemplar that might merit rejection. A "secularization" of disability was also in process, so that people could vacillate between the assumption that disability was divine punishment for personal guilt and the opinion that impairment resulted from random and impersonal fate due to explicable, natural causes.[27]

Palmer had his own understanding of events. The notion that God would allow or even instigate a natural disaster like the fever sounded to him like the worst kind of blasphemy. The divine Creator could not possibly be malicious without end, producing the human suffering that swept up Palmer's family along with thousands of other victims in the city. Palmer would have found greater consolation in the notion of an uncaring fate, an accident neither divinely ordained nor brought on by immoral human behavior. What he *did* frame in moral terms was the response to adversity. Required of him now, he realized, was stoic endurance, an uncomplaining courage that kept him upright in this time of pain and loss. He had written about this as "Alfred" five years before, when he had prized inner fortitude. Patient endurance of hardest fate "sheweth a noble soul," he had said, and "declareth to his Creator, that he can bear the part assigned to him." Strength of mind "is one of the highest blessings of nature, it is the richest possession below the skies." In the face of personal tragedy, moral backbone was essential. Even so, the fortitude Palmer sought did not, in his view, reside in the Christian faith. The "moral principle" preceded all invented religions and would outlast them. It rested on "a basis as durable as time," he believed, and was "independent of all the theological reveries of antiquity."[28]

Regardless of whatever resilience he could muster, Palmer's situation was dire. Twenty-nine years old, he was suddenly a blind widower with two little boys and no income. At some point he took his sons to Connecticut to be raised by his father; his sisters and their families lived nearby. Perhaps he promised to visit as often as he could. Then he returned to Philadelphia where, bereft of his family, he sat in the strange new quiet. At first he tried to resume his legal work, but it proved impossibly difficult. To practice law required sight, he said, "to investigate its intricate subtilties." After a year of struggle to make a living in Philadelphia, Palmer decided to return to the last place where things had been whole for his family, his health, and his reputation: Augusta. Friends collected money to help him "remove to Georgia, which he could not have done without assistance." One of the contributors was Israel Israel, the Universalist who had vetted Palmer in 1792 and found his Christian faith lacking. Palmer "had been angry with him for preventing his admission into their Church," Israel remembered. He donated to the travel fund so Palmer would know that although Israel "disapproved of his religious Sentiments[,] he felt for him as a man." Was it humbling for Palmer to accept money from the man who had deprived him of access to the Universalist congregation? Or did the gift contribute to a reconciliation? The two men must have made some kind of peace, because Israel, who had a tavern and an inn, was a person "at whose house Palmer staid when in Town." But for now Palmer was leaving Philadelphia for the second time in as many years, this time alone, impoverished, and struck by terrible losses.[29]

Back in Augusta by 1794, Palmer tried to reconstruct the semblance of a life. Late in the year he applied to the Augusta Board of Trustees for permission to deliver a series of lectures on morality and philosophy every other Sunday in St. Paul's Episcopal Church. This time, Reverend Boyd was ready to defend his turf from the returned interloper. The trustees refused Palmer's request with the explanation that the church had been founded as a religious house of worship. The unspoken message was that Palmer could no longer pretend to offer a proper religious service. But the trustees did grant him use of a room in the Richmond Academy for his lectures. Either signals got crossed or Palmer ignored the message, because in January 1795 he advertised in the *Augusta Chronicle* that he would lecture in St. Paul's Church on the next Sunday. The trustees quickly published their refusal of Palmer's request, after which Palmer was obliged to notify the public of a change in venue. He would speak in the academy after all.[30]

To survive financially, and perhaps psychologically as well, Palmer had to reestablish what he could offer the community. In Philadelphia he had relinquished the title of "Reverend" in favor of "Mr." and then "Citizen." Upon his return to Augusta, however, he took up the clerical title once more. It may have been the easiest thing to do. His acquaintances in

Georgia remembered him as a minister and probably addressed him as such. It was also a source of much-needed revenue. The greatest threat was always that he would be reduced to indigence. By spring 1795, the news made it all the way to Jedediah Morse in Massachusetts that Palmer was "dependent on Charity" for support. To avoid a fate of beggary, Palmer had to present himself as still a man of talent and worth. In June 1795, "Rev. Dr. Palmer" officiated at a marriage in Augusta, and the next month he delivered a public oration on the Fourth of July, possibly his first such speech delivered without the benefit of eyesight.[31]

Books for the blind did not yet exist. In Liverpool, England, the outspoken abolitionist and poet Edward Rushton had established a school for blind children in 1791. Blinded himself at age nineteen by a contagious eye disease contracted on a slave ship when he offered succor to infected Africans, Rushton took an active part in the radical political circles of Liverpool and London. He edited a newspaper, established a bookstore, and eventually became part of Elihu Palmer's transatlantic network of freethinkers. But the development of reading techniques for the visually impaired was in its infancy when Palmer lost his eyesight. Some people experimented with movable, raised characters, or with forming letters by pricking or stamping paper. In Augusta, however, Palmer had no access to such techniques. He would need to find other ways to share ideas and make a living.[32]

Political engagement became one way for Palmer to contribute something of value and feel himself part of a larger effort. He shared the Republican outrage about the Treaty of Amity, Commerce, and Navigation, then under consideration between the United States and Great Britain. Commonly called the Jay Treaty, the agreement supported trade between the two countries at the same time that it broke a wartime treaty with France. The deal proved to Democratic-Republicans that the Washington administration had gone terribly soft on the British monarchy. In Augusta, the town meeting appointed Palmer to a committee of fifteen men charged with determining whether the treaty would, if ratified, "be subversive of the sovereignty and independence of the said United States." (The committee found exactly that and recommended that President Washington withhold his signature.) Also on the committee was the former state governor, Edward Telfair, with whom Palmer had marched in the thanksgiving parade in 1789, and Reverend Boyd, now the uncontested minister of St. Paul's

Church. Palmer had made yet another comeback of sorts, at least in terms of attaining a position of public regard. His financial situation was precarious, but he could count himself among the most respected townsmen of Augusta.[33]

Maintaining his dignity as a blind person in public spaces required a whole new set of skills. Perhaps Palmer had already acquired a walking cane of the kind displayed in his later portrait. A cane would signal his impairment and invite others to come to his aid as he made his way through town. Linking arms with another person helped enormously, and he must have requested such guidance countless times. He probably memorized his path to the academy, the steps between buildings, and the location of ditches, fences, and hitching posts. He would have endured the indignity and bruises from stumbling into unexpected objects or falling off a curb. He learned which foods he could eat politely in public and which proved too unwieldy to try. Living alone was impossible. Boardinghouse life provided food, warmth, and company. The mistress might do his laundry, children could run errands, and housemates could share gossip, report on the weather outside, and read newspapers aloud. Palmer probably attended Masonic meetings once more and joined any reading or conversation circle to which he was invited. As he adjusted to his new situation, he used all the social tools at his disposal to build on existing relationships in Augusta, even as he learned new ways of navigating his world.

Not everyone had sympathy for the freethinker who had lost his family, his eyesight, and his independence. Ebenezer Hazard, the Presbyterian in Philadelphia who had supported the anonymous takedown of Palmer in print, wrote to Jedediah Morse in July 1795, enclosing "Palmer's Note as you desire." The note probably pertained to a loan and promised its repayment, because Hazard added flippantly that the note, "like [Palmer] himself, it will probably never be worth any Thing." Enmity for Palmer's religious ideas had sapped Hazard of any compassion for the man. Despite Palmer's tragic losses, Hazard dismissed him as a contemptible infidel. Such disdain would not have surprised Palmer, who associated just such meanness with the advocates of Calvinism. This was the "spirit of persecution" he had decried in 1792, seeing it as a defining trait among dogmatic, self-righteous Christians. With unintended irony, Hazard had written to Morse at the height of the yellow fever that "those who depend on Man alone for aid must be wretched indeed." Only those who trust in the Lord as "our Refuge, & our Fortress," Hazard said, are "enabled" to offer "Consolation & Support" to others.[34]

In Augusta, Palmer found genuine support and regained his footing. He learned he could still hold an audience with his public speaking. He had always preached well without notes, and now his blindness added to the effect, showcasing his talent. His lectures would have engaged his favorite topic, namely the principles that underlay both the natural world and human morality. Understanding the true foundations of morality was imperative for human happiness, he believed, and to share this concept became his inspiration, a mission that helped him endure even his considerable losses. In 1788, as a younger man, he had praised the virtue of resilience in the face of hardship. Now he knew about adversity firsthand. More than pride was needed to overcome such misfortune; a faith in something greater than oneself was required—and he had one. Palmer had faith in the power of reason to assist human progress toward future happiness. He believed he held crucial information that could help humanity advance toward that better future, and this conviction buoyed his spirits, channeled his energy, and gave him the courage to carry on. It was not easy to be blind, but Palmer "often said, that the accident had fallen upon the right person, upon one that was able to bear it; that many would have sunk under it; but that he could submit with firmness."[35]

CHAPTER 7

Fellowship

A NEW FRIENDSHIP in 1796 changed the course of Elihu Palmer's life. He had traveled from Augusta to Connecticut, possibly to visit one or both of his sons who, if they still lived, would then have been about three and five years old. On his way, Palmer tarried in New York City, where he met John Fellows, a freethinking bookseller five years his senior. It would have taken mere minutes for the men to realize they had compatible ideas about religion. That year, Fellows had published his essay *The Character and Doctrines of Jesus Christ*, a forty-page defense of the idea that Jesus had been entirely human. According to Fellows, the crucifixion did not kill Jesus, who was taken from the cross while still alive. No miraculous resurrection occurred. Jesus was, however, "a man of excellent understanding," Fellows wrote, "a good man and a warm patriot, desirous of restoring the liberty of his country, which had fallen under the Roman yoke." In fact, Jesus was a man after Fellows's own heart, a role model whose "republican spirit" was "very evident in his speeches and in his actions." The New York bookseller had no doubt that a divine "first cause, a creator of the universe" provided a heavenly future for every soul. Like Palmer, Fellows endorsed a liberal version of Christianity that celebrated the teachings of Jesus but dispensed with the Trinity, supernatural miracles, original sin, and eternal damnation.[1]

The two men found much to discuss. Fellows hailed from Sheffield, Massachusetts, and Palmer shared his story of preaching there in 1788 on his way to Long Island. By that time Fellows had left home, graduated from Yale (in the same class as Jedidiah Morse), and made his way to New York City. He would have recognized the townsman who had chided Palmer for telling the Sheffield churchgoers "to spend the day joyfully in innocent festivity, and to render themselves as happy as possible." Fellows and Palmer probably shared a good laugh at that, and Fellows later recounted with sarcastic italics that Palmer "was lectured by an attorney, a *sound believer*, at whose house he stopped, for giving such liberal advice."[2]

Fellows suggested a speaking opportunity for Palmer. The bookseller belonged to the local Democratic-Republican society, formed to "support and perpetuate the EQUAL RIGHTS OF MAN." Members came from "every class" of men and met monthly. Palmer, who had joined the Democratic Society of Pennsylvania three years before, readily agreed to address the group in a large assembly room on the following Sunday. The lecture must have gone well, because Palmer thought he might find an audience for his ideas in New York. He decided to pack up his life in Georgia, and by late summer 1796 he had moved to Manhattan. It would prove to be a turning point in his life as a freethinker.[3]

New York was smaller than Philadelphia, but even without eyesight Palmer could tell it was booming. We can imagine him on a bright autumn morning in 1796, stepping out of Benjamin Powell's large brick boardinghouse and getting his bearings. A block to the west, the ferryman called for passengers waiting to cross the Hudson to New Jersey, while gulls shrieked and swooped over the docks. Palmer turned his back to the river and faced the morning sunshine. He could feel the warmth and perhaps perceive the light. Sunny days made navigation easier. In the beginning, of course, someone had accompanied him on his walks. Perhaps his landlord's wife, a pleasant woman, had taught Palmer the safest ways to go. Eventually, he may have made his way without a companion, tapping his long cane in front of him, listening carefully to the sounds all around, and stopping frequently to ask for guidance. His favorite destination was John Fellows's bookstore and circulating library on Wall Street.[4]

The half-mile walk from Powell's boardinghouse to Fellows's bookstore brought Palmer in contact with a wide array of people, sounds, and smells. Walking east on Cortlandt Street, he passed shops, boardinghouses, and the tavern. He could not see the two- and three-story buildings he passed, the wooden houses with artisan shops at street level and living quarters upstairs behind dormer windows, or the older Dutch homes with stepped roof lines in the brick gables that faced the street. Nor could he see the carpenters, stonecutters, and grocers who plied their trade on the west side. But he could hear the bootblacks and buttermilk vendors and tea-water men calling out their wares, and the girls hawking hot corn in a singsong. Roaming pigs proved a hazard, but Palmer learned to mark their grunt and snuffle and stand his ground. Everywhere, too, were the smells of city life: the aroma from bakehouses, smokehouses, and livery stables; and the stench of garbage and human waste that fermented in the street gutters until Fridays when disgusted slaves carted it off in tubs on their heads and dumped it into the river. As he walked, Palmer picked up snatches of conversations—English spoken with an Irish lilt or a Scottish burr, also plenty of German and Dutch, and the French patois from Saint Domingue. New York bustled with newcomers like Palmer himself. He had arrived during a decade in which the population doubled in size. Carpenters and bricklayers extended the city northward two full blocks every year. In this place full of people from elsewhere, Palmer was among those looking for a fresh start.[5]

Two blocks down Cortlandt, Palmer turned right on Broadway, home to the upscale businesses frequented by moneyed New Yorkers. He headed south past the City Hotel, which filled an entire block. Iron-shod hooves and carriage wheels clattered on Belgian-block pavers. A swish of silk and the click of well-made heels signaled a customer entering a drygoods store. Across the street, friends hailed one another in front of the City Tavern. A few blocks down, Palmer reached Trinity Church, only recently rebuilt after the war. He felt merely scorn for the Episcopal institution, as well as for the other two dozen churches and one synagogue that stood within a square mile. Twenty years had passed since Americans declared their independence, yet they remained attached to superstitions that Palmer thought unworthy of the new republic. He turned his back to Trinity Church and waited for someone to help him across busy Broadway. He continued east on Wall Street's brick sidewalk, glad for any even walking surface. He passed Federal Hall, where George Washington had been inaugurated as the nation's first president. Palmer could remember with pride how impressed Washington had been with Palmer's students during the commencement ceremonies of Richmond Academy in Augusta in 1791. It was only five years ago, but it may have seemed another lifetime to Palmer—before the birth of his first child, before the public scandal in Philadelphia, before the yellow fever took away his wife, his eyesight, and his family life. Palmer at thirty-two had lost much, but he envisioned a greater future happiness for all living things and believed he could help it along.

New York buzzed with trade, but Palmer had little connection to the moving and selling of goods. On Wall Street he could hear men alighting from horse-drawn carriages, prepared to conduct business with the merchants and lawyers inside their fashionable three-story brick homes. At the end of the street, company directors, merchants, and auctioneers gathered upstairs in the elegant Tontine Coffee House, which doubled as the mercantile exchange. The Chamber of Commerce met in Bradford's Coffee House, while artisans and mechanics held their trade society meetings in taverns. All around him people plied their trades, but Palmer had nothing to do with the activity around manufactures, raw goods, imports, exports, and the bottom line. His métier was intellectual; his line of work involved books and the people who read them. Ideas would change the world, he believed. Only a liberation of the mind could bring lasting change to the political system or alter the social hierarchy that had rich men at the top and slaves at the bottom. Palmer did not need actual eyesight to help others to a greater vision. He needed only courage and an audience, and he found both at 60 Wall Street. Having arrived, Palmer climbed the steep stoop and entered the bookstore, calling out his greetings to the proprietor, his new freethinking friend.[6]

John Fellows had begun selling books three years earlier with a Frenchman named Hocquet Caritat. They had opened a bookstore and circulating library from which customers could borrow books, usually one at a time, for a small fee. Essentially a book rental service, the circulating library of this era existed to make a profit, and owners catered to the tastes of a broad readership by stocking popular novels and by opening their doors to women as well as men. Caritat and Fellows also featured the works of Condorcet, Voltaire, Diderot, and other recently translated contemporary French philosophers. Fellows corresponded with Thomas Paine in London, and with Joel Barlow, a family friend then serving as an American diplomat in Algiers. In 1792, Barlow and Paine had been elected to the French National Convention in revolutionary Paris. When Paine landed in prison, Barlow helped the first part of Paine's *Age of Reason* get into print. Fellows published and sold Barlow's political writings, as well as an inexpensive

FIGURE 5. Street map of Manhattan (detail), 1803. Elihu Palmer learned how to navigate in Manhattan without eyesight. In particular, he became familiar with the route from Powell's boarding house on Cortlandt, west of Broadway, to John Fellows's bookstore on Wall Street. Courtesy of the American Antiquarian Society.

edition of the *Age of Reason*. "In short," Fellows later remembered, "my store became notorious for containing what the Federalists considered heretical works." When Caritat departed for France in 1795, leaving Fellows in charge of the bookstore, financial troubles caused Fellows to part with the library and enter into partnership with someone else. That firm broke up in 1796, and Fellows tried the bookstore and library once more, opening in August at his new Wall Street location.[7]

By September, Palmer felt ready to resume public speaking. He would once more build his reputation as a lecturer, as he had in Augusta and Philadelphia, but this time without the advantage of vision. He would have to memorize his speeches or improvise. He reserved Louis Gaultier's spacious assembly room at 68 William Street and placed an advertisement in the local newspapers. On September 24, a Sunday, the "Rev. Elihu Palmer" would deliver "a Theological Discourse" at half past ten in the morning. As in Philadelphia, Palmer scheduled his lecture for the same day and time that others went to church, making his presentation an alternative to worship service, not a supplement. He needed to assert his credibility as a speaker, and a "Reverend" Palmer giving a "Theological Discourse" helped with that. Over the next few weeks, however, his advertisements changed. On Saturday, October 1, three New York newspapers announced that the "Rev. ELIHU PALMER, will deliver a Moral Discourse at Eleven o'clock To-morrow." Palmer had dropped the adjective "theological," and a month later he left off the title of "Reverend." In November he referred to himself simply as Mr. Palmer. The changes from "Reverend" to "Mr." and "Theological" to "Moral" suggest that Palmer felt ready to shed religious descriptors that no longer fit.[8]

One reason for the changing terminology may have been Palmer's encounter with the works of Thomas Paine. Multiple American editions of Paine's *Age of Reason* had appeared in 1794, the year Palmer moved to Augusta and struggled to regain his equilibrium. Perhaps someone there had read the *Age of Reason* to Palmer. If not, Fellows could now fill him in, for he had published three cheap editions of the essay. The jaw-dropping novelty of Paine's work was that he did not pretend to reclaim or improve Christianity, as so many freethinkers, including liberal Christians like Palmer, had done. In Paine's view, there was nothing about Christianity worth saving. He attacked the Bible as a pack of lies intended to frighten believers into submission. Christianity, he said, was of a piece with all other revealed religions based on fabricated stories of supernatural events. "All national institutions of churches," Paine wrote, "whether Jewish, Christian or Turkish, appear to me no other than human inventions, set up to terrify and enslave mankind, and monopolize power and profit."[9]

The *Age of Reason* was a revelation for Palmer. It challenged his long-held notion that the best option was to try to change Christianity from within by keeping only the moral teachings and none of the supernatural ones. Paine was outspoken and unapologetic in battering Christianity from a position *outside* the faith. He did not try to make Christianity more rational by removing the miracles, or more lenient by positing a universal salvation of souls. He dispensed with Christianity altogether, calling it not only wrong but *harmful*. Jesus was not an admirable human being, as John Fellows and others imagined; Jesus was a fool. To turn one's other cheek to an assailant, Paine said, is a prescription for "assassinating the dignity of forbearance." It encourages the abuser and reduces the victim to the status of a kicked dog, "sinking man into a spaniel." Paine did not invent this critique of Christianity, but *Age of Reason* was the first book Palmer encountered that used hostile and mocking language about even the gentlest teachings of the Christian faith. Moreover, Paine put his name to his work.[10]

Like everyone else, Palmer noticed that Paine attacked the foundational doctrines of Christianity in colorful, memorable street-language. The doctrine of original sin, for example, taught a man to think of himself "as an out-law, as an out-cast, as a beggar, as a mumper, as one thrown, as it were, on a dunghill, at an immense distance from his Creator, and who must make his approaches by creeping and cringing to intermediate beings." The result, Paine said, was an egregious ingratitude toward the bounties of creation. Man "calls himself a worm, and the fertile earth a dunghill; and all the blessings of life by the thankless name of vanities." If the doctrine of original sin was bad, even worse was that of atonement, the reconciliation of sinners with God through the sacrifice of Jesus, a story Paine found "blasphemously obscene." The innocent cannot pay the moral debts of the guilty, Paine said. The very idea of God condoning the crucifixion was absurd. "It is then no longer justice. It is indiscriminate revenge."[11]

Such offensive speech about Christianity crossed a new line, challenging long-standing assumptions about what could be printed and publicly said in the United States. After all, blasphemy was not protected speech. The New York state constitution protected "the free exercise and enjoyment of religious profession and worship, without discrimination or preference," as long as it was not "construed as to excuse acts of licentiousness, or justify practices inconsistent with the peace or safety of this State." What was Paine's denunciation of Holy Writ if not an immoral breach of the peace? Blasphemy remained an actionable offense, and as late as 1811, one John Ruggles spent three months behind bars and paid a fine of five hundred dollars for his assertion that "Jesus Christ was a bastard, and his mother must be a whore." For Fellows to reprint Paine's work, and for Palmer to reiterate such words in public, challenged deeply rooted cultural norms and flirted with legal action.[12]

As exciting for Palmer as the public disparagement of Christianity was Paine's description of a superior religion. "The only true religion," Paine claimed, "is deism," by which he meant, very simply, "the belief of one God, and an imitation of his moral character, or the practice of what are called moral virtues." Belief in God and good conduct was the sum of his religion. Scriptures of any kind are unnecessary, Paine said, because everyone can see the work of the divine Creator in the natural world: "THE WORD OF GOD IS THE CREATION WE BEHOLD." As to worship, Paine believed we can best serve God by "contributing to the happiness of the living creation that God has made." In Paine's view, moral duty required no theology, because every person is born with an inner moral compass and can readily perceive the difference between right and wrong. Acts of persecution and revenge were obviously wrong, as was "cruelty to animals." The so-called golden rule of treating others as one wished to be treated was obvious on its face and accepted in many cultures of the world, Paine said. Jesus was not the first or only one to explain it. In fact, belief in Jesus was a form of idolatry, the worship of a human being that Paine called "manism." Christian reverence of Jesus seemed to him "a species of atheism" because it "professes to believe in a man rather than in God. It is a compound made up chiefly of manism but with little deism, and is as near to atheism as twilight is to darkness."[13]

Paine's deism demonstrated to Palmer a different place from which to speak about God and religion, one that refused to fit within the confines of Christianity or use the language of polite society. As Paine said, "my own mind is my own church." That such a revelation came from a hero of the American Revolution, the greatest propagandist in that struggle, probably carried additional weight with Palmer. The revolutionary wordsmith had openly abjured the religion Palmer had struggled with for the last five years or more. Palmer's version of Christianity—absent the miracles, the doctrines, the Trinity—had left him without a church home. Paine's *Age of Reason* beckoned with a rational, minimalist, yet devout deism that spoke only of a Creator-God who merited gratitude and awe and asked only that one do right by one's fellow creatures. That fall, Palmer considered Paine's way of thinking about religion. The idea of a life force within all matter, an idea Palmer had combined with a liberal version of Christianity, could just as readily meld with the deist notion of a Creator-God. None of Palmer's convictions rested on accordance with the Bible at all. Paine had staked out a confident position outside of Christianity, and Palmer considered him "one of the first and best of writers, and probably the most useful man that ever existed upon the face of the earth."[14]

Palmer developed a voracious appetite for freethinking approaches to religion and morality, and Fellows's bookstore could satisfy it. Reading aloud was a popular part of socializing, and circulating libraries offered congenial spaces for reading and conversation. In his first winter in New York City, Palmer listened closely as acquaintances read the recently published English translations of works by the French philosophers Constantin-François Volney and the Marquis de Condorcet, as well as the writing of the English philosopher William Godwin. These writers saw the unprecedented political upheaval occurring around them and envisioned an equally fundamental change in social relations. Taking account of the long history of the human species and mapping out the gradual development of language, society, and religion, these philosophers projected an ongoing intellectual and moral development with no foreseeable limit. The path to full-fledged enlightenment would not be direct or short, they acknowledged, given the entrenched powers that benefitted from widespread ignorance and the deep-seated prejudices against unfamiliar ideas. Yet optimism about eventual happiness on a global scale seemed warranted now that reason had sprung its religious restraints and could freely and scientifically investigate the human condition. Palmer thrilled to this message. Paine's *Age of Reason* had suggested he need not fit his ideas within a Christian frame. Now Condorcet, Godwin, and Volney opened his mind to the moral investigations that could take place once the mind-fog of revealed religion had cleared.[15]

Palmer was taken with the writings of William Godwin, who placed no limits on the capacities of human beings. Godwin's *Enquiry Concerning Political Justice* (1793) proclaimed it absurd to set limits prematurely on the extent of human improvement. Palmer had embraced the idea of humanity's expansive potential for moral development when he read the works of Reverend Richard Price in or just after college. Now Godwin furthered Palmer's understanding of what might be possible, offering a vision of progress that eventually encompassed all of humanity. Palmer had already been inclined to see improvement in global terms, as his Fourth of July speech in 1788 made clear. Godwin confirmed the idea as eminently reasonable and added the language of human perfectibility.[16]

Even more inspiring was the work of Condorcet, who advanced the idea of a science of social existence. Social organization, moral conduct, and all other human affairs could be understood with the methods of science applied to society—what Condorcet called social mathematics. He proposed that by identifying the first principles underlying human nature and social organization, one could develop a reality-based scientific theory of how society should function to improve living conditions and achieve widespread human happiness. Condorcet expressed great optimism about the human capacity to learn. Granted, the physical and mental limitations of the human mind meant that no one would ever grasp the universe. But within the frame of being human, Condorcet wrote, "no bounds have been fixed to the improvement of the human faculties." Progress toward "the perfectability of man," as such, is "absolutely indefinite," limited only by whatever time the species has on this planet. He fondly imagined a future in which a free people will know "no other master than their reason" and when tyrants, slaves, and priests will exist only in history books and plays. The habitual practice of "moral goodness," along with the attainment of liberty, equality, universal education, and "everything truly important to the happiness of mankind," will achieve a free and happy human community, "the absolute perfection of the human species." The talk of scientifically identifiable principles underlying all social existence influenced Palmer deeply and became part of his own vocabulary.[17]

Most of all, Palmer acquired a high regard for Constantin-François Volney, a French philosopher who wrote an enormously popular book that described the gradual development of many of the world's religions. Volney adopted the dispassionate tone of an anthropologist, viewing all religions as equally subject to critical inquiry. He had become a religious skeptic when, as a medical student in Paris in the 1770s, he attended the salon of the freethinker Paul Henry Thiry, Baron d'Holbach. D'Holbach envisioned an entirely mechanistic universe without any deity at all. Influenced by the salon's irreverent conversations about religion, Volney travelled to Egypt and Syria and began his comparative study of the world's religions. Published in English in 1796, Volney's *Ruins* opens by doubting that there had ever been a personal revelation from God. Religions have no metaphysical origins, Volney said, but originated in the human desire to understand the powerful forces of nature. Earliest human reflections about nature gradually developed into nine "systems" of belief, each with its own distinctive way of understanding the relationship between the natural world and divine power.[18]

The sixth system, which Volney titled "the animated world," posited a vital force within all matter, a notion Palmer had encountered in his conversations with Isaac Ledyard on Long Island. Volney favored the sixth system, according to which the universe is made up entirely of matter in constant motion. He identified two strands of thought within this sixth system. One "sect" of theological philosophers believed that the elements of matter moved in a mechanical way, determined in their course by the properties internal to them. This view represents that of d'Holbach, whose deterministic materialism left no room for an unpredictable life force. Everything in the world occurred exactly as it must, d'Holbach said, according to matter's inherent properties. The world was a machine containing machines, all the way down to its smallest components. Human beings were no exception, and the notion of free will was only a naïve illusion.[19]

A second line of thought that had developed within the sixth system explained matter in motion differently, and in ways akin to Isaac Ledyard's idea of vibrant matter. Matter's activity resulted not from mechanical laws at work, according to this view, but instead from a divine power inseparable from matter. According to this ontology, "the whole universe was God," Volney explained. "God was at once effect and cause, agent and patient, moving principle and thing moved." Volney sided with this second model of matter in motion, speculating about a vital force he called a "luminous fluid, principle of warmth and motion, pervading the universe." Whether conceived of in its mechanistic or vitalist version, the sixth system saw matter itself as always in motion of its own accord, a notion that Volney supported, as did Palmer.[20]

Palmer seriously considered d'Holbach's entirely mechanistic and atheistic worldview. Upon much reflection, Palmer said, he still felt pressed "to the admission of an immortal principle, to the faint conception of an eternal being, whose perfections guarantee the existence and harmony of the universe." Where d'Holbach imagined every organism operating according to deterministic laws, Palmer perceived a mysterious life force at work in all matter. He may well have had Isaac Ledyard's *Essay on Matter* in mind. As Ledyard had explained, the unseen vital power eluded accurate description, and Palmer agreed that the "essence of such a being is inconceivable." We can have only faint glimmerings of that which animates the universe. "At present," Palmer maintained, "it is sufficient that we refer the universe, its laws, and order, to the divinity of thought emanating from the most perfect of all beings." His tentative articulation of the "immortal principle" defies easy categorization. The reference to a "perfect being" capable of "thought" suggests a distinct and sentient deity, a transcendent God. Yet Palmer also insisted that nothing existed above or beyond the singular substance of the universe. Today we might think of panentheism (a close relative to pantheism) as the appropriate term for Palmer's theological conception: the notion that God encompasses and infuses all things and is also beyond all things. In his day, Palmer recognized that the terms available to him could not adequately describe the vital power that keeps matter eternally in motion. The result, for him, was a wondrous thing, a mystery within the whole, a divine power that was both scientific fact and beyond all naming.[21]

Palmer found support for his cosmology in Volney's *Ruins*. Volney had arrived in the United States in 1795 and become a cause célèbre among the freethinking set. Based in Philadelphia, he traveled widely during his three years in the country. With Jefferson at Monticello, he worked on an English translation of his book. When Volney visited New York, he lived in the same boardinghouse as John Fellows, making a meeting with Palmer all but certain. Palmer learned best in conversation, and he would have relished talks with the cosmopolitan *philosophe*. Palmer concluded that "of all the books that ever were published, Volney's *Ruins* is pre-eminently entitled to the appellation of *Holy Writ, and ought to be appointed to be read in Churches.*"[22]

In New York City, Palmer did what he had done elsewhere: he established a forum for discussion and cultivated a community of freethinkers. A "small society was formed to aid his exertions," Fellows said, and Palmer insisted that it be called the Deistical Society of New York rather than the proposed alternative, the Theophilosophical Society. Palmer preferred the term "deistical" because it made plain that the group promoted something other than Christianity. The society would advance both "moral science and the religion of nature," Palmer explained. Its members proclaimed "the existence of one supreme Deity" and agreed that moral truths could be found in the universe rather than in any book of revelation. The group had in view "the destruction of superstition and fanaticism" and intended to nurture "a genuine natural morality—the practice of a pure and uncorrupted virtue—the cultivation of science and philosophy—the resurrection of reason, and the renovation of the intelligent world."[23]

The founding document of the Deistical Society presented an agenda of intellectual liberation. Its members pursued philosophy, not political engagement. While "political despotism of the earth is disappearing," Palmer wrote, freedom of the mind needed attention as well. "The slavery of the mind has been the most destructive of all slavery," in his view, and the cause was religion: "a dark and gloomy superstition." Palmer knew by now that "a few individuals" like himself could not suddenly establish "moral and mental felicity" for all humanity. But they could lay the foundation for the work of future generations. A central article of Palmer's faith asserted the moral and intellectual ability of people to improve their own nature, expand the circle of their concern, and achieve eventual, worldwide happiness. In contrast to Fitch's short-lived Deist Society in Philadelphia with its commitment to inoffensive freethinking exchange, Palmer intended a more purposefully pedagogical project. He had made up his mind about Christianity, including its most liberal versions, and he decided to attack the religion in its entirety, just as Paine had done.[24]

What better way to announce his newfound hostility toward Christianity than on Christmas Day? On December 25, 1796, in Gaultier's assembly hall,

Palmer listened as the audience took their seats. When it was time for him to speak, Palmer sounded much like Paine in both substance and style. It appears he had virtually memorized the *Age of Reason* and adopted Paine's sarcastic manner. "This, my friends, we are told is Christmas-day," Palmer began, and "an ignorant and astonished world are called upon to yield an unqualified credence to the mysterious dogmas of this mysterious religion." It was time to end the "mental stupidity" and "general torpor" created by an unthinking adherence to religious nonsense. Palmer's extended takedown of Christianity began, logically enough, with Jesus's improbable conception. The story that Jesus was "begotten by a ghost," Palmer said, collided with the claim that he was "the eternal Son of the Father, that is, of the Creator and Preserver of the universe." How could both things be true? How could an eternal being have a moment of conception? And did he have two fathers, both supernatural ones at that? No, Palmer told his listeners, the "simple truth is, that their pretended Saviour is nothing more than an illegitimate Jew." Any hopes of salvation through Jesus Christ rested therefore on "no better foundation than that of fornication or adultery." With such fighting words, adapted from Paine's *Age of Reason*, Palmer set the tone for the rest of his oration. If anyone wondered what Palmer would be willing to say on Christmas Day, they knew it now. He would hold back none of his derision.[25]

The life and death of Jesus had done no good in the world, Palmer said, "unless the horrid cruelties, the murderous wars and devastations, which had disgraced the annals of the Christian world, can be considered as blessings to mankind." The man who came to cleanse the world of sin had obviously failed, as abiding immorality and wretchedness made clear. A divine mission should have had a better outcome. Jesus had expressed on the cross his sense of abandonment and a plan gone awry. God had withheld "attention and support in this trying hour," Palmer said, and neither divine Father nor chosen Son exhibited the "spirit of fortitude and constancy" the moment required. Palmer found the whole story so improbable that it must have been fabricated. Just as fictitious were the torments of hell. The notion of eternal damnation slandered "the God of Nature as cruel and vindictive." This could never be true, and "hell is a bugbear of superstition."[26]

Palmer took on the foundational doctrines one at a time. In the manner of Paine, he subjected the Bible to a literalist reading, rejecting any metaphorical meaning and dwelling on the impossibility of biblical claims. The concept of original sin, for example, was inherently unfair, as it held all human beings responsible for a mistake made by Adam long ago. That Adam's violation should prove "eternally fatal to the human race" was atrociously unjust, Palmer said, because how could the transgression of one person be transferable to others who had nothing to do with it? Palmer used the mocking tone typical of Paine to make fun of the forbidden fruit—whether it was "an apple, a peach, or an orange, is not material"—and said the "story is almost too foolish to deserve a serious examination." The most egregious aspect of the doctrine of original sin, in Palmer's opinion, was the idea that Adam's transgression had introduced mortality. Blaming Adam for death is ludicrous, Palmer said, for mortality resides in the very nature of all living things. The "disorganization or physical death" of all animal life is unavoidable; the material composition of living things ensures their "subsequent derangement" and eventual "dissolution." Decay is inevitable, a natural fact, making death "as natural as life in the order of the world." The story that Adam's sin caused the death of previously immortal beings is pure fiction.[27]

The doctrine of atonement had just as many problems. The idea of a reconciliation between sinful humanity and God through the suffering and death of Jesus relied on a moral transference of sorts. This Palmer rejected entirely. One person cannot pay the moral debt of another, he said, echoing Paine. Furthermore, the sacrifice of an innocent being is abhorrent, making the torture of Jesus "a spectacle truly distressing." Worse, the sacrifice had not been effective. Even proponents of the doctrine agreed that atonement was only partial, reaching one tenth of the human race and dooming the rest to eternal torment. "Priests and fanatics of the world!" Palmer called out, was this their version of a perfect God? "Are murder, carnage, and injustice, the objects in which you delight?" Is it "only among miracles, ghosts, and crucified Gods that you delight to walk?"[28]

Palmer promoted instead a worshipful gratitude for the bounties of the natural world. "Oh! Prejudiced and superstitious man, look at the splendid beauties of nature, look at the vast machinery of the universe, and through these thou mayest discover the intelligent organizer of the whole, perfect in all his attributes, and worthy of thy adoration." Palmer combined the deism of Paine with the perfectibility of Godwin. An intelligent Creator-God, the "parent and friend of the whole human race," intended universal happiness.

Humanity would find that "the primary principles" underlying human nature "are sufficient for our improvement and ultimate perfectability." By perfectibility Palmer meant "the dignity and final improvement of the human species" and "the permanent happiness of sensitive creatures." The only thing required of humans, and it was demanding enough, was the practice of moral virtue.[29]

As a guide to virtue, Jesus did not help much. The moral teachings of the Christian religion Palmer found "inaccurate and incomplete, trifling, and often without utility." More often than not, Christian morality asks people to demean themselves and reward bullies. Turning the other cheek means "sacrificing the dignity of our character, and inviting fresh injuries." To offer love in response to persecution was unnatural, and who really does this? Echoing Paine, he asked: "Are you willing to surrender your natural dignity, to sink your nature to a level with the spaniel, in order to become a true christian?" Clearly, Christianity "does not draw its morality from the right source."[30]

Worse, Christianity had historically declared war on science, Palmer opined, and the two could not peacefully coexist. Either the world must "retrograde to a state of darkness," Palmer declared, or "the Christian religion must become wholly extinct." He had made his choice. For humankind to "progressively advance towards a state of perfectability, this system of religion, so injurious to its researches and so incompatible with the dignity and happiness of his nature, must be forever annihilated and destroyed." When that had occurred, humanity could "come home to nature, admire her splendid beauties" and her permanent laws, cultivate real virtue and "adhere to the practice of a pure and genuine morality." The end of religion would mean the beginning of human contentment. By late 1796, Palmer disavowed the Universalist and anti-Trinitarian versions of Christianity that he had previously advocated.[31]

Palmer had found a new way to speak about religion. No longer were individual clergymen, or even despotic ecclesiastical institutions, the problem. Now, he said that the most cherished Christian beliefs themselves were toxic. The faith's doctrines, not just its minions, corrupted morals and destroyed human happiness. In 1793, Palmer had criticized a church aligned with political tyrants, but he had pulled his punches, noting that some clergy were upright men of honor and good sense. He had not attacked

Christian tenets directly, nor had he targeted the person or the teachings of Jesus. Three years later, Palmer made no such concessions to the clergy, and he took on Christian doctrines full bore. He cast aside the language of liberal Christianity, the Universalism and Socinianism he had formerly promoted as a way of rationalizing the faith. Now he adopted deism as his mantle. With all the enthusiasm of a new convert, Palmer made Paine's polemical tone his own, attacking Christianity and calling for its demolition.

A God of Nature and his creatures—this was the classic language of deism. Palmer spoke of an "intelligent organizer of the whole, perfect in all his attributes, and worthy of thy adoration." At the same time, he gestured repeatedly toward nature as the source of morality, possibly harkening back to his conversations with Isaac Ledyard and more certainly to his recent discovery of Volney. Palmer asked Christians rhetorically: "Will you never learn wisdom from the book of nature, will you never derive instruction from the permanency of her laws?" All genuine morality can be found in "the nature and condition of rational beings." He touted the "correct, the elegant, the useful maxims of Confucius, Antoninus, Seneca, Price, and Volney," adding that the philosophers of the present day will greatly aid "the progressive improvement and real welfare of the human species." Someday, the names of "Paine, Volney, Barlow, Condorcet, and Godwin" will be revered as "among the greatest benefactors of the human race." Once religious superstition had faded away, humankind would "develop from the system of nature, the fundamental principles of his real felicity." Then reason, science, and "true philosophy" shall "render happy the great family of mankind." Palmer adopted the language of deism and kept his focus on the lessons from nature—not just the orderly workings of the natural world but also its very constitution, its eternal makeup.[32]

Casting his lot with Paine carried social costs for Palmer. Going public with his overtly anti-Christian opinions virtually ensured that he would not be invited into one of the most intellectually challenging groups of freethinkers in the city. The Friendly Club entertained freethought of all kinds, but it did so behind closed doors and banned gratuitous insults. At the center of the club was Elihu Hubbard Smith, a physician in his mid-twenties who read voraciously, wrote poetry and fiction, and edited the nation's first medical journal, the *Medical Repository*. Like Palmer, Smith admired the work of Godwin and believed in eventual human perfectibility. Palmer and Smith would have had much to discuss, but Smith and his cohort rejected as uncouth the abrasive style of Paine and Palmer. Granted, Smith had enjoyed reading aloud Paine's *Age of Reason* with two friends in April 1796. They had amused themselves "with this lively & humorous publication," which caused them "many hearty laughing-spells." But then Paine wrote a public letter that accused President Washington of failing to act when Paine was imprisoned in Paris. That letter was "full of impudence, egotism, misrepresentation, & falsehood," Smith felt. By the spring of 1797, Smith said he was "disgusted with the temper" in which the *Age of Reason* was written. Ridicule was mean-spirited and unjust, Smith thought, a "distortion of the thing ridiculed" for the sake of cheap lampooning. When Smith rejected polemic, he necessarily also decided against Palmer.[33]

The two men must have met. Smith regularly stopped by Fellows's establishment, visiting at least once or twice a month in the winter of 1796–97. Fellows even offered to make Smith a business partner, although nothing came of the idea. Yet Smith's diary, with its detailed account of the books he read and conversations he enjoyed, makes no mention of Palmer, who was also a fixture at Fellows's bookstore and library. Palmer had crossed an invisible line, placing himself beyond the polite society of the Friendly Club.[34]

If exclusion from the Friendly Club came with a sting, Palmer still felt himself to be in good company. In New York City he found freethinking friends, supporters, and an audience. Fellows's bookstore and library offered a cornucopia of freethinking philosophy and a space in which people could read aloud and discuss the writings of Volney, Condorcet, Godwin, and Paine. For the first time, Palmer could feel that he had a posse of freethinkers behind him—those in New York and also those, he may have felt, living and writing in Europe. The Friendly Club wouldn't have him? No matter, Palmer might have thought. They were too accommodating to Christianity anyway. Palmer created his own circle to promote deist religion and the freedom of even blasphemous speech. A new era was dawning for freethinkers, Palmer believed, and Christmas Day seemed as good a time as any to celebrate it.

CHAPTER 8

Sensitive Atoms

THEY WALKED TO the bookstore arm in arm, Elihu Palmer and a tall man wearing a threadbare Armenian coat. The man was of striking appearance, with prominent cheekbones, angled jaw, deep-set dark eyes, and unruly dark curls. John Stewart enjoyed being conspicuous, and his devil-may-care attitude appealed to Palmer. Older than Palmer by seventeen years—Stewart was pushing fifty—the Englishman had long ago asserted his independence from all convention. He had traveled through many parts of the world, gaining the nickname Walking Stewart, and he still sported the clothes he had acquired on his journeys, a "Hindoo costume," for example, and his Armenian coat. He liked to broadcast that he was fluent in eight languages, and he lectured incessantly. Reprints of his portrait could be purchased in bookstores in New York City. In some circles, Walking Stewart became a minor celebrity, and he stepped into the role with gusto. When he and Palmer entered John Fellows's bookstore on a February day in 1797, Stewart opened the conversation with a joke that set the men laughing. He would rather pray to his lecture audiences than to any God, he said.[1]

The eccentric Englishman would have a lasting impact on Palmer, adding an unexpected dimension to one of Palmer's favorite subjects: matter in eternal motion. Ever since his conversations with Isaac Ledyard on Long Island, Palmer had thought about the endless rotation of matter. Initially, Palmer combined the idea of eternal matter with a liberal version of Christianity and then, after encountering Thomas Paine's *Age of Reason*, with deism. Stewart, who disavowed all religions, added a distinctive conceptual twist to the idea of eternal matter, namely that the smallest particles—he called them atoms—registered sensations. Atoms were *sensate*, Stewart said, and their sensations never disappeared but instead accumulated in the singular substance that makes up the universe. The notion of sensitive atoms was new to Palmer, yet persuasive. With characteristic enthusiasm, he melded the concept with his existing ideas about an eternal substance. Palmer would continue to speak favorably of deism with its skepticism toward supernatural religion, and he may have considered himself a deist, a capacious category of thought without a particular creed. But what became central to Palmer's thinking, even without a proper label for it, was the idea of sensitive atoms. This insight was the key to a better future, he decided, for when the concept of sensate matter was widely understood, it would awaken a compassion so deep that people would naturally change their behavior and thereby transform the world.

Stewart did not publish his lectures, but the message that captured Palmer's imagination appeared in Stewart's 1795 poem, *The Revelation of Nature*. The poem opens with "nature's voice" describing the universe as matter in motion:

> Hear nature's voice, the universe I am,
> One whole of matter indistructible
> All modes of being my constituent parts;
> Connected links on matters circled chain.
> Exchanging modes, by death renewing life.[2]

The idea that the universe consisted of eternal, or "indistructible," matter in endless motion did not surprise Palmer, who had discussed this very concept with Isaac Ledyard and had since then read about it in his favorite book, Volney's *Ruins*. More surprising, however, was Stewart's description of *how* matter moved. All organisms continuously and involuntarily emit particles into their surroundings, Stewart said, and those particles merge instantly with other forms they encounter. Stewart remained vague about the process of "emission" and "absorption," but he described how a writer who takes a stroll unwittingly exudes atoms that become part of the air, the grass, the sheep grazing nearby. The transference is swift and ongoing. Soon one's particle might be part of another planet:

> The human atom that this moment writes,
> The next perhaps is bleating on the plain,

Figure 6. The frontispiece of William Thomas Brande's *The Life and Adventures of the Celebrated Walking Stewart: Including His Travels in the East Indies, Turkey, Germany, & America. By a Relative.* (London, 1822). John "Walking" Stewart believed he had glimpsed the workings of the natural world, but that most of humanity was not yet ready for the truth. Elihu Palmer was one of the few people Stewart convinced. Courtesy of the University of Minnesota Library.

Thence enters herb, or earth, or air,
Or moves thro' planets in the solar sphere.[3]

The most provocative idea that Stewart introduced, the one that pushed Palmer's thinking beyond the ideas of Ledyard and Volney, was the notion that individual atoms register sensation, including pain. When an atom jumps from one creature to the next, the atom carries those sensations to the organism it just joined. To explain what this means, Stewart asked his reader to imagine a person beating another creature. When atoms from the perpetrator jump to the victim, the perpetrator inflicts violence upon part of himself. Stewart put it this way:

> Think not O man! my dear coequal part,
> That change awaits a slow dissolving death;
> O no! that arm that dares uplift the goad
> On brute or man, some wretched atom flies
> (In flux emissive and absorptive changed)
> Ere falls the stroke, incorporate with brute.[4]

The oppressor instantly becomes the victim of his own actions:

> See matter transmute in the present life,
> The tyrant atom that prepares the rod,
> Next moment slave to feel the stroke it will'd,
> Whirl'd in emission and absorption's tides,
> The matter forcing turn to matter forc'd;
> Now jockey riding and now steed bestrode,
> Now Lord imposing and now Hind impos'd.[5]

Stewart's theory had far-reaching implications, in his view. Although individuals do not consciously experience the pain of another being or its atoms, and although individual consciousness does not survive the disintegration of the human form, yet the bare fact of sensitive matter remains, Stewart said, even without human memory of a sensation. Human consciousness is secondary, even irrelevant, to the sensations that are stored in matter, and the "annihilation of the human mode does not at all affect the interest of matter or nature." The recognition of this circumstance, he thought, was enough to change behavior. He used the example of a man plagued by gout. When the man eats, Stewart explained, the exchange of atoms in his stomach transfers his physical pain to the food he imbibes. Creatures must eat to survive, of course, but every *unnecessary* mouthful the sick man swallows "is gratuitous anguish, transferred to brute matter, his fellow being." To torture even a leaf of lettuce increases the pain in all of nature. Those who understand this, Stewart said, have a feeling of cosmic kinship, a sensibility apparent in the "homo-ousiast," or "man of nature," who "fears to communicate pain to the crust he eats." Thomas Paine once witnessed Stewart in London addressing the oysters on his plate. "I will change your predicament for the better," he told the mollusks. "I will make you a part of John Stewart." A person who feels for every "sensitive fellow being," Stewart said, "would lift the worm from the path, lest some heedless fool might crush it, and save the drowning fly from his tea cup." Certainly such a man can never be "the tyrant of his [own] species." All-embracing compassion and the careful avoidance of violence in everyday life made the enlightened man into "the universal self, or man-god."[6]

For Stewart, the very idea of shared and sensate matter was so compelling, so persuasive on its face, that he felt it required no empirical substantiation. The lack of corroboration from natural philosophers did not concern him in the least. In general, Stewart trusted his own thinking more than anything to be learned from books. He did read Locke, Bolingbroke, Rousseau, Mirabeau, and Pope, if only to point out their limitations. A self-proclaimed autodidact, Stewart disdained the scholarship "spun out in musty volumes of recorded error." He and Palmer could agree that what passed for learning in schools, the memorization of a "rubbish of detail," only "oppresses the judgment, and renders learned ignorance incurable." Stewart especially disdained analytical philosophy and all manner of logical propositions that led down rabbit holes of error. Precious few intellectual forerunners received his praise. Spinoza was one, the first human who "got a glimpse of the totality," Stewart said. The seventeenth-century Dutch philosopher held that everything that exists in the universe is made of one substance and that God and nature are two names for the same reality. Stewart appreciated this view, along with that of Helvétius, the materialist French philosopher who "pushed on Spinoza's doctrines." But Stewart felt himself a peer to these men, not an admiring follower, claiming that "long before their voices reached me, I had acquired a comprehensive view of the tree of existence." Needless to say, Stewart enjoyed a robust self-confidence.[7]

Where did Stewart, the London-born son of a Scottish cloth merchant, hear about sensate matter that makes up everything in the universe?

Certainly not in the two English boarding schools that expelled him. In search of adventure, the teenaged Stewart moved to Madras in 1763 to work as a clerk for the British East India Company. Shocked by the corruption he witnessed and bored with his employment, Stewart informed the company administrators that he was "born for nobler pursuits, and higher attainments, than to be a copier of invoices and bills of lading to a company of grocers, haberdashers, and cheesemongers." He gave up his job, set out to explore his surroundings, and wandered into territory governed by the anti-British ruler of Mysore, Hyder Ali. Essentially a captive, Stewart managed to become first an interpreter and then a military commander under Ali. Stewart took part in battles that left him wounded in one arm and with a visible dent in his skull. When he requested permission to seek out a European surgeon, Ali granted the request but, suspecting Stewart of treason, ordered his escorts to murder him at the border. Only a swift swim across a river saved Stewart from being killed.[8]

Clever and charismatic, Stewart became an aid and personal secretary to Muhammed Ali Khan Wallajah, the pro-British Nawab of Arcot. Proving himself capable, Stewart rose to the rank of prime minister. By the late 1770s, Stewart had saved £3000 and felt it was time to move on. He began the tour on foot that gave him the nickname Walking Stewart. He traversed India, the African continent, and many countries on the Adriatic and Mediterranean Seas before arriving in London in about 1783. Still restless, he set out again the following year to walk through much of Europe and central Asia before returning to London by 1790.[9]

On his travels, Stewart learned about a form of meditation that he described as "the paramount faculty of mind" and "a new source of mental powers." Distinct from common "reflection," which must focus on one thing at a time, this special kind of "contemplation comprehends all science" at once, and all subjects are "combined by wisdom into one system, human happiness or universal good." During the contemplative practice, the mind "dwells upon its object, till every possible relation is discovered, not in a particular and separate series, but in its universality of relation or unity, with all existence." In a meditative state, Stewart had a holistic experience, a sense of the unified whole. His friends remarked on "the profundity of his sitting habits." Stewart "sat in trance-like reverie," they noted, "pursuing his philosophic speculations."[10]

Stewart's contemplative practice could have had a variety of sources. In India he may have heard about a state of consciousness in which the sense of being a finite individual, a distinct and bounded self, dissolved into a feeling of oneness with the whole of reality. Perhaps Stewart learned about the Hindu concept of *Brahman*, the unity underlying the visible diversity of things. Then again, Stewart "spoke with horror of the religion of the Gentoo [Hindu] nation." He singled out ritual self-immolation, especially "women burning themselves on the same funeral pile with their husbands," and denounced the practice as delusional and on par with fanatic Christians who burned heretics at the stake. "The religion of the Gentoos" consisted only in rituals and "ceremonies," Stewart claimed, and had nothing to do with morality. Maybe Jainism appealed to him instead, with its claim that even the smallest animals experience pain and are worthy of utmost regard. The mandate to avoid harm to living beings pointed to vegetarianism, to which Stewart subscribed. He expressed his open admiration for the "Siamese" (in what is now Thailand) who believe, he said, that "the universe is one great body tending to promote its own good by the instrumentality of its parts, which are all eternal atoms co-equal, co-essential, co-interested." That Stewart used the same language of coequal atoms with which he described his own cosmology suggests his approval of the "Siamese," who develop "their different energies," presumably mental energies, "for the important purpose of augmenting good, and diminishing evil, through the whole mass of existence."[11]

Whatever the sources of his inspiration, Stewart did not understand himself as an adherent to any religion. He did not use the language of "God" except to describe the homo-ousiast as the man-God of nature. He referred to deism disparagingly. No sentient deity figured in Stewart's cosmology of eternally existent matter, no Creator-God observed human conduct, and certainly no divine judge sent souls to heaven or cast them into a fiery pit. Immaterial souls did not exist, and neither did heaven or hell. All religion was human invention, in his view, and he dispensed with any religious lens on the natural world. The unity of the universe was simply a natural fact. Even if he had learned meditation from religious practitioners, Stewart believed the powers of contemplation revealed an underlying physical reality that, once seen, could not be unseen. In fact, just one glimpse of the unity of the universe might nudge people away from their religious "imbecility" and replace all "bigotry" with gentle behavior toward all things. In his opinion, the natural effect of such contemplation made his message the "most important discovery and instruction, that ever was offered to human nature."[12]

If religion got in the way of insightful contemplation of nature, so too did science, in Stewart's view. In rejecting metaphysical explanations for natural phenomena, empiricists made the grave mistake of renouncing "all the energies of speculation," even those that, through analogy, go beyond individual experience to find cosmic truths that elude "the narrow circle of experimentalism." Stewart lamented the scientist of his day who, in the name of reason, "forbids the mind to receive any influence from the speculations of analogy, however intelligent or forcible, if carried beyond the measure of experience." The current "doctrine of experimentalism pervading the whole continent of Europe" cannot last, Stewart said. It is only the "fashion of a season among thoughtless wits and scientific idiots," because "it stands in direct opposition to the laws of intellectual power."[13]

Few conversation partners shared Stewart's critique of both religion and science, and when he visited the United States for the first time in 1791, he met with disapproval. Doctor Benjamin Rush in Philadelphia noted that Stewart "appears to be a man of strong powers, of great eloquence, much observation; but to have started without fixed principles on any subject." On the second day of Stewart's visit, over breakfast and again at teatime, Stewart regaled the physician with stories from his travels, and Rush recorded some of the details. Stewart had been called eccentric, he told Rush, but "while the centre of ordinary conduct was Error, he wished to be in a state of eccentricity from it for ever." On the third day, Rush wrote, Stewart visited in the morning "and for 15 minutes talked unintelligibly. I discovered that he was a materialist and an Atheist. He said 'he was in search of the origin of moral motion.'" Rush found the gregarious Stewart intriguing, perplexing, and misguided. Most Americans shook their heads at Stewart's ideas. Only those "acquainted with the writings of the celebrated European free-thinkers" could engage him at all, Stewart learned, and most responded "with apathy, and even dislike," especially in the country's interior, where he encountered "utter ignorance." Disappointed, Stewart returned to England.[14]

Back in London by early 1792, Stewart fell in with a group of freethinkers and social reformers, notably Thomas Paine, Joel Barlow, the American diplomat, and the English philosopher William Godwin. With the last, Stewart enjoyed regular conversations, sometimes several times a month, even after Godwin told Stewart about the "errors" in his thinking. Stewart's circle of freethinkers also included Mary Wollstonecraft, who that year published her feminist *The Vindication of the Rights of Woman*; the bookseller Thomas Clio Rickman; and John Oswald, a radical democrat, atheist, vegetarian, and animal rights advocate from Scotland. Stewart moved among intellectuals deeply interested in the exciting political developments underway in Britain and France.[15]

Oswald and Stewart had much to talk about, since Oswald had also traveled to India. He arrived in Bombay in 1782 as the officer of a Scottish infantry regiment sent to fight Hyder Ali, the same Mysore ruler for whom Stewart had fought in the 1770s. Oswald soon became disgusted with British colonialism, deserted the army, and lived with Brahmins, adopting some of their practices, including vegetarianism. A professed atheist and critic of Christianity, Oswald loved the Hindu concept of universal sympathy for all living creatures. He saw vegetarianism as part of radical democratic politics, a form of solidarity with other species as well as with people who could not afford to eat meat. Meat producers evicted poor tenant farmers to graze more animals instead, and inordinate amounts of grass and grain went into making meat for well-to-do carnivores. Oswald said that to eat meat was to participate in a system of economic oppression and social injustice. The same year his friend Thomas Paine published *Rights of Man*, Oswald made his views known in *The cry of Nature, or, an Appeal to mercy and to justice on behalf of the persecuted animals* (1791). He deplored the callous cruelty with which humans slaughtered, cut, chewed, and swallowed their fellow creatures, perversely overriding the natural law of universal sympathy.[16]

Stewart shared Oswald's vegetarianism, but the two men differed in their politics. Oswald moved to revolutionary France, joined the Jacobin Cercle Social, and was nominated along with Paine for honorary French citizenship. In his fervor to create an egalitarian society, Oswald called for the deaths of those who opposed this revolutionary vision. Killing was certainly evil, Oswald knew, but to assure peace the oppressors must be removed—by killing them. Paine supposedly put it this way to Oswald: "You have lived so long without tasting flesh, that you now have a most voracious appetite for blood." Oswald did indeed have a strange way of endorsing the deaths of people while eating his tenderly prepared roots and herbs. He secretly helped plan a French invasion of England, and in 1793 he organized and led the First Battalion of Volunteer Pikemen, who set out to quell royalist sympathizers in the Vendée region. The use of pikes in hand-to-hand combat meant killing in its most immediate and raw form, and Oswald died in battle for the revolutionary cause.[17]

John Stewart responded differently to revolution. Possibly at the urging of Paine, he decided to visit revolutionary Paris in 1792. At first, Stewart enjoyed the company of French philosophers and the resident English poet William Wordsworth, who was, in turn, impressed with Stewart's eloquence. Stewart supported the political changes afoot, but his enthusiasm gave way to alarm when he witnessed the surge in street violence and "the most dreadful symptoms of mob government." Revolutionaries confiscated his money, and Stewart left precipitously, deeply skeptical about the prospects for political revolution. By the time Oswald had died in battle and Paine sat in a Paris jail, Stewart was safely back in London. He would ever after advise against too much democracy and warn against sudden social reform, even about matters he considered egregiously immoral, such as British imperialism and African slavery. The "speculative philosopher," wrote Stewart, "is no revolutionist in action, but a reformer of sentiment in theory." He advocated only "peaceful, gradual, and safe change" that could occur "without violating laws, habits, or opinions, or demanding those sudden and painful sacrifices, which endanger the progress of perfectability, and threaten the return of barbarism."[18]

The key to peaceful transformation, Stewart said, was the fundamental shift in perspective that resulted from the habitual contemplation of the physical reality of the universe, the shared sensate matter that comprises the whole. The "reform of the mind will prepare the change of government, custom, and opinion," Stewart said, "without the anarchy of revolution." Stewart marveled that his friend Paine still "idolizes the discretion of the multitude, in that very country, where experience has fully evinced their folly, cruelty, and incapacity of popular government." In Stewart's opinion, only contemplative men of strong moral sense should lead reform efforts by coaxing others to understand the truth of nature. When human beings grasp that every act of charity or cruelty is, in a sense, paid forward to future versions of themselves, then bare self-interest will inevitably produce pacifism, vegetarianism, and universal sympathy with all living things. The insight of homo-ousia—that all of nature is made up of one, shared substance—evokes benevolence for all things, Stewart said. In response to the hope and danger of this revolutionary age, he promised fundamental change without the terrifying anarchy he had witnessed in France. Intellectually unorthodox and socially and politically conservative, Stewart claimed his ideas would remake the world without any violence at all.[19]

In 1795, Stewart turned his sights once more to North America. Perhaps this time Americans would give his gently radical homo-ousia a better hearing. He harbored great hopes for the United States as the seedbed for gradual and peaceful transformation. The physical size of the nation, Stewart thought, and its commitment to "absolute liberty of the press," made room for disagreements of any kind. He appreciated the many utopian communities under way. "Quakers, moravians, dunkers, etc. etc. have all established new institutions of domestic life," he noted, and some groups even held property in common. These religious communities could never fully succeed, Stewart thought, because they were based on religious "superstition." But at least such experiments could thrive without suppression or persecution. He harbored doubts about a democratic republic in which every male citizen had a political voice, and he openly preferred leadership by an elite. But at least political disagreements and social experiments could occur in America "without annihilating the domestic peace."[20]

American tolerance for social experimentation appealed to a man who flouted many norms. Stewart rejected as "human imbecility" the mind-numbing conformity of high society, the "irksome feasts of etiquette and expensive luxury," along with the "yawning tedium of fashionable life." Stewart wore his frayed coats in defiance of the "tyrant fashion" that deforms "personal beauty with ungraceful and costly ornaments of dress." He wished women would "desist from the ignorant and contemptible practice of rendering the body delicate, pale, languid, and genteel." Any man attracted to "a sickly countenance and constitution, must have a diseased mind," he said. If high society was bad, its educational institutions were worse. Parents placed their children in "prisons, called schools, where mephitic air and confinement debilitates the nervous system." No real learning occurred behind those walls. Rather, the "unintelligible sounds" of foreign languages were "stuffed into memory," preparing pupils to be hospital patients rather than "useful and happy citizens of social and perfectable life." Authentic, experiential learning was the birthright of every child, yet hens and geese did a better job of raising their chicks, Stewart opined.[21]

In New York City, Stewart and Palmer became close friends, as did John Fellows, who roomed with Stewart one winter and witnessed some of his unusual habits. Stewart liked to keep the window wide open, and he paced the room at night, "bathing in air," as he put it. He rose early to take long walks before breakfast, meditated for long periods, survived on bread, apples, and cheese, and talked constantly about sensitive matter. He shunned alcohol and avoided meat, convinced that a carnivorous diet "destroys the teeth" and causes indigestion, foggy judgment, a "ferocious" will, frayed nerves, and "premature old age." Stewart's understanding of sensate matter stoked his vegetarianism. Vegetables, "feeling no violence" when chewed and swallowed—in contrast to animal meat, which registers the brutality of mastication—better prepare the human body for its future forms. A person who has imbibed contented vegetables rather than miserable animals "sleeps into the euthanasia of a new modification," meaning the next shape the body's particles assume, "with the consolatory reflection" of having done as little harm as possible to other sensate beings. When Stewart did eat meat, he chose mutton, considering it "the most innocent animal used for food."[22]

Stewart's concerns about health extended to sexual intercourse. He found sex outside of marriage, as well as prostitution, morally uncomplicated. To avoid venereal disease, Stewart recommended "venereal preventative lotions" made of "alkalis, cautiously mixed," along with "strong soap and hot water" applied to the genitals immediately after intercourse. The unmarried Stewart said he knew from his own experience of the treatment's success. He also favored birth control. Assertive women could "prevail on their husbands, in the act of coition, to eject the semen from the womb," and he hoped unmarried youth would do the same. He was no libertine, however, and he told Benjamin Rush, perhaps with some pride, that his passions were "equable and his appetite for women so weak that he has lived 14 months without a connection with the sex."[23]

To speak and publish about such matters was unconventional, to say the least, and Fellows wondered if Stewart's head injury in India had caused

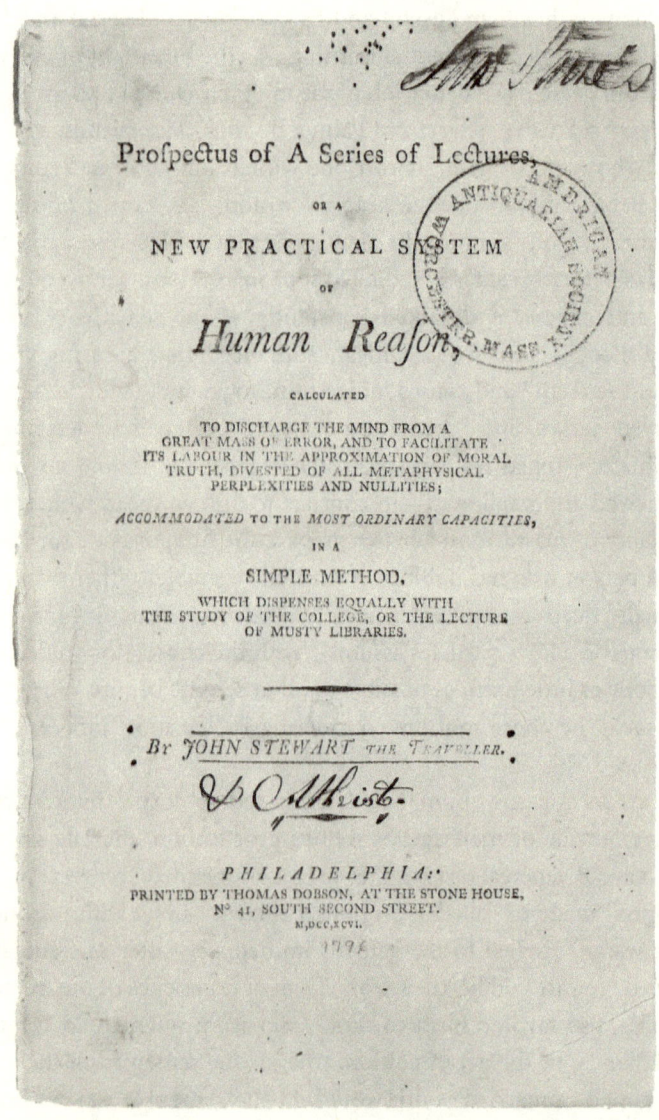

FIGURE 7. The title page of *Prospectus of a Series of Lectures, or a New Practical System of Human Reason*, by John Stewart (Philadelphia, 1796). John Stewart offered lectures that he considered the most valuable lesson ever offered to humankind. Courtesy of the American Antiquarian Society.

his "excentricity." Stewart considered himself a misunderstood genius, a man centuries ahead of his time and therefore doomed to be underappreciated by his peers. He described himself as a loner, yet he remained irrepressibly extroverted, and Fellows called him "a very pleasant companion." Stewart did not argue with people about their religious beliefs, and he welcomed critical engagement with his ideas. He was "never offended at having any of his opinions controverted," Fellows said, "but on the contrary expressed his approbation of it, saying that was the right way to elicit truth."[24]

One person, maybe the only person, who was fully persuaded by Stewart's discussion of sensate matter was Palmer. He took to paraphrasing Stewart's ideas without attribution and always as a statement of natural fact. When Palmer spoke, for example, about "the immortality of sensation in the aggregate mass of sensitive and intelligent life," he echoed Stewart. He accepted Stewart's claim that pain accumulates in the material universe with every act of violence, large or small. The pain which a man "inflicts upon sensitive existence," Palmer maintained, "will return upon himself with interest, and will pave the way for eternizing a system of misery fatal to the sensations of the whole animal world." Palmer explained that "our sensations are, at this moment, suffering under the cruel lash of ancient institutions," meaning that violence inflicted long ago had caused pain that reverberated in atoms throughout the ages and continued to be felt in the present. The "whole animal world are reciprocating with each other a system of extensive and perpetual wretchedness," Palmer said.[25]

Also following Stewart, Palmer believed that recognizing sensate atoms and the "constant interchange of matter with matter" held the key to a better future. With a shift in perspective one could imagine the "vast assemblage of living creatures, whose relations are reciprocal and reciprocated under a thousand different forms, and supported by a thousand different ligaments of an imperceptible nature." In this web of all life, "nothing is foreign or irrelative in the vast fabric to which we belong. Union is most intimate." Palmer had experienced feelings of an all-inclusive solidarity, and they brought him deep joy. "Man's highest happiness," he insisted, lay in "discovering his true connection with nature, and the eternal duration of this connection." On this point Palmer became impassioned. "If man had a comprehensive view of the successive changes of his existence, and a correct idea of the nature of sensation continually resulting from the renovation of organic forms, sympathy or universal benevolence, would become irresistibly impressive upon his moral powers, and form the basis of his subsequent conduct." The circle of one's compassion would extend to "the whole animal world, so as to exclude acts of cruelty, and annihilate every species of injustice." People would recognize that killing an insect or another human being differed only in matter of degree. "The child that is permitted in early life to run a pin through a fly," Palmer declared, "is already half prepared to run a dagger through the heart of his fellow creature!"[26]

The concept of singular matter left no doubt about human equality. No natural classes of men exist, Palmer said, as "nature has furnished no marks of preference by which to designate the master from the slave." All human beings belong "to the same species." The plainest, most incontrovertible truth in nature must be that "all mankind are entitled to equal rights; they are entitled to an equal just protection of their lives, their liberty, their property, and the means of procuring human felicity." Such talk of human equality, so commonplace in this revolutionary era, put Palmer in plenty of company. But he arrived at it through an uncommon route. He did not argue for natural rights granted by a divine creator, as Paine and so many others did. Rather, he posited that humans are made of fundamentally the same stuff, and that all appearances of difference, whether of race, gender, or otherwise, are epiphenomenal and of no lasting import.[27]

Like Stewart, Palmer saw meditation as the path to deeper knowledge about the world. If people could be brought to a "contemplation of nature—to a view of the powers of their own existence—to the beneficial results of intellectual operation—to love of self and love of species—to a clear view of individual with aggregate nature, every thing valuable would be accomplished." Religious doctrines and dogmas would be swept away, Palmer said, "like chaff before the wind." Meditative contemplation revealed to him the interconnectedness of all things, a connection that evoked in him an all-encompassing love, even an ecstatic feeling of oneness with the larger totality of being. He believed he had glimpsed the reality that lay below the surface appearances of things. The unity of the natural world and the principles by which it was organized appeared to him as both utterly magnificent and as simple, scientific fact—a material truth with the power to spark a transformative love.[28]

Palmer labored to articulate his sense of the world as a single living organism with its own generative force. The Earth is "a real being" with "powers" we should better understand, he said. The planet is the source of life, the "fountain of all terrestrial existence," and home to "millions of inferior beings, dependent upon the intrinsic and essential energies of the visible fountain." Palmer did not suggest planetary sentience or intention; rather, the world was a living system with a proclivity toward the proliferation and preservation of its interdependent parts. In contrast to the biblically proclaimed human dominion over nature, Palmer now saw humanity as a subset of the living creatures sustained by the Earth. Nature was the "indestructible fountain of knowledge" for an ignorant but teachable humanity. The physical world, and not homo sapiens, held the information most crucial to mankind, namely, the "universal knowledge of the origin, progress and destiny of his life."[29]

Feeling himself part of an age-old tradition, Palmer declared that the real philosophers of all ages had always focused on the concerns of "sensitive life." Philosophers in ancient Egypt, Persia, India, China, Greece, and Rome had made great inroads into the laws of nature. Ancient Greeks had understood the "coessential and the coeternal relationship of the whole material world." From Japan to the Roman Empire, philosophers had cared not about "the transmigration of souls; but [about] the transmutation of matter." Egyptian pharaohs had tried to foil the endless recombination of matter by building pyramids that would "seclude" their corpses "from all subsequent intercourse with the animal world." What a "preposterous and fallacious expectation!" Palmer exclaimed. Nothing can stop the eternal interaction of matter with itself.[30]

Christian theologians had suppressed ancient materialist philosophy for eighteen centuries, but Palmer thrilled to the fact that philosophers had picked up where the ancients had left off. "Thoughtful and contemplative men," Palmer said, "who have, in modern times, surveyed the system of the material world, recognize the same truths as were developed in former ages by many philosophers of the eastern hemisphere." British and French philosophers, in particular, had taken up the work. "Of all the men, however, whose philosophic researches have extended the farthest into the properties of the material world, John Stewart, a celebrated traveler of the present day, a single individual who has dared to despise all compromises with prejudices, appears to be entitled to the highest estimation." Palmer said Stewart "possesses a bold, contemplative and energetic understanding, and his enquiries into the nature of the human mind, the qualities of the material world, and the connection subsisting between the parts and the whole, have never been equaled by any individual, either in ancient or in modern times."[31]

Stewart's cosmology fit with and extended what Palmer had learned elsewhere. From the works of Richard Price, Condorcet, and William Godwin, Palmer had imbibed a hopeful assumption of human progress and eventual perfectibility. On Long Island, Isaac Ledyard had convinced Palmer to think about matter as eternally in motion. Volney's discussion of religion as a human invention and Paine's overt rejection of any revealed religion had enabled Palmer's break from even the most liberal forms of Christianity. Into this space came Stewart's practices of meditation and the idea of a universe of shared, sensate matter. By 1797, Palmer's understanding of the world combined ideas from these different thinkers, the most revered of whom was John Stewart.

Stewart's talk of sensate matter and jumping atoms persuaded Palmer but not others. The physician Elihu Hubbard Smith was browsing at Fellows's bookstore when he "picked up the last publication of the Traveller Stewart, in which I have read some to-day." While Smith was there, Stewart "came in, & I saw him, for the first time." Smith initially found Stewart impressive. "His countenance is fine—parts of it uncommonly so; & his voice is equally agreeable. He spake like a man of sense." But the favorable impression soon faded. Smith and two friends spent most of an evening "devoted to an attempt to solve one of Stuart—the Traveller's—unintelligibles, in his last publication." Alexander Anderson, a well-read medical student who enjoyed the works of Paine, Volney, Voltaire, and Condorcet, also found Stewart's work impossible to comprehend, and not for lack of trying. Intrigued by Stewart's "greatest absurdities," Anderson took the publication to a friend "and read the greatest part of it to him." The next day Anderson read a piece by Priestley on education, and Stewart did not fare well by comparison. "But how different this [Priestley] was from what I read to him yesterday," Anderson wrote in his diary. In Priestley's work "flow'd the dictates of pure morality, convey'd in a pleasing style," while Stewart "with an arrogant display of knowledge, undertook to modify *right* and *wrong* according to his own notion."[32]

The question of right and wrong, and how to know the difference, was precisely the point of contention, Palmer recognized. A democratic republic relied on a virtuous citizenry, all agreed, but he looked to *nonreligious* sources for a morality that was grounded in the facts of nature. A science of morality, like the kind Condorcet had promoted, required neither deity nor theology. "If a thousand Gods existed, or if nature existed independent of any," Palmer said, "the moral relation between man and man would remain exactly the same in either case." Morality "is founded in the properties of our nature, and it is as indestructible as the basis on which it rests." He meant that the physical interdependence of all beings called for ethical conduct: compassion, generosity, and nonviolence. Acknowledging the "reciprocation of matter" results in "the most unqualified and universal sympathy," and this sympathy, in turn, "ought to become the criterion of social institutions." When that happened, the problems of the world would melt away. It might take some time, as the "march of science is slow." But with a free press and "righteous political institutions," knowledge about the reciprocal relations in nature would spread, making eventual human perfectibility "as sure as the motion of the Earth round the Sun." One day, Palmer predicted, when "reason shall have wrought her perfect work, fools will blush and be silent—imposters will disappear, and the earth will become the habitation of human happiness."[33]

By the summer of 1797, Palmer was ready for another Fourth of July oration, possibly his first in four years. Ten of his supporters, including Philip Freneau, publisher, poet, and cousin to Isaac Ledyard, petitioned for access to the large courtroom in New York's city hall. Palmer intended to deliver his holiday speech there, but the request was denied on the grounds that he was "An Infidel." The freethinkers gathered instead in Gaultier's assembly room, Palmer's usual venue. Two newspapers announced that Palmer's political oration would begin at ten in the morning. He could assume a familiar and friendly audience, and, in fact, the event doubled as a fundraiser for him. With a veiled reference to his blindness, the newspaper explained that given "Mr. Palmer's peculiarly unfortunate situation, it is proposed by his friends to make a Collection on that day for his benefit."[34]

Standing at the front of the assembly room, perhaps guided there on a friend's arm, Palmer waited to hear the quiet that signaled an attentive audience. Then he began his optimistic message. Humankind is on the verge of comprehending matters of greatest concern, he announced. Philosophers in different countries were combining their efforts "to ameliorate the condition of the human race." One could already detect "in the progressive movements of intellectual power, the certain ruin, the inevitable destruction of those pernicious systems of error and superstition, of civil and religious despotism, which have so long desolated the world and degraded the character of man." The American Revolution was the perfect example of this trend in that the political struggle produced not only national independence but also the "gradual decay of superstition and fanaticism." Even the most violent wars cannot produce lasting change unless accompanied by just such intellectual liberation, Palmer claimed. This is precisely what made the American Revolution so meaningful, so unprecedented, in his view. The struggle for liberty involved more than the quest for political power; it entailed battling mental despotism and achieving intellectual emancipation and moral rejuvenation.[35]

The future looked bright, Palmer told his audience, because a new "science of morality" would soon produce a system of ethics based on the workings of nature. The physical makeup of the natural world, composed entirely of shared, sensate matter, meant that each individual action affected the whole—a fact that, once understood, brought with it both the obligation and the desire to reduce harm to other beings. The examination of the "whole mundane system of existence" will reveal the "primary principles by which all existence is influenced and governed." These insights will be "applied to the practical concerns of life," Palmer declared, and then "the whole world will assume a new aspect, cheering to the heart, and animating to the mind, of every intelligent being." Religion had long obscured material reality, Palmer said, but now "the charm is broken, the clouds of mysticism are dispersing, and the bright rays of truth are about to illuminate the world." To the anticipated charge of utopian thinking, Palmer spoke preemptively. "Say not that these are the dreams of delirium—the anticipation of unreasonable desires—No! the ground of such expectation" rested on the "progressive improvements already made." Success was virtually guaranteed, and soon "national prejudices and animosities" will disappear along with the "savage ferocity" they produce. Palmer quoted at length "the celebrated Condorcet," who had predicted the end of all wars and the advancement of women's rights. On this day of celebration, Palmer did not commemorate the American Revolution or its heroes. He did not speak of George Washington, John Adams, or other leading political figures. Instead, he lauded the international group of philosophers he judged most beneficial to all of humankind. "Paine, Volney, Barlow, Condorcet and Godwin," he said, "will be ranked among the greatest benefactors of the human race."[36]

In his speech on the previous Christmas, Palmer had targeted Christian beliefs and a corrupt clergy. Now he focused more positively on religion's replacement, namely the principles underlying human nature. He felt himself part of an international effort to acquire a more accurate understanding of the natural world. Framing his lectures as part of a project pursued by an international cohort of intellectuals, Palmer felt confident, even exuberant, about the future. He had rebounded from his devastating loss of sight. He felt buoyed by an appreciative audience and a circle of supporters. His focus on something greater than himself, on the future perfectibility of the human race, lifted his spirits.

Blindness remained a handicap, rendering Palmer financially unstable and dependent upon charity. Sometimes his impairment was used against him as grounds for dismissal. "I suppose you can see with a more penetrating eye than I can," mocked one critic of his speech. To offset barbs such as these, the editor of Palmer's published oration addressed "the *peculiar situation* of the Author" and defended Palmer's mental acuity. Someone working under "the total loss of sight" can hardly be expected to commit "ideas to paper with that nice precision, elegance, regularity or method" that vision facilitated. The ideas in Palmer's oration were "strong and vigorous, and frequently original," proving that "loss of sight does by no means impair the energy of the contemplative faculties of man." Other reviewers agreed. "Citizen Elihu Palmer" spoke well, one said. His "diction is correct and elegant; his elocution clear and sonorous—the effects of which are heightened by energetic and expressive gestures." Philip Freneau's *Time*

Piece, and Literary Companion reprinted the speech in two parts, and the playwright and novelist William Dunlap was surprised to find himself impressed by it. Dunlap, a member of the Friendly Club, had not thought much of Palmer, whose acerbic attacks on Christianity did not fit with the club's etiquette of civility, but Dunlap noted in his diary that Palmer's oration "gives me a higher idea of the man Than I had; indeed, it is energetic, philosophic & benevolent."[37]

Palmer had made a strong comeback from the disasters of 1793. He now had a clear sense of his own role in creating a better future. He was an educator, an advocate for the idea that natural principles underlay true morality. He would share with a wider public not only the anti-Christian critique he had learned from Paine, but also the mind-bending, euphoria-inducing, non-dualistic vision of the universe that ancient philosophers had long ago discovered. John Stewart had brought these insights back from his travels around the world, and they awaited a public airing in the United States. It required only a courageous speaker, one who did not fear the repudiation of the clergy or the rejection of higher society. Palmer was that man. Ready to bring his message to a broader audience, and willing to navigate unfamiliar terrain to do it, he prepared for a speaking tour.

PART III

Lightning Rod

CHAPTER 9

Specter of Infidelity

DAVID DENNISTON FEARED for his future as the editor of the newspaper in Newburgh, New York. He had welcomed the controversial Elihu Palmer to the small town on the Hudson River and arranged his public lectures. Ever since, Denniston had been hearing complaints about his support for religious infidelity. The Presbyterian minister and other prominent townspeople warned the region's residents that skepticism endangered not only their individual souls but also the political stability of the nation. In October 1797, twenty-three men signed a public letter that objected to Denniston's support for Palmer and cancelled their subscriptions to the town's only newspaper, the *Mirror*. The signers' concern was no petty matter. They viewed Palmer's lectures, and Denniston's advertisement of them, as part of a larger coordinated attack on the United States. Newburgh had fewer than three thousand inhabitants, but news of the local conflict spread when citizens of Orange County alerted friends in New York City, sixty miles away, about the nefarious designs of Denniston and Palmer.[1]

Religious infidelity and Republican treachery were of a piece in the minds of those who opposed Denniston. The son of a wealthy farmer in Orange County, Denniston was a staunch Democratic-Republican and kin to the powerful Clinton family, whose most famous members, Governor George Clinton and his up-and-coming nephew and secretary, DeWitt, held long tenure as Republican leaders in New York State. By the late 1790s, when the Terror in France had ended in the government takeover by an oligarchy, the aggressively imperialist Directory, Federalists saw ongoing Republican support for France as severely misguided. The trajectory was clear, Federalists said. Anarchic French atheism had produced destructive, revolutionary violence that only a strong national government could suppress. Religious infidelity in America would weaken morality and create similar havoc if it was not subdued. In Federalist opinion, the print scuffle in Newburgh over Denniston's support for Palmer's irreverent lectures was no mere trifle. It was one episode in the high-stakes struggle over the future of the republic.[2]

Republicans felt just as jittery about the nation's future, but for different reasons. They dreaded what they saw as the Federalists' "monarchist" tendencies to undermine democratic principles and the civil liberties of the people, particularly their freedom of speech, through repressive centralized government. What good was a social order that came at the cost of freely speaking one's mind? The First Amendment prevented only the federal government from infringing on freedom of speech and of the press, but Republican editors considered free speech a matter of principle that should extend to the states and every local government. As the century came to a close, a battle raged over what some considered forward-looking freethought and others called dangerous infidelity, by which they meant a repudiation of the Christian faith. The contest in Newburgh over Palmer's lectures and Denniston's support for them was part of a larger clash over freedom of speech. Ink was the weapon of choice, and the printable page was the staging ground for contests over religious opinions and reputations. In letters of protest and self-defense, in sermons and satirical spoofs, infidelity hovered as a specter over the page, haunting those who feared its power to lead Christian believers astray, as well as those who feared its religious effects not at all, but who dreaded the shade it cast on freethinkers' reputations.

Elihu Palmer became a catalyst in connecting freethinkers and galvanizing their opponents beyond the confines of New York City. The small town of Newburgh witnessed years of strife that was sparked by Palmer's transient presence in and after 1797. Previously obscure figures come to the fore in this telling, in particular the freethinking editor David Denniston, a vitalist physician named Phineas Hedges, and an opposed minister, Jonathan Freeman. In these local conflicts, what Palmer stood for in the minds of Newburgh citizens became more important than the man himself. He appeared in Newburgh in person on occasion but more frequently as a caricature in the pages of the local newspaper—both as the personification of infidelity and as the means to sully the reputation of his friends.

The warm reception Palmer received in Newburgh in the late summer of 1797 gave no warning of the contest to come. Denniston would have greeted him at the docks and helped him disembark from one of the sloops that sailed regularly between New York City and Newburgh. As they walked through town, probably arm in arm to prevent Palmer from stumbling, Denniston might have explained the noisy activity going on around them: loggers hauling cartloads of felled trees into town, men feeding logs into water-powered sawmills, shipbuilders hammering timber, and stevedores stacking lumber on boats bound for New York. Palmer may have inquired about townspeople who were open to rethinking religion. Who in Newburgh cared to examine the implausibility of Christian beliefs? Who was receptive to learning about the science of morality and the makeup of the universe? Denniston could name the local freethinkers, including three physicians, Charles Clinton, Phineas Hedges, and Elias Winfield, all of them Democratic-Republicans, as well as an array of artisans, merchants, and a retired military man. Denniston had requested and been denied access to the Presbyterian church for Palmer's lectures, but he obtained a room in the recently finished Academy, a public school intended "for the instruction of youth in literature and the principles of morality." There Palmer could lecture on the fallacies of the Christian religion, the truth of scientific principles of nature, and the possibility of human happiness on a global scale.[3]

Dr. Phineas Hedges, a Newburgh physician in his mid-thirties, would have found it easy to strike up a conversation with Palmer. Hedges advocated the kind of medical vitalism that had inspired Isaac Ledyard on Long Island. Like Ledyard, Hedges admired the writings of William Cullen, the Scottish professor who described a vital power within the human body. Hedges adopted Cullen's understanding of the *vis medicatrix*, a natural tendency within the human body toward the recuperation of health. The life force remained mysterious, Hedges admitted in his book on physiology. The vital power was not sentient in the way of a rational being, that is, not invested with intelligence or rationality, yet it was self-activating and autonomous in ways unlike any "inanimate automaton." Mystery prevailed, since the healing *vis medicatrix* does not act "uniformly, nor yet always successfully." But empirical observation proved beyond a doubt "the existence of the *vis natura*," a force working within individual organisms. Hedges took Cullen's claims beyond human physiology, believing the vital principle was "diffused throughout all nature." Not only do living creatures show evidence of the life force, Hedges said, "even inanimate matter seems to possess a principle of this kind." Palmer recognized these ideas instantly. He had discussed them with Dr. Ledyard years before and then, more recently, with John Stewart. These very concepts had propelled him down the path of freethought that brought him now to Newburgh.[4]

The healing principle acted not only within individual bodies, Hedges said, but also in larger systems, such as an entire society. "The affairs of states and kingdoms," he wrote, as if "by an invincible necessity, tend to a certain point, after arriving at which, by some invisible cause, take a contrary direction." In other words, society was like a body that operated according to natural laws of disease and healing. The cause of recovery was invisible but powerful nonetheless. The vital force that healed an individual body could also restore health to an ailing body politic. This was just the kind of thinking Palmer loved: the idea that a single principle underlay the workings of the physical, social, and moral universe.[5]

Hedges was a deist, easily combining the idea of a vital principle with that of a sentient Creator-God who made the *vis natura* part of all physiology. Hedges suggested as much when he wrote that the "author of man" had "bestowed" certain properties on the heart muscles, for example. A divine intelligence had built protective measures into its creation, Hedges explained, and "if providence had not wisely implanted the *vis medicatrix* in our constitution, we should fall an easy prey to the noxious agents that surround us." But the deity Hedges had in mind was nothing like the Christian notion of God, for which Hedges had only utter disrespect. In fact, Hedges could not speak ill enough of religion, and of Catholicism in particular. In a Fourth of July speech to fellow Republicans in 1795, he had described centuries of Christianity as "a long night of impenetrable darkness" during which "religious sophistry" kept the human mind "sunk almost to the level of the brute creation." Religious authorities had suppressed scientific inquiry, Hedges said, precisely because science proved the fundamental equality of all people, a fact that religious and civil despots sought to hide from public view. Sounding much like Thomas Paine, whose

Age of Reason had appeared the previous year, Hedges described religion in grotesque terms. This "prolific fountain of corruption disgorged its pestilential water over the whole European world," he said, and the "benighted" believers who drank deeply at this well of superstition suffered "a universal sleep and death of mind." Hedges and Palmer both saw their present moment as one of intellectual awakening from a long night of religious stupor. Unfettered by religious prejudice, Hedges asked, may we not grasp "the mysteries of animate and inanimate matter? May we not discover the secret spring of life and animation?"[6]

The physician was not sanguine about success, however. Unlike Palmer, who spoke of an inexorable movement toward eventual human perfectibility, Hedges feared that corruption might undermine the "great work of reformation" that had just begun. Economic inequality tainted the political system, he said, which disproportionately represented the interests of wealthy constituents over those of ordinary people. Even so, he held out hope that an education in vitalism could transform society by entirely peaceful means. Humankind was one social body infused with the same vital power, Hedges believed, and this insight fostered feelings of generosity and compassion on a global scale. He looked forward to a time when "benevolence shall gush in limpid streams from the heart consoling all the afflicted." Imagery from physiology lay near at hand, with benevolence pumping through the social body in the way blood flowed through the individual heart, circulating without conscious effort. Hedges also used an electrical metaphor: "Wisdom shall dart with electrical velocity from mind, enlightening and invigorating the whole family of man." Whether by hydraulic or electrical means, benevolence will course through the social body in just the way that vital forces animate the physical organism. Unlike Hobbes's version of the body politic ruled by the king at its head, Hedges offered a vitalist version in line with his Democratic-Republican politics. In his model of society, a singular and shared power equally infuses the whole. Eventually, Hedges imagined, liberty itself "shall pervade all hearts and all climes, and the large family of man join in one general chorus in commemoration of the 4th of July."[7]

When Palmer arrived in town, he found a hearing with confirmed freethinkers like Denniston and Hedges and with other Newburgh residents as well. John Johnston, a teenager in 1797, later recalled that Palmer "was brought to Newburgh under a promise of an annual salary, to detail from Sabbath to Sabbath the opinions of Voltaire, Paine, Rousseau, Godwin, and others of the same stamp." Denniston's *Mirror*, an "infidel paper," fueled religious doubt, according to Johnston, while Paine's *Age of Reason*, Matthew Tindal's *Christianity as Old as Creation*, "and other books of the same kind, were reprinted, and circulated with all diligence." Infidel publications appeared "in every tavern, or shop, or private house from which they were not positively excluded," Johnston said. Townspeople circulated "obscene prints and pictures" involving religious motifs, and "young persons, even children, were invited and decoyed to view these drawings, which were generally intended to throw ridicule on some portion of sacred history." A "gentleman in Orange County" described the "unparalleled zeal" with which editor Denniston and "a little junto of infidel brethren" in Newburgh attacked Christianity. They had "hired one Palmer, an apostate from the christian faith, to preach, as they termed it, and publicly to ridicule the doctrines of our holy religion. Indeed they spared no pains to insnare the unguarded." More than an occasional public nuisance, these freethinkers were "most indefatigable to render the whole village infidel." Defenders of the faith responded to Palmer's lectures with alarm. A "religious tornado," Denniston wrote, "has shaken the country, on account of Mr. Palmer."[8]

Opposition to Palmer continued to build in Newburgh even after he returned to Manhattan in September. The *Goshen Repository*, a Republican newspaper in a town twenty miles away, published a thinly veiled satire of Palmer as the religiously flip-flopping "Dr. Proteus." Written by a Newburgh resident under the initials "D. N.," the piece caricatured actual residents in Newburgh: two sons of a Quaker physician (possibly Phineas and Jonathan Hedges); "Capt. Leather-Chops," a young artillerist who is "warm in contest against the christian scheme"; "Mr. Stitch," the tailor; and the cobbler, "Mr. Strop." In the satirical piece, none of the befuddled freethinkers could say with certainty "what God it is the Doctor professes to worship." Mr. Strop thought maybe "the God Apollo, or Minerva," although he admitted that maybe "*Bacchus was the Doctor's favorite.*" Perhaps Dr. Proteus had no faith at all and was "a mere Camelon [chameleon] to suit the times." The lion's share of the piece goes to Denniston, or "Type," the satire's main target. Type waxes ecstatic as he remembers Proteus's lectures. "O! how I have seen the Doctor's pious soul take wing, mount up, and in a flow of eloquence, turn the witty jest, tell the pretty tale, take a grog and play the boon companion.—Not like your starch christians, talk of a hereafter, and accountability in man." Stamping out Christianity "is my souls desire," Type proclaims, and his newspaper will serve the cause, printing the "sarcastic sneer or anecdote; all designed to wound the cause of Christ."[9]

The barely veiled indictment of Type as an enemy to Christianity was only the opening shot against Denniston. Two weeks later, the *Goshen Repository* published a letter of reproach against the Newburgh editor. Three men had drafted a complaint and circulated it for signatures. The letter described Denniston as "an avowed enemy to Revealed Religion" who had "taken an active part" in supporting Palmer, who pretends to be a preacher but "who publicly ridicules the Bible and all that we hold sacred." The letter remembered George Washington's assertion that "religion, and morality are indispensable supports" for political prosperity and happiness. The signers had no "personal resentments" against Denniston but were motivated by a "sincere regard to our country, ourselves, and rising families." Addressing Denniston directly, the critics wrote that even in "the utmost stretch of charity we cannot number you among our patriots, as we consider your principles and practice subversive of man's highest and most dear interests." The undersigned wished to settle their accounts and cancel their subscription to the *Mirror*. Twenty-three men signed their names.[10]

His livelihood at stake, Denniston defended himself in the *Goshen Repository* in October and December. (These issues of the newspaper have apparently not survived.) His defense prompted more verbal attacks. D. N., the author of the Proteus satire, printed a response to Denniston's self-defense, chiding the editor for having a double standard regarding free speech. The signed letter of complaint accused Denniston "of being a zealous Deist," a charge Denniston could not possibly deny, because plenty in town had heard him ridicule the Bible and the divinity of Jesus. Why was Denniston sensitive on this point? D. N. found it odd that "when you are called Infidels, you take umbrage, and resent it as ill treatment." The signers of the letter had committed no offence; they simply spoke the truth as they saw it. Did Denniston "profess to be a stickler for Liberty; and yet deny your neighbors the liberty of conversing and making up their minds respecting your conduct as a public servant?" What a despicable double standard, D. N. implied.[11]

As to Denniston's charge of defamation—"What *good name* have we robbed you of?" D. N. scoffed. "You have long been known to be an inveterate Infidel, and as such, you ought not to be considered as a friend to the good morals and prosperity of your country." Denniston seemed to think that his gossiping neighbors were guilty of "*lifting high the relentless arm of persecution, and robbing him of his good name.*" Not at all, D. N. declared. The signers of the October 10 letter did not wish to disturb Denniston's "enjoyment of your private sentiments concerning religion," but they drew the line at sponsoring his public expressions of them. They refused to give their money to one "who like a canker-worm is preying on the very vitals of religion, and the dearest interests of our country."[12]

Taking for granted that "the principles of the gospel lie at the foundation of our civil constitutions, and the laws of our country," D. N. asserted that any attempt to "remove that main foundation stone endangers the whole." Denniston openly supported Elihu Palmer, "*who ridicules the Bible, and all that the christian holds sacred.*" Did Denniston not "invite that gentleman to Newburgh, conduct him through the streets, entertain him in your house, strive to have him admitted into the Church, and followed him from place to place, to hear his blasphemy?" And, D. N. needled, what even *is* that thing "you call *natural religion*?" The ancient Egyptians had "worshipped Cats and Dogs, Leeks and Onions, and no doubt they considered it *natural religion.*" Others worship "the Sun, Moon, and Stars, and they with Thomas Paine, would call it *natural religion.*" Exactly which fake version of religion did Denniston support?[13]

The infidel editor was nothing special, D. N. continued. For centuries, "Satan and Deists" had tried and failed to extinguish the Christian faith. Denniston was only the least of these, D. N. mocked, because the editor had folded quickly under pressure and then begged his critics to do to him as they would be done by. Where had Denniston found "this excellent *rule of Conduct*?" Surely not in the "scurrilous writings" of Paine, Voltaire, Bolingbroke, or Hume. No, the golden rule Denniston invoked was from the very Bible he opposed. This was sheer hypocrisy, and "it ill becomes you, sir, to take into your unhallowed Lips the solemn Precepts of the Gospel of Jesus, and make use of them to answer your particular purpose."

D. N. considered the matter settled: Denniston was a man of low character. Denniston saw it differently, of course, but he no longer had access to the pages of the *Goshen Repository*. The editor of that paper gave D. N. the last word and announced in the same issue that he would no longer print their feud over "*religious principles.*"[14]

Barred from the *Goshen Repository*, Denniston resorted to printing his self-defense in a pamphlet that ran to forty-six pages. He placed the confrontation in Newburgh in the context of the long, dark history of religious persecution. "The appearance of Mr. Palmer" as "a preacher of morality in this village" had stoked "all the malevolent enmity that hath in former ages defiled the human character, and darkened the horizon of human happiness." Surely, Denniston insisted, there is "no right, more unalienable than that of thought or of worshiping the great author of Nature, in that way which appears reasonable to the individual, and most acceptable to Deity." Denniston appealed directly "to those gentlemen who have withdrawn their subscriptions from the Mirror" and pressed them to consider once more "whether they acted by the charitable principle of benevolence," which Christianity "so strongly enforces and recommends," namely "the golden rule; *do unto others, as you would they should do unto you.*" Denniston added that he saw these words "not as of divine origin" but as "clearly discoverable and deducible from the laws of nature or of society." He tried to shame the boycotters of his paper by referencing Palmer's blindness. They had withdrawn their patronage from the *Mirror* solely because Denniston "shewed respect to a gentleman whose character is respectable, and whose situation in life deserves, and would command the sympathy of every friend to the unfortunate." Generous men would not punish an editor for such simple decency.[15]

Insisting on his patriotism, Denniston reminded his readers that the nation's founders had required no religious test for public office. "Are deism and patriotism irreconcilable? If so, the framers of our constitutions were deficient in their duty, in not exacting a test to office. But the wisdom of our councils happily was not disturbed with the ravings of fanaticism, nor the gloomy horrors of superstition." Denniston refuted the notion that the Bible underwrote the Constitution. The claim that "the gospel lays at the foundation of our civil constitutions" is "entirely new and unintelligible," as neither "the gospel or any principle of religion [is] incorporated in our federal or state constitutions." Remember, too, that "freedom of opinion on religious subjects" was granted "the utmost scope . . . by our wise and wholesome constitutions." His critics had not embraced the freedoms the Constitution was meant to protect.[16]

Because they had no principle to stand on, Denniston continued, his critics resorted to misleading slander. They "confound deism and atheism in the minds of their hearers" in an effort to make deists appear all the more "detestable." Natural religion did not, of course, involve worshipping onions or leeks, Denniston said, but rather meant "an adoration of Deity as the primary cause of all things," along with obedience to "the eternal rule of right and wrong, which he has instituted for the conduct and government of man." Religious institutions were superfluous, because "pouring out grateful effusions of heart to the Author of Nature, may be done without a formal and ostensible prayer." His opponents were no better than the religious tyrants of old in that they would use any "civil power" at their disposal to pursue the "sacrifice of heretics" while a "tornado of ecclesiastical wrath would fulminate from the pulpit." Denniston's hyperbole suggests his own feeling of persecution, now that his livelihood as Newburgh's printer was at stake. His self-vindication ended on a heroic note. The "liberal and tolerant example of America" allows for religious diversity, he said, and the "most contrary religious opinions may exist in society, without disturbing each others opinion and happiness," as long as all sides disavowed persecution. Denniston proclaimed to his "Fellow-citizens" that neither "fear of poverty" nor social contempt would induce him to forfeit his freedom of speech. He detested tyranny of all kinds, he wrote, and would risk everything "for the enjoyment of our opinions." He would not bow to public pressure, and the boycott of his paper would not break his spirit. Like his friend Palmer, the editor believed himself engaged in a longer struggle for freedom of religious expression.[17]

The publicity around religious freethought in Newburgh aggravated the town's new Presbyterian minister. Recently arrived in 1797, Reverend Jonathan Freeman's concern about unbelief spiked with Palmer's visit. Earlier in the year, in a sermon on what he designated "sinful practices," Freeman had prioritized religious disinterest. "Procrastination or postponing ye business of religion to a future period is ye cause of destruction to thousands," he lamented, "especially young people." Infidelity received only brief mention: "Many ruin their souls by imbibing false principles, especially ye principles of infidelity & by neglecting gospel ordinances." Clearly, infidelity misled some people, but complacency endangered far more souls. By December, however, Freeman was devoting increased attention to infidelity. On Sunday, December 24, he chose for his sermon text Matthew 28:6, "He is not here, for he is risen, as he said." Freeman's topic on this Christmas Eve was not the birth of Christ but the resurrection, precisely because this paramount doctrine "is much contested by infidels in ye present day." Freeman offered his parishioners a way to "strengthen your faith, & put arguments in your mouth to refute gainsayers."[18]

Freeman liked to say that infidels knew, deep down, that they were wrong and doomed to burn in hell. Every "deist under heaven" has been told "by his conscience that ye scriptures are ye word of God," Freeman said, and "every soul of them is afraid of this great truth." Skeptics seduced believers away from the Christian faith to have more fellowship in sin, to "bolster them up in their infidelity & silence ye remonstrances of conscience." Infidels would ultimately be forced to accept the truth of the Christian God, Freeman said, but this late recognition would not keep them from being "dashed to pieces by his iron rod, & consigned to ye torments of an eternal hell." Freeman imagined their destruction in vivid terms, perhaps relishing the thought. Then he announced that "I have now done with them." But Freeman could not leave the vexing freethinkers alone. Male competition may have increased the minister's antagonism toward the freethinkers. Freeman, Denniston, Palmer, and Hedges were all in their thirties, men vying for public stature. In the contest, Freeman became rather too aggressive, some thought. A man "of determined character," Freeman sometimes acted "from the impulse of his feelings rather than from deliberate judgment," his successor, John Johnston, recalled, and he "engaged in a newspaper controversy which embittered the feelings of many of the congregation."[19]

Fanning the flames of Freeman's anxiety was a curious and alarming book from Scotland then making the rounds among American ministers. John Robison, a professor of natural history in Edinburgh, had published his *Proofs of a Conspiracy against All the Religions and Governments of Europe, Carried on in the Secret Meetings of Free Masons, Illuminati, and Reading Societies*. In it, Robison explained that atheist French philosophers had infiltrated reading circles and Masonic lodges, using the gullible members to stage the French Revolution and overthrow both the monarchy and the Catholic Church. Other governments would be next. American ministers read the book and deduced that the Illuminati had already arrived on American shores. A contagious French atheism, they now understood, explained the rise of public expressions of religious skepticism in the United States. Palmer's lectures in Newburgh, and the support they received from the local newspaper, exemplified the danger Robison had warned about.[20]

As Jedidiah Morse in Massachusetts prepared a Fast Day sermon in May, 1798, he may have had his nemesis Palmer in mind. Morse had not forgotten their exasperating letter exchanges in 1791, when Palmer had taunted Morse for preaching a useless message of repentance. According to Morse's own understanding of the predestination of souls, Palmer had written, the saved were saved and the damned were damned, and nothing Morse said from the pulpit would change that. Morse might as well quit preaching, Palmer had mocked. The next year, Morse had cheered when Ashbel Green and his Philadelphia colleagues attacked Palmer in print as a hypocrite and infidel. Palmer had made a remarkable comeback from the yellow fever that robbed him of his family and his eyesight, but Morse had lost none of his hostility toward the man, and now Morse perceived that Palmer was part of an international conspiracy of infidels.

Morse warned his listeners in Boston and Charlestown of a "secretly operating *foreign influence* among us." Robison's *Proofs of a Conspiracy* had revealed a "deep-laid and extensive plan, which has for many years been in operation in Europe." To this plan, Morse said, "we may trace that torrent of irreligion, and abuse of every thing good and praise-worthy, which, at the present time, threatens to overwhelm the world." American-born conduits for French atheism "boldly denied" the existence of God, Morse said, and "deified and adored" Reason and Nature instead. Morse noted that Federalist politicians and Protestant clergy were "reviled and abused, in a singular manner, in similar language." Federalist leaders, although men of "great ability and incorruptible integrity," are "stigmatized continually, as unfriendly to the rights and liberties of the people."[21]

Stoking the general anxiety that summer of 1798 was the fear of war with France. Tension had been building ever since the United States government ceased paying on its wartime debt to France, with the argument that the loan had come from a regime that no longer existed. In response, French privateers began seizing American merchant ships, and the French government refused to receive the US minister sent to France in 1796. Relations continued to erode, and in April 1798 the American public heard the insulting news that French agents had demanded that US diplomats pay a large sum before political negotiations could begin. In July 1798, Congress rescinded its wartime treaties with France and authorized attacks on French warships found in American waters. Now the United States stood poised on the brink of another war. In this fearful moment, the Federalist administration under President Adams perceived critics as traitors. That summer Congress passed the Alien and Sedition Acts. The Sedition Act made it a crime to speak, write, or print anything "false, scandalous and malicious" about the US government, especially if done with an intent to bring its officials "into contempt or disrepute." Dozens of Republican editors were prosecuted for publishing criticism of Adams's administration, and some spent time in jail. Foreigners deemed dangerous found themselves deported. Republicans saw that the very liberties on which the nation was founded were being curtailed.[22]

As ministers continued to sound the alarm about domestic enemies, Reverend Freeman in Newburgh added his voice to the chorus. He, too, had read Robison's *Proofs of a Conspiracy*, and it cast Denniston and Palmer in a new light. They were, Freeman now believed, part of a larger atheist infiltration of America. He focused his Fast Day sermon in August on the dangers of organized infidelity. The "contagion" from infidel France had made significant inroads, Freeman warned, and many now profaned the Sabbath as merely "a superstitious custom generated by priestcraft." Local merchants, printers, and physicians plied their trades on Sundays rather than attend church services, he complained, and newspapers openly parroted French infidelity. Even government representatives had been infected with skepticism, and what could this be, Freeman asked, "but *aping* the atheistic legislature of France?" Freeman's main point was a political one: the United States should distance itself from France, that "centre of infidelity and atheism." Irreligion fed sedition, Freeman said, and in America "there is not one deist, who is not a *violent enemy* to our government, and a *warm* partizan for the French revolutionizers." Atheism led to anarchy, and American Christians should view France "with fear and trembling" and consider its influence "as the most deadly pestilence."[23]

Freeman missed the days when skeptics cowered in hiding. Not long ago, he reminded his congregants, "an infidel was justly deemed a monster; a disgrace to human nature." Those who doubted the Bible's divine origins maintained "profound silence on the subject." Shocking to realize, Freeman told his parishioners, that "you have lived to see—who could have thought it?—you have lived to see infidelity openly avowed. You have lived to see the religion of Jesus loaded with the most blasphemous ridicule, & horrid reproaches." But "still worse, if possible, you have lived to see an association of infidels formed for the purpose of destroying all civil government and religion in the world." The Illuminati, spawned in Germany and France, were on the move in America, and everywhere they went, they sought to undermine faith in God and belief in an afterlife. They undercut respect for government representatives, private property, and even the institution of marriage. Robison's *Proofs of a Conspiracy* revealed all this, Freeman said, and "every American who is a friend to his country, to liberty and religion, ought to be in possession of this book."[24]

Freethinkers no longer hid their sentiments—that much was true. When Freeman prophesied that Phineas Hedges would die young, just as the openly skeptical Ethan Allen had, Hedges responded with a letter that covered the entire first page of the *Mirror* and spilled onto the second. Freeman had issued the warning "*in terrorem* to frighten me into an acknowledgment of your clerical superiority," Hedges wrote, but he considered "the threat as a chimera & bugbear." Since when was Freeman a prophet? "Who gave you the prerogative of admonishing and warning people of the evil to come?" Hedges told Freeman to "look at the inveterate fury of your puerile, superstitious productions, your rancorous hatred to the progress of civil and religious liberty; contemplate the dirty lava emitted from the Crater of your combustible and effervescing intellect, and I fancy that if you are spiritually discerned, you can trace a more exact resemblance to a boar in combat." The days of feigning respect for a man of the cloth were over.[25]

The print battle continued when Palmer returned to Newburgh in November 1798. Writer D. N., possibly Freeman himself, once more revived the satire of Type and Dr. Proteus. Covering most of the front page of the *Goshen Repository* in January 1799, the piece announced that Dr. Proteus had returned to Newburgh to assess his disciples' progress in spreading the infidel word. In the essay, Type, the editor, boasts to Proteus that his newspaper had "teemed for a time, to serve the glorious cause" and that he had reprinted a book by the well-known English deist, Matthew Tindal. (Denniston had indeed published Tindal's *Christianity as Old as Creation* in 1798.) But Type had been compelled to "sacrifice" his press. Another character references Type's "political dissolution," which suggests that the boycott against Denniston as editor of the *Mirror* had been effective. (By October 1798, the editor was Philip van Horne.) Proteus feigns admiration for the self-sacrificing editor: "Your zeal is worthy of imitation," he tells Type, but in an aside the Doctor murmurs in a low voice, "O! what a fool, to throw away his living." Proteus embraces his own hypocrisy. He need only be assured bread, beef, "and plenty of good Madeira," he whispers to himself, to play the part of "Mahometan, Jew, Christian, or any thing else." In another aside, Proteus admits that Christianity might be true after all, in which case "Type must expect the worst of times," namely eternal hellfire for his heresy. With this piece of mockery, D. N. hoped to keep townspeople from attending Palmer's lecture.[26]

By the spring of 1799, Freeman's fear of a conspiracy against the United States verged on paranoia. He believed that European anarchists planned to destroy Christianity and all the civil governments on earth. The French, in particular, "are endeavoring to unhinge our government, destroy our independence & liberty, & to overturn our holy religion, which is infinitely more precious & valuable than all our civil privileges." Already much damage had been done. American infidels had welcomed the "hosts of Genets, Fauchets, Adets, Tallyrands & Volneys into our country, to create disorganization, insurrection, & opposition to government—to incite animosities & divisions—to disseminate their infidelity & atheism." Freeman believed the French had "employed" Thomas Paine to write the *Age of Reason* and then shipped fifteen thousand cheap copies to America to work its poison there. Volney sent copies of *The Ruins*, "as diabolical a book as ever was printed," then came over himself "to spread his infidelity & atheism" throughout the United States. The new nation teetered on the precipice of destruction because too many Americans had "embraced the demoralizing principles of the French revolutionists." Without an immediate and total break of political relations with France, Freeman warned, disaster for the United States was virtually guaranteed.[27]

As if to showcase the infidel takeover that Freeman envisioned, Phineas Hedges put himself on the ballot for the May election to the state assembly. The *Goshen Repository* slammed him as an infidel, and Hedges did not win a seat. But events in Newburgh soon took a more drastic turn. Palmer, scheduled to speak on July Fourth, was probably already in town when, as townspeople later told it, Hedges and other infidels gathered on Sunday, June 30, to enact a blasphemous spoof of the holy sacraments. Reverend Johnston, the eventual successor to Reverend Freeman, heard the story from others and recounted it in his memoir, years later. "So bold and outrageous had these infatuated men become," Johnston wrote, "that on a Sabbath after the Lord's Supper had been administered, they collected at a spring near the place of public worship, and, in mockery of what had been done in the church, gave a piece of bread and some water to a dog, using the words of our blessed Redeemer, when he instituted the holy supper." Only days after the sacrilege, Phineas Hedges, "the principle actor of this impious transaction," was dead. He had been in his room when suddenly he fell to the floor, "convulsed with awful spasms," and died "without being able to utter a word." Whether the thirty-four-year-old Hedges had taken poison or "whether it was the immediate act of God," Johnston did not pretend to know, but "the proximity of the sudden and awful death of this man to the impious transaction of the preceding Sabbath leads the mind into fearful conjectures."[28]

Word spread of the shocking events in Newburgh. In November, Jedidiah Morse received a letter from West Greenwich, Connecticut, reporting that a "Society" of "infidels" in Newburgh had "*even* practiced a mock ceremony of the Lords supper." More than three decades later, Abner Cunningham expanded the story to make Hedges's death one of many visited upon the infidels of Newburgh. Another participant in the canine communion was returning home, Cunningham wrote, when suddenly he "exclaimed, 'my bowels are on fire, die I must,'—and die he did, that same night." Hedges "was found a lifeless lump of clay in his bed, the next morning," and then Denniston, "their printer, fell in a fit within three days after, and died." Four others drowned, including "a well-educated man" whose remains were found in frozen water. Birds had "picked his bones above, and the inhabitants of the watery element had picked his bones below the ice." Cunningham continued on in this vein, with gruesome invention. David Denniston, at any rate, had not died—he moved to New York City instead. Decades later, two men who were in Newburgh that fateful summer agreed that Johnston and Cunningham had "exaggerated, especially in reference to the deaths of several of the participants" and that Johnston's account "comes to us somewhat colored perhaps by religious prejudice."[29]

At century's end, political and religious anxiety had melded into a potent force. Tense diplomacy with France and the fear of war compounded suspicions of a sinister foreign influence behind the spread of infidelity in the United States. Federalists saw religious freethought as potentially seditious, a threat to the political stability of the nation because moral conduct rested, in their view, on religious faith. The Alien and Sedition Acts, meanwhile, proved to Democratic-Republicans the authoritarian bent of the Federalists who disregarded the civil liberties of the American people. Anxiety ran high on both sides. In this context, Palmer and the Newburgh freethinkers became like a lightning rod, attracting the ire of ministers who sensed a larger danger afoot in the land. Freeman and his colleagues were right to recognize changes in the way freethinkers presented themselves in public. Palmer, for one, no longer confined his lectures to select audiences behind closed doors. He could imagine sharing his message even more broadly now. Not content to be a spectral presence in the press, the infidel written *about*, he would now do the writing himself. He set himself to authoring a book, and he continued his travels farther afield, bringing his message to new audiences.

CHAPTER 10

Controversy Among Freethinkers

In December 1800, readers of the *Augusta Herald* learned that a newspaper in New York City, the *Temple of Reason*, intended "to destroy all belief in the christian religion, and to establish Deism in the United States." The editor of the *Augusta Chronicle* could easily guess the identity of the man behind the publication. "From the sentiments and language of this paper, we think it probable that its principle editor is Mr. Elihu Palmer who is well known, and has been much respected in this place." Palmer, who had last lived in Augusta in 1796, continued to have a mixed reputation there. He was a man "whose talents might enable him to do much good to mankind," the editor thought, "but whose efforts we are sorry to have reason to fear, are directed to the material injury of society." The *Temple of Reason* was "sufficiently blasphemous, to excite general abhorrence at the undertaking," yet the misguided Palmer expected a favorable response. He "seems to flatter himself that he shall meet with encouragement," the editor wrote, and that "his *kind* of reason, will eventually prevail over what he calls prejudice and fanaticism."[1]

The editor in Augusta was mistaken; the man behind the *Temple of Reason* was not Palmer but instead an Irishman named Denis Driscol. Yet the Georgia editor touched on an important matter when he spoke of the "*kind* of reason" the newspaper promoted. Freethinkers of different persuasions, some Christian, others not, wrestled with the fact that there were different ways of reasoning and of rationally assessing religious claims to truth. How was one to parse truly miraculous occurrences from mundane events that simply awaited an explanation? How could one tell divine revelation from human fiction? Freethinkers disagreed mightily with one another over how to understand the Bible and when to see the hand of God at work in the world. All claimed reason for themselves, of course, yet what "*kind* of reason" to trust remained a matter of contention.

In 1801, Palmer engaged with the editor Denis Driscol and with one Reverend John Hargrove, the leader of a Christian sect called Swedenborgians, over the question of how one could know religious truth. All three rejected mainstream Protestantism with its Trinitarian doctrine of Father, Son, and Holy Spirit. Hargrove believed that this was reason enough for them to find common ground. But he had not factored in the countervailing pressures. In the attempt to garner public support and social legitimacy, freethinkers often prioritized being right over being respectful of others' opinions. Perhaps the stakes seemed too high for a welcoming pluralism. After all, for many people being right about religion meant building a moral nation (or not) in the near future and experiencing salvation (or not) in the eternal afterlife. Freethinkers like Palmer, Driscol, and Hargrove cared deeply about their differences of opinion, and these differences prevented them from making common cause against established religions.

For Denis Driscol, it had been a long road to New York City. As a young man, he had left his native Ireland to study in Spain for the Catholic priesthood. Theologically restless, he became an Anglican curate in Cork, Ireland. By the early 1790s, Driscol had shed Anglicanism and settled on a devout deism that featured a stern God with an Old Testament personality but no Biblical miracles and no mediating Savior-Son. Driscol threw himself into politics, supporting the French Revolution as well as agrarian reforms in colonized Ireland. For editing the *Cork Gazette* accordingly, he spent two years in jail on charges of seditious libel. Freed in 1796, an entirely unrepentant Driscol, age thirty-four, resumed his political work against British rule. Two years later, Irishmen wielding iron pikes and the rage of accumulated injustice took on the British Empire. When well-armed soldiers crushed the rebellion of the United Irishmen, Driscol joined the many who fled to the United States, arriving just in time for the presidential election between John Adams, a supposed monarchist from Massachusetts, and Thomas Jefferson, purportedly a Jacobin infidel from Virginia.[2]

Driscol founded the nation's first overtly deist newspaper in November 1800, during the last month of the drawn-out presidential election. The weekly *Temple of Reason* supported Jefferson, and its provocative title referenced the rationalist religion of the French revolutionaries. The "torrents of illiberal reflections and unqualified abuse poured forth every day, through the channels of bigotry and intolerance, against Deists, have provoked this publication," Driscol wrote in the newspaper's first issue. Deism needed a defender, and the *Temple of Reason* would demonstrate "the purity of our doctrines and the soundness of our principles," while "exposing at the same time, the corruption of those of our adversaries." The *Temple of Reason* would also print philosophical and moral "disquisitions" of many kinds, along with "political reflections." In short, the newspaper gave Driscol a public forum for all of his favorite opinions. In this he had the Constitution on his side, he said, since its "immortal framers" had protected the right to "private and public opinion" in matters of religion. Although the First Amendment pertained only to the federal government, Driscol took the principle of free speech as an ideal that applied more generally to the nation's inhabitants. The Constitution served as a "shield" against Christian zealots who tried to monopolize freedom of expression and "refuse safety and protection to any, but to themselves."[3]

The "Deist's Creed" on the second page emphasized obedience to divine rules. All people "are bound to adore, worship and obey" the God who made all things. The deity is perfect and merciful, Driscol said, yet the rules set down by this "Father of the Universe" must be followed. Every man must control his passions and "abstain from all debaucheries and abuses of himself, which tend either to the destruction of his own being, or to the disordering of his faculties." Driscol might have meant drunkenness, nonmarital sex, masturbation, gluttony, and more. In any case, he believed that a judging God kept track of every individual and would "testify his favor or displeasure" with "rewards and punishments in a life to come."[4]

Driscol viewed Palmer as a deist like himself, at least initially. In describing a fully human Jesus as the original deist, Driscol added: "What could Paine, Volney, Palmer, or any other avowed Deist of the day, say more." The *Temple of Reason* reported on Palmer's Sunday lecture series titled "Investigation of Moral Truth, or Free Enquiry upon all Religious Subjects," and the newspaper praised the "discriminating precision" with which Palmer discussed the "moral principles by which human existence ought to be governed." In December, the paper reported that Palmer had delivered an "able and philosophical discourse" to "a very numerous and respectable audience" on the impossibility of the biblical flood. A morally perfect God would not drown his own creation, Palmer had said, but even if God had orchestrated a deluge, no ark could possibly carry all the animals and the food needed for such a long voyage. The story of the flood was both morally and logistically impossible, Palmer explained. The reviewer, likely Driscol himself, reported that "the subject was handled in a masterly manner (as indeed, is every other) by this enlightened Deist."[5]

When Driscol and Palmer conversed at greater length, they recognized their different conceptions of the divine. Driscol did not like what he heard, and he denounced Palmer's idea of a divine force immanent in all matter. Even though Palmer allowed for a divine intelligence, his materialism struck Driscol as atheistic. Atheism was "the very opposite to Deism," Driscol said, in that it means "the absolute denial of the living God." An atheist says that "nothing exists in the Universe but matter—eternal matter! and that there is neither infinite intelligence, nor infinite wisdom; but that all the organization of the world is the result of fate—blind chance and the happy effects of atoms or elements modified into various shapes and forms!" Driscol held to his version of a transcendent deity, and he could only "pity or despise those" who could not tell the difference between deism and atheism. Presumably, his pity included Palmer.[6]

The Irish editor could not see, or would not acknowledge, that Palmer's cosmology hovered somewhere within and beyond Driscol's version of deism. Palmer *combined* a divine power with an entirely materialist cosmology. His book, *Principles of Nature*, just recently completed, described endless matter eternally in motion, beyond which nothing exists—precisely Driscol's definition of atheism. But Palmer firmly rejected atheism and presumed the eternal existence of a ubiquitous and divine power. Inconsistent in his descriptions of divinity, Palmer sometimes referred to a divine intelligence that sounded sentient and intentional, while at other times he reiterated that nothing existed outside of matter. He reached for a vocabulary that could elide Driscol's bounded categories of, on the one hand, a narrowly framed deism with a stern and judging God and, on the other, a lifeless and mechanical materialist atheism. Neither fit Palmer's thinking of divinely infused matter, a mysterious life force within all things in the universe. Given the absence of a vitalist idiom, Palmer resorted to using deist terminology, the most capacious religious vocabulary then available to him. For example, he titled a December lecture, "The Creation is the Bible of the Deist." He also continued to use a language of God. The cosmos he imagined was infused with an eternal and omnipresent power, and what should one call that, if not God? Palmer would have recognized, however, that Driscol's views of God were closer to those held by many Christians than they were to Palmer's conception of a divine life force in all matter.[7]

Critics did not care to parse the different versions of freethought. They knew enough already. The *Temple of Reason* was an "infamous and execrable" rag, one editor in Philadelphia wrote. A Georgetown editor spotted an attack on the Christian faith of its readers. The deist newspaper dared to say that Christianity offers only "delirium and vice" and "will never cease to generate the greatest evils among mankind." Driscol "boldly assails the divine character of the blessed REDEEMER," the editor continued, and will surely contend, as Godwin and others had, that "*there is no God*—that *Death is only an eternal Sleep.*" One editor in Harrisburg, Pennsylvania, let fly his raw anti-Irish bigotry, describing Driscol as "one of those vipers that has been brought to us frozen from the bogs of Ireland." Having been "restored to life by our fire-sides," Driscol offered only "Irish Gratitude," meaning, apparently, none at all. The editor hoped soon to see Driscol along with the printer William Duane "and many others, skipping like rats to their land of potatoes," where they might more easily be hanged than in the United States. These vicious sentiments showcased loathing for the uprising in Ireland (for which Driscol ought to be hanged) as well as for his deism. The Harrisburg editor felt that those who opposed Christianity and took up arms against British rule in Ireland did not deserve to live.[8]

Hateful speech had become the norm during the polarizing presidential campaign of 1800. Jefferson's supporters called out Federalists as closet monarchists who secretly loathed American democracy, while Adams's backers depicted Jefferson as a dangerous infidel, complete with horns and a tail. Hostile hyperbole narrowed the rhetorical field for those who saw bipartisanship as possible, reasonable, or even a good idea. Newspapers turned up the partisan heat like never before. Republican editors, in particular, had an ax to grind. The Sedition Act of 1798 had put more than a dozen editors in jail for criticizing the Adams administration, and the maltreatment had radicalized rather than cowed its victims. To persecuted printers, a nonpartisan approach to delivering the news now seemed outdated, dishonest, and dangerous. David Denniston moved from Newburgh to New York City and declared in his newly founded *American Citizen* that if impartiality meant "equal attachment to aristocracy as to republicanism," his newspaper must reject neutrality as "ruinous to the best interests of mankind." It would be far better to earn the trust of readers by speaking clearly for or against the presidential contestants, only one of whom could be a worthy leader. Open partisan politicking, once considered uncouth, had become necessary, even virtuous, in the fierce contest for the nation's future.[9]

Palmer knew what kind of abuse to expect, then, as he prepared his own book for the press. A blind man could write a book only with help, and that aid came from Mrs. Mary Powell, who, with her husband, Benjamin, ran the boardinghouse Palmer had lived in for some time. Mary Powell was adept at taking dictation, and Palmer spoke fluently, without frequent recourse to revision. In November 1800, he advertised that his book, *Principles of Nature; Or a Development of the Moral Causes of Happiness and Misery among the Human Species*, was finished and would "be put to press as soon as a sufficient number of subscribers appear, to defray the expenses." The book ran to about three hundred duodecimo pages (about seven by five inches), would include a "good likeness of the author," and cost one dollar. To whet the reader's appetite, Palmer noted that the book exposes "the errors of Ancient Systems of Theology" and will defuse the "unreasonable anxiety and terror" about a future state of "terror and torment." Palmer also mentioned his blindness. Although the author "labours under one of the severest of all human misfortunes, the total loss of sight," the advertisement read, he hoped to promote "the moral progress of the human race, by dissipating the clouds of superstition" which have for so long "obstructed the moral vision of the intelligent world." Insight did not require eyesight, he suggested. The book elucidated the universal principles undergirding all life and offered a morality based on the natural world, the true understanding of which would lead to happiness for all human beings. By May, the book had been printed and could be purchased in various locations in town.[10]

Eager to share his ideas beyond New York City, Palmer planned a trip to Philadelphia. Driscol had suspended the *Temple of Reason* in February for lack of funds and then resumed the paper in Philadelphia a few months later. The two men remained friendly, and when Palmer came to Philadelphia that summer, Driscol helped host Palmer and promote his lectures. At first, the prospects looked good for Palmer's visit. Members of the Universalist Church granted him permission to speak in their church on the evening of Sunday, July 5, 1801. But in a reprise of Palmer's expulsion from the Universalist pulpit nine years before, it was not to be. On the evening of the lecture, people arrived at the Universalist Church only to find a notice on the closed door. Mr. Palmer would not preach there after all, the notice said, "it being contrary to the wishes of the church." The question of Palmer's lecture had been put to a vote following the morning service, and a majority of "old women and bigots," in Driscol's words, had decided against it. Driscol derided the biblical stories that would have been welcome in place of Palmer's lecture on morality. The "magic tricks of Moses" or a story about "Jonah and the whale" would have met with loud applause, he mocked. If only Palmer would "abandon his reason" and adopt the "mad folly" of Christianity, if only he would "roar, and scream" his self-loathing as a sinner, then the church would have received him warmly. What a shame, the *Temple of Reason* lamented, "that the truth-searching and liberal parts of the community, and they are not few, should be deprived of the benefit and talents of men" who only wish to "promote the moral and intellectual happiness of their fellow-citizens." Driscol turned the Universalists' rejection of Palmer into a call for action. "It is painful to see superstition have her temples, and delusion its altars, while philosophy and truth have to wander abroad, like aliens or strangers in the land!" Perhaps the friends of truth "are *now* convinced of the necessity of erecting a building, where they may be sheltered and protected from the persecution of ignorance and the malice of bigotry."[11]

By barring Palmer from their pulpit, Driscol implied, the Universalists opened themselves to charges of doctrinaire rigidity and intolerance. They were not as liberal as they seemed. The belief that all souls will eventually be saved is "liberal and benevolent enough," he wrote, but their treatment of Palmer suggested that if salvation were up to them, they might make exceptions. "Those that would not admit Mr. Palmer and his hearers into their little church in Lombard-street," Driscol wrote, "would place a similar *notice* on the gates of heaven." The Universalists either preached a generosity of spirit they did not actually feel, Driscol said, or they were unwilling to put it into practice. They should "abandon their pretensions to universalism, or else act with more liberality and consistency in future."[12]

Did the closed door of the Universalist church trouble Palmer? It is hard to know. The Universalists' refusal to let him speak made for a déjà vu experience, but this time with a pleasant twist. In 1792, his candor with the Universalist spokesperson, Israel Israel, had deprived him of the last possible church home he could imagine for himself at the time. He had enjoyed preaching from a pulpit on the corruptions of Christianity. With no Unitarian meeting yet formed in Philadelphia, the Universalists were his last remaining hope. The fit was uncomfortable, but expulsion was worse. The next best option had been John Fitch's Deistical Society, but none of the society members stuck up for him in the character assassination that followed his announced lecture against the divinity of Jesus. Now, in 1801, Palmer's experience was dramatically different. For one thing, he was no longer trying to speak as a minister from within the Christian fold, and charges of ministerial hypocrisy could not stick. More important, Paine's *Age of Reason* with its outright rejection of Christianity, and the affirmation of the freethinking groups in New York City and Newburgh, had given Palmer a language of deism along with moral support and a thicker skin. This time, when the Universalists of Philadelphia once more barred Palmer from speaking, he had backup. Driscol mounted a quick defense of Palmer in his newspaper, denoting him a truth seeker and attacking as hollow the liberal pretensions of the Universalists. The shut door of the church showcased their close-mindedness, Driscol implied. But Palmer no longer needed the attention of the Universalists, or of any other Christian sect. He believed he could find more courageous, worthy audiences elsewhere.

Fair to say, neither Driscol nor Palmer demonstrated irenic forbearance themselves. Reverend John Hargrove found out the hard way that Driscol and Palmer harbored hostility toward even the most freethinking Christians. Hargrove had left the Trinitarian fold to become a Swedenborgian, which was then a small denomination. His rejection of the Trinity made him a kind of deist too, he thought. But when he tried to engage with Driscol and Palmer, he met with scorn. Generosity among freethinkers could be in short supply despite a strong rhetoric of religious tolerance, and when Driscol and Palmer derided the Swedenborgian minister, he responded in kind.

The Irish-born Hargrove had been a Methodist minister in Maryland when he decided in the 1790s to counter the writings of the Swedish scientist and mystic Emanuel Swedenborg. The Swedenborgian dissent from Christian orthodoxy centered on the Trinity, the tripartite Godhead agreed upon at the fourth-century Council of Nicaea. Swedenborg believed instead that God was singular and that Jesus was the manifestation of the one and only God. Powerful visions and dreams brought Swedenborg direct and personal messages from Jesus-as-God. In mystical experiences, Swedenborg traveled to heaven and to hell, spoke with angels and with people who had died, and received divine inspiration for his writings. He had it on the highest authority that the Second Coming had already taken place and was, in fact, an ongoing occurrence.[13]

As Hargrove read, he found Swedenborg surprisingly persuasive. Science and mystical religion melded easily in Hargrove's thinking, as it had for the denomination's founder. Swedenborg, a polymath in geometry, chemistry, physiology, and metallurgy, had conversed with angels, demons, and spirits from other planets, and his writings were directly inspired by divine revelation. Hargrove came to revere Swedenborg as a mystic and, like his role model, studied science. Hargrove wrote essays on the telescope, the air pump, an electrical machine, the Milky Way, and the properties of matter. He described atoms as eternal but inert, moved only by external forces such as gravity and electricity. Hargrove was a rational, mystical, and scientifically minded Christian all at once.[14]

After his conversion, Hargrove became the first minister of the New Jerusalem Church in Baltimore, the first Swedenborgian Church in the United States. Following Swedenborg, Hargrove believed "that GOD is ONE (and not three) both in essence and in person." Hargrove differed from Unitarians who also disavowed the holy Trinity, but whose singular God was distinct from Jesus. Unitarians debated whether Jesus was fully human or partially divine, but they knew he was not God. Hargrove's Jesus *was* God. Hargrove's non-Trinitarian faith was a reformed version of Christianity but was Christianity nonetheless, and Hargrove revered the Bible as the revealed word of God. Trinitarian Christians, however, the nation's Protestant majority, rejected Swedenborgianism as heretical. In Baltimore, Hargrove's former Methodist co-religionists were especially hostile, and their name-calling of Swedenborgians devolved to "false pretenders," "hypocrites," "ignorant understrappers," and "common prostitutes."[15]

In his opposition to Trinitarian orthodoxy, Hargrove thought he might make common cause with deists like Denis Driscol. Deists also envisioned a singular God and disavowed Trinitarian belief—shared assumptions, Hargrove thought, from which to begin a conversation. The mistake the deists made was akin to that of the Unitarians, he thought. Rather than recognizing Jesus as God, the Unitarians and deists demoted Jesus. Some deists still revered Jesus as a moral teacher and a role model, while others dismissed him as an imposter. Yet such errors need not preclude a reasoned conversation, and Hargrove hoped the readers of the *Temple of Reason* would reconsider his enlightened, rational, non-Trinitarian version of Christianity.

If Hargrove had been toying with the idea of contacting the editor of the *Temple of Reason*, the issue on June 17, 1801, pushed him to take action. The offending piece was John Hollis's "*Some Doubts Respecting the Death, Resurrection, and Ascension of Jesus Christ*," first published in 1797 for John Fellows and now serialized in the *Temple of Reason*. Jesus had been a good man and entirely human, Hollis had written. Hargrove reached for quill and paper to set the matter straight. Surely a man like Driscol could respect an enlightened form of Christianity and would recognize Hargrove as an ally in the push against misguided Trinitarianism. Driscol was a "good deist," Hargrove wrote to his fellow Irishman, a characterization Hargrove would "not disavow" for himself either. The world's future rested on "the united efforts of all the lovers of truth" of whatever persuasion, Hargrove continued. "*Reason* and *Religion* shall fully unite their sacred and all-powerful influence in promoting truth and righteousness." Hargrove expected a friendly response to his courteous letter. He imagined an ongoing conversation on the pages of the *Temple of Reason* in which Hargrove explained away any confusion about the Bible's narratives and cleared up any doubts regarding Jesus's divinity. If Driscol liked this first letter, Hargrove added, he would gladly follow it up with an explanation of "what became of the natural body of Jesus" after his death.[16]

Driscol rejected the idea out of hand. He declined to publish Hargrove's letter and printed instead that the *Temple of Reason* was "not established for every furious fanatic and wild visionary to *rant* and *cant* away in it." Reproducing Hargrove's letter would be akin to placing "arms into the hands of our religious and bigoted enemies," Driscol wrote in his newspaper. Surely that was taking "*impartiality too far*, and giving the advocates of superstition advantages" to which they were not entitled. After all, which Christian minister of whatever sect, "from the *old* to the *New Jerusalem*," will "open the doors of his church" to allow a deist to "combat and expose" Christian doctrine? None, Driscol wrote, because "not one is to be found." Hargrove should learn the creed "of a *real* deist," Driscol informed him, namely that "there is but one God!" Defending the category of deism from encroachment by the Swedenborgian minister, Driscol insisted that no deism worthy of the name allowed for a divine Jesus.[17]

Taken aback but persistent, Hargrove wrote a second letter to Driscol, noting that deists and Swedenborgians, with their shared opposition to dominant Trinitarians, should be able to have civil conversations about religion. But Driscol responded to Hargrove's second letter as he had to the first, publicly mocking the author's message without reprinting it. All Christians made the foundational mistake of believing the Bible was divine revelation, Driscol said, and there the folly begins. Yet no matter how "*absurd* in creed or *extravagant* in practice," such as "*naked exhibitions*, or *midnight orgies*," not one Christian sect admits to being "wild, extravagant, foolish or ridiculous." Every "dissenter is always in the right, and all the rest are unhappily in the wrong!" Driscol defended his decision not to print Hargrove's letters, saying that bigots did not deserve such generosity because they never responded in kind. Driscol referenced the Universalists' recent refusal to let Palmer speak in Philadelphia. "It is to be hoped, when Mr. Palmer visits Baltimore, that the members of the New Jerusalem will not act so." Driscol challenged Hargrove to "set the example of 'liberal' himself, before he can justly accuse others of illiberality."[18]

Frustrated by Driscol's refusal to engage in a real conversation on the printed page, Hargrove started his own newspaper. For the three months of its existence, the *Temple of Truth* reprinted Hargrove's missives to Driscol, along with the latter's disparaging replies. Just as important, Hargrove reviewed Palmer's lectures in Baltimore, using them as a way to explain the differences between reasonable and unreasonable methods of biblical interpretation. Throughout, Hargrove showcased his knowledge about scientific matters, asserting himself as a methodical, clear-eyed, rational thinker.[19]

Having heard Palmer speak in Baltimore before a "numerous and respectable audience," Hargrove conceded that Palmer "possesses considerable talents as an extempore speaker," even if his style was "rather *turgid and too rhetorical.*" Hargrove focused on the flaws in Palmer's thinking and countered them point by point. Palmer "need not tauntingly cry out, (as he did last Sunday night) why does not God work miracles now to overturn the present growing infidelity of the age?" Spectacular miracles were not necessary now that people are "capable of entering more intellectually into the evidences" for the Christian faith. God will overthrow infidelity "in his own good time," Hargrove wrote, by "THE EVIDENCE AND POWER OF GENUINE TRUTH." To Palmer's argument that miraculous intervention suggested a design flaw in God's creation, an impossibility if God was perfect, Hargrove replied: who are we as humans to claim to know all the divine laws of nature? Even Isaac Newton, that "profound Christian philosopher" who understood the laws of nature better than anyone, still "subscribed to the Christian system" and considered miracles "not incompatible or discordant to the grand and invariable laws of nature."[20]

Worst of all, in Hargrove's opinion, was Palmer's superficial and misguided method of biblical interpretation. Palmer defined the term "faith" in ways Hargrove found "very lame, imperfect, and discordant to the general tenor" of the Bible. Palmer's "pretended proofs" of the Bible's inaccuracy were always "a mere play on words," Hargrove complained, "an egregious abuse of the *letter* of the Scriptures." Like Paine, Palmer submitted the Scriptures to a literalist reading that exposed them as illogical and impossible. This was a tiresome sleight of hand, Hargrove thought, a cheap trick. Palmer was not honest, not trustworthy, in his reading of Scripture. But because Palmer might persuade some listeners, Hargrove published a lengthy counterargument, one that described true religion as mystical *and* rational.[21]

Pedantic insistence on only the most obvious and literal understanding of a biblical story would never do, Hargrove explained. Finite human reason was inadequate to the task of apprehending divine truth. One needed

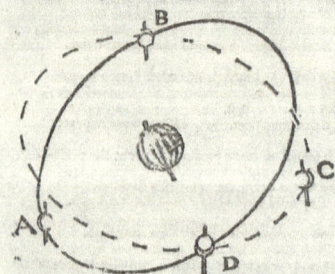

FIGURE 8. Pages from John Hargrove's newspaper, the *Temple of Truth*. The Swedenborgian minister presented himself as in equal part scientifically minded and religiously devout. He argued against Elihu Palmer's literalist reading of the Bible and explained how the biblical miracles were true.
Courtesy of the University of Minnesota Library.

a "spiritual method of interpreting the holy scriptures," a "spiritual apprehension." With an "inward perception" of the harmony within the Bible, "the apparent inconsistencies and absurdities of the letter vanish and no longer give offence." What seemed nonsensical to a superficial reader acquired "divine weight and consequence" when read with the heart as well as the mind. Palmer missed the difference between the mere letter of the

Gospel and the wisdom shimmering behind the word. Hargrove acknowledged that his own method of biblical interpretation might seem whimsical, indeterminate, and prone to error. A greater danger, however, lay in being too literal (as Jews were, he said). Hargrove believed in mystical access to divine truths, and he followed Swedenborg in claiming that God still spoke to believers. There are still "*out-pourings*, or *revelations*," he said, but only for those open to the message. Palmer misused his reason to block incoming messages from the Holy.[22]

In fact, Hargrove explained, Palmer perfectly demonstrated how *not* to interpret Scripture. Palmer had quoted the Gospel of Mark on the ability of true believers to cast out devils in Jesus's name, to speak with new tongues, take up serpents, drink "deadly things" without harm, and heal the sick with a laying on of hands. No living Christian could accomplish any of this, Palmer had said, so true believers must no longer exist. Ridiculous, Hargrove replied. Miracles had indeed ceased in the natural world, but they continued to operate in the spiritual world. Miracles worked on the *spirits* of believers. Palmer mistook heaven and hell to be physical places when in fact they exist within every human heart. Are we proud, covetous, or hateful? Wherever "evil affections" are, Hargrove said, there too is hell and the devil. But a man may "expel these evils from his heart," thereby casting out devils just as Mark had said, namely "in the name of Jesus; that is, by an appropriation of the *quality* of the *divine wisdom* of God manifested unto him." A man with a new heart speaks with a new tongue, one "fit to minister grace to his hearers." As to the serpents, Hargrove continued, these were obviously metaphorical images of evil influences—the deception of the senses, for example, or too great an attachment to material objects. So, too, the metaphor of drinking a "deadly thing." How ignorant to assume this meant a common poison that could kill the body! At issue here was not the physical body but *spiritual* sickness and death. A true believer could "drink errors, and false principles, either from bad books, bad company, or bad teachers, and yet not feel any hurt to his soul." Palmer's perversely literal reading of the Bible allowed him to mock the message. His notions were "subversive of all the sweets of experimental religion, and civil government: gloomy as the night, wavering as the wind, unsettled as the ocean, destructive as the pestilence, and perishing as the grass."[23]

To Hargrove's claim that Palmer's ideas were "subversive . . . of civil government," Driscol in Philadelphia had a quick comeback. Claims of political subversion had a "malicious drift," the deist editor said, and required a firm rebuttal. The Sedition Act had taught every Republican the very real threat that lurked behind the smear of treason. Even though Jefferson sat in the White House and the Sedition Act had lapsed in March, Driscol sprang to deism's defense. Driscol saw "no instance of deists having distracted the peace of a single community." Besides, "Mr. Palmer's principles are well known, and tried as Democratic," and he is "consequently a friend to all republican institutions." Insisting that "Mr. Palmer is no trimming priest, or temporizing patriot," Driscol rebuffed Hargrove's effort to meld religious skepticism with political subversion.[24]

There would be no agreement between Driscol and Hargrove—not on miracles, on Jesus, or on Palmer's lectures. The sparring continued until October, when the *Temple of Truth* folded. Hargrove had spent eight dollars of his own money (his annual salary might have been about a hundred dollars) plus "all his labor as chief editor" to produce the paper. He had anticipated "more extensive co-operation" from "christian brethren of various denominations" in the fight against Palmer's irreverence and Driscol's disdain. Hargrove recognized that his church stood on the edge of respectable Protestantism. The Swedenborgian belief in ongoing revelation and its anti-Trinitarianism put it there. Like Driscol, Hargrove saw bigotry and prejudice among established Christian sects, and as the leader of a marginal new church, he felt himself the target of their suspicion. Yet Hargrove had hoped his clerical compatriots would make common cause against infidelity despite their doctrinal differences. In this, he was disappointed. He had made "the most liberal proposals" to "many of the most influential characters of this city" and beyond (including Jedidiah Morse in Massachusetts), "but to no effect." Of all the clergy in Baltimore, only the Catholic bishop, John Carroll, had subscribed to Hargrove's newspaper. Not one Protestant minister joined his cause. Hargrove consoled himself that the members of his own New Jerusalem Church, along with "about 180 of his fellow citizens of other denominations, many of whom are the most enlightened and respectable citizens of Baltimore," had "nobly conquered the infernal spirits of bigotry and sectarian prejudice which have too long infested the church of Christ." Such prejudice, he might have added, tainted conversations among freethinkers as well. Mutual forbearance for another's opinion did not seem as important as demonstrating the superiority of one's own religious view, making it harder for freethinkers to forge alliances.[25]

Alert to substantive differences on religious truth and how to know it, freethinkers did not seek out common ground. Driscol loathed Hargrove's mystical reading of the Bible and his belief in Jesus-as-God, but he also rebuffed as atheistic Palmer's ideas of eternal matter. Hargrove saw himself occupying a position between the "fanaticism" of Trinitarian Christianity and the bankrupt rationalism of the "mere deist" who relies on only human reason. His religious truths were "too *rational* for the *mere fanatic*," Hargrove said, "and too *spiritual* for the *mere deist*." Palmer was happy to go along with Driscol's deism, but not with Hargrove's mystical Christianity. Everyone believed they had reason on their side. Maybe the stakes seemed too high to live and let live, to allow openly for the possibility of one's own error. This was no parlor game, after all. Public exchanges among religious liberals about their convictions were a bid for social respectability and influence. Driscol keenly felt the marginal status of deists who did not have their own established lecture halls. Giving space in his newspaper to Hargrove seemed like aiding the enemy. Hargrove, meanwhile, went to great lengths and personal expense to warn people about the insidious messages of Palmer and Driscol.[26]

Despite professions of support for religious freedom and tolerance, there was not much reaching across doctrinal aisles for these freethinkers. They found no single religious banner around which to unify. That was the thing about freedom of conscience: it might make for a church of one. As Thomas Paine put it, "My own mind is my own church." That self-reliance, while empowering on an individual level, got in the way of political alliances and left freethinkers vulnerable to political attack.[27]

CHAPTER 11

Weaponizing Freethought

THE LETTER FROM Paris addressed Elihu Palmer as "Dear Friend" and carried the date "February 21, 1802, since the Fable of Christ." The writer knew Palmer would appreciate his poke at Christianity. They had not yet met in person, but Thomas Paine had read *Principles of Nature* and wrote to compliment Palmer on "the excellent work you have published." Paine especially commended Palmer on his forthright prose: "I see you have thought deeply on the subject," Paine wrote, "and expressed your thoughts in a strong and clear style." In matters of religion, Paine continued, a "hinting and intimating manner of writing" fails to persuade. "It is necessary to be bold," he wrote. "Some people can be reasoned into sense, and others must be shocked into it. Say a bold thing that will stagger them, and they will begin to think." Paine shared with Palmer his plan to return to America in a few months, carrying with him new ammunition against Christianity. He had "a third part of the Age of Reason" ready to print upon arrival in the United States, and he believed it would "make a stronger impression than anything I have yet published on the subject." Paine closed his letter with "Yours in friendship." Praise from this famous revolutionary meant the world to Palmer, who admired and emulated Paine's *Age of Reason*. Palmer was almost three decades younger than his role model, but in the cause against Christianity, they were now colleagues.[1]

With his book as his calling card, Palmer could join the transatlantic network of freethinkers. He could ship the volume to London or Paris and hope to enter cosmopolitan conversations with the likes of Paine. But even as Palmer imagined himself as part of an international cohort of philosophers, he found himself ensnared by the bitter partisanship that continued to shape American politics after the election of Jefferson to the presidency.

In what Jefferson called the revolution of 1800, President John Adams relinquished the nation's highest office to his nemesis, enacting a peaceful transfer of power to his successor. Yet the transition remained fraught. Federalists continued to worry that the Francophile freethinker in the White House might unravel the nation's moral fabric. Republicans, meanwhile, fought among themselves for positions of political leadership. During this time of partisanship and strife, Palmer's openly anti-Christian writings and speeches and his friendly association with Paine made him a convenient target. Scandal mongers recognized that a sure way to inflict harm on political opponents was to associate them with Palmer. His freethought could be deployed for a partisan cause, weaponized in the contest for political influence.[2]

The year 1802 had gotten off to a fine start for Palmer, with no hint of the troubles to come. That winter he offered a new series of ten political lectures on Wednesday evenings that expanded his repertoire considerably beyond the familiar subjects of morality and theology. He discussed the Constitution of 1787 with its separation of powers ("the most rational system of government ever known in the world") and compared it favorably to the unwritten constitution in England, offering a "minute investigation of its Anglo-Saxon form, as well as the various mutations through which it passed." Then he "took a comprehensive view of the revolution in France, of the different constitutions which have been established in the republic, of the factions that have arisen, and of the usurper, Bonaparte." The synopses appeared in the *American Citizen*, curated by David Denniston, Palmer's freethinking friend who had moved from Newburgh to edit what was then New York City's only Republican newspaper. Of course Denniston offered favorable reports, yet he also had reason to be genuinely impressed with Palmer's ability to absorb and digest so much information through listening, and then, without recourse to written notes, deliver it in "a very pleasing and instructive manner." Denniston described Palmer's hour-long lectures as "truly philosophic, and consequently instructive," and his language as "elegant and impressive."[3]

Palmer's book, *Principles of Nature*, had sold well enough to warrant a second edition in May, with five new chapters. Two of these expressed more boldly than ever before the idea that all things are made of singular matter that registers sensation on the level of its atoms. A chapter titled "Universal Benevolence" explained the physical connection among all living creatures and the way that pain accrues in sensate matter. The final chapter, "Philosophical Immortality," described once more the "immortality of sensation in the aggregate mass of sensitive and intelligent life." Palmer was committed to the concept of sensate matter and believed that once people accepted this natural fact, their hearts, minds, and behavior would change for the better.[4]

Meanwhile, he nurtured his network of freethinkers. His blindness notwithstanding, Palmer traveled in teeth-rattling stage coaches and on listing boats. Upon arrival, he navigated unfamiliar streets, boardinghouses, and lecture platforms. In May and June, he lectured to Philadelphia audiences he could not see, listening for their responses to his message. Then he sailed once more up the Hudson River to Newburgh. The local society of freethinkers was "closely connected with the one in New-York," one critic reported. "President Palmer visits them frequently," and over the summer "they held secret meetings." Denniston probably accompanied Palmer on this trip, because Palmer was seen strolling through Newburgh "with Mr. David Denniston under one arm, and Mr. Charles Clinton under the other." Skeptics in town felt emboldened to take action. In what might be the first documented instance of objection to school prayer, freethinking parents in Newburgh removed their children "from a school, because the teacher would open and close with prayer." Affronted by the teacher's efforts to indoctrinate their children, the parents set up "another teacher in opposition to him." The freethinkers had momentum, and they pushed for freedom of conscience.[5]

All summer, Palmer heard the speculation about Paine's return to the United States, much of it hostile. Paine's standing had dropped precipitously since he left America in 1787, even though he had set sail for England as a celebrated hero, the most powerful propagandist of the American Revolution. In the dark days of the war, General Washington had called upon him to shore up the flagging spirits of the American troops. Paine penned *The American Crisis* by firelight in the field of battle, writing that these were "the times that try men's souls." He had inspired weary soldiers with words of heroic patriotism and promised the nation's eternal gratitude for their sacrifices. Now the nation's political leaders sought political stability, not more rebellion, and Paine, that eternal revolutionary, was no longer welcome. Many thought he was not even a true friend to the United States.

Two things had turned Americans against Paine. The first was his shockingly derisive treatment of Christianity. Few believed his claim that he wrote *Age of Reason* to offset the atheism that had bloomed during the French Revolution. Although he waxed eloquent about a benevolent Creator-God who merited gratitude for the life-sustaining bounty of the natural world, his descriptions of deist religion were swamped by his flamboyant denunciations of the Bible. Paine's relentless takedown of Christian beliefs and clergy made charges of atheism stick, and American common sense insisted that atheism and republicanism did not mix. The second blow to Paine's reputation came with his published tirade about President Washington's character. Washington had not intervened with French authorities during the eleven months Paine had spent in a Parisian jail, and in 1796 Paine dipped pen in bitter ink to call it a callous disregard for his life. Never mind that Washington had not fully known of Paine's situation. Paine saw a flaw in the president's constitution—an absence of heart. His "constitutional indifference" to other people made him incapable of friendship, Paine wrote. Some people had mistaken Washington's "cold, hermaphrodite faculty" for the admirable traits of "prudence, moderation and impartiality." But no—the president was simply a self-serving "hypocrite," reptilian at his core. Paine's public disrespect for the war-hero-turned-president went beyond what most Americans could tolerate. Even Paine's supporters stopped naming him in their celebratory toasts on feast days. For the party of Jefferson, Paine had become a liability.[6]

When Federalists learned that President Jefferson had invited Paine to sail on a US naval ship from France to the United States, their newspapers went on the attack. "So perfectly blasted is the reputation of Thomas Paine," wrote the Philadelphia *Gazette* in June 1802, that "even in Paris, he can associate only with the lowest and vilest of the rabble." Paine had been useful in the American Revolution, the *Gazette* conceded, but "in France he became the tool of the regicides" and had "joined to inflame the rabble in dragging their sovereign to the scaffold, and erecting the standard of Jacobinism on the ruins of the government." This claim was patently untrue. Citizen Paine had been arrested by his more radical comrades precisely because he had pleaded with the French Assembly to spare the life of the deposed king. But the *Gazette*'s larger point was that Paine threatened the political and social order. He had tried to destroy every government under which he had ever lived, the *Gazette* asserted, and had stoked the violence in France. Furthermore, the "corruptions of his private life are almost without example." Paine "used every exertion to corrupt the morals of youth," was drunk every day, and is "fast sinking into the grave," jeering and cursing the whole way. "This is the man whom we kindly invite to our shores!!!" The president was clearly out of his mind. Paine would bring with him "all his lewdness, infidelity, and democracy." Republicans saw through the Federalist strategy of tarring Jefferson with the brush of Paine. One Republican editor wrote that when "pell-mell, Jefferson, and Paine, and deism, and infidelity, are jumbled together without order or mercy, we can see in such noisy nonsense nothing but the yelpings of a set of [Federalist] bloodhounds."[7]

In this moment of intense partisan strife, Palmer's freethought proved as useful as Paine's for the purpose of discrediting anyone associated with him. A pamphlet attacking Palmer in September 1802 came not from a Federalist writer but from a supporter of the Republican vice president, Aaron Burr. The author, John Wood, set out to discredit Burr's Republican competition, New York governor George Clinton and his nephew, DeWitt Clinton, then a state senator and soon to be mayor of New York. Wood targeted the Clintonian Republicans by linking them to Palmer and his group of freethinkers. The title of the fifty-six page pamphlet, *A Full Exposition of the Clintonian Faction, and the Society of the Columbian Illuminati*, declared what lay within its pages. Wood raised the specter of conspiracy, renaming the Deistical Society of New York as the "Society of the Columbian Illuminati," and maligning it as a secretive and seditious group of infidels. In reviving the fears of atheist infiltration that had panicked Federalist clergy in and after 1798, Wood tapped into an abiding anxiety about the relationship between irreligion and immorality. But the real targets of Wood's pamphlet were the Clinton-allied Republicans who, Wood claimed, had supposedly joined the "Columbian Illuminati" in great numbers.[8]

In Wood's telling, the cultish "Illuminati" demanded an obedience to "President Palmer" that was antithetical to the intellectual independence required of any free citizen. Every member of the society supposedly vowed "a faithful and complete surrender" of their private judgment and pledged to serve the order with "my fortune, my honour and my blood." Admittance to the highest grade in the "Illuminati" required an oath of "perpetual silence, and unshaken loyalty, and submission to the order, in the person of our President." Wood suggested that the pro-Clinton Republicans who joined the "Illuminati"—he claimed to have a list of ninety-five!—had dedicated themselves to the deist cult rather than to the nation and its political institutions. Supporters' "love for Mr. De Witt Clinton, proceeds in a great measure from an idea that he is a deist," Wood said, and on that supposition these fanatics "will almost hazard their lives in his behalf." Wood implied that pro-Clinton Republicans had compromised their intellectual independence and their fealty to the nation and thereby forfeited their legitimacy as political leaders.[9]

Wood renamed and reimagined a group of religious freethinkers that really did exist, the Deistical Society of New York, to make a more persuasive and frightening case against the pro-Clinton Republicans. Because there are no membership lists or meeting minutes of the Deistical Society that Palmer founded in 1796, any full accounting of participants remains impossible. Were there really ninety-five? Philip Freneau, the freethinking poet (and cousin of Isaac Ledyard) participated in the society, as did Palmer's friends William Carver and David Denniston. No other members have been confirmed. The Deistical Society was not, in fact, a clandestine group, but in Wood's hands it became a franchise of the international "Illuminati" so vividly described by the Scottish professor John Robison. Robison's book, *Proofs of a Conspiracy Against All the Religions and Governments of Europe, Carried on in the Secret Meetings of Free Masons, Illuminati, and Reading Societies*, had alarmed American readers since its publication in 1798, and men like Jedidiah Morse were still convinced of its merits. Wood played on these fears, describing "President Palmer" as "the Weishaupt of the order," a reference to the German founder of the banned Order of the Illuminati in Bavaria. No longer would Reverend Morse have to learn from "foreign professors" like Robison about the infiltration of atheists, Wood claimed. Morse could simply write to the Republican mayor of New York, Edward Livingston, to learn how "Elihu Palmer, a blind preacher," and the editor David Denniston, had banded together with "many other zealous Clintonians" to oppose Christianity and ruin the republic.[10]

According to Wood, the "Columbian Illuminati" attracted radical riff-raff that hailed from both sides of the Atlantic. The Democratic-Republican Society of New York had disbanded, yet the "scattered dregs of these Jacobin infidels" had joined Palmer, said Wood, as had the "imported scum of the Edinburgh Convention" and the "banished rebels of Ireland," meaning United Irishmen like Denis Driscol, editor of the *Temple of Reason*. Radicals from different places brought to the nation "a combination of treachery, of indigence, of frenzy, intemperance, and every species of polluted baseness, for the purpose of combatting religion, virtue and wisdom." These schemers were neither "novices" nor "strangers to the art of cunning or deceit," Wood declared. They instituted secretive and mystical customs and codes, much like those of the freemasons. The members met according to grades and pledged "to renounce all form of worship whatever." Palmer's *Principles of Nature* was the required "text book" for the members, who had to declare their allegiance to the "whimsical jacobinism of Paine, and the wild philosophy of his disciple blind Palmer."[11]

Wood insisted that the greatest danger lay in the intended political takeover. Every member of the "Illuminati" was a Republican of the Clintonian persuasion. They planned to remove Christians from positions of political influence and "get all the public offices of the United States, filled with deists." One unnamed state legislator "who was foisted in by the Clinton interest, is an avowed supporter and hearer of the President Palmer; and for ought I know, also a member of the highest grade among the Illuminati." Wood's implied and readily understood point was that a deist could not also be a loyal citizen. If his pamphlet had done its work, Wood wrote, the "link which connects the infidels of New-York with the Clinton family, must now be obvious." The "mutual affection and sympathy which exist between Mr. Clinton and the Columbian Illuminati" served to discredit both.[12]

Federalists viewed with delight the internecine strife among Burrite and Clintonian Republicans. William Coleman, editor of the Federalist *New-York Evening Post*, used Wood's pamphlet to claim that *all* Republicans were equally enthralled with the "Illuminati." The entire Republican Party had a dangerous heretical bent, he and other Federalists suggested. That summer and into the fall, Coleman's newspaper repeatedly claimed that all Republicans, whether affiliated with Clinton or Burr, subscribed to deism in ways that cast doubt on their political loyalty. Palmer served as the figurehead of the cabal, the personified proof that Republicans had gone off the deep end in their romantic fawning about atheist French revolutionaries. No longer *free*thinkers, these Republicans had relinquished their intellectual independence and become *non*-thinkers: obedient acolytes to "President Palmer" in the same way that Republicans bowed and scraped to President Jefferson, the nation's most powerful infidel. The "Illuminati" had been frightening enough in 1798, when John Adams was in office, but Congress had responded then with the Alien and Sedition Acts. The danger from irreligion seemed much greater now with Jefferson in the White House. He might show the "Illuminati" an open door rather than sign a new version of the Sedition Act, which had been allowed to lapse. Federalists could not count on the new president to keep the nation safe from infidelity.[13]

Talk of the dangerous "Illuminati" and its "President Palmer" spread as newspapers from Maine to Virginia ran Wood's pamphlet in serial form. Readers in New Hampshire, Massachusetts, Connecticut, New York, Pennsylvania, and Washington DC learned that deists were making headway. "Almost every day brings fresh proofs of the existence of a *Deistical Society* in New-York," warned the *New-York Gazette*. "What may we not fear from an infidel club, over which Palmer presides?" The answer was "irreligion and civil confusion." And did this "infidel gang" have a replacement in mind for Vice President Aaron Burr? Perhaps even "the renowned Elihu Palmer himself, the President and Apostle of their society?" The newspaper promised to reprint extracts of Palmer's book "so the horrid tendency of the work may be more generally known." The *Gazette* went so far as to evoke the specter of Benedict Arnold by comparison. Arnold's treachery had endangered the civil liberties of Americans, but "had *Palmer* and his *band* succeeded, we must have been doomed to unspeakable miseries in this world, and deprived of all hope in the world to come." The *Alexandria Advertiser* in Virginia printed a series of excerpts from *Principles of Nature*, each one accompanied by the editor's titillating warning that they "cannot be read by any christian, without horror." Palmer posed a real danger, Federalist editors warned, and his clerical past made his apostasy worse. "It aggarvates the feelings to know that Mr. Palmer 'was once a public speaker in the cause of Christianity,'" one wrote. In the commonplace twinning of politics and religion, Palmer was described as a blasphemer with political clout. He stood "at the head of a *deistical* and *political* club, who have been unwearied in their attempts to destroy the Christian religion and all wholesome government."[14]

As the news flurry about Palmer and the "Columbian Illuminati" reached its crescendo, Paine sailed west from France. During the two-month trip, the sixty-five-year-old envisioned a hero's welcome, unaware that he had become persona non grata among his former friends in the United States. Republican newspapers had initially discounted as slander the Federalist disclosure that Jefferson had invited Paine to return. Only when faced with the published evidence of Jefferson's invitation did Republican newspapers change course and decide to remember Paine as a hero of '76.

Meanwhile, Federalist newspapers staged a revival of enmity toward Paine, using weapons of sarcasm and contempt. The Philadelphia *Gazette of the United States* referenced the "great Thomas Paine, the affectionate friend of our president, and the idol of such puny infidels as the editors of the *Temple of Reason*, the *Aurora*, and the *American Citizen*, etc." When Paine sailed into Baltimore Harbor on October 30, the paper predicted that the Democratic-Republican *Aurora* would serve as Paine's mouthpiece and impress upon "the youth of our country" that divine revelation "is a mere farce." No sooner had Paine gone ashore than the Baltimore *Republican; or, Anti-Democrat* described him tippling brandy and holding forth at Fulton's tavern, speaking of himself as an important "public character," while people gaped at their hero. The *New-York Evening Post* offered sarcastic congratulations on "the arrival of Thomas Paine, the *pacific*, and the *pious*." Surely now the nation's "political animosities" will be "greatly allayed, and personal hatreds and heart-burnings considerably assuaged by the benevolent exertions of that ingenious gentleman." Furthermore, "men of property" could look forward to "an ingenious plan for an equalization of wealth," and "an agrarian experiment upon those gentlemen who have too much land." Certainly Paine had not come to the United States to retire. "We cannot suppose that this flaming comet, whose fiery course has so long astonished and terrified mankind, will now stop its career." Rather, Paine was sure to "catch additional fire from its near approach to that sun of *political, moral,* and *religious* virtue Mr. Jefferson." The *Balance, and Columbian Repository* shared the rumor that Paine had arrived with a stack of constitutions that Napoleon had rejected as "too democratical," and that said Jefferson was sure to use one of them to replace the US Constitution.[15]

Paine's supporters took a stand too. David Denniston's *American Citizen* described Paine's warm reception in Baltimore "on account of his literary exertions, during the revolutionary struggle for American freedom." Denis Driscol's *Temple of Reason* celebrated that the "friend of liberty, and the apostle of the one only God, has arrived at Baltimore." While "christians already tremble for their Superstition" and clergy of all kinds "feel themselves in danger," the "friends of moral truth" will find in Paine "a firm supporter and advocate of genuine unsophisticated morality; and a powerful antagonist" against religious imposters. Paine later boasted to his friend in London, Thomas Clio Rickman, "I arrived at Baltimore on the 30th October, and you can have no idea of the agitation which my arrival occasioned. From New Hampshire to Georgia (an extent of 1500 miles), every newspaper was filled with applause or abuse."[16]

Within days of Paine's arrival, the press linked his name to Palmer's. The *Federal Gazette* quoted Denniston's *American Citizen*: "*We congratulate the friends of republican government on the arrival of Mr. Thomas Paine in the United States.*" The paper then satirically asked all Republicans: "*Do your hearts beat in unison with those disciples of Palmer?*" The implication was that Republicans joined Palmer's "disciples" in a fluttering anticipation of Paine's return. In other contexts, too, the names of Paine and Palmer appeared together. In December 1802, at a "respectable meeting" of booksellers in Philadelphia, the men raised their glasses and wished "*remorse and repentance to the man whose press or bookstore is like Pandora's box, fraught with destruction to the morals of society.*" Which writings caused moral decay? Paine's *Age of Reason*, of course, "an open, blasphemous attack on the Christian Religion," and "*Principles of Nature*, by Elihu Palmer, an Atheist, a work so very bad that no printer has ventured to put his name to it." This was followed by the *Temple of Reason*, "an avowedly Deistical newspaper."[17]

Reality set in for Paine when he made his way to Washington, DC, unpacked his bags at William Lovell's hotel, and then heard nothing from the president. They had been friends in Paris in the 1780s, and Paine looked forward to more wide-ranging conversations. As the days of waiting for an invitation from Jefferson turned into weeks of presidential silence, Paine occupied himself by publishing "Letters to the Citizens of the United States" in the *National Gazette*. He offered his opinion on political leaders like John Adams—"of a bewildered mind . . . John was not born for immortality"—and George Washington, a man "of such an icy and death-like constitution that he neither loved his friends nor hated his enemies." In a fury about self-serving power-mongers and with an eye to the silent Jefferson, Paine expressed his disdain for political opportunists. "In taking up any public matter," he told American readers in December, "I have never made it a consideration, and never will, whether it be popular or unpopular; but whether it be right or wrong." Was Jefferson reading Paine's missives to the public? If so, Paine had words for him: "I despise expedients, they are the gutter-hole of politics, and the sink where reputation dies."[18]

Jefferson had his own priorities, and they did not include an open embrace of Paine. Even after the election of 1800, Federalist newspapers continued to harp on Jefferson as a Frenchified infidel and to question whether American institutions would survive his presidency. Jefferson tried to appease his political foes. His inaugural speech deplored the vituperative political rhetoric of the late 1790s, pleaded for greater civility, and referenced a common ground. "Let us restore to social intercourse that harmony and affection without which liberty and even life itself are but dreary things," he said. Having banished religious intolerance, Americans should not allow "a political intolerance" just as "despotic, as wicked, and capable of as bitter and bloody persecutions." Americans disagreed over how to respond to the "convulsions" of revolutionary France, Jefferson said, but "difference of opinion is not a difference of principle." Americans remained "brethren of the same principle. We are all Republicans, we are all Federalists." In this effort to placate his opponents, Jefferson saw no place for a man as divisive as Paine.[19]

The attempted reconciliation with Federalists came at the cost of Jefferson's staunchest allies. He distanced himself from colleagues who remained unapologetically partisan, especially the Republican editors who had supported him, and he gave government publishing work to Federalist printers instead. To temper his image as an infidel, Jefferson showcased a mingling of religion and politics during his administration. Just weeks after Jefferson penned a letter to the Baptists in Connecticut that fully endorsed a "wall of separation between Church & State," he participated in a worship service in the chapel adjacent to the Hall of Representatives. Perhaps not by accident did newspapers report that Jefferson was "seen at church, and has assisted in singing the hundredth psalm." Such demonstrative support for religion did not reduce Federalist concerns about his freethought, however, and newspapers excoriated Jefferson for inviting Paine back to the United States.[20]

The president was still actively ignoring Paine's presence in the capital when a package came across his desk in December. Jefferson held in his hands Palmer's newly printed second edition of *Principles of Nature*. Bound in inexpensive cardboard covers with leather corners, it featured an attractive frontispiece with an engraved portrait of the author. The black and white image showed a youthful man seated in a vest and cutaway coat, with ruffles at his neck and wrists. A large tricorn hat covered straight brown hair. His round, smooth-cheeked face was in three-quarter profile, unseeing eyes cast downward. Long fingers held a thin walking cane. Palmer's book arrived with a note. "Sir," Palmer's message began, "I send you a Copy of the Second Edition of my Principles of Nature. I beg that you would accept of it as a mark of that profound respect which I entertain for premient"—perhaps he meant "preeminent"—"talants and Virtue." Palmer chose modest words next. "I know that the Book which I send you contains nothing new to you and furnishes only an evidence of sincere attachment to you and the Principles for which you have contended." Palmer presumed they shared an understanding of Christianity as fabricated and harmful, and he knew Jefferson supported freedom of conscience. Palmer wrote to the president as a peer, not an underling, and signed off simply with "Health & Respect."[21]

Jefferson did indeed have strong doubts about Christianity as it had been passed down through the ages, and he was perhaps even then thinking about revising the Bible to excise the supernatural parts. When not preoccupied with affairs of state, Jefferson cut out the sections of the New Testament he endorsed, and pasted them together to form a new book he called "The Philosophy of Jesus of Nazareth." (This text did not survive, although the mutilated Bibles did. In 1819 he would make a second version, called "The Life and Morals of Jesus of Nazareth," known today as the Jefferson Bible.) No miraculous occurrences made the cut. In Jefferson's version, Jesus was born, lived, and died the normal way, without angelic announcement, a virgin birth, supernatural miracles, or a resurrection. What remained in Jefferson's streamlined account was an entirely human Jesus who offered an unsurpassed code of moral conduct. This despite the fact that when Jesus was killed, he had not yet reached his peak ability, "his reason having not yet attained the *maximum* of its energy," and also despite the "unlettered and ignorant men" who carried on the missionary work but botched the message. So yes, Jefferson entertained religious freethought that others might consider heretical. In a private letter he advised his nephew to "fix reason firmly in her seat, and call to her tribunal every fact, every opinion. Question with boldness even the existence of a God; because, if there be one, he must more approve of the homage of reason, than that of blindfolded fear." Interested in religion and freethinking philosophy, Jefferson may well have read some or all of Palmer's book.[22]

But whatever Jefferson thought of *Principles of Nature*, he had no desire to be associated with its author. In the three months it took for the package to travel from New York City to the president's desk, Palmer had become infamous, accused of leading a secretive anti-Christian cult filled with New York Republicans. The president knew well how religious freethought could be weaponized in partisan conflicts, and he understood that any evidence of contact with Palmer would incite the opposition press. Jefferson, who really did engage in epistolary conversation across the Atlantic with freethinkers like Volney—just the kind of dialogue Palmer dreamed of joining—took care to keep these exchanges as private as possible. Rather than use his position to expand public conversations about religion, Jefferson decided to camouflage his religious freethought. He presided over a country riven by partisanship. This was no time, he might have thought, for friendly engagement with someone described in the newspapers as a danger to the nation.[23]

If Jefferson had any inclination to send a note acknowledging the arrival of Palmer's book, a visitor to the White House the following week reinforced his instinct not to write one. Reverend John Hargrove, the Swedenborgian minister who had critiqued Palmer's Baltimore lectures in August 1801, visited Jefferson on December 26, 1802. Hargrove and Jefferson had been corresponding since the minister wrote to congratulate the president-elect on his win. The minister's self-proclaimed Christian deism interested Jefferson, as did a shared passion for scientific instruments. Jefferson had invited Hargrove to speak to Congress about his faith, another reassuring show, perhaps, of Jefferson's pro-religion stance. As Jefferson and Hargrove conversed, even a casual mention of Palmer's name or the title of his recently arrived book would have elicited from Hargrove plentiful commentary about Palmer's rancorous anti-Christian message and his obtusely literal reading of the Bible. Instead of writing to Palmer, Jefferson simply jotted his initials into Palmer's book and shelved it in his library's section on moral philosophy alongside volumes from ancient Greece and Rome, deist tracts from England, and works by Spinoza and the French *philosophes*. In this moment of Federalist hostility toward his presidency, Jefferson could more safely converse with a mystical Swedenborgian minister than with someone like Palmer, who shared with Jefferson a deep respect for Volney and other freethinkers but who was politically toxic in the way of Paine.[24]

Jefferson did eventually invite Paine to the White House, but only after Paine wrote in January to express his disappointment at not receiving an audience with the president. Paine requested the return of his model bridges, the ones he had hoped to discuss with Jefferson, and said he planned to depart for Philadelphia and New York. Jefferson had "shown no disposition" toward a conversation with Paine and had, in fact, "by a sort of shyness, as if you stood in fear of federal observation, precluded it." To the implied charge of cowardice, Jefferson responded with an invitation for dinner and an overnight stay at the White House. But the message was clear: Jefferson would restrict his interactions with Paine and give Federalists no easy opportunity to crow once more about the president's affection for a cosmopolitan "infidelity" that endangered the nation.[25]

Jefferson's choice was full of irony, since one of his proudest achievements was the Virginia Statute for Religious Freedom. He had drafted the language that guaranteed in Virginia not only freedom of conscience but also the right to defend one's religious views publicly without discrimination or retribution of any kind. That legal document, and not his two-term presidency, was what Jefferson wanted remembered on his tombstone. Yet during his tenure in the nation's highest office, the politics of infidelity were such that even the president believed he had to choose between political influence and his own freedom of speech. A brief note of thanks for a book could cause public relations problems that Jefferson urgently wished to avoid.

Paine set out to find better allies than the one in the White House, and by the summer of 1803, he was in New York City. Palmer must have been thrilled to meet his role model, the man whose proud identification as a deist and scorching critique of the Bible had given Palmer a new perspective on even the most liberal forms of Christianity. Paine would have been glad to meet the New York freethinkers who were just then preparing to test freedom of religion in court. David Denniston had recently moved back to Newburgh, where he now edited a Republican newspaper called *Rights of Man*. Denniston had sued another Newburgh editor for breach of contract, and in July he stood in the Orange County courthouse, ready for the question he knew would come next. Before the judge heard a case, all parties had to swear the customary oath. The question put to Denniston was "Do you believe in a Supreme Being, and a future state of rewards and punishments?" Denniston refused to answer and objected that "the question was improper" and "one which the court had not authority to ask." The judge threatened to drop the case unless Denniston answered the question in the affirmative. Invoking the First Amendment and the Constitution of the State of New York, Denniston challenged the legality of the judge's threat and requested a hearing to determine the point. At the hearing, Denniston and his lawyer, William Ross, appeared before five judges. Ross made "a luminous display of the principles of the constitution and laws of our country," Denniston reported in his newspaper, demonstrating "the incompatibility" of the courtroom oath with the nation's "political institutions." The judges scheduled their resolution of Denniston's question for the last day of the court session. For now, Denniston could celebrate that he had not been shut down. The verdict was still out on whether his day in court could be abridged if he refused to swear a religious oath, but at least he had stood up for his freedom of conscience and of speech.[26]

The revolution of 1800 had done nothing to quell the potent politics of freethought, in which skepticism and heterodoxy appeared to many as dangerous and un-American. In August 1803, the *Recorder of the Times* in Newburgh continued the print battle that had begun when Denniston first hosted Palmer six years before. A long letter in that newspaper explained that since Denniston's return to Newburgh in 1803, the "infidels" in town had displayed "an *increased* and *more deep rooted* enmity against christianity." These men "are aspiring to office," the writer asserted, "and they have lately *sworn that they will rule the roost*—that they will *make their sentiments respected*, even if they have to *draw the sword.*" They only pretend to be champions of freedom, and while words of "democracy and republicanism are flowing in torrents from their tongues and pens, their hearts are under the absolute control of *aristocratic* principles of the most diabolical kind. Their whole conduct shews that they wish to reign *exclusively*. They wish none to enjoy liberty but *themselves*. They wish no press to be *free* but *their own.*" The freethinkers of Newburgh "have labored, and labored *hard*," the writer said, "to be made justices, judges, shariffs, and county clerks." These "men of no education" are "scrambling up the hill of power" only to establish "their infernal principles of deism." In the process, the region's Republicans had splintered. A "division among the republicans of the town of Newburgh, has for many years existed," the writer recalled, ever since Palmer had first came to town and Denniston had edited the Newburgh *Mirror* with an eye to "the destruction of the Christian system of Religion." The animosity that had developed among Republicans, and certainly between Republicans and Federalists, had carried over into the new century and continued to fester.[27]

CHAPTER 12

The Best Kind of Revolution

BAD ENOUGH, a Virginian wrote in an open letter in 1803, that "places have been assigned in our large cities, for Elihu Palmer and others, to preach publicly against Christianity." Now the "infamous Tom Paine" had returned to America and "joined the blasphemous pack of bloodhounds already in full cry," placing himself "at the head of the cut throats." The advertisement for Elihu Palmer's start-up newspaper, *Prospect; or, View of the Moral World*, served as just more evidence that the "horrors of infidelity" were upon the nation.[1]

For Palmer, by contrast, the moment was full of promise, both for himself personally and for the nation at large. Although he depended on the charity of friends to supplement his income from lectures, he had managed to avoid utter poverty, a fate that often came with loss of sight. By this time Palmer knew that standard-fare respectability would forever elude him— his overt hostility toward Christianity and his ideas about sensate, jumping atoms saw to that. But he enjoyed the companionship and esteem of free-thinking writers, booksellers, and printers. John "Walking" Stewart returned to New York City in late 1803 or early the next year. Navigating the relationship between Paine and Stewart had its challenges for Palmer, because his two friends disagreed about how best to achieve social change, and their religious views diverged as well. Yet Palmer cherished both Stewart and Paine and mediated between them. During these years he worked out his own position on the best method for social transformation, and he grappled with the important question of whether violence for the sake of revolution was ever justified. Being one freethinker among others boosted his courage, and his message gave him wings. The truth about nature, he thought, had the power to open hearts and dramatically change human behavior. At the height of his speaking power, full of ideas and ambition, he could not know he had entered his life's last chapter. Constitutionally optimistic, Palmer in these years must have been happy too.[2]

On a personal level he certainly was happy, for in October 1803 he married his friend and collaborator, Mary Powell. He was thirty-nine, she two years older. By then, Palmer had lived in the Powell boardinghouse on Cortlandt Street for several years, and Mary Powell had taken dictation for Palmer who, as John Fellows noted, "dictated as fast as a quick writer could copy, and in language that required little or no alteration." Mary and Elihu probably spent many hours drafting and polishing prose about religion and philosophy. Then her first husband, Benjamin Powell, died in 1801 or 1802. That Mary was willing to marry a man of Palmer's scandalous reputation— the "Columbian Illuminati" smear campaign had broken just the previous year—suggests her own commitment to the freethinking cause. Fellows described Mary Palmer as "a woman of good sense, and fine moral feelings" who "possessed as strong an interest as her husband in promoting the cause of truth." Their marriage was based on personal affection and philosophical camaraderie.[3]

The Palmers wed with another joint venture in mind. They would pick up where Denis Driscol's *Temple of Reason* had left off in February 1803, but they would bend the revived weekly toward Palmer's message. The new title, *Prospect; or, View of the Moral World*, conveyed Palmer's interest in sharing his understanding of morality, one based on the workings of nature. With the help of subscribers in New York City, Newburgh, Philadelphia, and Baltimore, who each advanced one dollar (half the annual price), the first *Prospect* appeared on Saturday, December 10, 1803, with Palmer's name on the masthead. His blindness might have made him all the more proud of his accomplishment. He probably had his wife's involvement at every turn.[4]

The weekly consisted of four octavo-sized sheets of paper (about six by nine inches) printed on both sides in a single column. The paper was entirely supported by its readers—Palmer ran no advertisements—and enlisting and keeping those subscribers would be crucial to the enterprise. In its run of sixty-five issues over more than a year, the *Prospect* printed a variety of material, much of it serialized: Palmer's systematic exegesis of the

Bible, reprinted essays by well-known authors, and pieces that he and others wrote specifically for the *Prospect*. Palmer numbered the pages consecutively, and he eventually had all the issues bound as a single book. He envisioned the compilation as a textbook of abiding value rather than as a commentary on the ephemeral news of the day.

An opening message "to the public" declared the significance of the paper they held in their hands. The world needed an education in morality, a "diffusing through the mass of society a clear knowledge" of the "nature and character" of human beings. This was the purpose of the *Prospect*, a publication of philosophical bent and reformist ambition. The paper would deliver the moral key that could unlock humanity's unlimited potential for intellectual and moral advancement. Readers familiar with Palmer's work would have recognized his one-two punch. First he planned to expose revealed religion as false, because only a mind liberated from superstition could absorb the truth. The *Prospect*'s "free, open, and bold" discussion of Christian theology would "be managed with decency," Palmer promised, and with "suitable respect for the opinions of every Christian sectary." (That promise proved false; the newspaper deployed the derisive sarcasm that Palmer had learned from Paine's *Age of Reason*.) Second, Palmer would present truths that empowered human beings to change the world for the better. To that end, the *Prospect* announced itself open to printing "all moral, philosophical, and literary productions, useful to society, and calculated to augment the science and happiness of human life." Palmer invited contributions from "scientific or thoughtful men in any part of the world" whose topics relate "to the cause of truth, virtue, and human happiness." It was to be a collection of freethought from various sources, a funneling of the world's truths into one place.[5]

The first issue of the *Prospect* featured an excerpt from John Stewart's *Great Essay to Systematize the Moral World*. All revealed religions were equally benighted, Stewart announced. He put Christians on the same level as the "inspired ideots" everywhere "who pretend to commune with supernatural beings" and who burn each other as "schismatics at opposite stakes." Stewart had found a better alternative among the "Siamese" in Indochina who believe "the universe is one great body tending to promote its own good by the instrumentality of its parts, which are all eternal atoms co-equal, co-essential, co-interested, in all good and evil, in time and

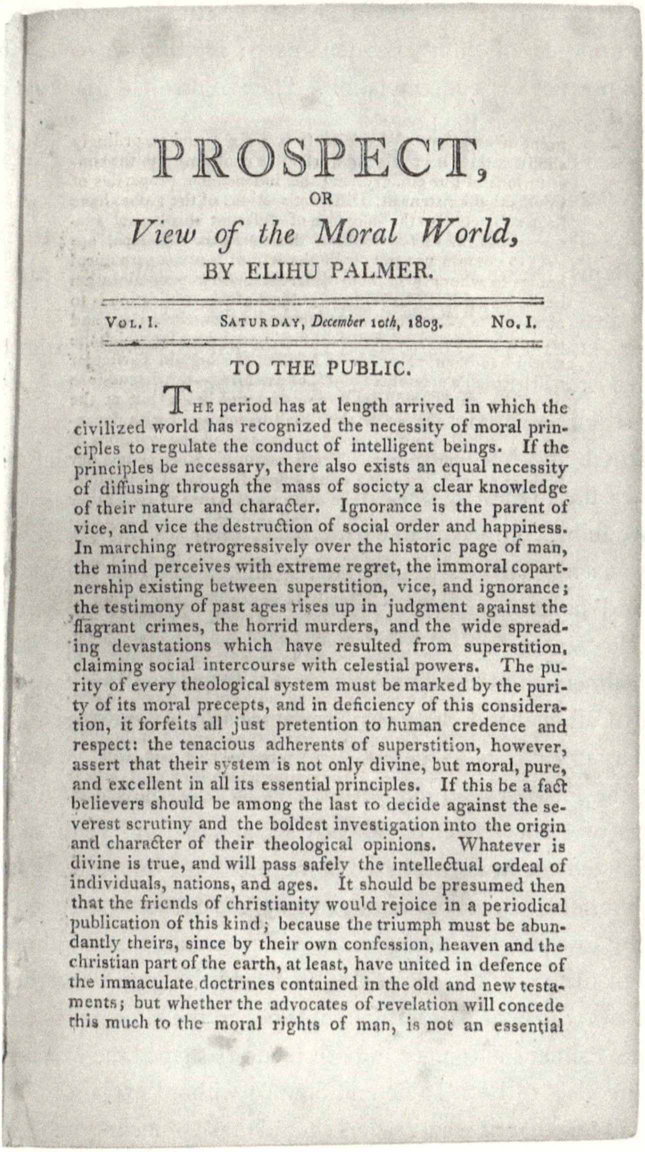

PROSPECT,

OR

View of the Moral World,

BY ELIHU PALMER.

| VOL. I. | SATURDAY, *December* 10th, 1803. | No. I. |

TO THE PUBLIC.

The period has at length arrived in which the civilized world has recognized the necessity of moral principles to regulate the conduct of intelligent beings. If the principles be necessary, there also exists an equal necessity of diffusing through the mass of society a clear knowledge of their nature and character. Ignorance is the parent of vice, and vice the destruction of social order and happiness. In marching retrogressively over the historic page of man, the mind perceives with extreme regret, the immoral copartnership existing between superstition, vice, and ignorance; the testimony of past ages rises up in judgment against the flagrant crimes, the horrid murders, and the wide spreading devastations which have resulted from superstition, claiming social intercourse with celestial powers. The purity of every theological system must be marked by the purity of its moral precepts, and in deficiency of this consideration, it forfeits all just pretention to human credence and respect: the tenacious adherents of superstition, however, assert that their system is not only divine, but moral, pure, and excellent in all its essential principles. If this be a fact believers should be among the last to decide against the severest scrutiny and the boldest investigation into the origin and character of their theological opinions. Whatever is divine is true, and will pass safely the intellectual ordeal of individuals, nations, and ages. It should be presumed then that the friends of christianity would rejoice in a periodical publication of this kind; because the triumph must be abundantly theirs, since by their own confession, heaven and the christian part of the earth, at least, have united in defence of the immaculate doctrines contained in the old and new testaments; but whether the advocates of revelation will concede this much to the moral rights of man, is not an essential

FIGURE 9. The first page of Elihu Palmer's weekly *Prospect*, which published a wide array of freethought "in the cause of truth, virtue, and human happiness." Courtesy of the American Antiquarian Society.

futurity." In his characteristic idiom, Stewart gestured toward a single living system composed of interdependent parts, a reality revealed, he said, through a practice of "contemplation." The *Prospect* had made its opening splash, with Stewart at the bow.[6]

The second issue of the *Prospect* defended the "principles of Deism." Because a "rancorous spirit" had stoked "a considerable share of popular odium" against deism, Palmer wished to explain its main features in the simplest terms. Deism posited "one perfect God, creator and preserver of the universe," whose immutable natural laws are never violated with miracles of any kind. This Creator-God is "entitled to the adoration of every intellectual agent throughout the regions of infinite space." Such adoration did not require any particular form of worship, only "the practice of a pure, natural, and uncorrupted virtue," which is "the essential duty, and constitutes the highest dignity of man." Deists maintained that human beings are fully "competent to all the great purposes of human existence" and that "science, virtue and happiness" will prevail once "christian superstition and fanaticism have ceased to spread desolation and carnage through the fair creation of God." Deism's benevolent Creator-God did not exhaust Palmer's thinking about religion or the cosmos, but it was certainly the best of all available religious positions, and he enthusiastically supported it as an antidote to religious superstition.[7]

That the *Prospect* featured both the lively materialism of Stewart and the deism of Paine reflected Palmer's social situation. With each of his unlike-minded mentors he shared some opinions, but not others, about politics, morality, and social reform. Paine and Stewart disagreed strongly about how to achieve a revolution in social relations, and Palmer played the part of mediator, the social glue that held the group together, as did John Fellows who boarded, at different times, in the same houses as Stewart and Paine. Palmer's allegiance to both mentors shaped the *Prospect*, which offered the ideas of both Paine and Stewart without explaining how their concepts fit together or what readers should make of incongruences. Palmer had always been a compiler of ideas, accumulating his favorite notions from Richard Price, Isaac Ledyard, Volney, Godwin, Condorcet, Paine, and Stewart, always without any apparent concern for consistency in the particulars but with a focus on the shared through-line: the conviction that humankind had the ability to create a much better earthly future.[8]

The *Prospect* offered a collage of freethought in an effort to deepen the philosophical education of the already-open-minded subscriber and—this was the conceit—to startle Christian readers into a more critical stance toward their faith. The eclectic collection of literature and philosophy offered a variety of ways to rethink religion and to ponder the sources of morality. The chapter "The Progress of the Christian Religion" from Gibbon's *Decline and Fall of the Roman Empire* appeared in the *Prospect*, as did an essay by William Godwin, "Of the suppression of erroneous opinions of Religion and Government," and another by d'Holbach (under the penname Mirabaud) titled "Man is only unhappy because he is ignorant of nature." Readers encountered Voltaire's "Certainty," Plutarch's "Of Superstition and Atheism," and excerpts from skeptical philosophers such as Hume, Raynal, and Helvétius. Palmer did not necessarily agree with all the works he reprinted. About Rousseau's famous "Profession of Faith of a Savoyard Curate," for example, Palmer editorialized that the piece was flawed and "not altogether correct" on matter and spirit but worth reprinting because it was not well known in America and still offered useful "sentiments of virtue." The array of essays made the point that the exploration of diverse philosophical and religious positions spelled intellectual freedom.[9]

Paine supported the *Prospect*, especially as a vehicle for his own agenda. In the spring of 1804, at age sixty-seven, Paine moved to New Rochelle, New York, where Congress had, twenty years prior, granted him a house and land for his wartime services. His "communications" for the *Prospect* defended deism and compared it favorably with Christianity on a point by point basis. In July, Paine sent John Fellows an essay for the *Prospect* with the comment that "if the plan mentioned in it is pursued, it will open a way to enlarge and give establishment to the deistical church."[10]

Palmer's voice can be most clearly heard in the systematic parsing of books in the Bible. Each one appeared to him inconsistent, unbelievable, and morally outrageous. In the book of Exodus, for example, God promises to "harden Pharoah's heart, and multiply my signs and wonders in the land of Egypt." Palmer condemned "the abominable profanity of charging God with hardening the heart of man," a move that displaced "the wicked actions of man upon the creator himself." And then God sent a plague of frogs? The God of the Jews was "loaded with immoral attributes which would disgrace even a common man." The scoffing literalism was familiar.

Paine had used it in *Age of Reason*, Driscol did the same in the *Temple of Reason*, and Palmer emulated it in his *Principles of Nature*. Serialized, this biting exegesis easily filled pages. Readers could begin in January with "Comments on Genesis," chapter 1, and work their way through weekly commentary on that book until May. Discussion of the book of Exodus carried readers through November. Conveniently for the editor, it would take years to get through all the books of the Bible.[11]

Using the *Prospect* as his mouthpiece, Palmer fought back against what he saw as the toxic effects of revealed religion. Fear was the "great instrument of ecclesiastical despotism," he wrote. Mankind is "afraid of his own powers, afraid to exercise his own faculties—he is terrified and alarmed when reflections arise in his mind hostile to the orthodox systems of antiquity." Not just fear of religious authorities paralyzes a person; the impulse to social conformity exerts pressure as well. A man is "dreadfully alarmed if any of his neighbours call in question any of his opinions." It took guts to be an outlier, Palmer knew. In the face of widespread conformity Palmer wondered, "when will man learn to exercise intellectual courage?" Worst of all, Palmer said, "He is afraid of God! What stupid mind was it that first invented the idea that human beings ought to tremble before the Supreme and benevolent Creator of the universe. There is but one thing that man ought to fear, and that is vice."[12]

With much pleasure Palmer addressed the Christian clergy as if they were reading his words and left speechless and ashamed by his irrefutable arguments. "Ye spiritual instructors of a lost and wicked world!" he exclaimed. Would they be proud to have authored "such a production" as Exodus, with all its bloodlust? False beliefs of a malicious God spread "desolation and death," making superstition an affliction "worse than the yellow fever." No doubt mindful of his own losses to that dread disease, Palmer suggested it was better to be blinded physically by fever than to be spiritually debilitated by false religion. When a pamphlet warned in 1804 against atheists and especially the "high Priest Elihu Palmer," he may even have been flattered. The pamphlet put Palmer in company with the "infamous contemptible outcast, *Paine*" and likened Palmer's work to the "more dangerous productions of Godwin," Thomas Jefferson, and Anacharsis Cloots, the Prussian cosmopolitan who disavowed all revealed religions and theorized a world government. Palmer belonged to the most dangerous freethinkers of the day, the pamphlet implied. With that, Palmer could feel he had joined those speaking truth to power.[13]

Palmer's book and newspaper and news of the thriving Deistical Society in New York might have been the reason for John Stewart's return to America. Few people in the English-speaking world understood and accepted his views about the foundational workings of nature, but Elihu and Mary Palmer were among those who did. He could converse with the Palmers at length about the constant and instantaneous exchange of sensate particles and the power of meditation to reveal the underlying unity of all matter.[14]

Stewart's presence made Palmer's life more enjoyable in some ways and more complicated in others. The complexity had to do with Stewart's relationship to Paine. The two men tugged at Palmer's philosophical and political positions, pulling him in different directions. Palmer admired both men, drew on their respective insights, and wished to include both in his cohort of freethinkers. But they had forceful personalities and strong differences of opinion. Palmer was the youngest of the three—he turned forty in 1804, to Stewart's fifty-seven years and Paine's sixty-seven—and he was a newcomer to their relationship of over a decade. Stewart and Paine had been close friends in London in the early 1790s, but their harrowing experiences in revolutionary Paris led them to draw different conclusions about the best means and pace of social change. Paine continued to support popular rebellion against authority, while Stewart retreated into an elitist abhorrence of the "mob." Stewart was "astonished" that Paine still "idolizes" the French "multitude" even after they had "fully evinced their folly, cruelty, and incapacity of popular government." On the matter of suffrage, Stewart said only Paine's "theoretic insanity" could support the idea of extending the vote to women, youths, and laborers. Everyone knew that women's "defective education" and minors' "inexperience" made them unfit to cast ballots. Manual laborers had an even "worse and more deficient education, than either minors or women." History proved to Stewart that "the great mass of the uneducated vulgar," if prematurely granted the vote, would "become the dupes of faction and demagogues, till misery and anarchy force them to seek an asylum in despotism."[15]

Far preferable for Stewart was incremental change wrought by the spreading insight that the cosmos is made of shared sensitive matter and that any pain inflicted on one creature will eventually be experienced by all. The improvements Stewart envisioned would be a long time coming but at least they would avoid revolutionary chaos and violence. Patience was in order. In fact, he considered his ideas so much ahead of their time that he wanted his works translated into Latin, the language he thought most likely to survive, and then buried seven or eight feet underground. By that method his books would not be destroyed by his ignorant and hostile contemporaries but would be preserved until humankind was ready to receive his wisdom. The location of the books should remain a closely guarded secret, handed down from one generation of freethinkers to the next, until people had advanced enough to make proper use of them. This might take a thousand years, Stewart thought, and in the meantime, he favored "experiments of human perfectability" in small communities that would fan out across the land. Survival in these isolated communities would depend on simple self-interest and mutual aid. Stewart decidedly rejected any "revolutionary policy" or the "vain and verbal codes of reformed morality!"[16]

But revolutionary policy was precisely Paine's specialty. Neither meditation about cosmic connections nor experimental communities in isolation would solve the problem of poverty and disenfranchisement, in Paine's practical view. One must address the gross inequalities of wealth, and the way to do it was through the legal establishment and the enforcement of economic reforms. Not that Paine envisioned complete material equality. "That property will ever be unequal is certain," he wrote. He did not care "how affluent some may be" as long as "none be miserable in consequences of it." But he saw a causal relationship between obscene wealth and wretched poverty. "One extreme produces the other: to make one rich many must be made poor," and Paine found it impossible to enjoy wealth as long as "so much misery is mingled in the scene." The disparity between rich and poor is a *moral* issue, Paine insisted, and as egregious as "dead and living bodies chained together." The urgent crisis of poverty could not wait a millennium while Stewart's books moldered underground.[17]

Human misery stemmed from specific causes, Paine wrote. Slavery was atrocious, of course, as was "paying too little for the labour" of workers, and the draconian penal system. "When, in countries that are called civilized, we see age going to the workhouse and youth to the gallows, something must be wrong in the system of government." Paine opposed the death penalty and asked pointedly: "Why is it, that scarcely any are executed but the poor?" The fleecing of the dispossessed was a system of "legal barbarity," Paine wrote, as was the monopolizing of wealth. The divine Creator had granted the land, air, and water to all people, and those deprived of their birthright's share should receive an indemnity of sorts. Paine figured out the practical details of such a plan, suggesting that a property tax paid into a national fund would give every person on their twenty-first birthday, and then again annually after the age of fifty, some compensation "for the loss of his or her natural inheritance." He also worked out, to the English pound, how progressive taxation could support a social welfare system and ameliorate the massive inequalities of wealth. These were pragmatic solutions to a moral problem in need of urgent redress. The poor and the unemployed, newly married couples, new mothers, schoolchildren, and the elderly all had a right to partake of the Creator's bounty, Paine insisted. His policy proposals should become law, he said, because philanthropy alone would never accomplish the work. Real change must be required, not requested, and to think otherwise—to count on some future universal benevolence as Stewart and Palmer did—was to misperceive human nature. Once the new economic policies were in place, people could come to see the wisdom of them—or not. Fairness was not a matter of consensus.[18]

The *Prospect* shows Palmer holding a position between those of Paine and Stewart. He admired Paine's creative and practical proposals, and he shared Paine's optimism about democratic self-governance. Palmer deplored the "system of plunder and robbery, which makes nine-tenths of the human race absolute slaves to support the other tenth in indolence, extravagance, pride, and luxury." He also agreed that, over time, "our political institutions must be changed, and placed upon the broad basis of universal liberty and universal justice." But he remained vague about what this political reform entailed. Congress would benefit from having one house instead of two, he thought, and the president should not have veto power over laws. Certainly slavery must be abolished and women's equality guaranteed. But these were general propositions, not signs of a deeper engagement with the details. Palmer left it to Paine to devise specific plans for social betterment. Palmer enjoyed the philosophical principles underlying morality, not the nitty-gritty of political strategy, institution building, legal reform, or economic planning.[19]

Ever the educator, Palmer placed the greatest emphasis on the importance of understanding the natural world. "Man's highest happiness," Palmer declared, lay in "discovering his true connection with nature, and the eternal duration of this connection." This insight would alter human behavior, he thought. He stated his conviction as clearly as possible: "If man had a comprehensive view of the successive changes of his existence, and a correct idea of the nature of sensation continually resulting from the renovation of organic forms," then "sympathy or universal benevolence, would become irresistibly impressive upon his moral powers, and form the basis of his subsequent conduct." This heightened compassion would end oppression of all kinds, including women's "inequality of rights" as well as slavery, which is "a complete abandonment of the principle of reciprocal justice, and a violation of the fundamental laws of Nature." Palmer wanted the same kind of social equality Paine did, but he preferred Stewart's approach: a gradual but deeply transformative education about shared, sensate matter that naturally produces universal benevolence and that will, in turn, accomplish a thoroughgoing and entirely peaceful revolution in social relations. It would take time for people to shed their religious prejudices and grasp that everything is made of the same sensate matter, Palmer thought, but he believed the eventual results would go well beyond Paine's proposals to redistribute wealth and would transform societies without shedding a drop of blood.[20]

But what was one to do, Palmer wondered, in the face of massive resistance to social change? The violence committed in the cause of justice preoccupied Palmer and his friends at length. Did revolutionary ends justify violent measures? The answers to that question showed diverging conceptions of human nature. Paine and Stewart had seen people at their most terrifying in revolutionary Paris. Paine had barely escaped the guillotine, and he saw former friends and colleagues turn on one another to save their own lives. Paine's plan for social improvement required no magnanimous humanitarian spirit. He focused on life's necessities, on a living wage and education, and on their guarantee through policy and law. Stewart, meanwhile, had given up on democratic self-government altogether, retreating into a fearful elitism and expecting very little from his contemporaries. Palmer was the most idealistic of the three. He believed in a transformative awareness of unified nature and in a future perfectibility of humankind. He held fast to the human capacity for empathy and generosity. With regard to social change, he positioned himself somewhere between his two most influential teachers. Like Stewart, Palmer favored gradual change through education, and like Paine, he continued to support the principles behind the French Revolution and the move toward popular democracy. Palmer acknowledged that the effort to root out tyranny "will lead to the application of force in the political revolutions of the world," and that some "benevolent philosophers," meaning Stewart, had called this measure into question. In an effort to think through his own position, Palmer was even then preparing for the press a political work with an "ample discussion on this point." The question of violence in the cause of liberation remained a vexing subject.[21]

The examples of France and Haiti loomed over the question of whether the ends of liberty justified violent means. Tens of thousands of people had lost their lives during years of terror in both places, with mixed results. France in 1803 was under the dictatorial rule of Napoleon Bonaparte. He would crown himself emperor the next year, the same year that the former French colony of Saint Domingue received international recognition (although not from the slaveholding president of the United States) as an independent country named Haiti, the first black-led government in the western hemisphere. The island's massive slave-led rebellion had, from its beginning in 1791, inspired enslaved Americans and instilled dread in their owners, who feared the revolution might spread to the United States. For Stewart it was not an open question about whether to support the chaos of violence and the carnage of war. For Palmer and Paine, however, the question was more nuanced—namely whether and how to position themselves as enlightened proponents of emancipatory revolution, which so often turned deadly.

In general, Paine opposed wars, especially those pursued by governments for their own self-aggrandizement. Monarchies, one of his favorite targets, had fomented a "perpetual system of war and expense" that "certainly is not the condition that Heaven intended for man." It was "ridiculous and absurd" he wrote, "to be at the expense of building navies, filling them with men, and then hauling them into the ocean, to try which can sink each other fastest." He condemned wars of territorial aggression and the nationalism that governments stoked to justify brutal colonialism. Nationalist hatred was a "savage idea," Paine said. Palmer agreed that such "narrow prejudice" is "subversive of the best interests of human society." Stewart, meanwhile, remained an unapologetic British nationalist.[22]

But what about democratic revolutions that turned violent? Paine considered these an aberration. He championed "a passive, rational, and costless revolution" brought about by citizens engaged in open, public debate and with proper representation in national conventions. In the new, enlightened era Paine envisioned, open discussion arbitrates any question, "private opinion yields with a good grace" to the majority, and "order is preserved uninterrupted." He presumed respect for the democratic process and majority rule. If only the French had adopted a constitution like the American one, Paine said, the violence that took over and produced "the execrable Reign of Terror" could have been avoided. The best revolutions were the peaceful ones.[23]

Palmer agreed that things had gone terribly wrong in France, yet "the revolution in its principal" remained for him an "object of attachment and admiration." He felt ambivalent and uncomfortable about violent measures, however. He avoided talking about warfare directly and chose poetic language instead, with personified Reason appearing as the agent of war. "Reason, righteous and immortal reason, with the arguments of the printing types in one hand, and the keen argument of the sword in the other, must attack the thrones and the hierarchies of the world, and level them with the dust of the earth." Palmer preferred to speak of education and its inevitable, if gradual, effects. "Ages must elapse" before liberation could be accomplished, Palmer said, but its "causes are already in operation." Crucial was a free press, although not without limits. Liberty of the press extended only to the truth, in Palmer's opinion. No one has the right to do wrong, "to indulge in calumny and detraction, in slander and falsehood, against the character of his fellow citizen." Palmer parsed it this way: "In matters of speculation and opinion, the press should be perfectly unrestrained; in matters of fact, its expressions should remain faithful to the reality and truth of the case." Lies are a form of "moral violence" and should be halted, he felt. Any honest press, by contrast, should have "absolutely unqualified and unrestrained" liberty to publish even "the boldest truths; whether these truths relate to the humble citizen, or to the man that is high in office." In America, "no officer of government, no legislative body" should be "exempted from the severest scrutiny."[24]

On the difficult question of violence, Palmer backed off and changed the subject. The best way to create lasting change, he said, was to share through books and other publications "the clearest views of the laws of nature," along with the "pernicious errors" of antiquated religion. This described his life's work: to reveal the falsity of revealed religion and the truth about all of nature. He remained convinced that humans would think, meditate, and educate their way to freedom, peace, and global contentment. Eventually, without any supernatural help at all, humankind would create an earthly paradise. Once religious superstition was cast aside, Palmer believed, "the reign of reason would commence, republican virtue would gloriously triumph," and "peace, truth, and national happiness become the unalienable inheritance of the human race."[25]

By the time Palmer suspended the *Prospect* in March 1805 for lack of funds, he could feel good about what he and Mary had accomplished over the last fifteen months. All told, the weekly paper had done quite well. His reliance on subscriptions to pay for type, ink, and paper had always been a gamble, and many newspapers, even those with advertising revenue, folded within two or three years. Palmer's last words in the newspaper were ones he could stand by: "Man! think freely; speak with boldness; discard religious nonentities; practice virtue; and enlarge the circle of human felicity."[26]

The shuttering of the *Prospect* gave Palmer more time for his other projects. The Deistical Society persevered, and while it left few traces of its activity, it continued to raise money to build a lecture hall called the Temple of Reason. The Palmers enjoyed the company of friends in New York, including John Stewart, John Fellows, one Charles Christian, a lawyer with the last name of Rose, and John Taylor, whom Mary Palmer called "my good friend" and, after her husband, "my next best friend." When Paine moved from New Rochelle back to Manhattan in 1805, he visited Palmer daily. A new acquaintance was the fiery Reverend John Foster (not the Massachusetts minister with whom Palmer studied after college), who was both an ardent Universalist and an irreverent lampooner of parts of the Bible. Paine told Fellows he was "glad that Palmer and Foster have got together. It will greatly help the cause on." Foster, who spoke in "deep and solemn tones, which were at times almost terrific," became an "open infidel," one critic remembered, and "the fellow-laborer of Elihu Palmer, the atheist." At the Universalist meeting house in Rose Street, Foster entertained his listeners with "burlesque dissertations on the historical part of the Scriptures." He also opened the church to Palmer for his lectures. "We have procured the Universal Church in Rose-street for the delivery of Deistical Discourses," Palmer reported to a friend, and Foster and "a great part of his people have become very friendly to our cause." The open welcome marked a notable shift from the days when Palmer was denied the pulpit in Philadelphia's Universalist meeting house. Back in 1792, when the newly organized Universalists appeared marginal and suspect to Calvinist Protestants, they had protected their reputations by avoiding freethinkers like Palmer. In the ensuing years, the Universalists had gained recognition as a legitimate sect within the expanding Protestant mainstream. Foster was unusual among Universalists for his open denigration of the Bible, yet even so, a committee of his congregants defended him in the local newspaper—a sign of the changing times. Palmer had more and more freethinking company in New York.[27]

Connections beyond New York City nourished him as well. An English merchant named Robert Hunter visited New York and befriended the Palmers. After Hunter returned home, Mary Palmer wrote to thank him for "your goodness in wishing Mr palmer to have his sight restored and your inviting him to go over the atlantic" as well as "many other proofs of sincere friendship." Hunter communicated with Edward Rushton in Liverpool about Palmer. Rushton was a radical abolitionist, poet, and bookseller who had lost his sight at nineteen when, as a shipmate, he had tended sick Africans on board a slaving ship and contracted an eye disease. Back in England, Rushton helped found a school for the blind in 1791 and would, in 1807, undergo eye surgery and partially regain his sight. Hunter and Rushton apparently hoped that Palmer might get medical help for his vision too. Palmer told Hunter he would visit England in two or three years when he had more money. For now, Hunter should share with his daughters the message from (forty-one-year-old) Palmer that "notwithstanding I am such an old blind fellow, that when I come I shall make them laugh." Palmer also asked that Hunter convey his "best respect to Edward Rushton and to any other thoughtful philanthropist within the sphere of your acquaintance." Palmer praised Rushton for his *Expostulatory Letter to George Washington*, which had reprimanded the American president in 1797 for proclaiming a love of freedom, and "Yet sir you are a slaveholder!" Palmer's greetings and good wishes to freethinkers he had not yet met forged affective ties of solidarity that extended across the ocean. These feelings of friendship encouraged Palmer to think of himself as part of a network of forward-looking cosmopolitans engaged in a shared project to free the intellect and thereby improve the world.[28]

Meanwhile, Palmer carried on with his lectures, orations, and speaking tours. In his Political Lecture series he probed a new range of subjects, including the "Moral and Political Consequences" of slavery, the "Rights of Man and the means of subverting unequal government," how best to defend "the genuine principles of Republicanism," and whether the "conflicting operation of Party Spirit in the United States will ultimately destroy the principles and existence of republicanism." He was also drafting a second book, "The Political World," which he hoped to complete in spring 1806, and he planned to resume publication of the *Prospect* in November. He was at the height of his powers as a speaker, and he still had much to say.[29]

In March 1806, Palmer reached for his traveling bag, ready for early spring weather in Philadelphia. Nothing suggested that this would be his last speaking tour: To Philadelphia, of all places, where the Universalists had shown him the door not once, but twice. Where he had been pressured and ridiculed after announcing a lecture against the divinity of Christ. Where he had lost his first wife to the yellow fever, and then his eyesight. Where he had failed, as a newly blinded lawyer, to support his two young sons. Philadelphia had been for him a place of challenges and personal failures, but it was also a city to which he had returned over and over again, determined and hopeful. Perhaps Mary joined him on this trip, but he often traveled without her, and maybe this time as well. He might have stayed once more in the inn belonging to his acquaintance Israel Israel, the Universalist who was just then the high sheriff of Philadelphia. Familiar surroundings helped Palmer to navigate by feel with less confusion.

While in Philadelphia, Palmer began to feel poorly and took to his bed. Had he visited a sick friend? He was known to do that. Word traveled as far as Liverpool, England, that Elihu and Mary Palmer had come to the aid of a sick and dying friend that very spring. "The conduct of Mr & Mrs Palmer on this trying occasion must endear them to every feeling Heart," wrote Edward Rushton. Most people "shrink from distress," he continued, "but Palmer the benevolent Palmer acted differently, he embraced Contagion, he risked his Life in an attempt to preserve his Friend." Whether or not a visit to a sick friend caused Palmer's illness, he came down with pleurisy, an inflammation of the lungs. No extant record shows whether Palmer, during the short span of his illness, received medical care. Perhaps a physician looked in on Palmer at his boardinghouse. At least one friend in town tended to him, and perhaps Mary was there as well.[30]

If Palmer recognized that he would not recover, he might have thought about what he once called the only consolation of man: that humans can expect the same kind of eternity as all other things. Just the previous year he had published a piece in the *Prospect* on death. "Whoever contemplates most thoroughly the laws and principles of the physical world," he wrote, "will be least susceptible of terrific apprehensions at the idea of corporeal dissolution. Organic structure is one of the great laws of nature; and disorganization, its counterpart, equally powerful, and equally universal." Palmer found it "astonishing" that this incontrovertible fact, for which there was clear evidence and no known alternative, had not "produced a more philosophical effect!" There was nothing to fear. "Death is only the commencement of a new mode of existence," he wrote, and the notion offered him "tranquility."[31]

After only a few days of illness, Palmer died on Monday, March 31, 1806. He was forty-one. No record reveals where he was buried. Perhaps his body was interred alongside other paupers in potters' field. At some point, his friends may have gathered in a ceremony appropriate for a man who believed the only eternal life was that of the atoms that made up his form. Palmer was sure the dissolution of a body did not alter "the inherent properties of the constituent parts. These parts form new relations, contract new alliances, and become susceptible of new pleasures." The building blocks of all living things are never lost, Palmer wrote, but are "destined to an immortality of being—to an everlasting routine of combining and dissolving action." He had expressed his beliefs often enough, and a friend who attended Palmer's sickbed reported that "*he died in the full confidence of the truth of those principles which he had inculcated in his discourses.*"[32]

Palmer may have been tranquil at the prospect of his own death, but for those left behind, it came as a shock. Having lived with such passion, and at the height of his energy for his many projects, he was suddenly gone, leaving his friends bereft and his wife reeling. For most of the last decade, Elihu and Mary Palmer had been partners in the cause of truth, laboring together for countless hours to bring his message to a wider public. His impaired vision had made him reliant upon her in ways large and small. Now Mary Palmer felt "greatly distresed and perplexed" after the loss of "My dearest My best of husbands."[33]

Newspapers in New York, Pennsylvania, and New England noted the death of the "well known moral and political lecturer." A few obituaries added that Palmer was esteemed or celebrated, while the *United States Gazette* in Philadelphia described him as the "noted apostle of Atheism." Closer to his hometown of Scotland, Connecticut, the *True Republican* of Norwich saluted "Citizen Elihu Palmer" as a "gentleman, philosopher, a sincere friend to liberty and *True* Republicanism, and still more as an honest man." Farthest away, the *Augusta Chronicle*, now edited by Denis Driscol, printed a tribute to Palmer who "preferred poverty" if it meant "candour," sincerity, "and the approbation of his own conscience," to any "riches and splendor purchased by hypocrisy." The most nuanced testimonial appeared in a Vermont newspaper with the pseudonym "An Enemy to Persecution." The writer, who claimed to know Palmer well, said that "as a public speaker he was excelled by few; his delivery was graceful, his voice strong and sonorous." But his unpopular opinions weakened the "support which his talents and industry merited," and his combative style only made things worse. Palmer "did not sufficiently respect the opinions of others," the eulogist said, and his bold attacks on Christianity "drove many from his lectures." As a person he was "rigidly moral, a philanthropist, and of course a zealous advocate for the liberty of mankind." He would not "swerve for a moment from what he thought right." Palmer could be intolerant and insulting, the writer implied, yet he hoped Palmer would be more charitably remembered for his philanthropic intentions and his "goodness of heart."[34]

Palmer himself would have preferred to have his *ideas* properly remembered, and for a while, they were. His book, *Principles of Nature*, was reprinted in New York and New Jersey in 1830 and 1840, and a final edition came out in London in 1841. Then it was forgotten. When historians took interest some ninety years later, they easily saw Palmer's support for deism, but they no longer recognized his concern for sensate, eternal matter. He would not mind being called a deist, but he would wish to call attention to the more important idea of sensate matter in constant reformulation. This notion would do the most to save the world, he thought, because it could change how people treated all other living beings. He understood himself as an educator, really still a preacher, who learned best in conversation and loved an audience. He created discussion groups everywhere he went, believing he could persuade his listeners of the crucial change in perception that would naturally bring forth benevolence. No political movement or institutional structure was required for the transformation. It could be achieved by teaching people to think critically about their religious assumptions and to open their minds to a new way of conceiving the whole of life. A clearer understanding of the natural world was the key to a better future, Palmer thought, because compassion would grow from an awareness of the shared fate of all things.[35]

By the time Palmer died in 1806, the world had changed dramatically since the days of his Calvinist childhood in a small town in colonial Connecticut. Not just the political nation had acquired independence, Palmer liked to say on the Fourth of July; every individual had the recognized right to intellectual freedom as well. When he started out as a minister, entering public life at the same time as the Constitution, he had presumed that freedom of religion and of speech had already been achieved. Only when his thinking moved beyond orthodoxy and he ventured to announce his ideas in public did he experience the informal means of pressure that still served to marginalize the bearers of heterodox ideas. When he decided to forge ahead anyway, his lectures and publications made him the foremost American example of a public freethinker, since Jefferson, obviously the more famous figure, had chosen a politic reserve. Palmer had come to play a symbolic role much larger than his relatively small following might suggest, although what he symbolized depended entirely on one's perspective. Some people were heartened by his bold talk, whereas others worried that his open disregard for Christianity would weaken the nation. In the nation's first culture war, which was waged over the extension or restriction of democracy and the expansion or curtailment of rights, the struggle for religious freedom always evoked its other side: the potential for a bewildering pluralism. Palmer experienced firsthand, in personal form, the contest taking place nationwide between religious multiplicity and a preference for conformity, between freedom of speech and the desire to contain it. In this volatile mix of openness and constraint, Palmer became a flashpoint. By enacting his right to free speech, he expanded what the public would tolerate, even as he fueled ongoing concerns about the effects of religious freethought.

Palmer was right about at least one thing. A pluralistic and democratic nation required a common ground for morality that did not presume any one, or even any, religious faith. Without a shared religion, with the insistence on free speech, and with a relatively uncontrolled print culture, cultural diversity was here to stay. What could serve as a foundation for ethical conduct in a religiously diverse democracy? Palmer offered his own particular answer: a morality based on the condition of being part of an interconnected natural world. He believed everyone could agree on this, once they allowed themselves to know it, namely that the shared material condition of all things prompted an ethics of compassion. The idea of a heartfelt benevolence for all living things did not gain many adherents in his lifetime, but it would live on into the future, changing form and inspiring others to imagine kinship on a cosmic scale.

EPILOGUE

Into the Future

When Elihu Palmer died unexpectedly in the spring of 1806, he left family members and many conversation partners behind. His widow immediately faced some difficult choices, because she had no fixed residence and no income. Mary Palmer put out a third edition of *Principles of Nature*, hoping for some revenue. She had to "sell my furniture to pay my rent the first of may," she told a friend, and was "in very bad health and really tired of my life." Her situation changed in July when Thomas Paine, who had returned to New York City, experienced something like a stroke, a "fit of apoplexy," he said, that "deprived me of all sense and motion." He described how the "fit took me on the stairs, as suddenly as if I had been shot through the head." He claimed his "mental faculties have remained as perfect as I ever enjoyed them." Even so, Paine was physically impaired and required care. "As soon as he recovered his senses he called for me," Mary reported, "and I have been with him ever since." He paid for Mary Palmer to take her own room at the places he stayed: Winship's boardinghouse at Coerlear's Hook, then the home of his friend, the English-born freethinker and ferrier, William Carver. Paine told Mary that she "must never leave him while he lives" and that he would include her in his will.[1]

Tending Paine could not have been an easy job. He could not walk or get in or out of bed without aid. He suffered from chronic discomfort and, some said, drank too much brandy. Paine's former ally and then enemy, James Cheetham, published descriptions of Paine as constantly inebriated, filthy, and rude. Much has been made of Paine's drinking ever since, with hostile gossip passing as evidence. William Carver, whose relationship with Paine soured over money, felt nonetheless that "Cheetham knew that he told a lie saying Paine was drunk." John Fellows said people lied terribly about Paine, who "was neither drunken nor filthy; he drank as other people did, and was a high-minded gentleman."²

Be that as it may, Paine continued to be an interlocutor for Mary Palmer, who had so recently lost her best conversation partner. Word made it as far as London, to the English freethinker and printer Richard Carlile, that "the widow of Elihu Palmer, was known frequently to be disputing the propriety of her husband's principles on materialism with Mr. Paine, and appealing to the arguments of Stewart as an authority: in which disputations she would frequently reduce Mr. Paine to the confession of 'it may be so.'" The account is apocryphal, but Mary Palmer may well have adopted Stewart's views of vital matter and engaged Paine in a serious and opinionated manner.³

By October 1807, Mary Palmer had moved in with her sister, a "Mrs. Holdron at Greenwich." Mary "appears very well off," said an acquaintance, who had heard "rumours that she is abt. taking another husband." She did not remarry. How well off could the forty-five-year-old widow be? Finding a haven with family was helpful, of course, but the conversation at her sister's house was stifling. Mary handed John Fellows her husband's unfinished book manuscript, "Political World," because her "bigoted sister" would have burned it had Mary not secreted it to Fellows for safekeeping. She and Fellows continued to visit Paine frequently, who spent his last days in the home of her married niece. Shortly before his death, Paine entrusted Mary with his last essay, the "reply to the Bishop of Llandaff," which Fellows reprinted in the short-lived freethinking newspaper he edited in 1810, the *Theophilanthropist*. Paine's will bequeathed one hundred dollars to "Mrs. Palmer, widow of Elihu Palmer." She continued to live in New York City, and probably remained friends with John Fellows and other freethinkers in town, until her death, in 1816, at the age of fifty-four.⁴

What of Elihu Palmer's two sons? Without knowing their names, they have been difficult to find in the archives. When Palmer died, his oldest son, if he still lived, would have been fourteen, the younger son around twelve. Fellows recounted that they lived with their grandfather in Connecticut, but Elihu Palmer Sr. left no will that might have revealed their names, and what happened to them remains unknown. Palmer Sr. lived in Scotland, Connecticut, until March 1810, when he died in the hamlet where he had lived for all of his eighty-two years. Palmer's brother, Nathan, continued to thrive in Wilkes-Barre, Pennsylvania, as a freethinking lawyer. He took various positions in municipal and state government and served as a state senator from 1808 to 1810. Then he moved with his family to Mt. Holly, New Jersey, and published the *New Jersey Mirror*. One son, Volney B. Palmer, changed the advertising business, making big money off the idea that only advertising could insure the independence and freedom of a press.[5]

John Stewart stayed in the United States long enough to publish another book in 1806, then he returned to England. Palmer had been his most admiring conversation partner in America. After Palmer's death, the Deistical Society lost much of its driving force and possibly any interest in hearing more from Stewart. Certainly Paine would not have been a reason for Stewart to stay in the United States. Although old friends, Stewart and Paine had disagreed about religion and politics for years, and Palmer was no longer there to mediate between them. Back in London, Stewart was surprised to receive a handsome sum for his services in India. The East India Company had settled the debts of the Nawab of Arcot and granted Stewart £10,000 in back pay. Stewart moved into a house at Charing Cross, decorated it with mirrors and chandeliers, and put on lavish salons that featured professional musicians, plentiful food and drink (of which he partook only sparingly), and his signature lectures. He walked many hours every day and could readily be found in St. James's Park or on Westminster Bridge discussing sensate atoms. He published more than thirty books, including *Roll of a Tennis Ball*, *Through the Moral World*, and his color-tinted portrait adorned shop windows. In his seventies, Stewart began to suffer poor health. He had often said that people should not long endure extreme suffering because it hurt not only them as individuals but also the entirety of matter, to which they transferred their torment. Should his own life ever become painful "without hope of remedy," he would end it. The "prospect of euthanasia" was liberating, he said, as it "casts a cheerful light" over life. When a visit to the seaside town of Margate did not relieve his symptoms, Stewart died at home in 1822, the day after his seventy-fifth birthday. An empty bottle of laudanum, an opium tincture, was found in his room.[6]

Stewart's friend Thomas De Quincey (known for his *Confessions of an English Opium Eater*) remembered him fondly. Of course one must read Stewart's works "with some indulgence," De Quincey admitted. The titles were pretentious, the composition "lax and imprecise," and the metaphysical speculations perhaps "untenable." But De Quincey found that "if Walking Stewart were at all crazy, he was so in a way which did not affect his natural genius and eloquence—but rather exalted them." Stewart was "a sublime visionary," De Quincey said, who struggled to convey ideas that remained "in a crude state—imperfect, obscure, half developed, and not producible to a popular audience. He was aware of this himself." Stewart had said that he "never found above ten individuals, over all the world," able to "take a comprehensive view of the tree of existence, or homo-ousia life." He would have been pleased to know that in 1842 his work appeared in a compendium of philosophical essays that included some by Spinoza, Helvétius, Pope, Paine, Palmer, and Bolingbroke. Readers browsing in bookstores in New York, New Jersey, Boston, and Philadelphia could read Stewart's essays and contemplate anew the notion that a shared, sensate substance composed all things.[7]

Palmer's name also lived on, for a while. At a commemorative celebration of Thomas Paine's birthday in New York in 1827, participants raised a glass to "the memory of Elihu Palmer, Voltaire, Hume, and all those deceased philosophers who, by their writings, contributed to subvert superstition, and vindicate the rights of humanity." Richard Carlile, the London printer, had heard Stewart's stories about Palmer and wished to learn more. Carlile took up correspondence with John Fellows, prompting Fellows to write his memoir about Palmer's life and to send it with the manuscript pages of Palmer's unfinished second book, "Political World." Carlile and his wife, Jane, stood trial in 1819 and then endured years of prison time and steep fines for publishing the "blasphemy" of Paine and Palmer. Upon his release in 1823, the intrepid Carlile once more published Paine's *Age of Reason* and Palmer's *Principles of Nature*, insisting on a freedom of speech that was not yet protected by English law.[8]

John Fellows remained a freethinker himself. No longer a bookseller, he made a living in various ways: as an auctioneer, as the superintendent of the Manhattan Water Works, then as the military storekeeper in New York. But he continued to advocate for his freethinking friends. In 1825, he sent Thomas Jefferson a copy of *The Theological Works of Thomas Paine*, purportedly printed by Richard Carlile in London but really, Fellows disclosed, by a bookseller in New York City who feared repercussions from religious critics. In his note to Jefferson, Fellows deplored the "shameful abuse which has been profusely bestowed upon Thomas Paine and his writings." In his reply to Fellows, Jefferson remembered the vehement opposition to Paine. That Paine had "encountered great abuse was a thing of course" in his day, Jefferson wrote, "nor has the genus irritabile vatum [irritable tribe of prophets] whom he bearded by these works, been found the most sparing of adversaries in the use of invective." Yet Paine's "political labors entitled him to the gratitude of his country," Jefferson continued, and "I never hesitated to bare [illegible] my . . ." The last phrase Jefferson crossed out, perhaps recalling that he had indeed hesitated to show his appreciation for Paine upon his return to the United States in 1802.[9]

When given the opportunity, Fellows published Palmer's unfinished work. Gilbert Vale, editor of the *Beacon*, asked Fellows to edit the newspaper briefly in 1841, and Fellows printed his memoir of Palmer's life along with three chapters of Palmer's manuscript, "Political World." In conversation, too, Fellows kept memories of older freethinkers alive. In his seventies, Fellows impressed a young man named Walt Whitman. The future poet remembered the older Fellows as "tall, with ruddy face, blue eyes, snowy hair, and a fine voice; neat in dress, an old-school gentleman, with a military air, who used to awe the crowd by his looks.'" Whitman considered it "the most happy good luck in my early days to fall in with superior men—the higher man of that past era," and he saw Fellows as "one of the finest of them all. He had been a bosom friend of Paine in his last days—Paine's last days. How good the stories he told! how well reflecting things as they must have been!" One good story would have been Elihu Palmer's astonishing life: a blind proselytizer dedicated to the concept that everything in the world is made of one substance and has a shared destiny. Whitman later wrote a poem with an opening Palmer would have loved. "I celebrate myself, and sing myself, / And what I assume you shall assume, / For every atom belonging to me as good belongs to you // . . . // My tongue, every atom of my blood, form'd from this soil, this air."[10]

Palmer's particular version of vitalism, inspired as it was by eighteenth-century European physiology and then furthered through the kind of meditation John Stewart learned about on his eastern travels, was only one iteration of the long-lived idea of a unified reality. In the nineteenth century, Romantic poets like Whitman, Transcendentalists like Ralph Waldo Emerson, and other adherents of a "religion of nature," differently imagined a creative force coursing through a harmonious universe. Palmer's conception of the world as a single, active whole was one variant of a cosmology that has had different names and distinctive manifestations, including Spinoza's monism and the modern-day deep ecology movement. When viewed within a larger chronological frame, Palmer's ideas are part of a story that has roots in ancient times and tendrils spiraling into an unknown future.[11]

By Whitman's day, religious freethought had come into its own as a public presence in the United States. Skeptics, utopianists, even outright atheists openly challenged the supernatural foundations of revealed religion. Yet disapproval for religious freethought never disappeared, and in some circles it became even more entrenched. By the 1820s, the American Bible Society and the American Tract Society had sold millions of proselytizing publications, and religiously inspired reform movements to abolish slavery and curb the consumption of alcohol began to sweep the country. Anxiety about the arrival of millions of immigrants from Ireland and Germany revived anti-Catholicism among Protestants who warned that "Popery" was immoral, dangerous, and incompatible with republican democracy. Protestants became, if anything, even more convinced of the nation's providential place in history and its divine mandate to enact a "manifest destiny" of white Protestant dominion over the entire continent. Religious prejudices found legal form, with restrictions placed on the civil rights of Catholics, Jews, freethinkers, and nonconformist Protestants like the Latter Day Saints. In moments of growing political rifts, Americans once more accused one another of harboring religious beliefs incompatible with patriotism. The hostility Palmer experienced in the 1790s, the enmity from Federalist Christians who referenced an invading atheist Illuminati and denounced religious freethinkers in the nation's first culture war, found new expression in the following decades. As before, anxious conspiracy thinking flourished alongside an irrepressible pluralism. Neither could vanquish the other.[12]

Palmer's long-held conviction—that the recognition of the fundamental unity of the world would produce a universal benevolence—now seems naïve. Certainly the future did not unfold as he expected. The staying power of supernatural religion would have surprised Palmer as much as Thomas

Jefferson, who proclaimed in 1822 that "I trust that there is not a *young man* now living in the United States who will not die an Unitarian." Both freethinkers underestimated the perseverance of deeply held faith in revealed religion. Religious bigotry and strife continued as well. More than two centuries after Palmer's death, his long-time Manhattan address, 71 Cortlandt Street, cannot be found on city maps because the street runs invisibly between the two commemorative reflecting pools where the World Trade Center once stood. The shocking, devastating violence that produced that memorial had its source, Palmer might have said, in the effort to discern the will of God from a book of miracles. To seek the divine in *any* written text was a crucial mistake, in his view. Miracles do occur, he thought, and constantly, but only as part of the natural world. Palmer agreed with Paine that "every thing is a miracle" and that "no one thing is a greater miracle than another. The elephant, though larger, is not a greater miracle than a mite; nor a mountain a greater miracle than an atom." This simple, marvelous fact becomes obvious, Palmer believed, with a larger awareness of the living whole.[13]

That shift in perspective also reveals an authentic morality grounded in something other than revealed religion. A democratic republic did indeed require a moral citizenry that complied with norms of civility and upheld the rule of law, but a working democracy did not need, and would not benefit from, a shared religion, Palmer thought. A self-governing people required instead unfettered freedom of conscience and of speech, along with the ability to tolerate a wide array of ideas. Such freedom would allow for discoveries of the natural world that could help humankind achieve social justice and move toward a better future.

Palmer understood that human perfectibility would take a while, yet the "spirit of persecution" that bears "hard upon the rights of conscience," as he had noted in 1792, lasted longer than he ever imagined. Religious pluralism had shaped the United States since its founding, but the fact of diversity did not ensure its acceptance, and freethought developed in tandem with intolerance. Palmer himself did not demonstrate the generosity he advocated. Still, he continued to promote the effort to make room for differences of religious opinion, to practice freedom of expression, and to act with compassion for all living things. The striving mattered, in his opinion. He believed it remained to those who came after him to fulfil the dream of a better future. That they would achieve it eventually, he had no doubt.[14]

NOTES

Prologue

1. John Wood, *A Full Exposition of the Clintonian Faction, and the Society of the Columbian Illuminati; with an account of the writer of the Narrative, and the characters of his certificate men, as also remarks on Warren's Pamphlet* (Newark: printed for the author, 1802).
2. *National Gazette* (Philadelphia), March 15, 1792, p. 159.
3. Benjamin Rush, "Address to the People of the United States," in *The American Museum, or Repository of Ancient and Modern Fugitive Pieces [. . .] for January, 1787* (Philadelphia: Carey, Stewart, 1790), 8–11, 8; From the *Gazette of the United States*, reprinted in the *Washington Federalist*, August 26, 1801, p. 3.
4. John Adams to Benjamin Rush, February 6, 1805, Founders Online, founders.archive.gov.
5. For a compelling account of the role that depictions of violence played in the partisanship of the 1790s, see Rachel Hope Cleves, *The Reign of Terror in America: Visions of Violence from Anti-Jacobinism to Antislavery* (Cambridge: Cambridge University Press, 2009), introduction, chaps. 1–2. A now classic exploration of the theme is John R. Howe Jr., "Republican Thought and Political Violence in the 1790s," *American Quarterly* 19 (1967): 147–165.
6. Kerry S. Walters, *Elihu Palmer's "Principles of Nature": Text and Commentary* (Wolfeboro, NH: Longwood Academic Press, 1990), 250. This reprint of the third edition from 1806 is the most conveniently available version of Palmer's book.
7. Walters, *Elihu Palmer's "Principles of Nature,"* 225.
8. On the Ruggles case and blasphemy law, see Sarah Barringer Gordon, "Blasphemy and the Law of Religious Liberty in Nineteenth-Century America," *American Quarterly* 52, no. 4 (December 2000): 682–719; Christopher Grasso, "The Boundaries of Toleration and Tolerance: Religious Infidelity in the Early American Republic," in *The First Prejudice: Religious Tolerance and Intolerance in Early America*, ed. Chris Beneke and Christopher S. Grenda (Philadelphia: University of Pennsylvania Press, 2011), 286–302.
9. [David Denniston], *General remarks, on the proceedings lately had in the adjacent country, relative to infidelity: comprehending the conduct of those persons who signed an address to the former editor of the Mirror; the writings of D. N. the conduct of the Goshen printer; together with some general observations. On the consequences of persecution.* (Newburgh, NY: David Denniston, 1798), 14.
10. G. Adolf Koch, *Republican Religion: The American Revolution and the Cult of Reason* (New York: Henry Holt, 1933), chap. 2; Herbert M. Morais, *Deism in Eighteenth Century America* (New York: Columbia University Press, 1934), chap. 5.
11. Henry F. May, *The Enlightenment in America*, (New York: Oxford University Press, 1976), 124; Kerry S. Walters, *The American Deists: Voices of Reason and Dissent in the Early Republic* (Lawrence: University Press of Kansas, 1992), 388. Walters located deism's end in 1811, so he did not include books that focus mostly on a later period, for example, Susan

Jacoby's *Freethinkers: A History of American Freethinkers* (New York: Metropolitan Books, 2004); or Catherine A. Albanese's wide-ranging *A Republic of Mind and Spirit: A Cultural History of American Metaphysical Religion* (New Haven, CT: Yale University Press, 2007). For more on Palmer as a deist, see "Introduction" in Walters, *Elihu Palmer's "Principles of Nature"*; Kerry S. Walters, *Revolutionary Deists: Early America's Rational Infidels* (New York: Prometheus Press, 2011), chap. 6; Terry J. Moore, "Neither True nor Divine: Elihu Palmer's Opposition to Christianity" (Ph.D. diss., New Orleans Baptist Theological Seminary, 1994). More recent descriptions of Palmer as a deist include Nathalie Caron, "Introduction to the Life and Work of a Militant American Deist: Elihu Palmer (1764–1806)," in *Religion et culture aux États-Unis*, Hélène Christol, ed., Annales Du Monde Anglophone 9 (Université de Province, 1999), 35–45; E. Brooks Holifield, *Theology in America: Christian Thought from the Age of the Puritans to the Civil War* (New Haven, CT: Yale University Press, 2003), 159–172; Eric Schlereth, "A Tale of Two Deists: John Fitch, Elihu Palmer, and the Boundary of Tolerable Religious Expression in Early National Philadelphia," *Pennsylvania Magazine of History and Biography* 132, no. 1 (January 2008): 5–31; Kirsten Fischer, "'Religion Governed by Terror': A Deist Critique of Fearful Christianity in the Early American Republic," *Revue Française D'Études Américaines* 125 (3e Trimestre 2010): 13–26; Eric R. Schlereth, *An Age of Infidels: The Politics of Religious Controversy in the Early United States* (Philadelphia: University of Pennsylvania Press, 2013); Christopher Grasso, *Skepticism and American Faith: From the Revolution to the Civil War* (New York: Oxford University Press, 2018). Palmer as deist also receives mention in Mark A. Noll, *America's God: From Jonathan Edwards to Abraham Lincoln* (New York: Oxford University Press, 2002); Matthew Stewart, *Nature's God: The Heretical Origins of the American Republic* (New York: W. W. Norton, 2014); Jonathan Israel, *The Expanding Blaze: How the American Revolution Ignited the World, 1775–1848* (Princeton, NJ: Princeton University Press, 2017); J. C. D. Clark, *Thomas Paine: Britain, America, and France in the Age of Enlightenment and Revolution* (Oxford: Oxford University Press, 2018). On the supposedly definitive end of deism as a movement in America, see Koch, *Republican Religion*, 292; Walters, *Revolutionary Deists*, 246; Noll, *America's God*, 143; Grasso, *Skepticism and American Faith*, 142–143.

12. [Isaac Ledyard], *An Essay on Matter* (Philadelphia, 1784); [John Stewart] *The Revelation of Nature, with the Prophecy of Reason* (New York: printed by Mott & Lyon, for the author. In the fifth year of intellectual existence, or the publication of the apocalypse of nature, 3000 years from the Grecian Olympiads, and 4800 from recorded knowledge of the Chinese tables of eclipses, beyond which chronology is lost in fable [1796]). A philosophy professor noticed in 1979 that Palmer "arrived at positions distinctly novel in American thought up to this time." Roderick S. French, "Elihu Palmer, Radical Deist, Radical Republican: A Reconsideration of American Freethought," in Studies in Eighteenth-Century Culture 8, ed. Roseann Runte (Madison: University of Wisconsin Press, 1979), 87–108, quote on 98. In 2010, I described Palmer as a deist; six years later, I insisted on his vitalism. It seems to me now that these categories are too rigid or perhaps beside the point. What matters is Palmer's understanding of sensate matter and its implication for humankind. See Fischer, "'Religion Governed by Terror'"; and Kirsten Fischer, "Vitalism in America: Elihu Palmer's Radical Religion in the Early Republic," *William and Mary Quarterly* 73, no. 3 (July 2016): 501–530.

Chapter 1

1. James Cogswell's Diary, 1781–1791, MS 34167, Connecticut Historical Society, Hartford, April 8, 1782 ("My mind"); James Cogswell, *The necessity of repentence in order to avoid destruction, considered and urged, in a sermon, occasioned by the unhappy and untimely death of Cotterel Smith, delivered at the Third Society in Windham, April 9, 1782* (Norwich, CT: John Trumbull, 1783), iii (all other quotes).

2. Historians have guessed that Palmer grew up in either Windham, Canterbury, or Norwich, Connecticut, but not in the hamlet of Scotland, which was his actual home. Palmer's close friend John Fellows also did not know. See John Fellows, comp., *Posthumous Pieces by Elihu Palmer [. . .]* (London: R. Carlile, 1824), 4. Lists of names on headstones in Windham County cemeteries led me to the village of Scotland. Lois Palmer's name among the church's communicants in 1753 and Elihu Palmer's baptism in 1764 (he was born August 7) are recorded in the Scotland Congregational Church records, vol. 2, reel 345, Connecticut State Library, Hartford. In 1783, the Scotland congregation had 186 members. The obituary for Elihu Palmer, Sr., remembered him as one of the "most valuable members" of his ecclesiastical society. *Windham Herald*, March 30, 1810. The protagonist of this book was Elihu Palmer III, and his father appears in the records as Elihu Palmer Jr., but the younger man never availed himself of the suffix "III" and signed his first publication as "Elihu Palmer, jun." To avoid confusion, the book refers to its protagonist as Elihu Palmer, or simply as Palmer, and to his father as Palmer Sr. One historian claims that Cogswell, like Ebenezer Devotion before him, "fitted young men for college and trained them for the ministry." Ellen D. Larned, *History of Windham County, Connecticut* (Worcester, MA: Charles Hamilton, 1874), 1: 572. Cogswell did not record in his diary that he tutored students, but it would have been normal for him to catechize children and prepare local school boys for college. He had, in earlier years, run a boarding school for boys out of his home.

3. George Whitefield, *A sermon on the eternity of hell-torments* (Boston: G. Rogers and D. Fowle, 1740), 3 ("Eternity"); George Whitefield, *The marks of the new-birth: A sermon preach'd by the Reverend Mr. George Whitefield* (Boston: G. Rogers and D. Fowle, 1740), 5 ("re-instamp"). On Nathan Cole dropping his tools in the rush to hear Whitefield preach, see Douglas L. Winiarski, *Darkness Falls on the Land of Light: Experiencing Religious Awakenings in Eighteenth-Century New England* (Chapel Hill: University of North Carolina Press, 2017), 133–139, and 139 ("heart wound"); Michael J. Crawford, "The Spiritual Travels of Nathan Cole," *William and Mary Quarterly* 33, no. 1 (January 1976): 89–126. The scholarship on religious revivals in the American colonies is extensive. On the religious experiences of ordinary people during the revivals, see especially Nathan O. Hatch, *The Democratization of American Christianity* (New Haven, CT: Yale University Press, 1989); Jon Butler, *Awash in a Sea of Faith: Christianizing the American People* (Cambridge, MA: Harvard University Press, 1990); Patricia Bonomi, *Under the Cope of Heaven: Religion, Society, and Politics in Colonial America*, updated ed. (Oxford: Oxford University Press, 2003); Susan Juster, *Disorderly Women: Sexual Politics and Evangelicalism in Revolutionary New England* (Ithaca, NY: Cornell University Press, 1994); Christine Leigh Heyrman, *Southern Cross: The Beginnings of the Bible Belt* (Chapel Hill: University of North Carolina Press, 1997).

4. Winiarski, *Darkness Falls on the Land of Light*, 137–138. On Whitefield's preaching style, see also Harry S. Stout, *The Divine Dramatist: George Whitefield and the Rise of Modern Evangelicalism* (Grand Rapids, MI: W. B. Eerdmans, 1991), 38–44; Frank Lambert, *"Pedlar in Divinity": George Whitefield and the Transatlantic Revivals, 1737–1770*, rev. ed. (Princeton, NJ: Princeton University Press, 2002); Thomas S. Kidd, *George Whitefield: America's Spiritual Founding Father* (New Haven, CT: Yale University Press, 2014). One of the revivalists' greatest critics, Reverend Charles Chauncy, worried that the revival was a satanic delusion. See Edward M. Griffin, *Old Brick: Charles Chauncy of Boston, 1705–1787* (Minneapolis: University of Minnesota Press, 1980), chap. 6.

5. For the American version of the long-standing debate over the role of reason in Christian theology, see E. Brooks Holifield, *Theology in America: Christian Thought from the Age of the Puritans to the Civil War* (New Haven, CT: Yale University Press, 2003).

6. On Wheelock, see Winiarski, *Darkness Falls on the Land of Light*, 171. Winiarski notes that Wheelock's 1741 letter contains one of the earliest references to the term "New Lights."

My discussion of the revivalists in the small villages of eastern Connecticut is indebted to the prodigious research presented in Winiarski's book. A lucid account of the different approaches among New Light ministers in Connecticut is Mark Valeri, *Law and Providence in Joseph Bellamy's New England: The Origins of the New Divinity in Revolutionary America* (Oxford: Oxford University Press, 1994).

7. Winiarski, *Darkness Falls on the Land of Light*, 294–295, 298 ("*Devil incarnate*"). See also Butler, *Awash in a Sea of Faith*, 182–186. On the dramatic and even devastating psychological toll of some conversion experiences, see Heyrman, *Southern Cross*.

8. Winiarski, *Darkness Falls on the Land of Light*, 252–53, 326. On the gendered nature of conversion experiences, see Juster, *Disorderly Women*. Juster in *Disorderly Women* and Heyrman in *Southern Cross* show that revivalist movements offered socially marginalized people a platform for spiritual authority but that by the end of the century the authority of white male preachers had been restored. For the argument that the religious revivals generally featured a conservative approach to authority, see Butler, *Awash in a Sea of Faith*, esp. 179–182; Amanda Porterfield, *Conceived in Doubt: Religion and Politics in the New American Nation* (Chicago: University of Chicago Press, 2012).

9. The Separates in Scotland are quoted in Ebenezer Devotion, *An answer of the pastor and brethren of the Third Church in Windham, to twelve articles, exhibited by several of its separating members, as reasons of their separation: shewing, that said members have unhappily mistook the occasions of their separation* (New London, CT: T. Green, 1747), 1. The Saybrook Platform organized regional associations of ministers and laymen to oversee the selection of new clergy. See C. C. Goen, *Revivalism and Separatism in New England, 1740–1800: Strict Congregationalists and Separate Baptists in the Great Awakening* (Middletown, CT, 1987), 38–40. For a nuanced discussion of the religious factions in revivalist Connecticut, see Valeri, *Law and Providence*, esp. chap. 1.

10. *A letter from the Associated Ministers of the County of Windham, to the people in the several societies in said county* (Boston: J. Draper, 1745), 6.

11. *Letter from the Associated Ministers*, 6.

12. *Boston Gazette* quoted in John W. Jeffries, "The Separation in the Canterbury Congregational Church: Religion: Family, and Politics in a Connecticut Town," *New England Quarterly* 52, no. 4 (December 1979): 522–549. My narration of the conflict in Canterbury relies heavily on Jeffries's article.

13. Jeffries, "Separation," 530. On the struggle in Canterbury, see also Goen, *Revivalism and Separatism*, 70–75, 115–123, 531; Larned, *History of Windham County*, 1: 437–444.

14. Winiarski, *Darkness Falls on the Land of Light*, 424. Brought before court magistrates in New London in November 1748, Wilkinson confessed her "vile and Prophain, Discorse and actions" and paid a fine. Winiarski, *Darkness Falls on the Land of Light*, 425. Wilkinson and her family belonged to a small group who believed themselves already resurrected, perfect, and immortal.

15. Winiarski, *Darkness Falls on the Land of Light*, 423–424, 427. When the Connecticut superior court rather surprisingly acquitted John and Mary of all murder charges, the two got married, remained in Canterbury, and started a new family.

16. James Cogswell, *The necessity of piety wisdom and labour, in order to acceptance with God in the work of the Gospel ministry. A sermon delivered at the ordination of the Reverend Mr. Josiah Whitney, Brooklyn in Pomfret, on the 4th day of February, 1756. By James Cogswell, A. M. Pastor of the church in Canterbury.* (New Haven, CT: James Parker and Company, 1757), 11. Cogswell's mild demeanor comes through in his diary. He does not record grudges or criticize others; he forgives insults and expresses gratitude and self-doubt. Others also described him as a mild-mannered, sociable, and pleasant person.

17. Cogswell, *Necessity of piety*, 16–20.

18. Quoted in Dave Richard Palmer, *George Washington and Benedict Arnold: A Tale of Two Patriots* (Washington DC: Regnery, 2006), 32–33. See also James K. Martin, *Benedict Arnold, Revolutionary Hero: An American Warrior Reconsidered* (New York: New York University Press, 1997), 26.

19. Larned, *History of Windham County*, 1: 459–460 ("did not preach"). On Rev. Devotion, see Mark A. Noll, "Ebenezer Devotion: Religion and Society in Revolutionary Connecticut," *Church History* 45, no. 3 (September 1976): 293–307; Kevin J. Hayes, "Portraits of the Mind: Ebenezer Devotion and Ezra Stiles," *New England Quarterly* 70, no. 4 (December 1997): 616–630.

20. Ebenezer Devotion, *An answer of the pastor and brethren of the Third Church in Windham, to twelve articles, exhibited by several of its separating members, as reasons of their separation: Shewing, that said members have unhappily mistook the occasions of their separation* (New London, CT: T. Green, 1747), 10. See also Larned, *History of Windham County*, 1: 459–464.

21. Larned, *History of Windham County*, 1: 459 ("deficient"). John Palmer and Elihu Palmer Sr. were related through their paternal grandfathers, who were brothers. At the age of eighty, Palmer Sr. was not among those listed who took Holy Communion. Perhaps he had become too frail to attend church service, or maybe he chose not to participate in the sacrament. His obituary said the ecclesiastical society "to which he belonged, has been deprived of one of its most valuable members. As he lived, so he ended his life, like *the good man*." *Windham Herald*, March 30, 1810, p. 3. The 1808 list of communicants is in the Scotland Congregational Church records, vol. 3, reel 345, Connecticut State Library.

22. The genealogical connection to Standish is laid out in *The Commemorative Biographical Record of Tolland and Windham Counties*, vol. 1 (Chicago: J. H. Beers, 1903). Elihu Palmer did not write about Myles Standish or any other family members, but his brother Nathan frequently referenced their Standish lineage, as Nathan's granddaughter remembered years later. See *New England Historical and Genealogical Register*, 30: 462. A critic later reported that Palmer's freethought had disgraced his lineage. "On his mother's side, his descent is said to have been from the Rev. John Robinson of Leyden, Holland, and the well known Miles Standish. What a falling off was this!!" George T. Chapman, *Sketches of the Alumni of Dartmouth College: From the First Graduation in 1771 to the Present Time; With a Brief History of the Institution* (Cambridge, MA: Riverside Press, 1867), 46–47.

23. On the Palmer family tree, see James R. Boylan and Williams Haynes, *Stonington Chronology 1649–1976: Being a Year-by-Year Record of the American Way of Life* (Chester, CT: published for the Stonington Historical Society by Pequot Press, 1976), 12–14. On Walter Palmer, see also Emily Wilder Leavitt, *Palmer Groups: John Melvin of Charlestown and Concord, Mass., and His Descendants* (1901–1905), 9–14. For Abigail Robinson's family line, see *Genealogical and Biographical Record of New London County, Connecticut* (Chicago: J. H. Beers, 1905), 425. For the ways in which English settlers encroached on Indian lands and eventually made their land claims permanent, see Jean M. O'Brien, *Dispossession by Degrees: Indian Land and Identity in Natick, Massachusetts, 1650–1790* (Cambridge: Cambridge University Press, 1997).

24. Windham Land Records and Deeds, vols. L–M, reel 5037; Town of Windham Deeds, General Index, 1706–1818, reel 5032, Connecticut State Library. William Floyd Willingham, "Windham, Connecticut: Profile of a Revolutionary Community, 1755–1818" (Ph.D. diss., Northwestern University, 1972), 41, 47, 50. Willingham explains that the highest town offices of moderator, selectman, and clerk were held by the wealthiest men, whereas other town offices were held by men of diverse economic standing. Brander and poundkeeper were among the least important offices but do not suggest low social ranking. Willingham, "Windham, Connecticut," 53–54.

25. The names and birthdays of the Palmer children are in *Commemorative Biographical Record of Tolland and Windham Counties*, 105. On eighteenth-century parents who grieved the loss of their children, see Linda A. Pollack, *Forgotten Children: Parent-Child Relations from 1500 to 1900* (Cambridge: Cambridge University Press, 1983), 133–134, 141.

26. That "Revnd Mr James Cogwell was Dismised from this Church" is in *Records of the Congregational Church in Canterbury, Connecticut, 1711–1844, Published Jointly by the Connecticut Historical Society and the Society of Mayflower Descendants in the State of Connecticut*. (Hartford, CT: Finlay Brothers, 1932), 152. That the position in Scotland came as a relief to Cogswell is apparent in a letter from his son: "I rejoyce at the favourable aspect of your affairs relative to Scotland." James Cogswell Jr. to Rev. James Cogswell Sr., January 17, 1772, Cogswell Family Papers, series 1, box 1, folder 2, Yale University Manuscripts and Archives, New Haven, CT. Rev. Cogswell accepted the call to the Scotland Church on January 27, 1772. See the Scotland Congregational Church records, vol. 2, reel 345, Connecticut State Library. That Cogswell moved into Martha Devotion's "pleasant homestead" is in Larned, *History of Windham County*, 2: 56. For Cogswell's appreciation of his second wife, Martha, see the Diary of James Cogswell, 1773–1775, in the George Waldo Papers, Yale University Manuscripts and Archives.

27. Cogswell's Diary, May 16, 1781 ("I fear"), August 30, 1781 ("did not pray"), October 3, 1782 ("politics"); September 25, 1781 ("Chore"); April 4, 1782 ("Hurry"); November 10, 1782 ("little sense"); May 5, 1782 ("some sense"; "pleasant to pray").

28. Willingham, "Windham, Connecticut," 127. In an election sermon to the General Assembly in Hartford, Cogswell said that true patriotism was motivated by religious principles and that faith-based patriotism fueled a righteous cause. See *A sermon, preached before the General Assembly of the colony of Connecticut, at Hartford, on the day of their anniversary election, May 9th, 1771. By James Cogswell, A. M. Pastor of the First Church in Canterbury* (New London, CT: Timothy Green, 1771).

29. Willingham, "Windham, Connecticut," 132–140. See also Oscar Zeichner, *Connecticut's Years of Controversy, 1750–1778* (Chapel Hill: University of North Carolina Press, 1949), chap. 10; Larned, *History of Windham County*, 2: 111–136.

30. Willingham, "Windham, Connecticut," 145. Between February 1777 and March 1778, twenty-seven Windham men paid the fine. Willingham, "Windham, Connecticut," 166. Seventy-six men with the last name Palmer, but none with the first name of Elihu or Thaddeus, are listed in Henry P. Johnston, *The Record of Connecticut Men in the Military and Naval Service During the War of Revolution: 1775–1783* (Hartford, CT, 1889). The records are incomplete, however. For example, the roll of noncommissioned officers and privates is missing for the Ninth Company (under Capt. Ebenezer Mosely of Windham), which was recruited in the first call for troops, in April and May 1775, as part of General Putnam's Third Regiment, recruited in Windham County. Samuel Huntington went on to serve as president of the Continental Congress from 1779 to 1781 and as state governor after 1786.

31. On wartime scarcity, inflation, and higher taxes, see Willingham, "Windham, Connecticut," chap. 6.

32. Cogswell's Diary, June 23, 1781. Robert A. Selig, *Rochambeau in Connecticut, Tracing His Journey: Historic and Architectural Survey* (Hartford, CT: Connecticut Historical Commission, 1999), 59, 61 (on army train and gear), 64 ("emerging place"). During the winter of 1780–81, several hundred French cavalry camped in the area, and the townspeople had to help supply them too. See Robert A. Selig, *Rochambeau's Cavalry: Lauzun's Legion in Connecticut, 1780–1781* (Hartford, CT: Connecticut Historical Commission, 2000), 30–34.

33. Cogswell's Diary, September 8, 1781; Larned, *History of Windham County*, 2: 202 (New London).

34. Cogswell's Diary, November 8, 1782.

35. Cogswell, *Necessity of repentence*, iii.
36. Cogswell, *Necessity of repentence*, iii.
37. Reverend Daniel Waldo, November 6, 1851, in William Sprague, *Annals of the American Pulpit* [. . .] (New York: Robert Carter & Brothers, 1857), 1: 447–448. For a description of Cogswell's preaching as "plain and practical, addressed to the understandings and consciences of his hearers," see Nathan Strong, *A Funeral Sermon* (Hartford, CT: Hudson and Goodwin, 1807), 15.
38. On the Connecticut nickname, see Walter Woodward, "The Unsteady Meaning of 'The Land of Steady Habits,'" https://connecticuthistory.org/the-unsteady-meaning-of-the-land-of-steady-habits/.
39. On the extensive library in the Devotion household, see Lance Mayer and Gay Myers, eds., *The Devotion Family: The Lives and Possessions of Three Generations in Eighteenth-Century Connecticut* (New London, CT: Lyman Allyn Art Museum, 1991), 61.
40. On Wheelock's efforts to found a missionary school for Indians that soon became a college for mostly Anglo-American boys, see James Axtell, "Eleazar Wheelock's Little Red School," in *The European and the Indian: Essays in the Ethnohistory of Colonial North America* (New York: Oxford University Press, 1981), 87–109; Colin Calloway, *The Indian History of an American Institution: Native Americans and Dartmouth* (Hanover, NH: Dartmouth College Press, 2010). Three Native American students attended in 1782, and none for the next fifteen years. See Leon B. Richardson, *History of Dartmouth College* (Hanover, NH: Dartmouth College Publications, 1932), 202. John Fellows said the charity fund that benefitted Palmer came from private donations and a state grant and was originally intended for Native American students but that these "soon became tired of the Greek and Latin languages, and left the college in disgust," making the funds available for "some of the white inhabitants." Fellows also recalled Palmer saying that he earned money by teaching in a school during college vacations. Fellows, *Posthumous Pieces*, 4–5. On financial aid and scholarships, see James Axtell, *The School upon a Hill: Education and Society in Colonial New England* (New Haven, CT: Yale University Press, 1974), 211. On the sons of farming families who attended college, often on scholarships, when land became scarce, see David F. Allmendinger Jr., *Paupers and Scholars: The Transformation of Student Life in Nineteenth-Century New England*, 4, 12. The annual average of graduates in New England is given on p. 10.

Chapter 2

1. The physical description of Palmer is based on his frontispiece portrait in Elihu Palmer, *Principles of Nature; or, A Development of the Moral Causes of Happiness and Misery Among the Human Species* (New York, 1802). On his voice, see John W. Francis, *New York During the Last Half Century: A Discourse in Commemoration of the Fifty-Third Anniversary of the New York Historical Society, and of the Dedication of their New Edifice (November 17, 1857)* (New York: John F. Trow, 1858), 90 ("pulmonary apparatus") and James Riker Jr., *The Annals of Newtown, in Queens County, New-York* [. . .] (New York: D. Fanshaw, 1852), 232 ("strong, musical voice"). This reconstruction of a confident debater is based on Palmer's membership in the United Fraternity, which staged frequent debates; his graduation with academic honors; and his lifetime proclivity for public speaking.
2. *Augusta Chronicle and Gazette of the State* (Georgia; hereafter *Augusta Chronicle*), November 14, 1789; see also November 21, 1789. Palmer published the essays under the pseudonym Alfred, as explained below.
3. For liberalizing tendencies within Calvinism in this period, see Conrad Wright, *The Beginnings of Unitarianism in America* (Boston: Beacon Press, 1955); E. Brooks Holifield, *Theology in America: Christian Thought from the Age of Puritans to the Civil War* (New Haven,

CT: Yale University Press, 2003), chap. 6; Peter S. Field, *The Crisis of the Standing Order: Clerical Intellectuals and Cultural Authority in Massachusetts, 1780–1833* (Amherst: University of Massachusetts Press, 1998), chap. 2. Field explains that the term "liberal" remained vaguely defined as an attitude of "openness, catholicity, and latitudinarian generosity to diverse doctrinal positions" (53).

4. Baxter Perry Smith, *The History of Dartmouth College* (Boston: Houghton, Osgood, 1878), 83–85; Leon B. Richardson, *History of Dartmouth College* (Hanover, NH: Dartmouth College Publications, 1932), 248–249, 376–377, 255; Joe W. Kraus, "The Development of a Curriculum in the Early American Colleges," *History of Education Quarterly* 1, no. 2 (June 1961): 64–76.

5. On the Socials, see Lois A. Krieger, *The Woodward Succession: A Brief History of the Dartmouth College Library, 1769–2002* (Hanover, NH: Dartmouth College Library, 2002), 4. Palmer was listed in the *Catalogue of the Members of the United Fraternity, Dartmouth College, August, 1818.* (Hanover, NH: Charles Spear, 1818), 17. Webster, class of 1801, is quoted in Richardson, *History of Dartmouth College*, 270. On college literary societies and their structured debates, see David Potter, "The Literary Society," in *History of Speech Education in America: Background Studies*, ed. Karl R. Wallace (New York: Appleton-Century-Crofts, 1954), 238–258; Thomas S. Harding, *College Literary Societies: Their Contribution to Higher Education in the United States, 1815–1876* (New York: Pageant Press International, 1971), chap. 1; Chris Grasso, *A Speaking Aristocracy: Transforming Public Discourse in Eighteenth-Century Connecticut* (Chapel Hill: University of North Carolina Press, 1999), 394–408; Catherine O'Donnell Kaplan, *Men of Letters in the Early Republic: Cultivating Forums of Citizenship* (Chapel Hill: University of North Carolina Press, 2008), 31–35. On rituals of male sociability in nineteenth-century college societies, see Nicholas L. Syrett, *The Company He Keeps: A History of White College Fraternities* (Chapel Hill: University of North Carolina Press, 2009).

6. *Catalogue of Books Belonging to the Library of the Social Friends* (Hanover, NH: Charles Spear, 1813), 11, 12, 16. Ethan Allen's *Reason, the Only Oracle of Man* came out in 1785, but only two hundred copies were sold, and Palmer never mentions it in his later work.

7. On the importation of freethinking books to the American colonies and their presence in college libraries, see Herbert M. Morais, *Deism in Eighteenth-Century America* (New York: Columbia University Press, 1934), chap. 2. The scholarship on English dissenters is extensive. See, for example, Knud Haakonssen, ed., *Enlightenment and Religion: Rational Dissent in Eighteenth-Century Britain*, (Cambridge: Cambridge University Press, 1996).

8. Pierre Viret had coined the term *déiste* in 1564 to refer to a group that was neither Christian nor atheist. In 1660, Blaise Pascal used *déisme* to describe the belief in a religion based on reason alone, without revelation. On deism in England, see Robert E. Sullivan, *John Toland and the Deist Controversy: A Study in Adaptations* (Cambridge, MA: Harvard University Press, 1982); Peter Byrne, *Natural Religion and the Nature of Religion: The Legacy of Deism* (London: Routledge, 1989); Peter Harrison, *"Religion" and the Religions in the English Enlightenment* (Cambridge: Cambridge University Press, 1990); J. A. I. Champion, *The Pillars of Priestcraft Shaken: The Church of England and Its Enemies, 1660–1730* (Cambridge: Cambridge University Press, 1992). Some historians use the term "deism" to mean "anti-Christian," but David Holmes points out that "some Deists renounced Christian belief more thoroughly than others" and that it was no contradiction in terms to be a Christian Deist. David L. Holmes, *The Faiths of the Founding Fathers* (Oxford University Press, 2006), 41. James Herrick writes that the "actual religious convictions of the Deists are so varied and complex as to raise questions about the descriptive usefulness of the term Deist, and controversy surrounds the theological commitments of even individual Deists." James A. Herrick, *The Radical Rhetoric of the English Deists: The Discourse of Skepticism, 1680–1750* (Columbia: University of South Carolina Press, 1997), 23–24. I do not capitalize "deism" because it was not a denomination

or a single set of beliefs. On deism in America, see Gerald R. McDermott, *Jonathan Edwards Confronts the Gods: Christian Theology, Enlightenment Religion, and Non-Christian Faiths* (Oxford: Oxford University Press, 2000); Ernest Cassara, *The Enlightenment in America* (Lanham, MD: University Press of America, 1975); Holifield, *Theology in America*, chap. 7, and the scholarship noted in my prologue.

9. John Toland, *Christianity Not Mysterious* (London, 1696), 132 ("has no interest"; "rash Presumption"), 173 ("unintelligible"), 145 ("*Knowledg*"). Palmer expressed admiration for Toland in his book, *Principles of Nature*, which came out in 1801. In the revised edition the following year, he expressed his admiration for Newton, Locke, d'Holbach, Rousseau, Voltaire, Hume, Tindal, and Bolingbroke, "together with twenty other philosophers of France and England" who "destroyed error by wholesale, and swept away the rubbish of ancient superstition." Palmer may have read some of these works in college. Kerry S. Walters, *Elihu Palmer's "Principles of Nature": Text and Commentary* (Wolfeboro, NH: Longwood Academic Press, 1990), 147, 179 ("twenty other").

10. Margaret C. Jacob, *The Radical Enlightenment: Pantheists, Freemasons and Republicans* (London: George Allen & Unwin, 1981), 36, 49–51, 152–155, 216–220. On the terms available to Toland, see Sullivan, *John Toland*, 209.

11. Richard Price, *Observations on the importance of the American Revolution, and the means of making it a benefit to the world* (Boston: Powars and Willis, 1784), 34–36, 21.

12. Price, *Observations*, 4, 7–8. Palmer's debt to Price becomes clear below.

13. On Arminianism as a theological movement in eighteenth-century New England, see Wright, *Beginnings of Unitarianism*.

14. Charles Chauncy, *The Mystery hid from Ages and Generations, made Manifest by the Gospel Revelation; Or, the Salvation of All Men* (London: for C. Dilly, 1784).

15. Chauncy, *Mystery hid*. On the opposing views of human nature at stake in the debate, as well as the perception of liberal religion as a delusional danger, see McDermott, *Jonathan Edwards*; Colin Wells, *The Devil and Doctor Dwight: Satire and Theology in the Early American Republic* (Chapel Hill: University of North Carolina Press, 2002). Wells offers the best analysis of Dwight's poem. The lines quoted here are from Wells, *Devil and Dr. Dwight*, 191.

16. Quotations from Richard J. Moss, *The Life of Jedidiah Morse: A Station of Particular Exposure* (Knoxville: University of Tennessee Press, 1995): Jedidiah Morse to his father, Jedidiah Morse Sr., January 6, 1782 ("Universal Depravity"), 18; March 15, 1781 ("exposed"), 19; June 24, 1783 ("gloomy") and November 7, 1783 ("degenerate"), 24. Morse's appreciation of "severe discipline" is quoted in Joseph W. Phillips, *Jedidiah Morse and New England Congregationalism* (New Brunswick, NJ: Rutgers University Press, 1983), 16.

17. *New-Hampshire Recorder*, September 25, 1787, p. 3. On the collapsing platform, see Richardson, *History of Dartmouth College*, 212; on the wigged audience, see Frederick Chase, *A History of Dartmouth College and the Town of Hanover New Hampshire* (Cambridge: Cambridge University Press, 1891), 1: 579. On commencement debates, see George V. Bohman, "Rhetorical Practice in Colonial America," in *History of Speech Education in America: Background Studies*, ed. Karl R. Wallace (New York: Appleton-Century-Crofts, 1954), 60–79. On the use of orations and debates to practice public controversy and to rehearse well-spoken male leadership, see Carolyn Eastman, *A Nation of Speechifiers: Making an American Public after the Revolution* (Chicago: University of Chicago Press, 2009), chap. 4, esp. 122–129.

18. *New-Hampshire Recorder*, September 25, 1787, p. 3 ("*ought a man*"); Virginia Statute for Religious Freedom (1786).

19. *Catalogue of the Members of the [Ph] B K Society; Alpha of New-Hampshire* (Hanover, NH: Moses Davis, 1806), 6. On the secret rituals of Phi Beta Kappa, see Samuel Eliot Morison, *Three Centuries of Harvard, 1636–1936* (Cambridge, MA: Harvard University Press, 1936), 181.

20. On the ad hoc training of ministers, see Walter Herbert Stowe, ed., *The Life and Letters of Bishop William White* (New York: Morehouse, 1937), 19, 196–197. That Palmer studied with "Rev. Dr. John Foster, of Massachusetts" is in Riker, *Annals of Newtown*, 232.

21. Earl Morse Wilbur, *A History of Unitarianism in Transylvania, England, and America* (Cambridge, MA: Harvard University Press, 1952), chap. 16; Wright, *Beginnings of Unitarianism*; Daniel Walker Howe, *The Unitarian Conscience: Harvard Moral Philosophy, 1805–1861* (Cambridge, MA: Harvard University Press, 1970); J. D. Bowers, *Joseph Priestley and English Unitarianism in America* (State College: Pennsylvania State University Press, 2009).

22. Wilbur, *History of Unitarianism*; J. Rixey Ruffin, *A Paradise of Reason: William Bentley and Enlightenment Christianity in the Early Republic* (Oxford: Oxford University Press, 2008). Bowers, in *Joseph Priestley*, explains that the Socinian view of a fully human Jesus was never as popular or accepted in the early United States as the Arian view that placed Christ ontologically somewhere between eternal God and mortal humans.

23. Holmes quoted in Samuel Adams Drake, *History of Middlesex County, Massachusetts* (Boston: Estes and Lauriat, 1880), 284, 283.

24. Hannah Webster Foster, *The Coquette and The Boarding School: Authoritative Texts Sources and Contexts, Criticism*, ed. Jennifer Harris and Bryan Waterman (New York: W. W. Norton, 2013), xx–xxi. For an analysis of Foster's description of marriage options for women, see Cathy N. Davidson, *Revolution and the Word: The Rise of the Novel in America* (New York: Oxford University Press, 1986), 140–150. On the common custom of reading aloud, especially before spectacles became commonplace in the late eighteenth century, see Abigail Williams, *The Social Life of Books: Reading Together in the Eighteenth-Century Home* (New Haven, CT: Yale University Press, 2017), esp. 66–68, 77.

25. Palmer "commenced preaching at Pittsfield, in Massachusetts; where he continued for some months." John Fellows, comp., *Posthumous Pieces by Elihu Palmer* [. . .] (London: R. Carlile, 1824), 5. And: "He preached some time in Pittsfield, Massachusetts, and then removed to Newtown, Long Island." James Carnahan, D. D., ed., *The Autobiography and Ministerial Life of the Rev. John Johnston, D. D.* (New York: M. W. Dodd, 1856), 90. On Allen, see Frank A. DeSorbo, "The Reverend Thomas Allen and Revolutionary Politics in Western Massachusetts" (Ph.D. diss., New York University, 1995), 39–50, 63–64. Allen claimed both orthodox principles and "a spirit of candor towards such as differ from them." Thomas Allen, *An Historical Sketch of the County of Berkshire, and Town of Pittsfield* (Boston: Belcher and Armstrong, 1808), 10. For an example of his deeply held faith in a perfect and merciful God who sent affliction to teach important lessons, see his funeral oration for his daughter, *Benefits of affliction: A funeral sermon; occasioned by the death of Mrs. Elizabeth White, consort of Mr. William P. White* [. . .] (Pittsfield: Chester Smith, 1798).

26. DeSorbo, "Reverend Thomas Allen," 172–175. On Allen as "slender, vigorous and active" and charged with "indiscreet zeal," see his son's description in William Sprague, *Annals of the American Pulpit* [. . .] (New York: Robert Carter & Brothers, 1857), 1: 610. An example of political sermonizing is Thomas Allen, *An Oration, Delivered at Pittsfield, July 4, 1803, Being the Anniversary of the Independence of the United States of America* (Pittsfield, MA: printed by Phinehas Allen, 1803). On the troubles in Pittsfield, see John L. Brooke, "To the Quiet of the People: Revolutionary Settlements and Civil Unrest in Western Massachusetts, 1774–1789," *William and Mary Quarterly* 46, no. 3 (July 1989): 425–462. On Allen as a leading constitutionalist, see Theodore M. Hammett, "Revolutionary Ideology in Massachusetts: Thomas Allen's 'Vindication' of the Berkshire Constitutionalists, 1778," *William and Mary Quarterly* 33, no. 3 (July 1976): 514–527.

27. *Berkshire Chronicle*, May 15, 1788, p. 1, May 22, 1788, pp. 1–2. "Alfred" published in the *Berkshire Chronicle* (Pittsfield) and the *Massachusetts Spy* (Worcester) only in May to October 1788, during months that Palmer was in Pittsfield, and "Alfred" published in the

Augusta Chronicle only in November and December 1789, during the time Palmer was in Augusta, Georgia. The topics are similar in all cases, featuring an emphasis on education and favorable references to Richard Price, and the style matches Palmer's. Alfred was not a common name at the time. A search in American newspapers in 1787 and 1788 shows that aside from the pen name, some ships named *Alfred*, and two remiss taxpayers in Vermont, the name appears only in connection with Alfred the Great, the ninth-century English ruler credited with promoting education for even non-noble boys and for supporting trial by jury. See, for example, the mention of King Alfred in an argument for jury trial coming out of Palmer's corner of Connecticut: "To the Inhabitants of the County of Windham" by a "constant customer" of the *Norwich Packet*, March 15, 1787. I suspect Palmer read this piece and knew the author. In October 1788, "Alfred" published three articles in the *Massachusetts Spy* that supported the new Constitution, its first ten amendments, and trial by jury.

28. *Berkshire Chronicle*, June 5, 1788, p. 1, June 12, 1788, p. 2, July 10, 1788, p. 2.

29. *Berkshire Chronicle*, June 19, 1788, p. 1 (on fortitude), June 26, 1788, p. 1 (on education).

30. On the importance of print for establishing a public persona in the early republic, see Bryan Waterman, *Republic of Intellect: The Friendly Club of New York City and the Making of American Literature* (Baltimore: Johns Hopkins University Press, 2007), esp. the introduction.

31. The *Berkshire Chronicle* makes no mention of a speech by Allen. A poem printed on July 31 mentions only Palmer's oration and that Parson Allen took part in the festive dinner afterward. On the performance of a natural aristocracy and virtuous patriotism in July 4th speeches, see David Waldstreicher, *In the Midst of Perpetual Fetes: The Making of American Nationalism, 1776–1820* (Chapel Hill: University of North Carolina Press, 1997), chap. 2, esp. 67–77; the discussion of the Albany street fight is on 99. Simon Newman explains that Independence Day celebrations had been local affairs during and just after the war and that a national political culture only emerged after ratification of the Constitution. Simon P. Newman, *Parades and Politics of the Street: Festive Culture in the Early American Republic* (Philadelphia: University of Pennsylvania Press, 1997), 38–43; Len Travers, *Celebrating the Fourth: Independence Day and the Rites of Nationalism in the Early Republic* (Amherst: University of Massachusetts Press, 1997), 48–50, 67–68. On the contested nature of the rituals of national unity, see Travers, *Celebrating the Fourth*, chap. 3; and Waldstreicher, *In the Midst of Perpetual Fetes*, chap. 2.

32. A description and engraving of the Pittsfield meetinghouse is in J. E. A. Smith, *The History of Pittsfield, Berkshire County, Massachusetts* (Boston: Lee and Shepard, 1869), 152–153, 156.

33. Elihu Palmer, *An oration pronounced in the Meeting House in Pittsfield, upon the Twelfth anniversary of the Independence of the United States of America* (Pittsfield, printed by Roger Storrs, 1788), 3. For the way local histories and orations engaged in the imaginary erasure of Indians, see Jean M. O'Brien, *Firsting and Lasting: Writing Indians Out of Existence in New England* (Minneapolis: University of Minnesota Press, 2010), esp. 55. At least one orator did find early settlers guilty of "forcibly or fraudulently depriving the natives of their possessions." See David Daggett, Esquire, *An oration, pronounced in the brick meeting-house, in the city of New-Haven, on the Fourth of July, A.D. 1787* (New Haven, CT: T. and S. Green, 1787), 4.

34. Palmer, *Oration*, 4. On the popular cosmopolitanism of the 1790s that prioritized the future of the human race over narrow national prejudices, and on the combination of patriotism with that cosmopolitanism, see Seth Cotlar, *Tom Paine's America: The Rise and Fall of Transatlantic Radicalism in the Early Republic* (Charlottesville: University of Virginia Press, 2011), 50–55, 80.

35. Palmer, *Oration*, 4. On the constitutional provisions for slavery, see David Waldstreicher, *Slavery's Constitution: From Revolution to Ratification* (New York: Hill & Wang, 2009).

36. Palmer, *Oration*, 8; Price, *Observations*, 68–69.

37. Palmer, *Oration*, 4–7. Here, too, Palmer had role models. The previous year, Joel Barlow had said, "The present is an age of philosophy; and America, the empire of reason. Here, neither the pageantry of courts not the glooms of superstition have dazzled or beclouded the mind." Joel Barlow, *An oration, delivered at the North Church in Hartford, at the meeting of the Connecticut Society of the Cincinnati, July 4th, 1787* (Hudson & Goodwin, 1787), 19. In *Observations* (22–23), Price gives examples of scientists unable to publish freely their theories of a heliocentric solar system lest they be hounded by church authorities. Palmer may have thought of these examples when he referenced the suppression of science.

38. Palmer, *Oration*, 5–7. Palmer's use of the term "asylum" borrows from Thomas Paine's *Common Sense* (1776): "This new world hath been the asylum for the persecuted lovers of civil and religious liberty from every part of Europe." On the self-interested framers, see Woody Holton, *Unruly Americans and the Origins of the Constitution* (New York: Hill and Wang, 2008).

39. Palmer, *Oration*, 8.

40. *Dunlap's American Daily Advertiser*, March 3, 1792, p. 3 ("Friends").

41. *Berkshire Chronicle*, July 31, 1788, August 7, 1788, August 21, 1788 (ads for his speech). The speech gives his name as "Elihu Palmer jun.. A. B.," referencing his college degree; *Berkshire Chronicle*, July 31, 1788, p. 4 (spoof), August 7, 1788, p. 3 (exhibition); *Massachusetts Spy*, October 16, 1788, p. 2, October 23, p. 2. The first and third of these articles by "Alfred" were republished in the *Massachusetts Gazette* (Boston), October 7, 1788, p. 1, October 28, 1788, p. 1.

42. Riker, *Annals of Newtown*, 232. Congregational ministers were often willing to preach under the Presbytery of New York.

43. Fellows, *Posthumous Pieces*, 5. On Sheffield, see James R. Miller, *Early Life in Sheffield, Berkshire County, Massachusetts: A Biography of its Ordinary People from Early Times to 1860* (Sheffield, MA: Sheffield Historical Society, 2002).

44. An advertisement in 1792 described Palmer as a "Preacher of Universal Salvation"; see *Dunlap's American Daily Advertiser*, March 3, 1792, p. 3. That same month Palmer declared that "I never professed to be an advocate for the divinity of Jesus Christ—I have spoken publicly against it, both in Georgia and Connecticut, long before I ever preached in this city [Philadelphia]. And if anyone here supposed I believed it, it is because he has not given attention to the public discourses which I have delivered." *Federal Gazette*, March 22, 1792, p. 2.

Chapter 3

1. On Newtown, which preceded modern-day Elmhurst, see Vincent F. Seyfried and William Asadorian, *Old Queens, N. Y., in Early Photographs: 261 Prints* (New York: Dover, 1991), 23, 25. At Dartmouth, Palmer had prepared for the Congregational ministry, but Congregationalists also preached under the Presbytery of New York City.

2. This paragraph is based on what John Fellows said Palmer had told him. John Fellows, comp., *Posthumous Pieces of Elihu Palmer [. . .]* (London: R. Carlile, 1824), 5.

3. Cass Ledyard Ruxton Shaw, *The Ledyard Family in America* (West Kennebunk, ME: Phoenix Publications, 1993).

4. [Isaac Ledyard], *An Essay on Matter* (Philadelphia, 1784), n.p., 1.

5. [Ledyard], *Essay on Matter*, n.p.

6. Francis J. Sypher Jr., *New York State Society of the Cincinnati: Biographies of Original Members and Other Continental Officers* (Fishkill, NY: New York State Society of the Cincinnati, 2004), 261–263. On Bard's contributions to medical training, see James J. Walsh, *History of Medicine in New York: Three Centuries of Medical Progress* (New York: National Americana Society, 1919), 1: 45–46, 50; G. K. Dickenson, "Doctor John Bard (1716–1799): A Short Biography and History of His Times, with a Unique Case of Extra-Uterine Fetus Correctly Diagnosed and Successfully Treated," *American Journal of Obstetrics and Diseases of Women and Children* 78, no. 6 (December 1, 1918): 796–803. Because there is no autobiographical material from Ledyard, his path toward vitalism is based on this reconstruction of his medical training at King's College.

7. Theodore M. Brown, "From Mechanism to Vitalism in Eighteenth-Century English Physiology," *Journal of the History of Biology* 7, no. 2 (Autumn 1974): 179–216. See also Robert Schofield, *Mechanism and Materialism: British Natural Philosophy in an Age of Reason* (Princeton, NJ: Princeton University Press, 1970), 191, 209. On medical vitalism in Europe, see Roselyne Rey, *Naissance et développement du vitalisme en France de la deuxième moité du 18e siècle a la fin du Premier Empire* (Oxford: Oxford University Press, 2000); Catherine Packham, *Eighteenth-Century Vitalism: Bodies, Culture, Politics* (Basingstoke, UK: Palgrave Macmillan, 2013), chap. 3; Elizabeth A. Williams, *A Cultural History of Medical Vitalism in Enlightenment Montpellier* (Aldershot, UK: Ashgate, 2003); Elizabeth A. Williams, *The Physical and the Moral: Anthropology, Physiology, and Philosophical Medicine in France, 1750–1850* (Cambridge: Cambridge University Press, 1994); Peter Hanns Reill, *Vitalizing Nature in the Enlightenment* (Berkeley: University of California Press, 2005); Hubert Steinke, *Irritating Experiments: Haller's Concept and the European Controversy on Irritability and Sensibility, 1750–90* (Amsterdam: Rodopi, 2005), 199–218; Ann Thomson, *Bodies of Thought: Science, Religion, and the Soul in the Early Enlightenment* (Oxford: Oxford University Press, 2008), esp. chap. 2. See also Margaret C. Jacob, *Scientific Culture and the Making of the Industrial West* (New York: Oxford University Press, 1997), esp. chap. 4. For the long history of natural philosophy that allowed for self-activating matter, see Jessica Riskin, *The Restless Clock: A History of the Centuries-Long Argument over What Makes Living Things Tick* (Chicago: University of Chicago Press, 2016).

8. Benjamin Rush, *An eulogium in honor of the late Dr. William Cullen, professor of the practice of physic in the University of Edinburgh* (Philadelphia: printed by Thomas Dobson, 1790), 23. A concise synopsis of the physiological theories Cullen and Whytt is in Packham, *Eighteenth-Century Vitalism*, 104–105.

9. Walsh, *History of Medicine*, 45 (numbers of degrees); Rush, *Eulogium*, 23.

10. On John and William Bartram, see Nina Reid-Maroney, *Philadelphia's Enlightenment, 1740–1800: Kingdom of Christ, Empire of Reason* (Westport, CT: Greenwood Press, 2001), chap. 2, quotes on 40, 44. For Jonathan Edwards's understanding of God's presence in and communication through nature, see Janice Knight, "Learning the Language of God: Jonathan Edwards and the Typology of Nature," *William and Mary Quarterly*, 3rd ser., 48, no. 4 (October 1991): 531–551. For Edwards's rebuttal of mechanistic explanations of nature and his talk about divinely driven atoms, see Avihu Zakai, "Jonathan Edwards and the Language of Nature: The Re-enchantment of the World in the Age of Scientific Reasoning," *Journal of Religious History* 26, no. 1 (February 2002): 15–41. The deistically inclined Benjamin Franklin described electricity's properties as akin to those of a vitalist substance. On Franklin, see Jessica Riskin, *Science in the Age of Sensibility: The Sentimental Empiricists of the French Enlightenment* (Chicago: University of Chicago press, 2001), chap. 3; James Delbourgo, *A Most Amazing Scene of Wonders: Electricity and Enlightenment in Early America* (Cambridge, MA: Harvard University Press, 2006), 45.

11. Benjamin Rush, *A plan for the establishment of public schools and the diffusion of knowledge in Pennsylvania* (Philadelphia: Thomas Dobson, 1786), 15 ("there can be no virtue");

Rush, *Eulogium*, 35 ("Revelation"). All other quotes from Rush, Edinburgh Journal, quoted in Stephen Fried, *Rush: Revolution, Madness, and the Visionary Doctor Who Became a Founding Father* (New York: Crown, 2018), 50. On Rush's medical vitalism, see Jason Frank, "Sympathy and Separation: Benjamin Rush and the Contagious Public," *Modern Intellectual History* 6, no. 1 (April 2009): 27–57; Sari Altschuler, "From Blood Vessels to Global Networks of Exchange: The Physiology of Benjamin Rush's Early Republic," *Journal of the Early Republic* 32, no. 2 (Summer 2012): 207–231.

12. Peter Middleton, *A medical discourse, or An historical inquiry into the ancient and present state of medicine: the substance of which was delivered at opening the medical school, in the city of New-York* (New York: Hugh Gaine, 1769), 56–57.

13. Physicians in Montpellier, a center of vitalist inquiry, contributed many essays to the *Encyclopédie*. See Williams, *Cultural History of Medical Vitalism*, chap. 4. On Diderot as an outspoken advocate of the Lucretian view of a world without design or purpose, see Eric Baker, "Lucretius in the European Enlightenment," in *Cambridge Companion to Lucretius*, ed. Stuart Gillespie and Philip Hardie, 278–279; and J. W. Schmidt, "Diderot and Lucretius: The *De rerum natura* and Lucretius's legacy in Diderot's scientific, aesthetic, and ethical thought," *Studies on Voltaire and the Eighteenth Century* 208 (1982): 183–294. Packham's multifaceted *Eighteenth-Century Vitalism* studies the language of vital nature in the literature and poetry of Erasmus Darwin and Mary Wollstonecraft and also in moral philosophy, economics, and political writing. Peter Hanns Reill argues for a specifically eighteenth-century vitalist language of nature that should not be confused with the mechanism that precedes it or the romantic transcendentalism that follows. See his *Vitalizing Nature in the Enlightenment* (Berkeley: University of California Press, 2005).

14. John Ledyard to Isaac Ledyard, January 15, 1782, John Ledyard Papers, Correspondence, 1772–1790, folder 1, New-York Historical Society, New York. That Ledyard entered the medical department of the army in March 1776 is in Walsh, *History of Medicine*, 37. One colleague remembered Ledyard as "educated abroad, intellectual and honorable" and that at war's end he was second in rank in the medical purveying department. See R. M. Wyckoff, M.D., "Kings County in 1776," in *Proceedings of the Medical Society of the County of Kings* (New York: Wheat & Cornett, 1876), 1: 157.

15. [Ledyard], *Essay on Matter*, 25 ("exchange of matter"), 7 ("Ignorant"), 8 ("Notwithstanding"), 23 ("hateful").

16. [Ledyard], *Essay on Matter*, 25–26.

17. [Ledyard], *Essay on Matter*, 12 ("possessed"), 14 ("actuates"), 7 ("co-existent"), 2 ("waste"), 11 ("CHANGE").

18. [Ledyard], *Essay on Matter*, 15 ("there is a God"), 16 ("impiously attempt").

19. [Ledyard], *Essay on Matter*, 15 ("best idea"), 16 ("a subject," "REASON"). Ledyard's idea of God can be described as nonpersonal monotheism. See Michael Levine, *Pantheism: A Non-theistic Concept of Deity* (London: Routledge, 1994), 3, 26–28, 95, 115–116, 147.

20. *An Accurate and Complete Description of Sleep, In a Discourse delivered before the Medical Society, September 1782, and now published in Answer to an anonymous pamphlet just published in Philadelphia, entitled An Essay on Matter: Wherein the Author's Design is supposed to be an attack on the Christian Religion; By the Author of the late Piece entitled, New System of Philosophy, etc.* (New York, printed for the author, 1784), 3–4.

21. [Charles Henry Wharton], *A reply to An address to the Roman Catholics of the United States of America: By the author of A letter to the Roman Catholics of the city of Worcester; To which are annexed a few observations on a late pamphlet entitled An essay on matter in a letter to a friend.* (Philadelphia: Charles Cist, 1785).

22. Dwight quoted in Colin Wells, *The Devil and Doctor Dwight: Satire and Theology in the Early American Republic* (Chapel Hill: University of North Carolina, 2002), 197. Wells explains the lines on Ledyard on p. 233.

23. On Ledyard's farm in Newtown, see James Riker Jr., *The Annals of Newtown, in Queens County, New-York* [...] (New York, 1852), 223.

24. Elihu Palmer, *An oration pronounced in the Meeting House in Pittsfield, upon the Twelfth anniversary of the Independence of the United States of America* (Pittsfield, Roger Storrs, 1788), 7 ("Sons of Science"); Kerry S. Walters, *Elihu Palmer's "Principles of Nature": Text and Commentary* (Wolfeboro, NH: Longwood Academic Press, 1990), 85 ("clear and correct"), 250–52 ("corroborate," 250).

25. Elihu Palmer to Jedidiah Morse, September 25, 1791, Gratz Collection, Historical Society of Pennsylvania, Philadelphia; Jefferson, *Notes on the State of Virginia* (Philadelphia: Prichard and Hall, 1788).

26. Walters, *Elihu Palmer's "Principles of Nature,"* 141 ("laws of nature," "truth"), 85 ("essence"), 86 ("sufficient"), 250 ("essential power," "all is alive"). Palmer, "Political World," in John Fellows, comp., *Posthumous Pieces by Elihu Palmer* [...] (London: R. Carlile, 1824), 21 ("not a single," "thinking"). Palmer was both entirely materialist *and* theist at the same time, in the way some scholars describe Spinoza's conception of God as the universal substance. See, for example, Lynn Avery Hunt, Margaret C. Jacob, and W. W. Mijnhardt, *The Book That Changed Europe: Picart and Bernard's Religious Ceremonies of the World* (Cambridge, MA: Harvard University Press, 2010), 285–293, and 363n28. (Palmer nowhere mentions Spinoza.) Michael Levine states that pantheists can view the divine as both immanent and transcendent, as long as the deity is not thought to be a personal one; see Levine, *Pantheism*, 3, 95, 115–116, 147. Palmer's sense of the divine was a kind of panentheism (a term coined in the nineteenth century), which posits that the divine pervades the universe and also extends beyond it. See John Culp, "Panentheism" in *The Stanford Encyclopedia of Philosophy*, ed. Edward N. Zalta (Summer 2017 Edition), https://plato.stanford.edu/archives/sum2017/entries/panentheism/. On belief in the sacred within nature, see Catherine L. Albanese, *Nature Religion in America: From the Algonkian Indians to the New Age* (Chicago: University of Chicago Press, 1990).

27. Walters, *Elihu Palmer's "Principles of Nature,"* 248 ("shape or form," "mighty power"), 223 (all following quotes).

28. Riker Jr., *Annals of Newtown*, 232. Riker Jr., who was born in 1822, recorded what he had been told about Palmer.

29. Riker Jr., *Annals of Newtown*, 232 ("displayed," "ardor," "soon discovered"); Fellows, *Posthumous Pieces*, 5–6 ("peculiar").

30. Riker Jr., *Annals of Newtown*, 232; Wyckoff, "Kings County in 1776," 157 ("intellectual"); Walsh, *History of Medicine*, 102 ("intellectual"). That Palmer arrived in Newtown in 1788 and stayed until 1789 is in William H. Henrickson, *A Brief History of the First Presbyterian Church of Newtown, Long Island* (n.p., 1902), 33–34.

Chapter 4

1. Report from Augusta, Georgia, dated November 28, 1789, in the *Daily Advertiser* (New York), January 1, 1790, p. 2. An excerpt also appeared in the *Pennsylvania Packet, and Daily Advertiser* (Philadelphia), January 8, 1790, p. 3.

2. Jedidiah Morse, *The American Universal Geography* [...] (Boston: Isaiah Thomas, 1793), 614. On the "middling folk," see Stuart M. Blumin, *The Emergence of the Middle Class: Social Experience in the American City, 1760–1900* (Cambridge: Cambridge University Press, 1989), chap. 2, esp. 37–38. On the art of performing gentility in vivacious, clever, polite conversation, see Richard L. Bushman, *The Refinement of America: Persons, Houses, Cities* (New York: Vintage, 1993), 80–89.

3. *Augusta Chronicle and Gazette of the State* (Georgia; hereafter *Augusta Chronicle*), July 18, 1789, p. 2 (chaplain), July 25, 1789, p. 3 ("applause," "Resolved").

4. Anton-Hermann Chroust, *The Rise of the Legal Profession in America*. Vol. 2: *The Revolution and the Post-Revolutionary Era* (Norman: University of Oklahoma Press, 1965), chap. 1, 272–273. For Palmer's "study of 'jurisprudence,'" while in the state of Georgia," see "From the Federal Gazette," *General Advertiser* (Philadelphia), March 24, 1791, p. 2.

5. Durwood T. Stokes, "Adam Boyd," in *Dictionary of North Carolina Biography*, 6 vols., ed. William S. Powell (Chapel Hill: University of North Carolina Press, 1979–1996), https://www.ncpedia.org/biography/boyd-adam. John Fellows's description of Boyd as an "honest good sort of man" must have come from Palmer, along with the information that Palmer "had a more numerous auditory than the parson of the parish." See John Fellows, comp., *Posthumous Pieces by Elihu Palmer* [. . .] (London: R. Carlile, 1824), 7. For Boyd's speaking style, see his solicitous but dreary address to students, which opens by saying he is "advanced in years, and oppressed with variety of affliction," and "hastening fast" to the grave (Boyd was fifty-four at the time): Adam Boyd, *For the benefit of youth. Four discourses delivered before the pupils of the Richmond Academy; one on, Remember thy creator, &c. and three on, The Lord's Prayer* (Augusta, GA: A. McMillan, 1793), 1.

6. Mention of Boyd's July 4th address is in the *Augusta Chronicle*, July 11, 1789. Palmer was asked to teach religious classes at Saint Paul's Church: https://www.saintpauls.org/1784-1821/. At the public examination in October, Palmer's pupils again impressed the trustees and "acquitted themselves with real applause, affording credit to the professors in this branch." *Augusta Chronicle*, November 7, 1789, p. 3.

7. *Augusta Chronicle*, November 14, 1789, p. 1 ("mechanically," "strong mind"), November 21, 1789, p. 1 ("invincible," "assist").

8. *Augusta Chronicle*, December 19, 1789, p. 1.

9. *Augusta Chronicle*, December 19, 1789, p. 1. Richard Price's *Sermons on the Christian Doctrine* and *The Evidence for a Future Period of Improvement in the State of Mankind*, both published in 1787, argue for the indefinite perfectibility of humankind.

10. *Augusta Chronicle*, December 19, 1789, p. 4; Earl L. Bell and Kenneth C. Crabbe, *The Augusta Chronicle: Indomitable Voice of Dixie, 1785–1960* (Athens: University of Georgia Press, 1960), 32 (on the Augusta Library Society); James Raven, "Social Libraries and Library Societies in Eighteenth-Century North America," in *Institutions of Reading: The Social Life of Libraries in the United States*, ed. Thomas Augst and Kenneth Carpenter (Amherst: University of Massachusetts Press, 2007), 24–52. On subscription libraries and book clubs as spaces of sociability, see Abigail Williams, *The Social Life of Books: Reading Together in the Eighteenth-Century Home* (New Haven, CT: Yale University Press, 2017), 110–122.

11. *Augusta Chronicle*, January 1, 1790, June 19, 1790, June 26, 1790. On American freemasons' sense of themselves as a beacon of enlightenment in the new republic, see Steven C. Bullock, *Revolutionary Brotherhood: Freemasonry and the Transformation of the American Social Order, 1730–1840* (Chapel Hill: University of North Carolina Press, 1996), chap. 5.

12. Jedediah Morse, *The American Universal Geography*, 3rd ed. (Boston: Isaiah Thomas and Ebenezer T. Andrews, 1796), 1: 697. For Palmer's work on the *Geography*, see Elihu Palmer to Jedidiah Morse, June 29, 1791, Gratz Collection, Historical Society of Pennsylvania, Philadelphia.

13. Morse described himself as a "moderate Calvinist" and a Federalist in a drafted letter to Professor Ebeling in Hamburg, March 5, 1801, Morse Family Papers, Yale University Manuscripts and Archives, New Haven, CT. On Morse's conflicted allegiance to both prosperity and piety, and on his strong opposition to liberal Protestantism, see Richard J. Moss, *The Life of Jedidiah Morse: A Station of Particular Exposure* (Knoxville: University of Tennessee Press, 1995), chaps. 4–5. See also Robert V. Rohli and Merrill L. Johnson, "The Legacy of Jedidiah Morse in Early American Geography Education: Forgotten and/or Forgettable Geographer?"

Geographical Review 106, no. 3 (July 2016): 465–483. Morse's father warned him not to prioritize his *Geography* over his congregation, but to no avail. Joseph Phillips, *Jedidiah Morse and New England Congregationalism* (New Brunswick, NJ: Rutgers University Press, 1983), 19–32, 35.

14. *Augusta Chronicle*, January 29, 1790, p. 2 ("ladies"), March 27, 1790, p. 3, April 3, 1790, p. 2, July 10, 1790 p. 3.

15. The Richmond County census of 1791 shows 4,116 slaves in a population of 11,317. Charles C. Jones, *Memorial History of Augusta, Georgia, from Its Settlement in 1735 to the Close of the Eighteenth Century* (Syracuse: D. Mason, 1890), 148. That Cogswell owned (probably three) slaves is in the *Diary of James Cogswell, 1773–1775*, April 16, 1775, Yale University Manuscripts and Archives.

16. *Augusta Chronicle*, July 18, 1789, p. 4.

17. *Augusta Chronicle*, July 25, 1789, p. 3 ("GANG"); August 15, 1789, p. 3 (seven-year-old); August 22, 1789, p. 4 ("John").

18. For the steam engine patent, see *The National Cyclopædia of American Biography* (New York: James T. White, 1899), 9: 434. Briggs later became a member of the American Philosophical Society, was appointed by President Jefferson as surveyor general of the Mississippi Territory, and was one of the cofounders, along with then secretary of state James Madison, of the American Board of Agriculture. Maryland Archives Biographical Series, http://msa.maryland.gov/megafile/msa/speccol/sc3500/sc3520/015800/015898/html/15898bio.html.

19. Isaac Briggs to Abolition Society, September 10, 1790, in the Pennsylvania Abolition Society Papers, Historical Society of Pennsylvania. Palmer and Briggs were members as of January 3, 1791. See the *Centennial Anniversary of the Pennsylvania Society, for Promoting the Abolition of Slavery* [. . .] (Philadelphia: Grant, Faires, and Rodgers, 1875), 56; Kerry S. Walters, *Elihu Palmer's "Principles of Nature": Text and Commentary* (Wolfeboro, NH: Longwood Academic Press, 1990), 124–125 ("immoral opinion").

20. "Diary of Rev. James Cogswell, Scotland, Connecticut, 1781–1791," Gallaudet University, Deaf Rare Materials, microfilm 132 (copy of the original diary held in the Connecticut Historical Society, Hartford), February 23, 1788 ("in Company"), September 19, 1788 ("extolled"), August 17, 1790 ("dissatisfied"), August 20, 1790 ("not like Mr Palmer"). Palmer took a leave of absence from Richmond Academy to visit "the eastern states." Minutes of Trustees, May 5, 1790, referenced in Charles Guy Cordle, "An Ante-bellum Academy: The Academy of Richmond County, 1783–1863" (master's thesis, University of Georgia, 1935), 13.

21. Cogswell's Diary, August 29, 1790 ("very good," "savored," "ingenious"), August 30, 1790 ("Exceptions").

22. John Fellows said Palmer had married and that the couple had two sons. Searching for "Palmer" in newspapers led me to "Shipping News," *Middlesex Gazette, Or, Foederal Adviser* (Middletown, CT), October 2, 1790, p. 3 (*Juno*). For the marriages of Thaddeus and Nathan Palmer, along with the incorrect statement that "Elihu, who was a clergyman of the Congregational church and who was blind, never married," see *Commemorative Biographical Record of Tolland and Windham Counties, Connecticut: Containing Biographical Sketches of Prominent and Representative Citizens and of Many of the Early Settled Families* (Chicago: J. H. Beers, 1903), 106.

23. *Augusta Chronicle & Gazette*, May 21, 1791; February 18, 1792; Clark Howell, *History of Georgia* (Chicago: S. J. Clarke, 1926), 1: 445 (declamation contest and awards). Augusta, and presumably Palmer too, participated in the sentimental spectacle of Washington's 1791 tour as described in David Waldstreicher, *In the Midst of Perpetual Fetes: The Making of American Nationalism, 1776–1820* (Chapel Hill: University of North Carolina Press, 1997), 117–126.

24. Elihu Palmer (writing from Canterbury) to Jedidiah Morse, June 29, 1791, Gratz Collection.
25. Cogswell's Diary, March 7, 1791 ("Deist"); March 3, 1791 ("folly"); June 17, 1791 ("Spalding girl").
26. Cogswell's Diary, July 31, 1791 ("prevail"); August 23, 1791 ("preached at Canterbury"). Palmer said he had "spoken publicly against" the divinity of Jesus Christ, "both in Georgia and Connecticut." *Federal Gazette and Philadelphia Daily Advertiser*, March 22, 1792, p. 2. On the "Infidelity and Universalism" that had "come in with the Revolution and drawn multitudes from the religious faith of their fathers," see Ellen D. Larned, *History of Windham County, Connecticut* (Worcester, MA: Charles Hamilton, 1874), 1: 221.
27. Elihu Palmer to Jedidiah Morse, June 29, 1791, Gratz Collection.
28. Fellows, *Posthumous Pieces*, 6 ("extensive field"); Elihu Palmer to Jedidiah Morse, September 25, 1791, Gratz Collection. Palmer advertised Morse's Geography in the *Augusta Chronicle* on April 3, May 7, and May 14, 1791. Starting on May 28 and continuing into September, W. Williamson placed the ads for Morse's *Geography*.
29. Elihu Palmer to Jedidiah Morse, September 25, 1791, Gratz Collection.
30. Elihu Palmer to Jedidiah Morse, September 25, 1791, Gratz Collection.
31. Elihu Palmer to Jedidiah Morse, September 25, 1791, Gratz Collection. Palmer may have been making oblique reference to the six months Morse spent in Midway, Georgia, in 1787. For reasons that are unclear, his time there was not satisfactory. See Moss, *Life of Jedidiah Morse*, 26, 36.
32. Elihu Palmer to Jedidiah Morse, September 25, 1791, Gratz Collection.
33. Elihu Palmer to Jedidiah Morse, September 25, 1791, Gratz Collection.
34. Elihu Palmer to Jedidiah Morse, September 25, 1791, Gratz Collection; Moss, *Life of Jedidiah Morse*, 41 ("not employed"); Fellows, *Posthumous Pieces*, 5 ("joyfully").

Chapter 5

1. *National Gazette* (Philadelphia), March 15, 1792, p. 159 ("Mr. Palmer desires"); *General Advertiser* (Philadelphia), March 17, 1792, p. 3 ("tenor of the agreement"); Frank D. Prager, ed. *The Autobiography of John Fitch* (Philadelphia: American Philosophical Society, 1976), 139 ("frightened"). Eric R. Schlereth describes the "Palmer controversy" in *An Age of Infidels: The Politics of Religious Controversy in the Early United States* (Philadelphia: University of Pennsylvania Press, 2013), 37–44; and "A Tale of Two Deists: John Fitch, Elihu Palmer, and the Boundary of Tolerable Religious Expression in Early National Philadelphia," *Pennsylvania Magazine of History and Biography* 132, no. 1 (January 2008): 5–31. Despite some errors in Schlereth's account, his larger argument stands, which is that Philadelphians discerned proper from improper speech and policed the latter as defined less by its content and more by its venue, whether uttered in public or private.
2. Freedom of religion and of speech had uneven support in the early republic, including in Pennsylvania. See Leonard W. Levy, *Emergence of a Free Press* (New York: Oxford University Press, 1985), chap. 7. The Philadelphia clergy who targeted Palmer for his open heresy did not use the power of the law, but they could have. See Sarah Barringer Gordon, "Blasphemy and the Law of Religious Liberty in Nineteenth-Century America," *American Quarterly* 52, no. 4 (December 2000): 682–719; Christopher Grasso, "The Boundaries of Toleration and Tolerance: Religious Infidelity in the Early American Republic," in *The First Prejudice: Religious Tolerance and Intolerance in Early America*, ed. Chris Beneke and Christopher S. Grenda (Philadelphia: University of Pennsylvania Press, 2011), 286–302. For the earlier history, see Susan Juster, "Heretics, Blasphemers, and Sabbath Breakers: The Prosecution of Religious Crime in Early America," in *The First Prejudice*, 123–142.

3. Billy G. Smith, *The "Lower Sort": Philadelphia's Laboring People, 1750–1800* (Ithaca, NY: Cornell University Press, 1990), 60–61, chap. 3. See also Gary B. Nash, *Forging Freedom: The Formation of Philadelphia's Black Community, 1720–1840* (Cambridge, MA: Harvard University Press, 1988); Ronald Schultz, *The Republic of Labor: Philadelphia Artisans and the Politics of Class, 1720–1830* (New York: Oxford University Press, 1993), esp. 131 on the Universalist Church. On the calls of street vendors, see *The Cries of Philadelphia* (Philadelphia: Johnson and Warner, 1810).

4. The Palmers moved to town after the Philadelphia Directory for 1791 had been completed. They may have moved to the neighborhood in which they resided when the next directory was compiled. In 1793, they lived at 400 Front Street in the Northern Liberties neighborhood. James Hardie, *The Philadelphia directory and register* [. . .] (Philadelphia: Thomas Dobson, 1793), 109; Dell Upton, *Another City: Urban Life and Urban Spaces in the New American Republic* (New Haven, CT: Yale University Press, 2008), 25, 42, 163–164, 166. For photographs of the kind of house the Palmers lived in, see Smith, "*Lower Sort*," 159, 161.

5. Prager, *Autobiography of John Fitch*, 138 ("great applause"). Ebenezer Hazard to Jedidiah Morse, April 20, 1795, Gratz Collection, Historical Society of Pennsylvania, Philadelphia (all other quotes). Israel Israel told the story about Palmer to Ebenezer Hazard in 1795, and Hazard conveyed it as an amusing anecdote to his friend Jedidiah Morse. The quotation is Hazard's paraphrasing of what Israel relayed to him. Fellows remembered that Palmer "became disgusted with preaching from pulpits, where the morose, vindictive, and uncharitable tenets of Calvin were generally inculcated, and expected by the hearers." John Fellows, comp., *Posthumous Pieces by Elihu Palmer* [. . .] (London: R. Carlile, 1824), 6. On the Philadelphia Universalists, see Russell E. Miller, *The Larger Hope: The First Century of the Universalist Church in America* (Boston: Unitarian Universalist Association, 1986), 76–77; Ann Lee Bressler, *The Universalist Movement in America, 1770–1880* (New York: Oxford University Press, 2001), chap. 1; David Robinson, *The Unitarians and the Universalists* (Westport, CT: Greenwood Press, 1985), chap. 2.

6. Ebenezer Hazard to Jedidiah Morse, April 20, 1795, Gratz Collection. On the Calvinist understanding of Universalism as yet another dangerous delusion, see Colin Wells, *The Devil and Doctor Dwight: Satire and Theology in the Early American Republic* (Chapel Hill: University of North Carolina Press, 2002), chaps. 1–2, esp. 36–37, 55–57.

7. Ebenezer Hazard to Jedidiah Morse, April 20, 1795, Gratz Collection.

8. Prager, *Autobiography of John Fitch*, 138.

9. Prager, *Autobiography of John Fitch*, 25. On Fitch, see also Schlereth, *Age of Infidels*, 33–35.

10. Prager, *Autobiography of John Fitch*, 125 ("word of honor"), 126 ("Midwives"), 128 ("world").

11. Prager, *Autobiography of John Fitch*, 123–124 ("despicable"); Thompson Westcott, *The Life of John Fitch, the Inventor of the Steam Boat* (Philadelphia: J. B. Lippincott, 1857), 411–412 (Westcott's quotes).

12. Prager, *Autobiography of John Fitch*, 120–123.

13. Prager, *Autobiography of John Fitch*, 121.

14. Prager, *Autobiography of John Fitch*, 130–132. Christopher Grasso sees Palmer as the person "who did the most to try to institutionalize deism in America" and claims Palmer "took his first steps toward trying to institutionalize it in Philadelphia in the early 1790s." Christopher Grasso, *Skepticism and American Faith: From the Revolution to the Civil War* (New York: Oxford University Press, 2018), 100, 109. But Fitch, not Palmer, founded the Deistical Society and developed detailed plans for the group, as Grasso also shows (110). No evidence from Palmer's stay in Philadelphia suggests that he took steps to build deist institutions.

15. Ashbel Green, *The Life of Ashbel Green, V. D. M.: Begun to Be Written by Himself in His Eighty-Second Year and Continued to His Eighty-Fourth* (New York: Carter, 1849), 319–320. It is a guess that John Smith and Ashbel Green coauthored the anonymous letter that appeared in the *Gazette of the United States* (Philadelphia), March 14, 1792, p. 1. The letter advised Philadelphia editors against printing "infidel" texts that cause "great injury" to readers who learn primarily from newspapers about politics and religion. Newspapers should not be party to "cramming impiety down our throats." Perhaps coincidentally, Palmer on the very next day advertised his "Discourse [. . .] against the divinity of Jesus Christ" in the *National Gazette*.

16. Prager, *Autobiography of John Fitch*, 138.

17. *Dunlap's American Daily Advertiser* (Philadelphia), March 3, 1792, p. 3. Fitch explained that "we got his Christian [Universalist] followers to take a large roome for him to speak in Church alley where he is to deliver a sermon tomorrow preached out of the Bible and I expect that very few if any of our society of those who are in town will neglect attending." Prager, *Autobiography of John Fitch*, 138.

18. Prager, *Autobiography of John Fitch*, 139.

19. Prager, *Autobiography of John Fitch*, 138.

20. William White, "The Autobiography of William White," ed. Walter Herbert Stowe, *Historical Magazine of the Protestant Episcopal Church* 22 (1953): 381–415; Deborah Mathias Gough, *Christ Church, Philadelphia: The Nation's Church in a Changing City* (Philadelphia: University of Pennsylvania Press, 1995), 102.

21. *General Advertiser*, March 17, 1792, p. 3. Prager, *Autobiography of John Fitch*, 139.

22. Constitution of the Commonwealth of Pennsylvania (1790), article 9, section 3 ("to worship"), section 4 ("no person, who acknowledges the being of a God and a future state of rewards and punishments, shall, on account of his religious sentiments, be disqualified to hold any office or place of trust or profit under this commonwealth."), section 7 ("free communication").

23. *General Advertiser*, March 17, 1792, p. 3. Palmer's response was dated March 16. The landlord approached him either that day or on the previous one (when the newspaper ad appeared).

24. Ebenezer Hazard in Philadelphia to Jedidiah Morse in Charlestown, January 21, 1792, Gratz Collection; Green, *Life of Ashbel Green*, 319; *Gazette of the United States*, March 14, 1792; Robert Annan, *Brief Animadversions on the Doctrine of Universal Salvation* (Philadelphia, 1787), 36, 38.

25. *Federal Gazette and Philadelphia Daily Advertiser*, March 19, 1792, p. 3.

26. *Federal Gazette and Philadelphia Daily Advertiser*, March 19, 1792, p. 3.

27. *Federal Gazette and Philadelphia Daily Advertiser*, March 19, 1792, p. 3.

28. *Federal Gazette and Philadelphia Daily Advertiser*, March 22, 1792, p. 2.

29. *Federal Gazette and Philadelphia Daily Advertiser*, March 22, 1792, p. 2.

30. Eliphaz Liberalissimus [pseud.], *A Letter to the Preacher of Liberal Sentiments, Containing Among Other Important Matters, A Liberal Man's Confession of Faith* (Philadelphia, 1792), 9–10. One copy of the pamphlet has a handwritten note on the title page: "alias the Rev[d] Ashbel Green DD!!" This tip led me to Green's, *Life of Ashbel Green*, 319–320, for his version of these events.

31. Liberalissimus, *Letter to the Preacher*, 11–12.

32. Green, *Life of Ashbel Green*, 320; Ebenezer Hazard to Jedidiah Morse, April 29, 1792, Morse Family Papers, Yale University Manuscripts and Archives, New Haven, CT.

33. *State Gazette of South Carolina*, May 3, 1792, p. 2. As early as 1776, Timothy Dwight described Americans as having a unique national identity with a shared religion. He said Americans "have the same religion, the same manners, the same interests, the same language,

and the same essential forms and principles of civic government." Timothy Dwight, *A valedictory address to the young gentlemen, who commenced Bachelors of Arts, at Yale-College, July 25th. 1776* (New Haven, CT: Thomas and Samuel Green, 1776). Palmer also used the language of civil religion in his July 4th speeches, beginning with his first in 1788, but for him the national achievement that mattered most was intellectual and religious liberty, not uniformity.

34. Elihu Palmer to Jedidiah Morse, August 20, 1792, and Jedidiah Morse to Ashbel Green, September 1, 1792, both in Gratz Collection. Morse had briefly sojourned in Philadelphia in 1788 and befriended Ashbel Green and Ebenezer Hazard (whose niece Morse married the following year).

35. Fellows, *Posthumous Pieces*, 6. Scholars insist on Palmer's deism (also "militant deism" and "organized deism") even when it conflicts with the sources. Schlereth says that by "the early 1790s, Palmer had jettisoned his fairly heterodox Christian faith for an unabashed adherence to deism," and that Palmer "first openly embraced deism while in Augusta." Schlereth quotes Palmer's statement to Morse that in Augusta Palmer "openly avowed the universal and Socinian doctrines. I believe them both." But Schlereth argues that "although Palmer described himself as a Socinian to Morse, his views at the time were much closer to deism." Schlereth, *Age of Infidels*, 36 ("unabashed"), 252n38 ("Socinian"). The trouble lies in imagining deism as a clearly bounded set of beliefs that are mutually exclusive from other (Christian) forms of freethinking. Deism in this time period was instead a questioning, skeptical, irreverent state of mind that, like Fitch's Deistical Society, pushed against received orthodoxy and social taboos of many kinds. Palmer was deistically inclined in that sense, and likely had been since his college days, but we have no reason to doubt his claims that he held Socinian and Universalist beliefs, especially since none of his extant letters or speeches from this time use the word "deism" for himself or others. In March 1792, Palmer still drew on biblical texts to deliver what Fitch called a "sermon" on universal salvation. Ashbel Green also remembered Palmer as a "Universalist and Socinian preacher." Green's stated concern was not deism but "infidel principles." Green and his colleagues saw Unitarians and Universalists advocating infidel principles that were as dangerous as deism, because they challenged fundamental tenets of Calvinism.

36. John D. Kilbourne and James Taylor, "Memoir of Bishop White by James Taylor," *Pennsylvania Magazine of History and Biography* 92, no. 1 (January 1968): 51, 52.

Chapter 6

1. On the high rents in Philadelphia, see Mathew Carey, *A short account of the malignant fever, lately prevalent in Philadelphia* [. . .], 4th ed. (Philadelphia: printed by the author, 1794), 9–10. John Fellows, comp., *Posthumous Pieces by Elihu Palmer* (London: R. Carlile, 1824), 7. Fellows inadvertently conflated Palmer's 1792 departure from Philadelphia with an incident that occurred there years later. What mattered was Palmer's feeling of being persecuted for the free expression of his religious ideas.

2. *Berkshire Chronicle* (Pittsfield, MA), June 19, 1788, p. 1.

3. On becoming a lawyer, see *Rules and Orders for Regulating the Practice of the County Courts of the Common Pleas, in the State of Pennsylvania* (Lancaster, PA: J. Bailey and W. Dickson, 1792), 3. By spring 1793, Palmer was a lawyer, so he must have done one of the required years of understudy in Wilkes-Barre.

4. The genealogical connection to Standish is laid out in *Commemorative Biographical Record of Tolland and Windham Counties*, vol. 1 (Chicago: J. H. Beers, 1903). The recounting of Nathan Palmer's claim to this lineage is in the *New England Historical and Genealogical Register* 30: 462. On the Susquehanna Company, see Donna Bingham Munger, *Connecticut's Pennsylvania "Colony" 1754–1810: Susquehanna Company Proprietors, Settlers and Claimants*

(Westminster, MD: Heritage Books, 2007). For an example of Nathan Palmer's provocative fighting style, in which he mocked his adversary for untamed rage while boasting of his own genteel self-control, see *Wilkesbarre Gazette, and Luzerne Advertiser*, March 18, 1800.

5. George Peck, D.D., *Early Methodism Within the Bounds of the Old Genesee Conference from 1788 to 1828, or, The First Forty Years of Wesleyan Evangelism in Northern Pennsylvania, Central and Western New York, and Canada* [. . .] (New York: Carlton & Porter, 1860), 123. Nathan's expressions of a non-Christian deism are in the *Wilkesbarre Gazette*. The buildings in town are described in Isaac A. Chapman, *A Sketch of the History of Wyoming* (Wilkesbarre, PA: Sharp D. Lewis, 1830), 198.

6. On the Democratic-Republican societies that began organizing in Philadelphia in April 1793 and replaced deferential rhetoric such as "Sir" and "your humble servant" with egalitarian phrasing like "Citizen" and "Fellow Citizens," see Albrecht Koschnik, *"Let a Common Interest Bind Us Together": Associations, Partisanship, and Culture in Philadelphia, 1775–1840* (Charlottesville: University of Virginia Press, 2007), 22–26. On Americans who adopted the "Citizen" form of address, see also Seth Cotlar, *Tom Paine's America: The Rise and Fall of Transatlantic Radicalism in the Early Republic* (Charlottesville: University of Virginia Press, 2011), 53.

7. Elihu Palmer to Jedidiah Morse, August 20, 1792 ("real friend"), and Elihu Palmer to Jedidiah Morse, March 28, 1793, both in Gratz Collection, Historical Society of Pennsylvania, Philadelphia. Morse had replied to Palmer on September 18, 1792, and when the letter arrived in Philadelphia, Palmer was no longer in town to receive it.

8. James Hardie, *The Philadelphia directory and register* [. . .] (Philadelphia: Thomas Dobson, 1793), 109; Elihu Palmer to Mathew Carey, July 25, 1793, Mathew Carey Correspondence, Historical Society of Pennsylvania.

9. Elihu Palmer to Mathew Carey, June 21, 1793 ("five dollars"), July 8, 1793 ("my Brother"), July 25, 1793 ("extremely glad"), Mathew Carey Correspondence.

10. On partisan July 4th celebrations, see Simon P. Newman, *Parades and the Politics of the Street: Festive Culture in the Early American Republic* (Philadelphia: University of Pennsylvania Press, 1997), chaps. 3–4; Len Travers, *Celebrating the Fourth: Independence Day and the Rites of Nationalism in the Early Republic* (Amherst: University of Massachusetts Press, 1997), 88–106. On the way Democratic-Republicans linked American patriotism with support for the French Revolution, see David Waldstreicher, *In the Midst of Perpetual Fetes: The Making of American Nationalism, 1776–1820* (Chapel Hill: University of North Carolina Press, 1997), 126–135; Cotlar, *Tom Paine's America*, 67–81. On the rising Federalist anxiety in the 1790s about violence in France and the possible importation of anarchy to the United States, see Rachel Hope Cleves, *The Reign of Terror in America: Visions of Violence from Anti-Jacobinism to Antislavery* (Cambridge: Cambridge University Press, 2009), chap. 2.

11. On the increase of partisanship and an openly politicized public sphere, see Koschnik, *"Let a Common Interest,"* 28–29; James Roger Sharp, *American Politics in the Early Republic: The New Nation in Crisis* (New Haven, CT: Yale University Press, 1993), chap. 3. On editors mentioning free speech, see Cotlar, *Tom Paine's America*, 176. On the sketchy protections of freedom of speech in the early Republic, see Leonard W. Levy, *Emergence of a Free Press* (Oxford: Oxford University Press, 1985).

12. *Pennsylvania Gazette* (Philadelphia), July 10, 1793 ("pleasing situation," "bower") quoted in Travers, *Celebrating the Fourth*, 117. Elihu Palmer, "Extracts from an Oration, Delivered at Federal Point, near Philadelphia, *on the* Fourth *of* July, 1793, *by* Elihu Palmer, citizen of Pennsylvania; and published by request of those who heard it," in *Political miscellany* [. . .] (New York: G. Forman, 1793), 22. Palmer was listed as a "lawyer" on the membership roll of the Democratic Society of Pennsylvania. See Philip S. Foner, *The Democratic-Republican Societies, 1790–1800: A Documentary Sourcebook of Constitutions, Declarations, Addresses, Resolutions, and Toasts* (Westport, CT: Greenwood Press, 1976), 441.

13. Palmer, "Extracts from an Oration," 23–24.
14. Palmer, "Extracts from an Oration," 24.
15. Palmer, "Extracts from an Oration," 25.
16. Palmer, "Extracts from an Oration," 26. On eighteenth-century moral sciences, see Keith Michael Baker, *Condorcet: From Natural Philosophy to Social Mathematics* (Chicago: University of Chicago Press, 1975); Jessica Riskin, *Science in the Age of Sensibility: The Sentimental Empiricists of the French Enlightenment* (Chicago: University of Chicago Press, 2002), 4–5.
17. Benjamin Rush to Julia Stockton Rush, August 21, 1793, August 25, 1793, August 29, 1793, in *Letters of Benjamin Rush*, ed. L. H. Butterfield (Princeton, NJ: Princeton University Press, 1951), 2: 637 ("fatigued"), 640 ("histories"), 644 ("chilly fitt" and all following quotes). The discovery that yellow fever was spread by infected mosquitoes was made a century later.
18. *Minutes of the proceedings of the committee, appointed on the 14th September, 1793, by the citizens of Philadelphia, the Northern Liberties and the District of Southwark, to attend to and alleviate the sufferings of the afflicted with the malignant fever, prevalent, in the city and its vicinity, with an appendix* (Philadelphia: Aitken & Son, 1794), 127 ("Front street"); Carey, *Short account*, 16–18.
19. Carey, *Short account*, 21–23; Ebenezer Hazard to Jedidiah Morse, September 20, 1793, Gratz Collection. See also J. H. Powell, *Bring Out Your Dead: The Great Plague of Yellow Fever in Philadelphia in 1793* (1949; repr., Philadelphia, 1993); J. Worth Estes and Billy G. Smith, eds., *A Melancholy Scene of Devastation: The Public Response to the 1793 Philadelphia Yellow Fever Epidemic* (Canton, MA: Science History Publications, 1997).
20. Ebenezer Hazard to Ashbel Green, October 12, 1793 ("such Demand"), Society Collection, Historical Society of Pennsylvania; Ebenezer Hazard to Robert Ralston, October 25, 1793 ("seven down," "*four Dollars*"), Hazard Family Papers, Historical Society of Pennsylvania. See [Absalom Jones and Richard Allen], *A Narrative of the Proceedings of the Black People During the Late Awful Calamity in Philadelphia, in the Year 1793* (Philadelphia: for the authors, by William W. Woodward, 1794). On mortality rates, see Susan E. Klepp, "Seasoning and Society: Racial Differences in Mortality in Eighteenth-Century Philadelphia," *William and Mary Quarterly*, 3rd ser., 51, no. 3 (July 1991): 480–487; 490–491.
21. Benjamin Rush to Julia Stockton Rush, August 25, 1793, in *Letters of Benjamin Rush*, 641.
22. Ebenezer Hazard to Ashbel Green, October 12, 1793, Society Collection.
23. "Elihu Palmer's wife" is listed among the dead in Carey, *Short account*, 150. She is not listed among those buried between August 1 and November 8 in the many graveyards of Philadelphia. See *Minutes of the proceedings of the committee, appointed on the 14th September, 1793*, n.p.; Dell Upton, *Another City: Urban Life and Urban Spaces in the New American Republic* (New Haven, CT: Yale University Press, 2008), 117, (potter's field). The Philadelphia potter's field is now Washington Square.
24. Fellows, *Posthumous Pieces*, 7. Others also opposed Rush's bleeding treatments. Ebenezer Hazard, once the doctor's close friend, believed Rush took more blood than was medically sound. See L. H. Butterfield, "The Reputation of Benjamin Rush," *Pennsylvania History* 17, no. 1 (January 1950): 6–7.
25. Fellows, *Posthumous Pieces*, 7 ("grope"); *Temple of Reason*, November 29, 1800, p. 32 ("total loss").
26. Fellows, *Posthumous Pieces*, 7 ("little sympathy"). Rush told John Fellows that Palmer "was opposed to being bled, which, had he submitted to, the Doctor thinks would have prevented the melancholy result." See ibid. The quotes from Governor Mifflin and the clergy are in Carey, *Short account*, 41–42. On blindness in the Bible, see Beth Omansky, *Borderlands*

of Blindness (Boulder, CO: Lynne Rienner, 2011), 128–133; Moshe Barasch, *Blindness: The History of a Mental Image in Western Thought* (New York: Routledge, 2001).

27. On shifting understandings of disability, see Lennard J. Davis, "Dr. Johnson, Amelia, and the Discourse of Disability in the Eighteenth Century," in *"Defects": Engendering the Modern Body*, ed. Helen Deutsch and Felicity Nussbaum (Ann Arbor: University of Michigan Press, 2000), 54–74, esp. 60–62; Roger Lund, "Laughing at Cripples: Ridicule, Deformity and the Argument from Design," *Eighteenth-Century Studies* 39, no. 1 (2005): 91–114, esp. 94–98. On efforts to disguise physical impairment, see Jennifer Van Horn, "George Washington's Dentures: Disability, Deception, and the Republican Body," *Early American Studies: An Interdisciplinary Journal* 14, no. 1 (Winter 2016): 2–47.

28. *Berkshire Chronicle*, June 19, 1788, p. 1 ("noble soul," "highest blessing"). Kerry S. Walters, *Elihu Palmer's "Principles of Nature": Text and Commentary* (Wolfeboro, NH: Longwood Academic Press, 1990), 78 ("moral principle," "basis").

29. Fellows, *Posthumous Pieces*, 7 ("subtilties"); Ebenezer Hazard to Jedediah Morse, April 20, 1795 (Israel Israel), Gratz Collection.

30. Charles Guy Cordle, "An Ante-Bellum Academy: The Academy of Richmond County, 1783–1863" (master's thesis, University of Georgia, 1935), 81. Adam Boyd was still the rector and minister of St. Paul's Church. See *Augusta Chronicle and Gazette of the State* (Georgia; hereafter *Augusta Chronicle*), October 4, 1794, p. 3, April 11, 1795, p. 3, July 11, 1795, p. 2.

31. Ebenezer Hazard to Jedediah Morse, April 20, 1795 ("dependent"), Gratz Collection; *Augusta Chronicle*, June 20, 1795, p. 3 (marriage), July 4, 1795, p. 3. (oration).

32. Franca Dellarosa, *Talking Revolution: Edward Rushton's Rebellious Poetics, 1782–1814* (Liverpool University Press, 2014). The Scottish poet, Thomas Blacklock, also blind, described efforts to develop systems of reading before Louis Braille came up with his method in the nineteenth century. See *Poems by the late Reverend Dr. Thomas Blacklock; together with an essay on the education of the blind. To which is prefixed a new account of the life and writings of the author* (Edinburgh: Alexander Chapman, 1793), 229–231, 237–239 (on pin pricks and moveable type).

33. *Augusta Chronicle*, August 29, 1795, p. 3. The committee report, with Palmer as one of the fifteen committee members, appeared in the *Augusta Chronicle*, September 5, 1795, p. 2, and was reprinted in the *Aurora General Advertiser* (Philadelphia), September 30, 1795, p. 3.

34. Ebenezer Hazard to Jedediah Morse, July 4, 1795 (Palmer's Note), and Ebenezer Hazard to Jedediah Morse, Sept 20, 1793 ("Refuge"), both in Gratz Collection.

35. Fellows, "Memoir," *Posthumous Pieces*, 7.

Chapter 7

1. [John Fellows], *The Character and Doctrines of Jesus Christ, from the author's Manuscript. To which is added Reasons for Scepticism in Revealed Religion, by John Hollis. Also, the History of the Man After God's own Heart* (New York: printed for John Fellows, 1796), 20 ("excellent,"), 39 ("first cause"). John Fellows recalled that Palmer "undertook a visit to his friends in Connecticut; and stopping in his way at New York, the writer [Fellows] for the first time, became acquainted with him, in the year 1796 or 1797." John Fellows, comp., *Posthumous Pieces by Elihu Palmer* [. . .] (London: R. Carlile, 1824), 7–8. It is an optimistic projection that one or both of Palmer's sons still lived with their grandfather in Scotland, Connecticut; their names and fates remain unknown.

2. Fellows, "Memoir," in *Posthumous Pieces*, 5.

3. Alfred F. Young, *The Democratic Republicans of New York: The Origins, 1763–1797* (Chapel Hill: University of North Carolina Press, 1967), 395 ("EQUAL," and "every class"); Fellows, "Memoir," in *Posthumous Pieces*, 8 (large assembly room); Sidney I. Pomerantz, *New*

York: An American City, 1783–1803; A Study of Urban Life (New York: Columbia University Press, 1938), 389 (Palmer spoke to the Democratic Republican society). For Palmer's membership in the Democratic Societies of Pennsylvania and New York, see Philip S. Foner, *The Democratic-Republican Societies, 1790–1800: A Documentary Sourcebook of Constitutions, Declarations, Addresses, Resolutions, and Toasts* (Westport, CT: Greenwood Press, 1976), 441 (Pennsylvania), 13 (New York).

 4. Aside from Fellows's account of meeting Palmer in 1796, there is no written trace of Palmer between his committee work in Augusta in September 1795 and his advertised lectures in New York a year later. That Palmer boarded at Benjamin Powell's by July 1798 is in a letter from John Fellows to Horatio Gates, July 11, 1798, New-York Historical Society, New York. This narrative presupposes that Palmer moved into Powell's house when he arrived in New York in 1796. Benjamin Powell's brick home on 71 Cortlandt Street featured eight fireplaces, two "good rooms," and a kitchen on the first floor, three rooms on the second floor, and "one room ceiled and plastered in the garret." See the *Daily Advertiser* (New York), March 25, 1794, p. 3. The house served as a tavern and a depot for the New York–Philadelphia mail stage, and Powell boarded horses in his livery stable. He was a man of business, and his literate wife, Mary, may have kept the books or taken her husband's dictation, as she did for Palmer. The couple had accumulated some wealth, enough for someone to steal, and in 1793 Benjamin Powell offered ten dollars reward for the return of pilfered goods, including monogrammed silver spoons and notes of debt written out to him. He reported the theft in the *New-York Daily Gazette*, May 13, 1793, p. 4.

 5. Thomas E. V. Smith, *The City of New York in the Year of Washington's Inauguration 1789* (New York: Anson D. F. Randolph, 1889), 107, 121 (tavern), 9 (waste collectors); Young, *Democratic Republicans*, 469–472 (on immigration and urban growth).

 6. Details about New York City are in Eric Homberger, *The Historical Atlas of New York City: A Visual Celebration of Nearly 400 Years of New York City's History* (New York: Henry Holt, 1994); Elizabeth Blackmar, *Manhattan for Rent, 1785–1850* (Ithaca, NY: Cornell University Press, 1898), chap. 2; Smith, *City of New York*, 17 (Belgian-block pavers).

 7. George L. Stevens, "John Fellows: A Minor American Deist" (master's thesis, University of Maryland, 1956), 7. The *Daily Advertiser*, June 14, 1793, p. 2: "Fellows proposes circulating a LIBRARY in this city." In 1796 Fellows moved his bookstore to 60 Wall Street and advertised that he had "concluded to re-establish his LIBRARY." See the *Minerva, & Mercantile Evening Advertiser* (New York), August 5, 1796, p. 3. On circulating libraries in the early Republic, see David Kaser, *A Book for a Sixpence: The Circulating Library in America* (Pittsburgh: Beta Phi Mu, 1980). On the business of bookshops, see Steven Carl Smith, *An Empire of Print: The New York Publishing Trade in the Early American Republic* (University Park: Pennsylvania State University Press, 2017), esp. chap. 3.

 8. Palmer advertised his lectures in the *Minerva, & Mercantile Evening Advertiser* on September 24, October 1, October 8, and November 5, 1796, p. 3 for each; *Argus* (New York; Greenleaf's *New Daily Advertiser*), October 1, 1796, p. 3; *Weekly Museum* (New York), October 1, 1796, p. 3. For Louis Gautier, see David Longworth, *Longworth's American Almanac, New-York Register, and City Directory, for the Twenty-second Year of American Independence* [. . .] (New York, 1797), 186. It must have been a stately room, because Alexander Hamilton called a meeting there in 1798 for the "officers of the late army and navy of the United States."

 9. Thomas Paine, *Age of Reason*, in *Thomas Paine: Collected Writings*, ed. Eric Foner (New York: Library of America, 1995), 666. Several historians have wrongly assumed that Palmer was the anonymous author of *The Examiners Examined: Being a Defence of the Age of Reason* (New York: printed for the author and sold by L. Wayland and J. Fellows, 1794). Aside from the fact that Palmer in 1794 was adapting to life without vision and possibly moved from Philadelphia to Augusta that year, the anonymous author claimed to be "intimately

acquainted" with Paine, who was last in the United States in April 1787. At that time, Palmer was a student in Hanover, New Hampshire. Palmer never claims to have met Paine before his return to the United States in 1802. Also, Fellows sold the pamphlet in 1794 but said he met Palmer for the first time in 1796. Finally, Fellows did not mention *Examiners Examined* to Carlile, who asked about Palmer's publications. For more on this, see Terry Jonathan Moore, "Neither True nor Divine: Elihu Palmer's Opposition to Christianity," (Ph.D. diss., New Orleans Baptist Theological Seminary, 1994), 43.

10. Paine, *Age of Reason*, 823.

11. Paine, *Age of Reason*, 685 ("out-law," "worm"), 792 ("blasphemously obscene"), 685 ("indiscriminate").

12. On the legal discrimination of freethinkers in the early United States, see Sarah Barringer Gordon, "Blasphemy and the Law of Religious Liberty in Nineteenth-Century America," *American Quarterly* 52, no. 4 (December 2000): 682–719; Christopher Grasso, "The Boundaries of Toleration and Tolerance: Religious Infidelity in the Early American Republic," in *The First Prejudice: Religious Tolerance and Intolerance in Early America*, ed. Chris Beneke and Christopher S. Grenda (Philadelphia: University of Pennsylvania Press, 2011), 286–302.

13. Paine, *Age of Reason*, 806 ("only true religion"), 686 ("WORD OF GOD"), 712 ("contributing"), 719 ("cruelty"), 690–691 ("manism").

14. Paine, *Age of Reason*, 666 ("own mind"); Kerry S. Walters, *Elihu Palmer's "Principles of Nature": Text and Commentary* (Wolfeboro, NH: Longwood Academic Press, 1990), 179 ("first and best").

15. A year after his arrival in New York City, Palmer said he considered "Paine, Volney, Barlow, Condorcet, and Godwin" to be "among the greatest benefactors of the human race." See Elihu Palmer, *An Enquiry Relative to the Moral and Political Improvement of the Human Species* (New York: John Crookes, 1797). One acquaintance surmised Palmer had "readers." See John W. Francis, *New York During the Last Half Century* [. . .] (New York: John F. Trow, 1857), 91. It stands to reason that Fellows's bookstore became the place where Palmer heard these books read aloud. On the widespread practice of sociable reading and bookstores as noisy places, see Abigail Williams, *The Social Life of Books: Reading Together in the Eighteenth-Century Home* (New Haven, CT: Yale University Press, 2017), esp. chap. 4.

16. On "perfectible" man, see William Godwin, *An Enquiry Concerning Political Justice*, ed. K. Codell Carter (Oxford: Clarendon Press, 1971), 58–60. The book was first published in 1793 and could well have been what Palmer found praiseworthy in 1797.

17. *Outlines of an Historical View of the Progress of the Human Mind: Being a Posthumous Work of the Late M. de Condorcet* (Philadelphia: printed by Lang and Ustick, for M. Carey, H. & P. Rice, J. Ormrod, B. F. Bache, and J. Fellows, New-York, 1796), 11 ("no bounds," "perfectability"), 258 ("no other master"), 279 ("moral goodness"), 266 ("truly important," "absolute perfection"). John Fellows was involved in the American printing of *Outlines*, which would have been available at his bookstore. On Condorcet's science of society, see the indispensable Keith Michael Baker, *Condorcet: From Natural Philosophy to Social Mathematics* (Chicago: University of Chicago Press, 1975).

18. Constantin-François Volney, *The ruins: or a survey of the revolutions of empires*, translated from the French (New York: printed by William A. Davis, 1796), 197. Kerry S. Walters writes that Volney "exerted a major influence on Palmer," who "considered Volney, along with Tom Paine, one of the greatest thinkers of his age, and cites him in the *Principles* more than any other author." Walters, *Elihu Palmer's "Principles of Nature,"* 273–275, note 8. Palmer would have been familiar with the genre of comparative religious ethnography. For a much published precursor to Volney's study, see Lynn Avery Hunt, Margaret C. Jacob, and W. W. Mijnhardt, *The Book That Changed Europe: Picart and Bernard's Religious Ceremonies of the World* (Cambridge, MA: Harvard University Press, 2010). An early encyclopedic description

of world religions by an American author was Hannah Adams, *An Alphabetical Compendium of the Various Sects Which Have Appeared in the World from the Beginning of the Christian Era to the Present Day* (Boston: B. Edes & Sons, 1784).

19. Volney, *Ruins*, 246. An English translation of d'Holbach's *System of Nature* was published in London in 1795 and was available in New York in 1797, if not before. See James E. Cronin, ed., *The Diary of Elihu Hubbard Smith (1771–1798)* (Philadelphia: American Philosophical Society, 1973), 388.

20. Volney, *Ruins*, 245–247. In a footnote added to the 1796 edition of *Ruins*, Volney wrote: "The more I consider what the ancients understood by ether, and spirit, and what the indians call akache, the stronger do I find the analogy between it and electrical fluid. A luminous fluid, principle of warmth and motion, pervading the universe, forming the matter of the stars, having small round particles, which insinuate themselves into bodies, and fill them by dilating itself, be their extent what it will, what can more strongly resemble electricity?" (245–246). Volney clearly rejected any belief system that separates the animating power, however conceived, from "inert" matter (249–254).

21. Walters, *Elihu Palmer's "Principles of Nature,"* 85–86.

22. That Fellows shared a house with Volney is in Gilbert Vale's obituary of Fellows, quoted in Stevens, "John Fellows," 95; Walters, *Elihu Palmer's "Principles of Nature,"* 157 (*Holy Writ*). Volney spent three weeks with Thomas Jefferson in Charlottesville. On Volney's friendship with Jefferson, see François Furstenberg, *When the United States Spoke French: Five Refugees Who Shaped a Nation* (New York: Penguin Books, 2015), esp. 310, 356; Nathalie Caron, "Friendship, Secrecy, Transatlantic Networks and the Enlightenment: The Jefferson-Barlow Version of Volney's *Ruines* (Paris, 1802)," *Mémoires du livre / Studies in Book Culture* 11, no. 1 (fall 2019), https://www.erudit.org/fr/revues/memoires/2019-v11-n1-memoires05099/10669 40ar/.

23. "Principles of the Deistical Society of the State of New York," appended in Fellows, *Posthumous Pieces*, 11. Not much is known about the membership or activity of the group, because the only extant descriptions are hostile ones (described in a later chapter herein), but Palmer did seem to be the central figure. Fellows called Palmer the "founder" of the group and said the principles were "drawn up by Mr. Palmer." Fellows, *Posthumous Pieces*, 9.

24. "Principles of the Deistical Society of the State of New York," 12.

25. Elihu Palmer, *Original Sin, Atonement, Faith, &c.: A Christmas Discourse delivered in New-York, December 1796* (New York, 1806), 3, 5–6. Palmer echoed Paine: the Bible taught that the mother of Jesus was "debauched by a ghost." Paine, *Age of Reason*, 792.

26. Palmer, *Original Sin*, 6, 9, 15–16.

27. Palmer, *Original Sin*, 11–15.

28. Palmer, *Original Sin*, 16, 19–20. Palmer again echoed Paine: "Moral justice cannot take the innocent for the guilty even if the innocent would offer itself. To suppose justice to do this, is to destroy the principle of its existence, which is the thing itself. It is then no longer justice. It is indiscriminate revenge." Paine, *Age of Reason*, 685.

29. Palmer, *Original Sin*, 20, 22.

30. Palmer, *Original Sin*, 29–30. Paine considered loving one's enemies "feigned morality" as it offers "a premium for crime," and "no man expects to be loved himself for his crime or for his enmity." Paine, *Age of Reason*, 823.

31. Palmer, *Original Sin*, 34, 36.

32. Palmer, *Original Sin*, 20, 29–34.

33. Cronin, *Diary of Elihu Hubbard Smith*: April 13, 1796, p. 156 ("lively"); December 25, 1796, p. 278 ("impudence"); Elihu Hubbard Smith to John Williams, April 15, 1797, p. 309 ("disgusted"); Elihu Hubbard Smith to Theodore Dwight, November 22, 1796, p. 263 ("distortion"). On the Friendly Club, see Bryan Waterman, *Republic of Intellect: The Friendly Club of*

New York City and the Making of American Literature (Baltimore: Johns Hopkins University Press, 2007); Catherine O'Donnell Kaplan, *Men of Letters in the Early Republic: Cultivating Forums of Citizenship* (Chapel Hill: University of North Carolina Press, 2008). On literate sociability, see also Thomas Augst, *The Clerk's Tale: Young Men and Moral Life in Nineteenth-Century America* (Chicago: University of Chicago Press, 2003).

34. Smith noted regular visits to Fellows's library between December 1796 and March 1797. Fellows made him a business proposal in February. See Cronin, *Diary of Elihu Hubbard Smith*, 289.

Chapter 8

1. The conversation in Fellows's bookstore was noted in Jane R. Pomeroy, ed., *Alexander Anderson's New York City Diary, 1793 to 1799* (New Castle, DE: Oak Knoll Press, American Antiquarian Society, 2014), February 20, 1797, 1: 485. John Fellows to Julius Ames, October 7, 1842 ("Hindoo costume"), Mss Collection, New-York Historical Society, New York. In December 1795, Stewart gave a series of twelve weekly "Conversations" in Oellers Hotel, in Philadelphia. The next year he issued a sixteen-page pamphlet that sketched the lectures he had on offer: *Prospectus of a series of lectures* [. . .] *By John Stewart the traveller* (Philadelphia: Thomas Dobson, 1796). James Sharples made a pastel likeness of John Stewart in 1796. See the *Catalogue (with biographical notes and illustrations) of the Sharples collection of pastel portraits and oil paintings, etc.*, compiled by Richard Quick, Superintendent of the Bristol Art Gallery (Bristol, UK: 1900), no. 18.

2. [John Stewart] *The Revelation of Nature, with the Prophecy of Reason* (New York: printed by Mott & Lyon, for the author. In the fifth year of intellectual existence, or the publication of the apocalypse of nature, 3000 years from the Grecian Olympiads, and 4800 from recorded knowledge of the Chinese tables of eclipses, beyond which chronology is lost in fable [1795]), 3. Stewart used a calendar that began in 1790 with his publication of the *Apocalypse of Nature: wherein the Source of Moral Motion is discovered* (London: Ridgway, 1790).

3. [Stewart], *Revelation of Nature*, 6.

4. [Stewart], *Revelation of Nature*, 4.

5. [Stewart], *Revelation of Nature*, 13.

6. John Stewart, *The Philosophy of Sense; or, Book of Nature: Revealing the Laws of the Intellectual World, founded on the Laws of the Physical World:* [. . .] *By John Stewart, the Traveller. From the Era of its own Publication, in the 7000th Year of Astronomical History, taken from the Chinese Tables* (London: printed for the author, 4 Cockspur Street), xvi ("annihilation"); [Stewart], *Revelation of Nature*, xiii–xiv ("gratuitous," "homo-ousiast"). Paine's anecdote about the oysters is in John Fellows to Julius Ames, October 7, 1842, New-York Historical Society.

7. [Stewart], *Revelation of Nature*, preface, 14. A friend later said that Stewart held "a sort of rude and unscientific Spinosism" and "expressed it coarsely and in a way most likely to give offence." See Thomas de Quincey, "Walking Stewart," in *The Works of Thomas de Quincey*, ed. Frederick Burwick (London: Pickering & Chatto, 2000), 3: 136.

8. Stewart's letter, on file with the East India Company, was quoted in the obituary for John Stewart, *Gentleman's Magazine* 92, no. 1 (March 1822): 279–280. For other British and American travelers in India at this time, see Anna Clark and Aaron Windel, "The Early Roots of Liberal Imperialism: 'The Science of a Legislator' in Eighteenth-Century India," *Journal of Colonialism and Colonial History* 14, no. 2 (Summer 2013), http://doi.org/10.1353/cch.2013.0025; Jonathan Eacott, *Selling Empire: India in the Making of Britain and America, 1600–1830* (Chapel Hill: University of North Carolina Press, 2016); Michael A. Verney, "An Eye for Prices, An

Eye for Souls: American Merchants and Missionaries in the Indian Subcontinent, 1784–1838," in *India in the American Imaginary: 1780s–1880s*, ed. Anupama Arora and Rajender Kaur (New York: Palgrave Macmillan, 2017), 41–74.

9. For Stewart's life and ideas, see G. Adolf Koch, *Republican Religion: The American Revolution and the Cult of Reason* (New York: Henry Holt, 1933), 148–167; Bertrand Harris Bronson, "Walking Stewart," in *Facets of the Enlightenment: Studies in English Literature and Its Contexts* (Berkeley: University of California Press, 1968), 266–297; Tristram Stuart, *The Bloodless Revolution: A Cultural History of Vegetarianism from 1600 to Modern Times* (New York: W. W. Norton, 2006), chap. 24; Gregory Claeys, "'The Only Man of Nature That Ever Appeared in the World': John Stewart and the Trajectories of Social Radicalism, 1790–1822," *Journal of British Studies* 53, no. 3 (July 2014): 636–659; Kirsten Fischer, "Cosmic Kinship: John Stewart's 'Sensate Matter' in the Early Republic," *Common-Place* 15, no. 3 (Spring 2015), http://www.common-place-archives.org/vol-15/no-03/fischer/#.VwJj4_krKo1.

10. Stewart, *Prospectus*, 7–8; Bertrand H. Bronson, "Walking Stewart," in *Essays and Studies by the Members of the Department of English* (Berkeley: University of California Publications in English, 1943), 135–136 ("profundity," "speculations"). Stewart spoke frequently of analogous thinking as a way to understand truths that go beyond immediate personal experience.

11. George W. Corner, ed., *The Autobiography of Benjamin Rush: His "Travels Through life" Together with His Commonplace Book for 1789–1813*, Memoirs of the American Philosophical Society 25 (Princeton, NJ: Princeton University Press, 1948), 92 ("spoke with horror"); *Prospect* December 10, 1803, p. 5 ("Siamese"). For the persuasive argument that early American representations of "the religion of the Hindoos" say more about what it meant to be American at the time than anything about religion as it was actually practiced in India, see Michael J. Altman, *Heathen, Hindoo, Hindu: American Representations of India, 1721–1893* (Oxford: Oxford University Press, 2017), prologue. The same would be true for an eighteenth-century Englishman's views of what might seem to be Buddhist practices, a term Stewart does not use. On the extended Western "discovery" of what we now call Buddhism, but that Diderot and Volney, for example, thought of as a pan-Asiatic religion that did not neatly distinguish Hinduism from Buddhism, see Urs App, *The Birth of Orientalism* (Philadelphia: University of Pennsylvania Press, 2010), esp. 183–187 (Diderot), 463–479 (Volney). See also Lynn Avery Hunt, Margaret C. Jacob, and W. W. Mijnhardt, *The Book That Changed Europe: Picart and Bernard's Religious Ceremonies of the World* (Cambridge, MA: Harvard University Press, 2010), chap. 9. On religious vegetarianism in India, see Rod Preece, *Sins of the Flesh: A History of Ethical Vegetarian Thought* (Vancouver: UBC Press, 2008), chap. 2.

12. *Prospect*, December 10, 1803, p. 5 ("imbecility"); Stewart, *Prospectus*, 4 ("most important"). Stewart spoke of impermanent ideas, "from Deism to Dogism, from Monarchy to Democracy." *Prospect*, February 23, 1805, p. 61.

13. Stewart, *Philosophy of Sense*, xvii. Stewart explains why contemporary philosophers have "retrograded" in their powers of intellect compared to ancient sages. It has to do with ignorance about the meditative powers of the mind. Our current "high state of scientific knowledge, co-existent with the low state of mental imbecility, is caused by the progress of science itself, which makes the modern [science] all [about] memory, while the ancient was all imagination, operating upon observation and reflection, to produce meditative memory, or the recollection of the greatest quantity of relations, constituting the evidence of all subjects, discovered by a long course of deliberation, and restored instantaneously to the view of the mind, by what may be called meditative, distinguished from reminiscent or recordative memory of other men's ideas, and not of our own." Stewart, *Philosophy of Sense*, 271.

14. Corner, *Autobiography of Benjamin Rush*, 209 ("strong powers"), 210 ("Error"), 212 ("unintelligibly"). Back in England, Stewart recounted his experiences to a relative (probably his brother-in-law, who provided some financial support), a professor of chemistry at the

Royal Institution in London. [William Thomas Brande], *The Life and Adventures of the Celebrated Walking Stewart: Including his Travels in the East Indies, Turkey, Germany, & America. By a Relative* (London: J. Davy, 1822). Brande anonymously published this commemorative pamphlet shortly after Stewart's death. For more on Stewart's biography, see de Quincey, "Walking Stewart," 132–142; John Taylor, *Records of My Life* (London: Edward Bull, Holles Street, 1832), 1: 284–294; J. W. C., *Materialism: A Sketch of the Life and Writings of John Stewart (Better Known as Walking Stewart)* (London: Farrah and Dunbar, 1861), 3–16.

15. Victoria Myers, David O'Shaughnessy, and Mark Philp, eds., *The Diary of William Godwin* (Oxford: Oxford Digital Library, 2010), August 10, 1792, http://godwindiary.bodleian .ox.ac.uk. Godwin recorded that he had seventy conversations with Stewart over the course of a quarter century. On Stewart's place in the London circle, see also Claeys, "'Only Man of Nature'"; David V. Erdman, *Commerce des Lumières: John Oswald and the British in Paris, 1790–1793* (Columbia: University of Missouri Press, 1986), 118–119. On the networks of English radicals in the 1790s, see Marilyn Butler, ed., *Burke, Paine, Godwin, and the Revolution Controversy* (Cambridge: Cambridge University Press, 1984), introductory essay; Mark Philp, *Reforming Ideas in Britain: Politics and Language in the Shadow of the French Revolution, 1789–1815* (Cambridge: Cambridge University Press, 2014).

16. John Oswald, *The cry of nature, or, an Appeal to mercy and to justice on behalf of the persecuted animals* (London, 1791). On Oswald, see Stuart, *Bloodless Revolution*, 295–312. On English advocates of vegetarianism in the 1790s, including Oswald, Stewart, and sometimes Godwin, see Preece, *Sins of the Flesh*, chap. 10.

17. Stuart, *Bloodless Revolution*, 298.

18. Stewart, *Scripture of Reason and Nature*, xix–xx ("dreadful"), quoted in Bronson, *Facets of the Enlightenment*, 274; Stewart, *Prospectus*, 13 ("speculative philosopher").

19. Stewart, *Prospectus*, 14 ("reform"); [Stewart], *Revelation of Nature*, xxxiii–xxxiv ("idolizes"). Stewart was not unusual in his assumption that universal benevolence would spread naturally, even without the aid of legal, economic, or other reforms. See Sarah Knott, *Sensibility and the American Revolution* (Chapel Hill: University of North Carolina Press, 2009); Jessica Riskin, *Science in the Age of Sensibility: The Sentimental Empiricists of the French Enlightenment* (Chicago: University of Chicago Press, 2002); Evan Radcliffe, "Revolutionary Writing, Moral Philosophy, and Universal Benevolence in the Eighteenth Century," *Journal of the History of Ideas* 54 (1993): 221–240.

20. [Stewart], *Revelation of Nature*, xxxi ("absolute liberty"), xi ("Quakers").

21. *Prospect*, February 23, 1805, pp. 59–60, 63.

22. John Fellows to Mr. Julius Ames, New York, October 7, 1842 ("bathing"), New-York Historical Society; [Stewart], *Revelation of Nature*, 64 ("teeth"). On his diet of apples and cheese, see Corner, *Autobiography of Benjamin Rush*, 209.

23. [Stewart], *Revelation of Nature*, 63 ("lotions"), 60 ("prevail"); Corner, *Autobiography of Benjamin Rush*, 209 ("equable"). Stewart would have known of a wide variety of popular treatments for venereal disease in eighteenth-century London, one of which was the washing he described. See Randolph Trumbach, *Sex and the Gender Revolution* (Chicago: University of Chicago Press, 1998), 1: chap. 7, esp. 198, 204. On the growing acceptance of nonmarital sex in some English circles in this time period, see Faramerz Dabhoiwala, *The Origins of Sex: A History of the First Sexual Revolution* (Oxford: Oxford University Press, 2012), chap. 2, esp. 104–116.

24. John Fellows to Mr. Julius Ames, New York, October 7, 1842, New-York Historical Society. That Stewart "never liked to talk upon the subject of religion" is in Taylor, *Records of My Life*, 1:291. Stewart described his efforts to avoid anger and ill humor and cultivate "joyful sensations of peace towards others, and peace with self, which was the great principle of moral health" and "enlightened consciousness." John Stewart, *Opus Maximum* (London, 1803), xxii–

xxvi. An expression of his perceived singularity is in the title of his book, *The Harp of Apollo: Exhibiting the harmonies of the intelligible and universal laws of nature [. . .] By John Stewart, the Traveller; And only Man of Nature that ever appeared in the World; whose Studies were pursued, not in Libraries or Colleges, but in the great Volume of Life, in the most extensive Travels ever performed by Man. In the Era 7000 of Astronomical History, taken from the Chinese Tables* (London: Printed by S. Gosnell, Little Queen Street, 1812.)

25. Kerry S. Walters, *Elihu Palmer's "Principles of Nature": Text and Commentary* (Wolfeboro, NH: Longwood Academic Press, 1990), 267 ("immortality"), 225 (all following quotes). Palmer did not apparently follow Stewart in becoming a vegetarian, because in 1805 Palmer reported the low price of "good Beef." See Elihu Palmer to Robert Hunter, September 6, 1805, Robert Hunter Correspondence, Manuscripts and Archives Division, New York Public Library, Astor, Lenox, and Tilden Foundations, New York.

26. Walters, *Elihu Palmer's "Principles of Nature,"* 223–225.

27. Palmer, "Political World," in Fellows, *Posthumous Pieces*, 32–33.

28. *Prospect*, January 5, 1805, p. 3.

29. *Prospect*, January 5, 1805, p. 2 ("real being," "fountain," "millions"); Palmer, "Political World," in John Fellows, comp., *Posthumous Pieces by Elihu Palmer [. . .]* (London: R. Carlile, 1824), 13 ("indestructible fountain"); *Prospect*, January 5, 1805, p. 2 ("universal knowledge"). Palmer, like Paine, left open the possibility of life on other planets.

30. Palmer, "Political World," in Fellows, *Posthumous Pieces*, 17. See also *Prospect*, January 5, 1805, p. 2.

31. Palmer, "Political World," in Fellows, *Posthumous Pieces*, 18–19. Understanding John Stewart is the key to understanding Palmer. Historians have sequestered Palmer into a more familiar deism, but to do so misses what is most interesting about his thinking, namely the ideas about sensate matter that he thought could achieve social transformation without incurring violence. For the most recent insistence on the primacy of standard-fare deism in Palmer's thinking, see Christopher Grasso, *Skepticism and American Faith: From the Revolution to the Civil War* (New York: Oxford University Press, 2018), 100–106.

32. James E. Cronin, ed., *Diary of Elihu Hubbard Smith, (1771–1798)* (Philadelphia: American Philosophical Society, 1973), 154, Saturday the 9th [either April or July], 1796; Pomeroy, *Alexander Anderson's New York City Diary*, July 1, 1796, 429 ("greatest absurdities"), 430 ("how different").

33. Walters, *Elihu Palmer's "Principles of Nature,"* 220–221 ("thousand gods"), 221 ("is founded"); Palmer, "Political World," in Fellows, *Posthumous Pieces*, 15 ("reciprocation"). *Prospect*, January 28, 1804, p. 58 ("march of science"); *Prospect*, January 14, 1804, p. 42 ("reason").

34. Koch, *Republican Religion*, 81 ("An Infidel"); *Diary and Mercantile Advertiser* (New York), July 3, 1797, p. 2. The notice ran again in the *Daily Advertiser* (New York), July 4, 1797, p. 3.

35. Elihu Palmer, *An enquiry relative to the moral & political improvement of the human species* (New York: printed by John Crookes, 1797), 35, 37.

36. Palmer, *Enquiry*, 45–47. For Condorcet's ideas about gender equality, see David Williams, *Condorcet and Modernity* (Cambridge: Cambridge University Press, 2004), 158–171.

37. *Time Piece, and Literary Companion* (New York), August 2, 1797, 245–246 ("penetrating eye"); Palmer, *An enquiry*, title page; *Diary and Mercantile Advertiser*, July 7, 1797, p. 3 ("Citizen"); *Time Piece, and Literary Companion*, July 24, 1797, p. 230, July 26, 1797, pp. 233–234; *Diary of William Dunlap (1766–1839) The Memoirs of a Dramatist, Theatrical Manager, Painter, Critic, Novelist, and Historian* (New York: New-York Historical Society, 1931), 1: 126, August 2, 1797 ("higher idea").

Chapter 9

1. The signed letter of protest appeared in the *Goshen Repository* (Goshen, NY), October 10, 1797, p. 3. The *Mirror* was started in September 1797 by Philip Van Horne, with Denniston as editor. See E. M. Ruttenber and L. H. Clark, *History of Orange County, New York, with Illustrations and Biographical Sketches of Many of Its Pioneers and Prominent Men* (Philadelphia: Everts & Peck, 1881), 269. On the Newburgh controversy, see also Eric R. Schlereth, *An Age of Infidels: The Politics of Religious Controversy in the Early United States* (Philadelphia: University of Pennsylvania Press, 2013), 98–102.

2. Denniston's precise relationship to the Clinton family is unclear. One Elizabeth Denniston married a Charles Clinton in Ireland, and the two immigrated to colonial New York. Their youngest son was George, the future governor of New York, and DeWitt was their grandson. Many Clintons and Dennistons emigrated from Ireland in the eighteenth- century, and many were born in New York. Charles Clinton, a Newburgh physician, accompanied Palmer and Denniston around town.

3. E. M. Ruttenber, *History of the Town of Newburgh* (Newburgh: E. M. Ruttenber, 1859), 86 (lumber industry); Eugene P. Link, *Democratic-Republican Societies, 1790–1800* (New York: Columbia University Press, 1942), 82 (Clinton, Hedges, Winfield). The freethinking "Colonel" is described in the *Goshen Repository*, January 15, 1799, p. 1. The Academy is described in "Extract of a Letter from a Gentleman in Orange County, March 10, to His Friend in This City," *Evening Post* (New York), May 24, 1803, p. 3.

4. Phinehas Hedges, *Strictures on the Elementa Medicinæ of Doctor Brown* (Goshen, NY: David M. Westcott, 1795), 30 ("inanimate automaton," "uniformly," "*vis natura*"), 25 ("diffused," "inanimate matter"). Hedges described himself as a "disciple of Cullen." Hedges, *Strictures*, 3. Hedges's first name was variously spelled "Phineas" or "Phinehas." No written evidence proves that Hedges and Palmer met, but because Hedges was known as a religious freethinker in this small town, a meeting seems all but certain.

5. Hedges, *Strictures*, 28.

6. Hedges, *Strictures*, 30 ("author of man"); 106 ("providence"); Phineas Hedges, *An Oration, Delivered before the Republican Society, of Ulster County, and other Citizens, Convened at the House of Daniel Smith, in the Town of Montgomery, for the purpose of celebrating the Anniversary of American Independence, The 4th of July, 1795* (Goshen, NY: David M. Westcott, 1795), 5 ("long night," "prolific," "benighted"), 12 ("mysteries").

7. Hedges, *Oration*, 13 ("great work"), 16 (all other quotes).

8. *The Autobiography and Ministerial Life of the Rev. John Johnston, D.D.*, ed. James Carnahan, D.D. (New York: M. W. Dodd, 1856), 91–92 ("brought," "obscene"). Johnston served as the minister in Newburgh from 1806 until his death in 1855. "Extract of a Letter," 3 ("unparalleled," "hired," "indefatigable"); [David Denniston], *General remarks, on the proceedings lately had in the adjacent country, relative to infidelity: comprehending the conduct of those persons who signed an address to the former editor of the Mirror; the writings of D. N. the conduct of the Goshen printer; together with some general observations. On the consequences of persecution* (Newburgh, NY: David Denniston, 1798), 14 ("tornado"). At least one woman supported Palmer—a tavern keeper named Dolly. See John Scarlett, *The Fate of Infidelity; or, the Dealings of Providence with Modern Infidels [. . .] By a Converted Infidel* (New York: Edward Walker, 1848), 18.

9. *Goshen Repository*, September 26, 1797, p. 1. A man in Newburgh with the initials D. N. requested that the piece be published in the *Goshen Repository*. At the time, Newburgh's only paper was edited by Denniston, who would not have printed the piece. On Palmer's return to New York to resume his lectures, see *Diary and Mercantile Advertiser* (New York), September 14, 1797, p. 3; *Time Piece, and Literary Companion* (New York), September 15, 1797, p. 4.

On the split among Orange County Republicans over Denniston's support for Palmer, see *Recorder of the Times* (Newburgh, NY), August 3, 1803, p. 3.

10. *Goshen Repository*, October 10, 1797, p. 3.
11. *Goshen Repository*, December 19, 1797, p. 2.
12. *Goshen Repository*, December 19, 1797, p. 2.
13. *Goshen Repository*, December 19, 1797, p. 2.
14. *Goshen Repository*, December 19, 1797, pp. 2–3.
15. [Denniston], *General remarks*, 7–9.
16. [Denniston], *General remarks*, 10 ("irreconcilable"), 21 (all other quotes).
17. [Denniston], *General remarks*, 13 ("confound"), 24 ("adoration"), 32 ("pouring out"), 22 ("sacrifice," "tornado"), 42 ("liberal and tolerant"); 45 ("Fellow-citizens").
18. Freeman's sermon on sinful practices was not dated but was numbered (no. 164, 2nd ser.) and preceded sermons 171–173, on infidelity, that he gave in December 1797. Quote on p. 10. Freeman sermon no. 171, ser. 1, December 24, 1797, p. 5, "Jonathan Freeman Sermons, 1798–1822," microfilm, Presbyterian Historical Society, New York.
19. Freeman sermon no. 173, ser. 3, January 1798, p. 16, "Jonathan Freeman Sermons, 1798–1822"; *Autobiography and Ministerial Life*, 87–88. Rev. Jonathan Freeman served in Newburgh from 1797 until 1805 (he was replaced by Rev. John Johnston, D.D., who started in 1806). Most of the participants in the print war published under pennames: D. N., A Christian Soldier, An Investigator, etc. It seems likely, based on Johnston's recollection of Freeman's involvement, that Freeman was D. N.
20. John Robison, *Proofs of a Conspiracy against All the Religions and Governments of Europe, Carried on in the Secret Meetings of Free Masons, Illuminati, and Reading Societies. Collected from Good Authorities* (New York: George Forman, 1798). On the way in which Federalists recast cosmopolitanism as treason, see Seth Cotlar *Tom Paine's America: The Rise and Fall of Transatlantic Radicalism in the Early Republic* (Charlottesville: University of Virginia Press, 2011), chap. 3. For the targeting of the Friendly Club as a cosmopolitan literary society, see Bryan Waterman, *Republic of Intellect: The Friendly Club of New York City and the Making of American Literature* (Baltimore: Johns Hopkins University Press, 2007), chap. 2, esp. 71–76.
21. Jedidiah Morse, *A sermon, delivered at the New North Church in Boston, in the morning, and in the afternoon at Charlestown, May 9th, 1798, being the day recommended by John Adams, president of the United States of America, for solemn humiliation, fasting and prayer*, (Boston: Samuel Hall, 1798) 13, 18–20; Timothy Dwight, *The nature, and danger, of infidel philosophy, exhibited in two discourses, addressed to the candidates for the Baccalaureate, in Yale College, by the Rev. Timothy Dwight, D. D. president of Yale College; September 9th, 1797* (New Haven: George Bunce, 1798). On the Illuminati conspiracy, see Vernon Stauffer, *New England and the Bavarian Illuminati* (New York: Columbia University Press, 1918), 199–228; Gary Nash, "The American Clergy and the French Revolution," *William and Mary Quarterly* 22, no. 3 (July 1965): 392–412; Joseph W. Phillips, *Jedidiah Morse and New England Congregationalism* (New Brunswick, NJ: Rutgers University Press, 1983), chap. 3, esp. 73–101; Larry Tise, *The American Counterrevolution: A Retreat from Liberty, 1783–1800* (Mechanicsburg, PA: Stackpole Books, 1998), chaps. 18–19; Michael Leinesch, "The Illusion of the Illuminati: The Counterconspiratorial Origins of Post-Revolutionary Conservatism," in *Revolutionary Histories: Transatlantic Cultural Nationalism, 1775–1815*, ed. W. M. Verhoeven (New York: Palgrave, 2002), 152–165; Rachel Hope Cleves, *The Reign of Terror in America: Visions of Violence from Anti-Jacobinism to Antislavery* (Cambridge: Cambridge University Press, 2009), 91–103; Cotlar, *Tom Paine's America*, 105–111; Jonathan J. Den Hartog, *Patriotism and Piety: Federalist Politics and Religious Struggle in the New American Nation* (Charlottesville: University of Virginia Press, 2015), 45–69.

22. Seth Cotlar makes the compelling case that the Alien and Sedition Acts were the legal dimension of the larger Federalist project in 1798 to delegitimize as foreign and dangerously "Jacobin" a radical democratic tradition that had emerged in America as well as elsewhere. See Seth Cotlar, "The Federalists' Transatlantic Cultural Offensive of 1798," in *Beyond the Founders: New Approaches to the Political History of the Early American Republic*, ed. Jeffrey L. Pasley, Andrew W. Robertson, and David Waldstreicher (Chapel Hill: University of North Carolina Press, 2004), 276–79. On the prosecution of Republican editors, see Wendell Bird, *Criminal Dissent: Prosecution under the Alien and Seditions Acts of 1798* (Cambridge, MA: Harvard University Press, 2020). That the political repression of Republican editors only increased their radicalism and resistance is demonstrated in Jeffrey L. Pasley, *"The Tyranny of Printers": Newspaper Politics in the Early American Republic* (Charlottesville: University of Virginia Press, 2001), chaps. 5–6.

23. Jonathan Freeman, *A sermon delivered at New-Windsor and Bethlehem, August 30. 1798. Being the day appointed by the General Assembly of the Presbyterian Church, in the United States of America: to be observed as a day of solemn humiliation, fasting and prayer, in all the churches under their care* (New Windsor: Jacob Schultz, 1799), 16 ("contagion," "superstitious"), 21 ("*aping*"), 38 ("*violent enemy*"), 46 ("fear and trembling," "pestilence"). Jedidiah Morse and his colleagues similarly noted the unprecedentedly *public* nature of infidelity, as "Atheists dared openly to avow their detestable principles" and "infidels were so numerous, so fast increasing, so bold, insidious, and industrious in disseminating their opinions." See the Circular Letter, printed April 15, 1799, MS 358, Morse Family Papers, Yale University Manuscripts and Archives, New Haven, CT.

24. Freeman, *Sermon delivered at New-Windsor*, 25–26.

25. *Mirror* (Newburgh, NY), October 22, 1798, p. 1. The *Mirror* also published favorable pieces on the United Irishmen (November 26, 1798, p. 2) and Toussant L'Ouverture (December 10, 1798, p. 2).

26. *Goshen Repository*, January 15, 1799, p. 1. Proteus says "The sloop E— is my favorite for passage—her Master, *friendly soul*; I have flattering hopes that in due time I shall initiate him into the faith." This reference put pressure on John Anderson, ship master of the *Eliza*, to refuse service to Palmer. Anderson ran biweekly ads and time tables for the *Eliza* in the *Goshen Repository* from May through December, 1797.

27. Jonathan Freeman, "A Sermon shewing that the President has ample authority to appoint a fast; And pointing out the duties of Americans, which arise from the contaminating Iniquities, the insidious arts, and nefarious policy of the French Nation. Delivered on the National Fast, April 25, 1799. In the church of Bethlehem & of New Windsor, by Jonathan Freeman, Pastor of said churches," doc. 24, pp. 22, 28, "Jonathan Freeman Sermons, 1798–1822." An asterisk leads to a note referencing Dr. Morse's sermon of November 1798. For examples of Federalist fear that the union might not survive the seditious attacks of infidels, see Samuel Austin to Jedidiah Morse, February 11, 1799; Jedidiah Morse Sr. to his son, Rev. Jedidiah Morse Jr., March 23, 1799; Jedidiah Morse Jr. to Jedidiah Morse Sr., November 24, 1801, all in MS 358, Morse Family Papers.

28. On the May election, see the *Goshen Repository*, May 21, 1799, pp. 1–2, May 27, 1799, p. 3; *Autobiography and Ministerial Life*, pp. 92–93.

29. Zechariah Lewis to Jedidiah Morse, November 27, 1799, MS 358, Morse Family Papers; Ruttenber, *History of the Town of Newburgh*, 89; Abner Cunningham, *Practical Infidelity Portrayed and the Judgments of God Made Manifest: An Address Submitted to the Consideration of Robert D. Owen, Kneeland, Houston, and Others of the Infidel Party, in the City of New York* (New York: Daniel Coolidge, 1836), 46–47. Cunningham included a tale involving Palmer: "A neighbor of mine, a proselyte to blind Palmer, rose in the morning," told his children that "he had a presentiment that he should never see them again. He went out, and not more than

about forty rods from his own house, he mounted a hay-stack—a sudden flash of lightening struck him—he fell, never again to rise. I myself saw the flash, and felt the shock." Cunningham, *Practical Infidelity*, 26. John Scarlett, claiming to be a converted infidel, retold Cunningham's version of events. Scarlett, *Fate of Infidelity*.

Chapter 10

1. *Augusta Herald* (Georgia), December 17, 1800, p. 3.

2. On Driscol, see Michael Durey, "Irish Deism and Jefferson's Republic: Denis Driscol in Ireland and America 1793–1810," *Eire-Ireland* 25, no. 4 (Winter 1990): 56–76; David A. Wilson, *United Irishmen, United States: Immigrant Radicals in the Early Republic* (Ithaca, NY: Cornell University Press, 1998), chap. 3; Eric R. Schlereth, *An Age of Infidels: The Politics of Religious Controversy in the Early United States* (Philadelphia: University of Pennsylvania Press, 2013), 110–118.

3. *Temple of Reason*, November 8, 1800, p. 1. Palmer apparently offered Driscol moral support and some useful connections. The Deistical Society of New York supported Driscol's publication, and Palmer's friend and collaborator from Newburgh, David Denniston, loaned Driscol the press on which the paper's first issues were inked. Denniston had moved from Newburgh to New York City and in 1800 founded the *American Citizen*, then the city's only Republican newspaper. Some historians have claimed that Palmer was the founder and editor of the *Temple of Reason*, but no evidence supports this. After three months of publication in New York City (November 8, 1800–February 7, 1801), Driscol suspended the newspaper and moved it to Philadelphia.

4. *Temple of Reason*, November 8, 1800, p. 2.

5. *Temple of Reason*, November 22, 1800, p. 17 ("Paine"), November 8, 1800, p. 7 ("Investigation"), December 6, 1800, p. 39 ("able").

6. *Temple of Reason*, December 20, 1800, pp. 54–55. Palmer rejected atheism. When a reviewer of his book, *Principles of Nature*, said "Mr. Palmer is as determined an Atheist as any of them," Palmer responded with a footnote in the second edition. For believers, he wrote, "the Christian God is like a man, perhaps like one of the New York Reviewers." But in Palmer's view, "the mighty power by which the universe is sustained" must forever elude definition, and "of the shape or form of this power, the New York Reviewers have as little idea *as the author of the Principles of Nature*." Theism, Palmer implied, did not require that divine power appear as anything like a personal God. See Kerry S. Walters, *Elihu Palmer's "Principles of Nature": Text and Commentary* (Wolfeboro, NH: Longwood Academic Press, 1990), 247–248.

7. *Temple of Reason*, December 20, 1800, p. 55 ("Creation is the Bible").

8. *Gazette of the United States, and Daily Advertiser* (Philadelphia, PA), December 6, 1800, p. 3 ("infamous"); *Washington Federalist* (Georgetown, District of Columbia), December 2, 1800, p. 2 ("delirium"); *Oracle of Dauphin and Harrisburgh Advertiser* (Pennsylvania), December 29, 1800, p. 3 ("vipers").

9. *American Citizen*, March 10, 1800, p. 2. For Federalist depictions of Jefferson as an atheist Jacobin, see Charles F. O'Brien, "The Religious Issue in the Presidential Campaign of 1800," *Essex Institute Historical Collections* 107 (January 1971): 82–93. On the intensified partisanship in newspapers after the Alien and Sedition Acts, see Jeffrey L. Pasley, *"The Tyranny of Printers": Newspaper Politics in the Early American Republic* (Charlottesville: University of Virginia Press, 2001), chaps. 6–7; Schlereth, *Age of Infidels*, chap. 4.

10. *Temple of Reason*, November 29, 1800, p. 32. The portrait mentioned in the advertisement appeared in the second edition in 1802. An ad in *American Citizen*, May 21, 1801, p. 1,

announced that the book was available for purchase. It is unconfirmed but likely that Mary Powell penned Palmer's book. John Fellows described her taking dictation for Palmer, and their collaboration probably began during the years Palmer was a boarder (since at least 1798). John Fellows, comp., *Posthumous Pieces by Elihu Palmer* (London: R. Carlile, 1824), 9.

11. *Temple of Reason*, July 8, 1801, p. 207. Driscol had reason to think the Theophilanthropists in Philadelphia, a society of deists, would welcome him. For their founding, see *Temple of Reason*, December 13, 1800, p. 46.

12. *Temple of Reason*, July 8, 1801, p. 207.

13. A biographical sketch of John Hargrove is in *New Jerusalem Magazine* 14, no. 12 (August 1841): 485–491. See also Marguerite Beck Block, *The New Church in the New World: A Study of Swedenborgianism in America* (New York: Swedenborg Publishing Association, 1984), 90–93; Christopher Grasso, *Skepticism and American Faith: From the Revolution to the Civil War* (New York: Oxford University Press, 2018), 130–140.

14. John Hargrove, "September 5th, 1801, Palmer versus Revealed Religion," in *The Temple of Truth; or, A Vindication of Various Passages and Doctrines of the Holy Scriptures: Lately Impeached in a Deistical Publication [the Temple of Reason, ed. By D. Driscol] Printed in Philadelphia; Together with a Reply to Two Theological Lectures, Delivered in Baltimore Last September, by Mr. Palmer* (Baltimore: Warner & Hanna, 1801), 65–69.

15. Hargrove, "August 1st, 1801, To the Public," *Temple of Truth*, 3 ("GOD is ONE"); Terry D. Bilhartz, *Urban Religion and the Second Great Awakening: Church and Society in Early National Baltimore* (Madison, NJ: Fairleigh Dickinson University Press, 1986), 119 ("false pretenders").

16. Hargrove, "August 1st, 1801," 1. Hargrove was responding to Driscol's reprint of John Hollis's *Some Doubts Respecting the Death, Resurrection, and Ascension of Jesus Christ* (New York: Printed for John Fellows, 1797.)

17. *Temple of Reason*, July 1, 1801, p. 199.

18. Hargrove, "August 1st, 1801," 7–10; *Temple of Reason*, July 15, 1801, p. 215.

19. Hargrove, "August 15th, 1801," *Temple of Truth*, 18–23.

20. Hargrove, "September 5th, 1801," 65–69. Driscol responded to Hargrove in *Temple of Reason*, August 26, 1801, p. 263, September 9, 1801, p. 279.

21. Hargrove, "September 12th, 1801, More of Mr. Palmer," *Temple of Truth*, 81–91.

22. Hargrove, "September 19th, 1801, On the True Nature, Dignity, and Stile of the Sacred Scriptures," *Temple of Truth*, 100–101, 103 ("out-pourings").

23. Hargrove, "September 12th, 1801," 84–91. Hargrove used blindness, perhaps not accidentally, as an example: "It is surely full as great a miracle that a man who for years has been blind to the malignant nature and fatal consequences of vice and immorality, should be restored to his spiritual sight, whereby he trembles at, and flies from, his former wicked practices" (84). Hargrove uses the term "mere-deist," as in the "mere-deist esteems it enthusiasm to believe in our bibles at all." Presumably Hargrove was another kind of deist (84).

24. *Temple of Reason*, September 23, 1801, 295.

25. Hargrove, "October 17, 1801, Selected and Important Distinctions Between Adulterated Reason and Genuine Truth, [continued from p. 155.]," *Temple of Truth*, 174–175. The last piece in the *Temple of Truth*, on October 31, 1801, opens with an extract from the *Temple of Reason* and offers a final reply. Hargrove sent his newspaper to Jedidiah Morse in February 1802. Morse would have been very interested in Hargrove's critique of Palmer's lectures, but he did not reply to Hargrove until September. While Morse disliked Palmer, he was not quick to embrace the anti-Trinitarian Hargrove, either. John Hargrove to Jedidiah Morse, February 20, 1802, Morse Family Papers, Yale University Manuscripts and Archives, New Haven, CT.

26. Hargrove, "October 17th, 1801," 174–175.

27. Thomas Paine, *Age of Reason*, in *Thomas Paine: Collected Writings*, ed. Eric Foner (New York: Library of America, 1995), 666.

Chapter 11

1. Thomas Paine to Elihu Palmer, February 21, 1802, in *The Complete Writings of Thomas Paine*, ed. Philip Sheldon Foner (New York: Citadel Press, 1945), 2:1426.

2. Thomas Jefferson to Spencer Roane, September 6, 1819, Founders Online, founders.archive.gov. For the extended argument that both Christians and deists used religious opinions to define patriotism and treason in the 1790s and early 1800s, and that in so doing "they actually fashioned a new vocabulary of religious intolerance," see Eric R. Schlereth, *An Age of Infidels: The Politics of Religious Controversy in the Early United States* (Philadelphia: University of Pennsylvania Press, 2013), chaps. 3–4, quote on 108.

3. *American Citizen* (New York), January 19, 1802, p. 2 ("elegant and impressive"), January 27, 1802, p. 2 (all other quotes). The list of topics appeared in the *American Citizen* on January 2, 1802, p. 2.

4. Kerry S. Walters, *Elihu Palmer's "Principles of Nature": Text and Commentary* (Wolfeboro, NH: Longwood Academic Press, 1990), chap. 20. Chapters 20 and 26 are especially replete with descriptions of the constant interchange of eternal, sensate matter.

5. *New York Gazette*, September 22, 1802, p. 2.

6. For American reactions to Paine's deism, see Patrick W. Hughes, "Irreligion Made Easy: The Reaction to Thomas Paine's The Age of Reason," in *New Directions in Thomas Paine Studies*, ed. Scott Cleary and Ivy Linton Stabell (Houndsmills, UK: Palgrave Macmillan 2016), 109–131. On the public letter to Washington and Paine's subsequent fall from grace as an American hero, not only among Federalists but also among Democratic-Republicans, see Simon P. Newman, "Paine, Jefferson, and Revolutionary Radicalism in Early National America," in *Paine and Jefferson in the Age of Revolutions*, ed. Simon P. Newman and Peter S. Onuf (Charlottesville: University of Virginia Press, 2013), 71–94.

7. *Gazette of the United States* (Philadelphia), June 19, 1802, p. 2; *Democratic Republican, or, Anti-Aristocrat* (Baltimore, Maryland), August 13, 1802 ("pell-mell"), quoted in Schlereth, *Age of Infidels*, 137. For Jefferson's letter of invitation to Paine, dated March 18, 1801, see Moncure D. Conway, *The Life of Thomas Paine* (repr., New York: Benjamin Blom, 1969), 275–276. The *New-York Evening Post*, August 9, 1802, p. 3, denounced Jefferson for inviting Paine. Defenses of Paine appeared in newspapers such as: the German-language *Der Readinger Adler* (Reading, PA), August 31, 1802, p. 2; *National Aegis* (Worcester, MA), Sept 8, 1802, p. 4; *Vermont Gazette* (Bennington), September 13, 1802, p. 3; *American Citizen*, September 15, 1802, p. 2.

8. John Wood, *A Full Exposition of the Clintonian Faction, and the Society of the Columbian Illuminati: With an Account of the Writer of the Narrative, and the Characters of His Certificate Men, as also Remarks' on Warren's Pamphlet* (Newark, NJ: printed for the author, 1802). For discussion of Wood's pamphlet, see Evan Cornog, *The Birth of Empire: DeWitt Clinton and the American Experience, 1769–1828* (New York: Oxford University Press, 1998), 41–42; Schlereth, *Age of Infidels*, 130–141; Christopher Grasso, *Skepticism and American Faith: From the Revolution to the Civil War* (New York: Oxford University Press, 2018), 128–130.

9. Wood, *Full Exposition*, 45–46.

10. Wood, *Full Exposition*, 31 ("Weishaupt"), 27 ("foreign professors," "zealous Clintonians"). The book by John Robison, discussed at greater length in Chapter 9, was *Proofs of a Conspiracy Against All the Religions and Governments of Europe, Carried on in the Secret Meetings of Free Masons, Illuminati, and Reading Societies. Collected from Good Authorities* (New York: George Forman, 1798). For Morse's ongoing defense of Robison's book, see his drafted

letter to Professor Ebeling, March 5, 1801, and his drafted letter, possibly to Timothy Dwight, April 17, 1801, Morse Family Papers, Yale University Manuscripts and Archives, New Haven, CT. Sidney Pomerantz argued that Denniston's editorship of the *American Citizen*, along with his familial relationship to DeWitt Clinton (it seems they were cousins), "gave the Federalists a pretext to play upon the fears of religiously conservative New Yorkers by linking the entire Republican Party with the Deistic movement, a technique of warfare that was being resorted to by the opponents of Jeffersonianism throughout the country." See Sidney I. Pomerantz, *New York, An American City, 1783–1803: A Study of Urban Life* (New York: Columbia University Press, 1938), 389.

11. Wood, *Full Exposition*, 27 ("dregs"), 28 ("scum," "rebels," "treachery," "novices"), 37 ("renounce"), 32 ("text book"), 36 ("whimsical").

12. Wood, *Full Exposition*, 44–48.

13. On Coleman's deft use of Wood's pamphlet to tar all Republicans, see Schlereth, *Age of Infidels*, 132–136.

14. *New-York Gazette and General Advertiser*, September 25, 1802, p. 2 ("fresh proofs"), October 18, 1802, p. 2 ("infidel club"), October 7, 1802, p. 2 ("horrid"), September 18, 1802 (*"Palmer"*); *Alexandria Advertiser and Commercial Intelligencer*, October 18, 1802, p. 3 ("without horror," "aggravates," *"deistical"*). Wood's pamphlet ran in other newspapers, including the *Spectator*, September 16, 1802, p. 2; *Republican; or, Anti-Democrat* (Baltimore), September 17, 1802, p. 2; *Philadelphia Gazette and Daily Advertiser*, September 18, 1802, p. 2; *New-York Evening Post*, September 10, 1802, p. 3. Responses from David Denniston and William Carver appeared in the *New-York Evening Post* on September 18, 1802, p. 2. Excerpts from Palmer's book appeared in the *Alexandria Advertiser*, October 27, 1802, p. 3, November 12, 1802, p. 2, November 17, 1802, p. 3. The *Temple of Reason* responded in defense of Palmer on September 25 and October 2, 1802. Palmer continued to advertise his lectures in the *American Citizen*, October 2, 1802, p. 1, December 28, 1802, p. 3.

15. *Gazette of the United States* (Philadelphia), October 30, 1802, p. 2 ("great Thomas Paine"); *New York Gazette* (republished from the Baltimore *Republican; or, Anti-Democrat*), November 4, 1802 ("public character"); *New-York Evening Post*, November 4, 1802 (*"pacific"*); *Balance, and Columbian Repository*, November 9, 1802, p. 358 ("too democratical"). For the argument that newspaper editors focused on Paine's return primarily as a way to attack the Jefferson administration, see Jerry W. Knudson, "The Rage Around Tom Paine: Newspaper Reaction to His Homecoming in 1802," *New York Historical Society Quarterly* 53, no. 1 (January 1969): 34–63.

16. *American Citizen*, November 4, 1802; *Temple of Reason*, November 6, 1802, p. 287; Paine to Thomas Clio Rickman March 8, 1803, Thomas Paine National Historical Association, New Rochelle, NY, http://thomaspaine.org/letters/other/to-thomas-clio-rickman-march-8-1803.html.

17. *Federal Gazette* (Baltimore), November 8, 1802, p. 3 (*"disciples"*). The booksellers' toast appeared in the *New-York Herald*, December 19, 1802, p. 3, and the *New-York Evening Post*, December 16, 1802, p. 3.

18. Thomas Paine in the *National Intelligencer*, November 22, 1802 (Adams), November 29, 1802 (Washington), December 6, 1802 ("gutter-hole").

19. Thomas Jefferson, first inaugural address, March 4, 1801. For ongoing Federalist attacks on President Jefferson's religious beliefs, see Constance B. Schulz, "'Of Bigotry and Politics in Religion': Jefferson's Religion, the Federalist Press, and the Syllabus," *Virginia Magazine of History and Biography* 91, no. 1 (January 1983): 73–91.

20. Thomas Jefferson to the Danbury Baptists Association, January 1, 1802 ("wall"), Founders Online, founders.archive.gov; *Port Folio* (Philadelphia), January 23, 1802 ("assisted"), quoted in James H. Hutson, "Thomas Jefferson's Letter to the Danbury Baptists:

A Controversy Rejoined," *William and Mary Quarterly* 56, no. 4 (October 1999): 775–790, quote on 785. Seth Cotlar demonstrates that once Jefferson was in office, he and other powerful Democrats tried to appease the Federalists by denouncing more radically democratic constituents, including Republican editors, as dangerous and un-American "Jacobins." Seth Cotlar, *Tom Paine's America: The Rise and Fall of Transatlantic Radicalism in the Early Republic* (Charlottesville: University of Virginia Press, 2011), 206–214.

21. Elihu Palmer to Thomas Jefferson, September 1, 1802, Thomas Jefferson Papers, ser. 1, General Correspondence, 1651–1827, Library of Congress, Washington, DC, [1–2], http://www.loc.gov/resource/mtj1.027_0006_0007/?sp=1. Jefferson noted receipt of Palmer's book on December 19, 1802. The re-bound copy is now in the Library of Congress. See E. Millicent Sowerby, ed. and comp., *Catalogue of the Library of Thomas Jefferson*, 5 vols. (Washington, DC: Library of Congress, 1952–1959, 2:24–25. Palmer might have learned in conversation with Volney of Jefferson's interest in materialism. By the 1820s, Jefferson told John Adams that "to talk of *immaterial* existences is to talk of *nothings*. to say that the human soul, angels, god, are immaterial, is to say they are *nothings*, or that there is no god, no angels, no soul." He spoke of his "creed of materialism." See Thomas Jefferson to John Adams, August 15, 1820, Founders Online, founders.archive.gov. On Jefferson's friendship and correspondence with Volney, see Nathalie Caron, "Friendship, Secrecy, Transatlantic Networks and the Enlightenment: The Jefferson-Barlow Version of Volney's *Ruines* (Paris, 1802)," *Mémoires du livre / Studies in Book Culture* 11, no. 1 (fall 2019), https://www.erudit.org/fr/revues/memoires/2019-v11-n1-memoires05099/1066940ar/.

22. Thomas Jefferson, "Syllabus of an Estimate of the Merit of the Doctrines of Jesus, Compared with Those of Others," appended to a letter to Benjamin Rush, April 21, 1803 ("his reason"); Thomas Jefferson to Peter Carr, August 10, 1787 ("Fix reason"), both in *Thomas Jefferson: Writings*, ed. Merrill D. Peterson (New York: Library of America, 1984), 1125, 902. See also Paul Conklin, "The Religious Pilgrimage of Thomas Jefferson," in *Jeffersonian Legacies*, ed. Peter Onuf (Charlottesville: University Press of Virginia, 1993); Edwin S. Gaustad, *Sworn on the Altar of God: A Religious Biography of Thomas Jefferson* (Grand Rapids, MI: Eerdmans, 1996).

23. Even before Jefferson received his copy of Palmer's book, the Federalist *New-York Evening Post* claimed the "Theistical Society of New York" sent the volume to Jefferson "and received an answer." *New-York Evening Post*, September 10, 1802, p. 2.

24. Palmer's book arrived December 19, 1802, and Hargrove lectured on December 26, 1802.

25. Thomas Paine to Thomas Jefferson, January 12, 1803, in Conway, *Life of Thomas Paine*, 282.

26. Paine had arrived in New York City by August 1803 and lived in a boardinghouse in the city that winter. See Conway, *Life of Thomas Paine*, 287; *Rights of Man* (Newburgh), September 12, 1803, p. 2. No ruling occurred because Denniston died on December 13, 1803, of a lung infection at the age of thirty-six. On Denniston's court case, see also Grasso, *Skepticism and American Faith*, 116–117. For the ongoing, if sporadic, abridgement of legal rights for refusal to swear a courtroom oath, see Christopher Grasso, "The Boundaries of Toleration and Tolerance: Religious Infidelity in the Early American Republic," in *The First Prejudice: Religious Tolerance and Intolerance in Early America*, ed. Chris Beneke and Christopher S. Grenda (Philadelphia: University of Pennsylvania Press, 2011), 286–302.

27. *Recorder of the Times* (Newburgh, NY), August 3, 1803, pp. 2–3.

Chapter 12

1. Mr. William Baker's letter to his fellow citizens in Prince George County, Virginia, appeared in the *Washington Federalist* (Georgetown, DC) on August 12, 1803 (p. 3) and was

excerpted in the *Alexandria Advertiser and Commercial Intelligencer* (Virginia) September 5, 1803 (p. 3) and the *Dartmouth Gazette* (Hanover, NH), September 10, 1803 (pp. 1–2).

2. Evidence for Stewart's presence in the United States is that he proposed to speak in Ballston Spa, New York, in July and August 1804. See the handwritten note on his 1804 advertisement for the Lyceum, or School of Philosophy, American Antiquarian Society (Worcester, MA). Stewart's distance to Paine's deism appears in his statement that all belief systems are impermanent, "from Deism to Dogism, from Monarchy to Democracy." *Prospect; or, View of the Moral World* (hereafter *Prospect*), February 23, 1805, p. 61.

3. "Married, in the city of New-York, on the 19th ult., by the Rev. Mr. Wall, Mr. Elihu Palmer, to Mrs Mary Powell." *Republican; or, Anti-Democrat* (Baltimore), November 2, 1803, p. 3; John Fellows, comp., *Posthumous Pieces by Elihu Palmer* [. . .] (London: R. Carlile, 1824), 9 ("dictated"), 3–4 ("woman of good sense"). In 1802, neither Benjamin nor Mary Powell appeared in the city directory, but Elihu Palmer, their long-term boarder, was listed as "preacher of Natural Religion, 71 Cortlandt" in *Longworth's American Almanac, New York Register, and City Directory, for the Twenty Seventh Year of American Independence* (New York: D. Longworth, 1802), 285. Mary Powell and Elihu Palmer were still there in April 1803. See *American Citizen* (New York), April 16, 1803, p. 2. But by 1804 they had married, moved out, and become boarders themselves. Possibly Mary had to sell the house to pay off Benjamin's debts. See *John Langdon and Son's New York City Directory, from May 1, 1804 to May 1, 1805* (New York: William W. Vermilye, 1804).

4. The last issue of the *Temple of Reason* came with the note that "Mr. Palmer, in a few weeks, intends to revive it in New-York." *Temple of Reason*, February 19, 1803. Mixed with Palmer's excitement about the *Prospect* was the sad news that his friend, David Denniston, likely never saw it. Denniston died in Newburgh on December 13, 1803 of a lung infection. Isaac Ledyard also died that year in August, age forty-eight, of yellow fever. Francis J. Sypher Jr., *New York State Society of the Cincinnati: Biographies of Original Members and Other Continental Officers* (Fishkill, NY: New York State Society of the Cincinnati, 2004), 261–263.

5. *Prospect*, December 10, 1803, pp. 1–2.

6. *Prospect*, December 10, 1803, pp. 5–6.

7. *Prospect*, December 17, 1803, pp. 1–2. (Issue no. 3 picks up the page numbering as if no. 2 had continued with 9–16.)

8. That John Fellows lived in the same boardinghouse as Paine "above a twelvemonth," and that the two men were intimate friends, is in Gilbert Vale, *The Life of Thomas Paine* [. . .] (New York: published by the author, Beacon Office, 1841), 12. That it was 1804 when Paine and Fellows boarded at the house of James Wilburn in Gold Street, is in George L. Stevens, "John Fellows: A Minor American Deist" (master's thesis, University of Maryland, 1956), 50–51. That Fellows roomed with Stewart is in the letter from John Fellows to Mr. Julius Ames, New York, October 7, 1842, New-York Historical Society, New York.

9. *Prospect*, May 5, 1804, p. 171 ("not altogether").

10. Thomas Paine to John Fellows, July 9, 1804, Thomas Paine National Historical Association, New Rochelle, NY. The association's web page lists seventeen pieces that it says were written by Paine for the *Prospect* in 1804 alone: http://thomaspaine.org/essays/religion/prospect-papers.html. See also Moncure D. Conway, *The Life of Thomas Paine* (repr., New York: Benjamin Blom, 1969), 301–302. By 1804, the Palmers boarded at 26 Chatham Street, and Palmer was still listed as "teacher of natural religion." See *John Langdon and Son's New York City Directory, 1805*, n.p. When Thomas Paine boarded at William Carver's house in Chatham Street beginning in fall 1805, Elihu and Mary Palmer still "boarded in the same street." See Vale, *Life of Thomas Paine*, 148.

11. *Prospect*, June 16, 1804, p. 217 ("Pharoah's heart," "abominable," "wicked," "loaded"), June 23, 1804, p. 226 (frogs).

12. *Prospect*, August 4, 1804, pp. 274–275.

13. *Prospect*, November 24, 1804, pp. 401–402 ("Ye spiritual," "yellow fever"); Robert Cooper, *Signs of the Times* [. . .] (Carlisle, PA, 1804), 3 ("high Priest"). Critics noticed that Palmer offered something other than deism. Although Palmer was "evidently assisted by Paine" in producing his *Principles of Nature*, Palmer had "outstripped his master and gave a system of atheism." See the *Albany Centinel* (New York), October 14, 1803, p. 3. A later critic wrote that "for gross blasphemy and infidelity," Palmer's work "far surpassed Tom Paine's Age of Reason, and all other deistical and atheistical works that ever preceded it." See *Tickler* (Philadelphia), May 24, 1809, pp. 2–3. Palmer rejected atheism outright, however. See Kerry S. Walters, *Elihu Palmer's "Principles of Nature": Text and Commentary* (Wolfeboro, NH: Longwood Academic Press, 1990), 85–86, 247–248.

14. For Stewart's admission that he "never found above ten individuals, over all the world" who grasped "the tree of existence, or homo-ousia life," see [John Stewart] *The Revelation of Nature, with the Prophecy of Reason* (New York: printed by Mott & Lyon, for the author. In the fifth year of intellectual existence, or the publication of the apocalypse of nature, 3000 years from the Grecian Olympiads, and 4800 from recorded knowledge of the Chinese tables of eclipses, beyond which chronology is lost in fable [1795]), 101. For the claim that Mary Palmer, too, shared Stewart's views, see James Cheetham, *The Life of Thomas Paine, Author of Common Sense, The Crisis, Rights of Man, &c. &c. &c.* (New York : Southwick and Pelsue, 1809), 187; *Republican*, March 15, 1822, p. 325.

15. [Stewart], *Revelation of Nature*, xxxiii–xxxiv ("astonished," "idolizes"), viii (theoretic insanity), ix (all other quotes).

16. John Stewart, *Opus Maximum* (London: J. Ginger, 1803), vi. Stewart expressed his ideas years before Charles Fourier developed his version of utopian socialism and intentional communities. Gregory Claeys explains that Stewart represents a transition to secular social reform of the kind Robert Owen made famous just a few decades later. Gregory Claeys, "'The Only Man of Nature That Ever Appeared in the World': John Stewart and the Trajectories of Social Radicalism, 1790–1822," *Journal of British Studies* 53, no. 3 (July 2014): 636–659.

17. Paine, *Dissertation on First Principles in Government*, 462 ("property"); Paine, *The Rights of Man*, 349 ("One extreme"); Paine, *Agrarian Justice*, 482 ("affluent," "One extreme," "dead and living"), all in *The Thomas Paine Reader*, ed. Michael Foot and Isaac Kramnick (London: Penguin Books, 1987). On popular conversations in the United States about how to achieve economic justice, see Seth Cotlar, *Tom Paine's America: The Rise and Fall of Transatlantic Radicalism in the Early Republic* (Charlottesville: University of Virginia Press, 2011), chap. 4; Michael Zuckert, "Two Paths from Revolution: Jefferson, Paine, and the Radicalization of Enlightenment Thought," in *Paine and Jefferson in the Age of Revolutions*, ed. Simon P. Newman and Peter S. Onuf (Charlottesville: University of Virginia Press, 2013), 252–276, esp. 259.

18. Paine, *Agrarian Justice*, 485 ("paying too little"), 478 ("natural inheritance"); Paine, *Rights of Man*, 314 ("countries," "Why is it," "legal barbarity"). Paine strongly opposed the death penalty in *Rights of Man* (397–398). Scholars disagree over whether and how Paine's religious beliefs informed his politics. Ruth Bloch describes the utopianism of Paine, Palmer, and Stewart in Ruth H. Bloch, *Visionary Republic: Millennial Themes in American Thought, 1756–1800* (Cambridge: Cambridge University Press, 1985), chap. 8. Eric Foner describes Paine as a secular millenialist who "transformed the language of an impending millennium into the secular vision of a utopia in the New World." Eric Foner, *Tom Paine and Revolutionary America* (Oxford: Oxford University Press, 1976), 81, 216. Gregory Claeys sees Paine's "rights of man" as a "secular reassertion of the Christian ideal of equality," in *New Directions in Thomas Paine Studies*, ed. Scott Cleary and Ivy Linton Stabell (New York: Palgrave Macmillan, 2016), 101. Scholars who see Paine's deism motivating his political activism include Harry

Hayden Clark, "An Historical Interpretation of Thomas Paine's Religion," *University of California Chronicle* 35 (1933): 56–87; Nathalie Caron, *Thomas Paine contre l'imposture des prêtres* (Paris: L'Harmattan, 1998); Vikki J. Vickers, *"My Pen and My Soul Have Ever Gone Together": Thomas Paine and the American Revolution* (New York: Routledge, 2006).

19. Walters, *Elihu Palmer's "Principles of Nature,"* 180 ("plunder and robbery"), 226 ("political institutions"). Palmer's solution to "avarice" and "political lethargy" was first and foremost an intellectual one: "The activity of the mind, and the progress of science are the sources to which benevolence will resort, and on which it must ultimately rest its hopes, for the cure of such direful calamities." Elihu Palmer, *The political happiness of nations; an oration. Delivered at the city of New-York, on the Fourth July, twenty-fourth anniversary of American independence* (The press—The friend of liberty and the scourge of tyrants 1800), 20 ("avarice"). See also Palmer's political lectures as summarized in the *American Citizen*, January 19, 1802, p. 2, January 27, 1802, p. 2, February 11, 1802, p. 2.

20. Walters, *Elihu Palmer's "Principles of Nature,"* 223 ("highest happiness"), 225 ("comprehensive"), 124–125 ("abandonment"). Palmer's statement on the "prejudices which have established between the sexes an inequality of rights" is a direct quote from Condorcet, *Outlines of an Historical View of the Progress of the Human Mind* [. . .] (Philadelphia, 1796), 280. For Palmer, the most practical source of social progress lay in the "efforts of a philosophic mind." See Elihu Palmer, *An Enquiry Relative to the Moral and Political Improvement of the Human Species* (New York: John Crookes, 1797), 23.

21. Walters, *Elihu Palmer's "Principles of Nature,"* 175. Palmer blamed revolutionary violence on "those who have rendered the revolution necessary," i.e., on the people in positions of power who refused to relinquish it. See the review of his lecture in the *American Citizen*, February 11, 1802, p. 2.

22. Paine, *Rights of Man*, 265 ("perpetual system"), 358 ("ridiculous and absurd"), 359 (critique of British colonialism), 262 ("savage idea"), 306–307; See also Paine's letter to John Inskeep in 1806 in *The Complete Writings of Thomas Paine*, ed. Philip S. Foner (New York: Citadel Press, 1945), 2:737. Walters, *Elihu Palmer's "Principles of Nature,"* p. 226 ("narrow prejudice").

23. Paine, *Rights of Man*, 360–361 ("passive"), 363 ("private opinion"); Paine, *Agrarian Justice*, 473 ("execrable").

24. Elihu Palmer, *The Political Happiness of Nations; An Oration. Delivered at the City of New York, on the Fourth July, Twenty-Fourth Anniversary of American Independence* (New York, 1800), 13 ("revolution," "object"); Walters, *Elihu Palmer's "Principles of Nature,"* 175 ("Reason," "Ages," "causes"); Elihu Palmer, "Political World," in Fellows, *Posthumous Pieces*, 28–30 ("indulge," all other quotes).

25. *Prospect*, January 5, 1805, p. 4 ("clearest views," "pernicious error"); Walters, *Elihu Palmer's "Principles of Nature,"* 22 ("reign of reason").

26. *Prospect*, March 30, 1805, p. 100. On the financial challenges of the printing business, see Jeffrey L. Pasley, *"The Tyranny of Printers": Newspaper Politics in the Early American Republic* (Charlottesville: University of Virginia Press, 2001). Palmer would not have known this, but Thomas Jefferson had acquired an issue of the *Prospect* (June 2, 1804) as well as John Stewart's *The Dawn of Sense: The Moral or Intellectual Last Will and Testament of John Stewart, the Only Man of Nature That Ever Appeared in the World* (London, 1810); *Catalogue of the Library of Thomas Jefferson*, comp. E. Millicent Sowerby, (Washington, DC: Library of Congress, 1952–1959), 2: 179 (*Prospect*), 57 (*Dawn of Sense*).

27. Mary Palmer to Robert Hunter, September 3, 1806 ("next best friend"); Elihu Palmer to Robert Hunter, September 6, 1805 ("Rose-street"), both in Robert Hunter Correspondence, Manuscripts and Archives Division, New York Public Library, Astor, Lenox, and Tilden Foundations, New York; Thomas Paine to John Fellows, July 31, 1805 ("glad"), quoted in Conway,

Life of Thomas Paine, 300. For the listing of Palmer's friends, and that Palmer and Foster called each other "Brother," see Conway, *Life of Thomas Paine*, 301. That Paine visited Palmer daily in 1805 is in Vale, *Life of Thomas Paine*, 148. On Foster, see Samuel Hopkins Emery, *History of Taunton, Massachusetts: From its Settlement to the Present Time* (Syracuse: D. Mason, 1893), 228 ("solemn," "open infidel," burlesque"). In 1807, a grand jury in New York indicted Foster on charges of blasphemy. The outcome is unknown, but he was unrepentant and apparently acquitted. See Thomas Haynes to Robert Hunter, October 30, 1807, Robert Hunter Correspondence.

28. Mary Palmer to Robert Hunter, September 3, 1806 ("your goodness"); Elihu Palmer to Robert Hunter, September 6, 1805 ("notwithstanding," "best respect"), both in Robert Hunter Correspondence. Expostulatory Letter to George Washington from Edward Rushton, February 20, 1797 ("Yet sir"), Founders Online, founders.archive.gov. On Rushton's blindness and his connections with radical intellectuals in Liverpool and London, see Franca Dellarosa, *Talking Revolution: Edward Rushton's Rebellious Poetics, 1782–1814* (Liverpool: Liverpool University Press, 2014), introduction and chap. 1. On Palmer's cosmopolitanism, see Eric R. Schlereth, *An Age of Infidels: The Politics of Religious Controversy in the Early United States* (Philadelphia: University of Pennsylvania Press, 2013), 95–98. On cosmopolitanism, see also Cotlar, *Tom Paine's America*, chap. 2; Philipp Ziesche, *Cosmopolitan Patriots: Americans in Paris in the Age of Revolution* (Charlottesville: University of Virginia Press, 2010).

29. *American Citizen*, February 7, 1804, p. 3 ("Moral"), February 21, 1804, p. 2 ("Rights of Man"), July 4, 1805, p. 2 ("genuine"), January 29, 1806, p. 3 ("conflicting"). On Palmer's plans to complete "Political World" and resume the *Prospect*, see Elihu Palmer to Hunter, September 6, 1805, Robert Hunter Correspondence.

30. Edward Rushton to Robert Hunter, April 21, 1806. Robert Hunter Correspondence. Rushton could not have heard the news of Palmer's death in only three weeks. The hospital on Pine Street did not accept contagious patients, nor did Palmer receive treatment from the Philadelphia Dispensary, whose doctors offered house calls and pharmaceuticals for the poor. A list of dispensary patients, their illnesses, and outcomes shows that no patient treated by the dispensary for pleurisy in 1806 died of the disease. Outpatients at Dispensary, 1797–1817, vol. #195-B, 93. Pennsylvania Hospital Historic Collections, Philadelphia. Benjamin Rush also did not treat Palmer. Rush kept two, sometimes three, medical ledgers simultaneously, and none lists Palmer. Rush Family Papers, Historical Society of Pennsylvania, Philadelphia.

31. *Prospect*, February 9, 1805, pp. 42–43.

32. Palmer, "Political World," 21 ("inherent properties"); *Green Mountain Patriot* (Peacham, VT), May 20, 1806, p. 1 (*"he died"*). He is not listed in *Index to Registration of Deaths, City of Philadelphia, 1803–1860*, ed. Charles Barker (Philadelphia: Philadelphia Department of Records, 1962) https://www.familysearch.org/search/catalog/250135?availability= Family%20History%20Library.

33. Mary Palmer to Robert Hunter, Sept. 3, 1806, Robert Hunter Correspondence.

34. *Merrimack Magazine and Ladies' Literary Cabinet* (Massachusetts), April 12, 1806, p. 140 ("well known"); *United States Gazette* (Philadelphia), April 2, 1802, p. 3 ("apostle of Atheism"); *True Republican* (Norwich, CT), April 30, 1806, p. 3 ("Citizen Elihu Palmer"); *Augusta Chronicle*, April 26, 1806, p. 3 ("preferred poverty"); *Green Mountain Patriot*, May 20, 1806, p. 1 ("Enemy to Persecution").

35. Palmer's book was reprinted in England in 1819 and 1823. George Henry Evans published Palmer's *Principles of Nature* in New York (1830) and New Jersey (1840), and a final London edition appeared in 1841. Then Palmer's book did not appear in print for nearly 150 years. In 1990, the philosophy professor Kerry S. Walters republished the third edition of Palmer's *Principles of Nature*. Since then, scanned facsimiles of the book have appeared as small print runs, on-demand publishing, or on internet archives and open libraries. See, for

example, Truth Seeker Co., Inc., 2010; Nabu Press, 2012; Theclassics.Us, 2013; Forgotten Books, 2016.

Epilogue

1. Moncure D. Conway, *The Life of Thomas Paine*, (repr., New York: Benjamin Blom, 1969), 305–306 ("fit of apoplexy," "took me," "mental faculties"); that "Mrs. Elihu Palmer, in her penury, was employed by Paine to attend to his rooms, etc., during a few months of illness," is on 316; Mary Palmer to Robert Hunter, Sept. 3, 1806 ("sell my," "As soon," "never leave"), Robert Hunter Correspondence, Manuscripts and Archives Division, New York Public Library, New York Astor, Lenox, and Tilden Foundations. That Mary Palmer tended the ailing Paine and that William Carver charged Paine for a twenty-two-week stay for himself, and twelve weeks for Mrs. Palmer, is noted in Gilbert Vale, *Life of Thomas Paine* [. . .] (New York: published by the author, Beacon Office, 1841), 148–150.

2. Conway, *Life of Thomas Paine*, p. 312 ("Cheetham"), 325 (Fellows's quote).

3. Richard Carlile, *Republican*, March 15, 1822, p. 325. The dialogue between Paine and Mary Palmer is recounted in James Cheetham, *The Life of Thomas Paine* (New York: Southwick and Pelsue, 1809), 186–187.

4. Thomas Haynes to Robert Hunter, c/o Edward Rushton, bookseller, Liverpool, October 30, 1807 ("Mrs. Holdron"), Robert Hunter Correspondence; John Fellows, comp., *Posthumous Pieces of Elihu Palmer* (London: R. Carlile, 1824), 3 ("bigoted sister"); Conway, *Life of Thomas Paine*, 303 (Mary Palmer published Paine's essay), 319 (home of her niece); will of Thomas Paine, Thomas Paine National Historical Association, New Rochelle, NY, http://thomaspaine.org/essays/other/the-will-of-thomas-paine.html (bequeathed). Mary Palmer's obituary appeared in the *New-York Weekly Museum*, November 9, 1816, p. 31.

5. One Benjamin Franklin Palmer, born in the right time frame to be one of Elihu Palmer's sons, turned out to be a cousin from the Stonington branch of the Palmer family. See *The Diary of Benjamin F. Palmer, Privateersman*, Acorn Club Publications 11 (New Haven, CT: Tuttle, Morehouse & Taylor, 1914); *Windham Herald* (Windham, CT), March 30, 1810, (obituary of Palmer Sr.); Donald R. Holland, "Volney B. Palmer: The Nation's First Advertising Agency Man," *Pennsylvania Magazine of History and Biography* 98, no. 3 (July 1974): 353–381. Volney's older brother, Strange N. Palmer, became a state senator in New Jersey, as did Strange's grandson, Robert M. Palmer, who served as President Lincoln's minister to Argentina.

6. John Stewart, *Opus Maximum* (London, 1803), xxii, 228 ("cheerful"). The introduction to an 1842 reprint of Stewart's work mentions that his pamphlet, *The Conquest of the Moral World*, was "written and printed in America, 1806." A New York acquaintance noted in October 1807 that Stewart had left for Liverpool about twelve months ago. See Thomas Haynes to Robert Hunter, October 30, 1807, Robert Hunter Correspondence. The Deistical Society continued for "some years" after Palmer's death and then closed; see Fellows, *Posthumous Pieces*, 9; John Stewart, *Roll of a Tennis Ball, Through the Moral World* (Dublin, 1812). On Stewart's life back in London, see Gregory Claeys, "'The Only Man of Nature That Ever Appeared in the World': 'Walking' John Stewart and the Trajectories of Social Radicalism, 1790–1822," *Journal of British Studies* 53, no. 3 (July 2014): 636–659; Bertrand Harris Bronson, "Walking Stewart," in *Facets of the Enlightenment: Studies in English Literature and Its Contexts* (Berkeley: University of California Press, 1968), 266–297; [William Thomas Brande], *The Life and Adventures of the Celebrated Walking Stewart: Including his Travels in the East Indies, Turkey, Germany, & America; By a Relative.* (London: Printed for E. Wheatley . . . by J. Davy, 1822); "John Stewart, Esquire: Better Known by the Name of Walking Stewart," in *The Annual Biography and Obituary, For the Year 1823* (London, 1823), 101–109.

7. Thomas de Quincey, "Walking Stewart" (1823), in *The Works of Thomas de Quincey* (London: Pickering & Chatto, 2000), 3: 132–142. De Quincey believed that Stewart was not

prosecuted for blasphemy because the authorities deemed him crazy. Both Stewart's and Palmer's essays were reprinted in *The Bible of Nature and Substance of Virtue: Condensed from the Scriptures of Eminent Cosmians, Pantheists and Physiphilanthropists, of Various Ages and Climes* (Albany, NY: C. van Benthuysen, 1842).

8. G. Adolf Koch, *Republican Religion: The American Revolution and the Cult of Reason* (New York: Henry Holt, 1933), 298. Carlile knew of the friendship between Stewart and Palmer and believed "the Principles of Nature, by Elihu Palmer originated from this intimacy." Richard Carlile, *Republican*, March 15, 1822, p. 325. On Carlile, see Joel H. Wiener, *Radicalism and Freethought in Nineteenth-Century Britain: The Life of Richard Carlile* (Westport, CT: Greenwood Press, 1983); and Joss Marsh, *Word Crimes: Blasphemy, Culture, and Literature in Nineteenth-Century England* (Chicago: University of Chicago Press, 1998), chap. 1.

9. John Fellows to Thomas Jefferson, October 3, 1825; Thomas Jefferson to John Fellows, March 9, 1826; both in Thomas Jefferson Papers, Series 1: General Correspondence, Library of Congress, Washington, DC.

10. *Beacon* (New York), November 5, 1836; Horace Traubel, *With Walt Whitman in Camden* (New York: M. Kennerley, 1914), 139. Whitman also quoted in Conway, *Life of Paine*, 325; "Song of Myself," in Walt Whitman, *Selected Poems* (New York: Charles L. Webster, 1892), 110. Fellows published a book of his own, *An Exposition of the Mysteries, or, Religious Dogmas and Customs of the Ancient Egyptians, Pythagorans, and Druids* (New York: printed for the author, 1835) that sought to demystify Masonic ritual and depict freemasons as unthreatening to the nation. Fellows died in 1844 at age eighty-five. For details of his life, see George L. Stevens, "John Fellows: A Minor American Deist," (master's thesis, University of Maryland, 1956).

11. On vitalism and Romanticism, see Sharon Rustin, *Shelley and Vitality* (Houndsmills, UK: Palgrave, 2005); and Denise Gigante, *Life: Organic Form and Romanticism* (New Haven, CT: Yale University Press, 2009). On various kinds of belief in sacred nature, see Catherine L. Albanese, *Nature Religion in America: From the Algonkian Indians to the New Age* (Chicago: University of Chicago Press, 1990). For the longer history of thinking about self-activating matter, see Jessica Riskin, *The Restless Clock: A History of the Centuries-Long Argument over What Makes Living Things Tick* (Chicago: University of Chicago Press, 2016). For the deep ecology movement, see Carolyn Merchant, *Radical Ecology: The Search for a Livable World*, 2nd ed. (New York: Routledge, 2005). The idea of active matter is receiving increased attention from scholars of "new materialism," who describe "thing-power" as the active impulsion of matter, a propensity or striving of sorts that occurs even without sentience. For example, the unpredictable ways of electricity, the slow but ceaseless action of rust, and the transformation within a compost pile show that agency lies not in humans alone and that nonhuman materials play a role in public life. These scholars suggest that we live and act in a world that is the product of the interplay of human and nonhuman forces. See Jane Bennett, *Vibrant Matter: A Political Ecology of Things* (Durham, NC: Duke University Press, 2010); and Timothy LeCain, *The Matter of History: How Things Create the Past* (Cambridge: Cambridge University Press, 2017).

12. Recent work on nineteenth-century religious freethinkers includes Leigh Eric Schmidt, *Village Atheists: How America's Unbelievers Made Their Way in a Godly Nation* (Princeton, NJ: Princeton University Press, 2016); and Christopher Grasso, *Skepticism and American Faith: From the Revolution to the Civil War* (New York: Oxford University Press, 2018). On Protestant pushback and the limits to religious freedom in the nineteenth century, see David Sehat, *The Myth of American Religious Freedom* (Oxford: Oxford University Press, 2011).

13. Thomas Jefferson to Dr. Benjamin Waterhouse, June 26, 1822, Founders Online, founders.archivee.gov; Thomas Paine, *Age of Reason*, in Eric Foner, ed., *Thomas Paine: Collected Writings* (New York: The Library of America, 1995), 713.

14. *General Advertiser* (Philadelphia), March 17, 1792, p. 3.

INDEX

Figures are indicated by page numbers followed by *fig*.

abolition, 50, 79–80, 231–32. *See also* Philadelphia Abolition Society
Adams, John, 3, 4, 118, 191, 194, 207, 213, 216
African Americans: in Augusta, 78–79; in Connecticut, 18, 23, 78; in New York City, 134; in Philadelphia, 92–93, 102, 121–22; yellow fever and, 122. *See also* abolition; Allen, Richard; Jones, Absalom; slavery
Age of Reason (Paine): controversy over, 149, 178, 187; deism and, 66; influence on Palmer, 137–40, 144–45, 147–48, 150, 197, 206; publication of, 5, 135, 137; rejection of Christianity in, 137–38, 197
Aitkin, Robert, 100
Alien and Sedition Acts, 185, 189, 194, 204
Allen, Ethan, 186
Allen, Richard, 122
Allen, Thomas, 45–46, 48–49, 51
American Bible Society, 247
American Citizen, 195, 207, 215
American Geography (Morse), 76–77, 83–84, 110, 116, 119
American politics: election of 1800, 191, 206–7; French relations and, 184–85, 188–89; impact of French Revolution, 115, 117; partisanship in, 4, 195, 206–7, 209–11; political sermons and, 46, 49, 51; politics of freethought and, 185–86, 220–21; ratification of the Constitution and, 48; Revolutionary war and, 49, 51, 168. *See also* Democratic-Republican societies; Federalists; Republicans

American Revolution, 14, 26–27, 39, 49, 51, 55
American Tract Society, 247
Anderson, Alexander, 166–67
Annan, Robert, 100
Arch Street Ferry, Philadelphia (Birch), 94*fig*.
Arianism, 44, 258n22
Arminianism, 40, 47
Arnold, Benedict, 22, 29, 31, 213
atheism: deism and, 66–67, 193; French revolutionaries and, 174, 183–86; "manism" and, 139; Paine and, 209
Augusta Chronicle, 74–76, 190, 239

Bache, Benjamin Franklin, 193
Bard, John, 57, 65
Bard, Samuel, 57
Barlow, Joel, 135, 157
Bartram, John, 60
Bartram, William, 60
Bentley, William, 44
Berkshire Chronicle, 46, 52
Bible: Hargrove's interpretation of, 201–3; Paine's criticism of, 137–38; Palmer's literalist reading of, 145–48, 201–3, 227–28; as the revealed word of God, 94; theologically trained study of, 22–23
Birch, William, 94*fig*.
blasphemy: laws against, 5–6, 139, 245; Paine and, 215; Palmer and, 102, 145; public tolerance for, 112; views on Palmer's blindness and, 126

blindness: financial instability and, 169; Palmer's adjustment to, 2, 129–31, 195, 207–8, 228, 236–37; yellow fever and, 125–27
Boarding School, The (H. Foster), 45
bookstore and circulating library, 76, 135, 137, 140, 149, 215. *See also* Caritat, Hocquet; Fellows, John; Friendly Club; Smith, Elihu Hubbard
Boyd, Adam, 73–74, 128–29
Brande, William Thomas, 152*fig.*
Briggs, Isaac, 79–80
Bruno, Giordano, 38
Burr, Aaron, 210, 213

Calvinism: defenders of, 41; dissenters and, 37, 40; doctrinal disputes and, 35; Palmer's rejection of, 52, 56, 85–87; Palmer's upbringing in, 2, 26, 240; predestination and, 40, 85; Universalism and, 95
Carey, Mathew, 116–17, 121–22
Caritat, Hocquet, 135, 137
Carlile, Jane, 245
Carlile, Richard, 243, 245
Carroll, John, 204
Carver, William, 211, 242
Chauncy, Charles, 40–41
Cheetham, James, 242
Christianity: dissenters and, 37–40, 72; liberal versions of, 39–40, 112; vitalism and, 60–61. *See also* Calvinism; Congregational Church; Protestantism; religious doctrines; religious revivalism
Christianity as Old as Creation (Tindal), 178
Christianity Not Mysterious (Toland), 38
Churches Believing in the Salvation of All Men. *See* Universalism
civil religion, 109–10, 119
Clinton, Charles, 175, 208
Clinton, DeWitt, 173, 210–11
Clinton, George, 173, 210
Cogswell, Alice Fitch, 21, 25
Cogswell, James, 16*fig.*; belief in sin and redemption, 30–31; influence on Palmer, 13–15, 32–33; ministerial authority and, 21–23, 32; Palmer family and, 25–27; on Palmer's preaching, 80–82; on religious revivalism, 15, 18–21; on Revolutionary war, 26–27, 29–30; Separatist ouster of, 25; slave ownership of, 78; theological training and, 19–20, 22
Coleman, William, 212
Condorcet, Jean-Antoine-Nicolas de Caritat, 135, 140–41, 149
Congregational Church, 13, 18–19, 23, 35, 40, 44
Coquette, The (H. Foster), 45
cosmopolitanism, 49, 169, 234
Cullen, William, 59–60, 62, 125, 175–76
Cunningham, Abner, 188–89

Dartmouth College, 33–38, 255n40
Darwin, Erasmus, 61
Davenport, James, 17–18, 20
deism: atheism and, 66, 193; disavowal of holy Trinity by, 199; Driscol and, 190–93; forms of, 256n8–57n8, 269n35; impact of, 7; Paine and, 139–40; Palmer and, 1, 148, 192–94, 197, 226, 267n14, 269n35; as religious infidelity, 41; religious skepticism and, 7–8, 37–38, 41
Deistical Society of New York, 144, 210–11, 213
Deist Society of Philadelphia, 96–100
Democratic-Republican societies, 118, 133. *See also* Republicans
Denniston, David: *American Citizen*, 195, 207, 215; attacks on, 173, 178–82, 185; defense of religious expression, 181–82; Deistical Society and, 211; freethought and, 174–75, 177–78, 183; *Mirror*, 173, 178–79, 181, 187; religious oaths and, 220; *Rights of Man*, 220; support for Palmer, 173–75, 181–82, 207–8
De Quincey, Thomas, 244–45
Devotion, Ebenezer, 18, 20, 23, 25, 78
Devotion, Martha, 25–26
d'Holbach, Paul Henry Thiry, 142–43, 227
Diderot, Denis, 61, 135
Driscol, Denis: *Cork Gazette*, 191; criticism of Hargrove, 200, 204–5; criticism of Universalists, 196–97; deism and, 192–94, 200, 204; freethinker disagreements and, 191, 197–98, 200; *Temple of Reason*, 190, 192, 194–96, 199, 212, 215
Duane, William, 194
Dunlap, William, 170
Dwight, Timothy, 41, 65, 112

education: clerical, 43; legal, 69, 114; medical, 57, 59–61; standards and ideals, 14, 34–36,

46–48, 74, 234–35; Stewart's critique of, 154, 160–61. *See also* Dartmouth College; Richmond Academy
Edwards, Jonathan, 60
Emerson, Ralph Waldo, 246
Episcopal Church, 44, 71, 73–74, 91–92, 101–2
Essay on Matter, An (Ledyard), 56–57, 58*fig.*, 62, 64–66, 143

Federalists: Alien and Sedition Acts, 185, 189; anti-freethought, 174, 189, 194; anti-revolution and, 116–18, 173–74; attacks on Jefferson, 209–10, 216; attacks on Paine, 214–15; Democratic-Republican critique of, 7, 118, 174, 189, 194; *Federal Gazette*, 106, 215; Jefferson's appeasement of, 216–17, 287n20; Palmer and, 51, 114, 118, 120; religious faith and, 189, 207
Fellows, John: *Beacon*, 246; bookstore of, 135, 137, 140, 149; *Character and Doctrines of Jesus Christ*, 132; freethought and, 132, 245; friendship with Paine, 135, 137, 242–43, 246; friendship with Palmer, 114, 124–26, 132–33, 135, 226, 235, 245; on Palmer's preaching, 53, 111, 132–33; political writings and, 137, 140; publication of "Political World," 246; Stewart and, 161, 163; *Theophilanthropist*, 243
First Amendment, 5, 103, 216
First Great Awakening, 14. *See also* religious revivalism
Fitch, John, 96–98, 100, 102, 111
Foster, Hannah Webster, 43, 45
Foster, John (Congregationalist minister), 43–45
Foster, John (Universalist minister), 235–36
Fourth of July, 48–49, 78, 118, 167, 176–77, 188
Fox, George, 98
Franklin, Benjamin, 7, 39, 99
freedom of conscience, 36–37, 67, 219
freedom of speech: blasphemy laws and, 5–6; Democratic-Republicans and, 117; infringement of, 92, 103–4; limitations of, 6, 234–35; newspaper editors and, 117, 174; Palmer's insistence on, 240–41
Freeman, James, 44
Freeman, Jonathan, 174, 182–83, 185–89
Freemasonry, 76
freethought: church leader opposition to, 99–100; college campuses and, 37, 41; disagreement among, 190–91, 193–94, 197–201, 204–5; human capacity and, 141; Newburgh lectures and, 173–82; objection to school prayer, 208; partisanship and, 189, 207, 210–11; in Philadelphia, 96–99; politics of, 220–21; public tolerance for, 7, 112, 173–75, 241, 247; as religious infidelity, 99, 112; social costs of, 6, 99, 112; theological philosophers and, 140–44
French Revolution, 3, 115, 117, 186, 233–34
Freneau, Philip, 167, 169–70, 211
Friendly Club, 148–49, 170

Gage, Thomas, 27
Gay, Ebenezer, 43
Gazette (Philadelphia), 209–10, 213–14
gender: condition of women, 43, 45, 231–32; male contest for authority, 41–42, 74, 84–87, 183; male sociability, 36, 43, 75–76, 140–44, 148–49
General Atlas (Carey), 116
Gibbons, Edward, 227
Godwin, William, 140–41, 149, 158, 227
Goethe, Johann, 61
Goshen Repository, 178–79, 181, 187–88
Green, Ashbel: correspondence with Hazard, 122–23; *Letter to the Preacher of Liberal Sentiments*, 109*fig.*; public ridiculing of Palmer, 99–100, 104, 107–8, 110, 113; on Universalist infidelity, 112

Haiti, 4, 233. *See also* Saint Domingue slave rebellion
Hargrove, John: biblical interpretation and, 201–3; critique of Palmer by, 200–203; freethinker disagreements and, 191, 197, 199–200, 204–5; Jefferson and, 218–19; opposition to Trinitarian doctrines, 198–99; Swedenborgians and, 191, 197–99, 203–4; *Temple of Truth*, 200, 202*fig.*, 204
Hazard, Ebenezer: correspondence with Green, 122–23; correspondence with Morse, 108, 122, 130–31; on Palmer and Universalism, 95; public ridiculing of Palmer, 100, 104, 108, 112
Hedges, Phineas, 174–77, 183, 186, 188
Helvétius, 154, 227
heresy: Arian and, 44; freethought and, 218; Palmer on, 85–86, 106, 110; Socinian view of Jesus and, 102, 105; Universalism and, 94–95. *See also* blasphemy

298　Index

Hollis, John, 199
Holmes, Oliver Wendell, 45
Hume, David, 36, 227
Hunter, Robert, 236
Huntington, Samuel, 27

Illuminati conspiracy, 1, 184, 186, 210–14
Israel, Israel, 94–95, 121, 128

Jay Treaty, 129
Jefferson, Thomas: appeasement of Federalists, 216–17, 287n20; deism and, 7; election of 1800, 191–92, 194, 204, 206–7; Federalist attacks on, 209–10, 216–17; freedom of conscience and, 36–37, 67, 219; freethought and, 99, 213, 217–19; Hargrove and, 218–19; *Notes on the State of Virginia*, 36; Paine and, 209–10, 214, 216–17, 219, 245–46; Unitarianism and, 247–48
Johnston, John, 178, 183, 188–89
Jones, Absalom, 122
Judaism, prejudice against, 84, 203

Krafft, Mary, 96–97

Ledyard, Isaac: *Essay on Matter*, 56–57, 58*fig.*, 62, 64–66, 143; materialism and, 62–65; medical education and, 57, 59, 61; Palmer and, 55–56, 64, 66, 69; on sensate matter, 8, 151; vitalism and, 56–57, 59, 61–62, 66, 68, 125, 142–43
Ledyard, John, 56, 62
Letters to Serena (Toland), 38
Letter to the Preacher of Liberal Sentiments, A (Green), 109*fig.*, 110
liberal theology: Palmer and, 53–54, 66–67, 72; Unitarianism and, 43–44; Universalism and, 40
Life and Adventures of the Celebrated Walking Stewart, The (Brande), 152*fig.*
Lindsey, Theophilus, 44
Livingston, Edward, 211
Locke, John, 36
Longstreet, William, 79

matter, 38, 56–57, 61, 67, 142–43, 293n11. *See also* sensate matter; vitalism
Mayhew, Jonathan, 44
meditative contemplation, 155–56, 164
Middleton, Peter, 57, 61–62

miracles: dissenters and, 36–37, 56, 132; Hargrove on, 201–3; Palmer on, 67, 140, 201, 248; Universalism and, 95
Mirror (Newburgh, NY), 173, 178–79, 181, 187. *See also* Denniston, David
morality: Christianity and, 147; natural world and, 2, 4, 131, 146–48, 167, 195, 223–24, 241; Protestantism and, 5, 9; religious faith and, 3–4, 14, 147, 189; religious freedom and, 3, 5; science of, 120, 141, 167–69; sensate matter and, 5; traditional church authority and, 18–19
Morse, Jedidiah: correspondence with Palmer, 82–86, 110, 115–16; fears of atheist conspiracy, 184, 211; on Palmer's infidelity, 112, 184; theological disagreements with Palmer, 41–42, 72, 77, 84–87, 108, 110, 184. *See also American Geography* (Morse)

National Gazette, 1, 91, 101, 216
nationalism. *See* cosmopolitanism; Fourth of July
Native Americans, 18, 24, 49
natural world: divine power and, 139, 142; divine revelation and, 60; morality and, 2, 4, 120, 131, 146–48, 167, 195, 223–24, 241; scientific principles of, 164, 169; sensate matter and, 168, 232, 240
New Jerusalem Church (Baltimore), 198, 204
New Light revivalism, 17, 32–33, 55, 60
newspapers: battle over freethought in, 178–82, 186–88, 194–95; deist, 190–92; freedom of speech and, 5, 92, 103, 174; Palmer's complaint of religious persecution in, 103–4; Palmer's essays in, 46, 52, 74–75; persecution of Republican editors, 185, 194; ridiculing of Palmer in, 104–8, 178–79
New York City, 133–35, 136*fig.*, 137, 144
Nisbet, Charles, 108

Old Light ministers, 18, 23
Oswald, John, 158–59

Paine, Elisha, 19–20, 40
Paine, Solomon, 19–20, 23
Paine, Thomas: *American Crisis*, 208; American turn against, 208–10, 214–16; on the Bible, 227; correspondence with Palmer, 206; critique of Christianity by, 2, 5–6, 9, 137–40, 209; deism and, 139–40; Fellows

Index

and, 135, 137, 243, 246; on inequalities of wealth, 230–31; influence on Palmer, 137–40, 144–45, 147–48, 206, 222; Jefferson and, 209–10, 214, 217, 219, 245–46; Mary Palmer's care for, 242–43; revolution and, 233–34; *Rights of Man*, 158; Stewart and, 154, 157, 244; support for *Prospect*, 227. *See also Age of Reason* (Paine)

Palmer, Elihu: anti-Federalism and, 118, 120; blindness from yellow fever, 2, 125–27, 129–30, 169, 195, 207–8, 228, 236–37; church leader opposition to, 1–2, 5, 91–92, 101–3, 110–11; death of, 238–39, 242; death of first wife, 124–25; deism and, 7–9, 148, 192–94, 197, 226, 267n14, 269n35; on ethical conduct, 2, 4–5, 9–10; Fellows and, 114, 124–26, 132–33, 135, 226, 245; Fitch and, 100–102, 111; free speech and, 6, 104, 117, 241; freethinker philosophy and, 140–44, 148–49, 169, 174, 190–91, 240–41; human equality and, 164; on human perfectibility, 75, 166, 169, 177, 232–33, 235, 248; idealism of, 232–33; marriage to Mary Powell, 223; meditative contemplation and, 164; ministry in Augusta, 128–29, 131; on miracles, 140, 201, 248; on morality, 120, 222–24, 248; Morse and, 41–42, 72, 77, 82–87, 110, 115–16, 119, 184; natural world and, 164–65, 169, 195, 232, 240–41, 247; Paine's influence on, 137–40, 144–45, 147–48, 206, 222; political engagement and, 129–30; proto-Unitarian beliefs, 111; as public freethinker, 2, 6–7, 111, 115, 144–48; public oratory and, 117–20, 137, 167–70; public ridiculing of, 104–13; rejection of Christianity, 2, 5–6, 8–9, 145–48; on religious freedom, 1, 5, 52, 87, 119; religious persecution complaint, 103–8; resilience and, 127, 131, 170; retreat from Philadelphia, 113–15; revolution and, 232, 234; science of morality and, 167–69; sensate matter and, 4–5, 8, 150–54, 161, 163–64, 166, 193, 240, 279n31; social respectability and, 129–30; Socinian view of Jesus and, 66, 83–85, 95, 101–2, 105, 269n35; Stewart's influence on, 150–54, 161, 163, 166, 170, 222, 229; Universalism and, 93–96, 100, 147, 269n35; vitalism and, 4–5, 163–65, 246–47

—*Early career*: critique of slavery, 78–79; first marriage, 81–83; law studies, 72–73, 93;

Ledyard and, 55–56, 64, 66, 69; liberal theology and, 66–67; ministry in Augusta, 73–74, 77–78, 82; ministry in Newtown, 53–57, 68–70; public oratory and, 71–72, 74; Richmond Academy employment, 72–73, 82; social respectability and, 76, 78–80; unconventional ideas and, 68–69; vitalism and, 57, 66–68

—*Education and youth*: clerical training and, 35, 41, 43; church authority and, 13–15, 31; Dartmouth College and, 33–34, 42–43, 255n40; Federalist sympathies, 51–52; on freedom of conscience, 50; impact of Revolutionary war, 27–30; intellectual stimulation in college, 36–37; liberal theology and, 53–54; mentorship with Rev. Allen, 45–49; mentorship with Rev. Foster, 43–45; oration on American freedom, 48–52; Price's influence on, 39–40; public persona in early writings, 46–48, 52–53; Puritan lineage of, 24; Rev. Cogswell's influence on, 13–15, 26, 32–33

—*Lecture tours*: attacks on Denniston, 173, 179–82, 185; Baltimore, 200–201; controversy over, 173, 182–83, 188–89; discrediting of freethought, 210–11; hostility toward Hargrove, 197–98; Illuminati accusations and, 210–14; Newburgh, 173–84, 186–89, 208; Philadelphia, 195–97, 208, 237–38; political lectures of, 207, 237; public ridiculing of, 178–79; religious infidelity accusations, 173–74, 178–79, 182–85

—*Writings*: *American Geography*, 83–84, 110, 116; *Augusta Chronicle* essays, 74–75; *Berkshire Chronicle* essays, 46, 52; *An enquiry relative to the moral & political improvement of the human species*, 168–69; "Extracts from an Oration, Delivered at Federal Point, near Philadelphia, on the Fourth of July, 1793," 118–20; *Federal Gazette and Philadelphia Daily Advertiser*, 106–7; *General Advertiser*, 102–4; *Massachusetts Spy* essays, 52; *An oration pronounced in the Meeting House in Pittsfield, upon the Twelfth anniversary of the Independence of the United States of America*, 49–52; *Original Sin, Atonement, Faith, &c.: A Christmas Discourse delivered in New-York, December 1796*, 145–48; "Political World, The," 237, 243, 246; *Prospect; or,*

Palmer, Elihu (*continued*)
    View of the Moral World, 222–24, 225*fig.*, 226–29, 231, 235. *See also Principles of Nature* (Palmer)
Palmer, Elihu, Sr. (father), 14, 24–28, 31, 243
Palmer, John, 24
Palmer, Lois Foster, 14, 24–25
Palmer, Mary Powell: care of Paine, 242–43; collaboration with Palmer, 223, 229, 235–36; death of Palmer and, 239; marriage to Palmer, 223; work on *Principles of Nature*, 195
Palmer, Nathan, 24, 26, 81, 112–15, 243–44
Palmer, Thaddeus, 26–28, 81
Palmer, Volney B., 244
panentheism, 143, 263n26
pantheism, 39
Pantheisticon (Toland), 38
perfectibility, 9, 75, 141, 146–47, 169, 248. *See also* Condorcet, Jean-Antoine-Nicolas de Caritat; Godwin, William; Price, Richard
Philadelphia: diverse economic life in, 92–93; freethinkers in, 96–100; opposition to freethought in, 99–100; Palmer's lectures in, 195–97, 208, 237–38; religious denominations in, 93; yellow fever in, 121–25
Philadelphia Abolition Society, 79
"Political World, The" (Palmer), 237, 243, 246
Pope, Alexander, 61
Powell, Benjamin, 133, 195, 223
Powell, Mary. *See* Palmer, Mary Powell
predestination, 37, 40–41, 85
Presbyterian Church: Newtown and, 55–56, 69; Philadelphia and, 99–100, 104
Price, Richard, 39–40, 50, 52, 75, 78
Priestley, Joseph, 44, 111, 167
Principles of Nature (Palmer): condemnation of, 215; exegesis of the Bible in, 228; Illuminati accusations and, 212–13; influence of Ledyard on, 66; Jefferson and, 217–18; morality based on natural world in, 195; Paine on, 206; publication of, 7, 195, 239–40, 242, 245; on sensate matter, 193, 207–8; understanding of God in, 67
Proofs of a Conspiracy against All the Religions and Governments of Europe (Robison), 183–86, 211
Prospect; or, View of the Moral World, 222–24, 225*fig.*, 226–29, 231, 235

Prospectus of a Series of Lectures (Stewart), 162*fig.*
Protestantism: anti-Catholicism and, 247; Calvinism and, 2, 26, 35, 37, 40–41; doctrinal disputes, 35; freethought and, 112; morality and, 5, 9; religious dissenters and, 37; religious liberals and, 6, 9, 35; religious revivalism and, 14–15, 17–21, 23; traditional church authority and, 18–19; Trinitarian doctrine and, 198–99. *See also* Congregational Church

Quakers, 79, 93, 160

religious doctrines: Arianism, 44, 258n22; Arminianism, 40; Congregationalism, 13, 18–19, 23, 35, 40, 44; Socinianism, 44, 54, 66, 80, 101–2, 105, 258n22, 269n35; Swedenborgianism, 198–99; Trinitarianism, 37, 44; Unitarianism, 43–44, 198; Universalism, 93–95. *See also* Calvinism
religious establishment, 18–19
religious experience, 13–15, 17–18, 64, 67–68, 163–65
religious freedom, 1, 3, 5, 7, 52, 87, 119, 205, 216
religious infidelity: deism as, 41; fears of European conspiracy for, 183–88; freedom of speech and, 174; freethought as, 99, 112; Palmer and, 101, 104, 126, 173–74, 178–79, 182–85; social order and, 174
religious intolerance, 192, 200, 204–5
religious revivalism: beliefs of salvation and perfectionism, 20–21; defiance of official church by, 19–20; emotional experience and, 14–15, 17–20; extemporaneous prayer and, 18; Old Light condemnation of, 23; regeneration and, 17, 19; religious authority and, 18; Separatists and, 18, 23–25; spiritual authority and, 252n8; traveling ministers and, 15
religious skepticism, 8, 37–38, 40–41, 60–61, 99
Republicans: attacks on Palmer, 210–12; critique of Adams administration, 185, 194; critique of Federalists, 7, 118, 120; critique of Washington administration, 117; free speech and, 174; Illuminati accusations and, 210–13; Jay Treaty and, 129; leadership battles among, 207; Palmer's oratory and,

115, 117–18, 133; politics of freethought and, 177, 221; support for France, 117, 173. *See also* Democratic-Republican societies
Revelation of Nature, The (Stewart), 151–53
Richmond Academy, 71–73, 82, 128
Rickman, Thomas Clio, 158, 215
Rights of Man (newspaper), 220
Rights of Man (Paine), 158
Riker, James, 69
Riker, John, 55, 68
Robison, John, 183–86, 211
Rochambeau, Jean-Baptiste, 28
Rodgers, John, 53
Rousseau, Jean-Jacques, 36, 227
Ruggles, John, 5, 139
Ruins (Volney), 142–44, 151, 187
Rush, Benjamin: on body's vital force, 59–61, 125; on need for moral citizenry, 3, 4; on Palmer's blindness, 126; Stewart and, 157, 161; yellow fever treatment and, 120–21, 123–25
Rushton, Edward, 129, 236–37

Saint Domingue slave rebellion, 4, 110, 117, 233
Saybrook Platform, 18–19
school prayer, 208
sensate matter: Ledyard on, 8, 151; morality and, 5; natural world and, 168, 232, 240; Palmer on, 4–5, 8, 150–54, 161, 163–64, 166, 193, 240, 279n31; revolutionaries and, 160; Stewart on, 150–55, 159–60, 163, 166, 229–30
Shays's Rebellion, 46, 51
slavery, 23, 50–51, 78–80, 134. *See also* abolition; African Americans
Smith, Elihu Hubbard, 148–49, 166
Smith, John Blair, 100, 104, 106, 112
Smith, Mary, 21
Smith, Mehetabel, 21
Smith, Samuel Stanhope, 104
social order, 3–4, 24, 174
Society of Deist Natural Philosophers (Universal Society). *See* Deist Society of Philadelphia
Society of Social Friends (Dartmouth), 36
Society of Universal Baptists. *See* Universalism
Socinianism: as heresy, 102, 112; liberal Protestantism and, 80; Palmer and, 54, 66, 84–85, 101–2, 104–5, 148, 269n35; views of Jesus and, 44, 258n22
Spinoza, Benedict de, 38, 154
Standish, Myles, 24, 114
Stewart, John "Walking," 152*fig.*; De Quincey and, 244–45; disavowal of religion by, 150, 156–57, 224, 226; Fellows and, 161, 163; freethinkers and, 157–58, 229; *Great Essay to Systematize the Moral World*, 224; influence on Palmer, 150–54, 161, 163, 166, 170, 222; meditative contemplation and, 155–56; Paine and, 154, 244; *Prospectus of a Series of Lectures*, 162*fig.*; *Revelation of Nature*, 151; revolutionaries and, 159; *Roll of a Tennis Ball Through the Moral World*, 244; sensate matter and, 8, 150–55, 159–60, 163, 166, 229–30, 245; social experimentation interests, 160; travels of, 155; vegetarianism and, 158, 161
Stiles, Ezra, 41
Stoicism, 47–48
St. Paul's Episcopal Church (Augusta, GA), 71, 73–74
Swedenborg, Emanuel, 198
Swedenborgians, 191, 197–99, 204. *See also* Hargrove, John

Taylor, John, 235
Telfair, Edward, 71, 129
Temple of Reason, 190, 192, 194–96, 199–200, 212, 215
Temple of Truth, 200, 202*fig.*, 204
Tennent, Gilbert, 17
Theological Works of Thomas Paine, The, 245
Time Piece, and Literary Companion (Freneau), 169–70
Tindal, Matthew, 178, 187
Toland, John, 38–39
Transcendentalism, 246
Triumph of Infidelity, The (Dwight), 41, 65
Trumbull, Jonathan, 28

Unitarianism, 43–44, 111, 198–99
United Fraternity (Dartmouth), 36
United Irishmen, 191, 194
Universalism: acceptance of Palmer, 236; Calvinist critique of, 94–95; Jesus as divine savior in, 93–95; rejection of Palmer, 93–96, 100, 196–97; universal salvation and, 40–41, 95

Universal Society (Deist Society), 96. *See also* Fitch, John
Utopian communities, 160

Vale, Gilbert, 246
vegetarianism, 158, 160–61
Virginia Statute for Religious Freedom, 219
vitalism: Christianity and, 57, 60, 66–67; Ledyard and, 56–57, 59, 61–62, 66, 68, 125, 142–43; literature and, 61; matter and, 56–57, 62; medical, 57, 59–61, 175–76; religious doubt and, 60–61; social transformation and, 4–5, 159–60, 163–65, 177, 229–30, 240–41
Voigt, Henry, 96–98
Volney, Constantin-François, 140–44, 149, 151, 187
Voltaire, 135, 227

Washington, George: Democratic-Republican critique of, 117–18, 129; Paine and, 149, 208–9, 216; Revolutionary war and, 28; thanksgiving proclamation, 71; visit to Richmond Academy, 82, 134
Webster, Daniel, 36
Webster, Hannah. *See* Foster, Hannah Webster
Wharton, Charles Henry, 65
Wheelock, Eleazar, 17, 33, 35
Wheelock, John, 35, 42
White, William, 91, 101–2, 105, 111–12, 119
Whitefield, George, 15, 17, 55
Whitman, Walt, 246–47
Whytt, Robert, 59
Wilkinson, Mary, 20–21
Winfield, Elias, 175
Witherspoon, John, 104, 108
Wollstonecraft, Mary, 61, 158
Wood, John, 210–12
Wordsworth, William, 159

Yale College, 41–42
yellow fever, 121–25

ACKNOWLEDGMENTS

My thanks begin with the archivists and librarians who preserve and provide access to the archival sources that made this book possible. I first encountered the work of Elihu Palmer at the marvelous American Antiquarian Society in Worcester, Massachusetts, where I did much of my research over numerous visits. I appreciate the expert staff at the AAS, including Ashley Cataldo, Curator of Manuscripts, who procured images for the book. The staff at the Library Company of Philadelphia, especially Librarian James Green and Ann McShane (now at Emory University), provided valuable assistance, as did the archivists at the Historical Society of Pennsylvania. Special thanks to Mariam Touba and Tammy Kiter at the New-York Historical Society, to Stacey Peeples at the Pennsylvania Hospital Historic Collections, Philadelphia, and to James R. Miller at the Sheffield Historical Society in Massachusetts. I appreciate the help I received from archivists at the Berkshire Athenaeum in Pittsfield, the Connecticut State Library and Archives, the Historical Society in Hartford, the Yale University Manuscripts and Archives, the New York Public Library, Gallaudet University, the Library of Congress, and the University of Wisconsin Archive. Kevin P. Ring Sr. in Scotland, Connecticut, sent helpful information by email, as did Carol Waggoner-Angleton, Special Collections librarian at Augusta University's Reese Library, and Peter Carini and Laura Schieb at the Rauner Special Collections Library at Dartmouth College. I am grateful to the excellent staff at the University of Minnesota's Wilson Library. My thanks go to Marguerite Ragnow and Timothy Johnson at UMN's James Ford Bell Library, and to Jennifer Claybourne in the Digital Library Services Department. The Interlibrary Loan Department, I know for a fact, can procure most any text on the planet. I am grateful to the unsung people who digitized vast amounts of primary source material, and to the University of

Minnesota for providing access to the indispensable online Early American Imprint Series and Early American Newspaper Series.

Fellowships that enabled research trips and time away from teaching were essential to the reading, thinking, and writing that went into this book. The University of Minnesota generously provided research funding and leave time, including a McKnight Research Fellowship, a salary supplement during a fellowship, and stipends for research travel. The project took shape during the two years I spent as a visiting scholar at the Heidelberg Center for American Studies (HCA) in Germany. The first year was sponsored by a Deutsche Bank Fellowship, the second by a Fulbright Fellowship. The visionary founding director of the HCA, Detlef Junker, supported this project before it was clear what it would become, and I am grateful for his hospitality and that of Anja van der Schrieck-Junker and the colleagues at the HCA. There I received constructive feedback on early versions of my work, and I learned valuable lessons from the graduate students who took my seminar on religion and politics. I enjoyed sharing an office with Charles Postel, and I especially thank Anja Schüler and Manfred Berg for making Heidelberg a second home for me and my family. A fellowship from the Society for Historians of the Early American Republic sponsored a month at the Library Company and the Historical Society of Pennsylvania, and a Kate B. and Hall J. Peterson Research Fellowship supported research at the AAS one summer. Heartfelt thanks to these institutions and to the people who wrote letters on my behalf for these and other grants, including Nathalie Caron, William Chafe, Stephen Prothero, and JB Shank. My thanks also to UMN History Department chair, Ann Waltner, and the College of Liberal Arts for finding funds to help with printing costs.

Sometimes support for my work came in unexpected form. When I spent a research leave helping my mother care for my beloved father in the last months of his life, the department chair Elaine Tyler May and the department's Advisory Committee recognized the exigency of the moment and offered material and moral support. A most unusual gift came from my mother, Nancy Fischer. When I received a sabbatical at reduced pay, she supplemented my salary so I could take the leave from teaching. Her big-hearted generosity is the reason the book is done.

Many people have commented on my work and made it better. A long time ago, Alfred Young at the Newberry Library in Chicago supported my idea for the book, and I hope he would have liked the final result. At conferences I received constructive feedback from the audiences and commentators: Chris Beneke, John Brooke, Nathalie Caron, Joyce Chaplin, John Corrigan, Seth Cotlar, Christopher Hodson, Philippe Murillo, Monica Najar, Barbara Oberg, Janet Polasky, Amanda Porterfield, Kyle Roberts, Jonathan Sassi, Eric Schlereth, Leigh Eric Schmidt, Jon Sensbach, Maurizio Valsania, and Vikki Vickers. For their comments on individual chapters, I thank Nathalie Caron, Kathrinne Duffy, Nancy Fischer, Ann Little, Margaret Newell, Catharina Schuchmann, and members of the Atlantic History Workshop at New York University. Douglas Winiarski generously shared his unparalleled expertise with me on Chapter 1. Peter Wood recommended good books and has inspired me with his own writing. Talented writers of creative nonfiction—Mackenzie Epping, Laura Flynn, Jennifer Bowen, Rachel Moritz, and Angela Pelster-Wiebe—made excellent suggestions on two chapters. Gordon Legge and Leslye Orr helped me imagine how Palmer navigated his world without vision. Beth Cleary and the writers who gathered at the East Side Freedom Library in Saint Paul offered encouragement and the gift of creative quietude.

Colleagues and students at the University of Minnesota have inspired me for many years. Several chapters benefited from the exceptional Atlantic History Workshop, cofounded by my colleagues Katharine Gerbner and then-graduate student Joanne Jahnke-Wegner. From them and the other workshop participants I received valuable comments. Thanks to all of you! A shout out goes to Jason Eden at St. Cloud State, who sent detailed suggestions by email. JB Shank has encouraged me all along, and I appreciate his intellectual range and his generous feedback on several chapters. Helena Pohlandt-McCormick shared creative insights on an early chapter and provided strong moral support throughout. My thanks to participants in a summer colloquium of the Religious Studies Program at the University of Minnesota, and to the many undergraduates who took my course "Religion and the American Culture Wars" and grappled with longstanding American anxieties about freethought.

Parts of the book appeared previously in somewhat different form as "'Religion Governed by Terror': A Deist Critique of Fearful Christianity in the Early American Republic," *Revue Française D'Études Américaines* 125 (3e Trimestre 2010): 13–26; "Cosmic Kinship: John Stewart's 'Sensate Matter' in the Early Republic," *Common-place: The Journal of Early American Life* (Spring 2015), http://www.common-place-archives.org/vol-15/no-03/fischer/; and "Vitalism in America: Elihu Palmer's Radical Religion in the Early Republic," *William and Mary Quarterly* 73, no. 3 (July 2016): 501–530. I am grateful to editors Nathalie Caron, Amanda Porterfield, and Joshua Piker, respectively, and to the diligent outside readers for those publications, whose rigorous engagement with my work pushed me to clarify my arguments. I appreciate the publishers' permission to include revised versions here.

I am fortunate beyond words to have had brilliant readers of the entire manuscript. For years, Anne Carter, Anna Clark, and Kate Solomonson helped the book evolve. When I handed them pages of formless textual exegesis, they offered enthusiastic encouragement and concrete suggestions with nary a sign of bewildered exhaustion. At the very end, they read and commented on the whole manuscript, and I hope they recognize their influence on every page. Lisa Norling went beyond every norm of collegiality when she read the first full rough draft well before it was a pleasure to do so, and her visionary suggestions helped immensely. Drew Ross is an exceptionally talented editor whose thought-provoking questions invited me to imagine Palmer's experience and write for nonspecialist readers. Our extended conversations about Palmer's freethought helped me clarify what I most wanted to say. If the book is engaging to read, Drew is the reason, and I am grateful he took so much time from his own writing to think about mine. The unsurpassable reviewers for the press, Seth Cotlar and Erik Seeman, entered into the project and pushed on it from within, so to speak, furthering my sense of what it might say. Their guidance gave me direction for the next round of revision, and I returned to their inspiring comments over and over again. Barbara Welke's steadfast encouragement has been crucial to the book's progress. Her suggestions on the penultimate draft pushed me to place Palmer in the larger context of his time, and to clarify the stakes of his struggle. I am deeply grateful to all of these readers for their intellectual generosity.

Robert Lockhart at the University of Pennsylvania Press initiated our conversations about Palmer, waited patiently for chapters, then skillfully guided the manuscript through the review process. His sage advice about content and style improved the whole. I had the good fortune to have

Gail Schmitt assigned to my manuscript, a top-notch copyeditor whose meticulous review and fine sense of language refined the final version in ways large and small. My thanks also to managing editor, Lily Palladino, and the team at the University of Pennsylvania Press for turning computer files into a book, and to Melissa Stearns Hyde for the index.

A far-flung community of freethinkers sustains me with their friendship: Herman Bennett, Nick Biddle, Mara Brown, Nathalie Caron, Bill Chafe, Lorna Chafe, Heidi Clark-Goldfeld, Beth Cleary, Mary Ellen Curtin, Nancy Dilts, Janne Eller-Isaacs, Rob Eller-Isaacs, Carolin Emcke, Sabine Engel, Hartwig Fischer, Lisa Friedman, Christina Greene, Gurleen Grewal, Stephanie Guitard, KP Hong, Elisabeth Jay, Kathryn Jay, Ann Little, Louise Livesay-Al, Saje Mathieu, Caroline McDaniel, Helena Pohlandt-McCormick, Jennifer Morgan, Perri Morgan, Dan Philippon, Catharina Schuchmann, Susan Tobin, Kate Tucker, Tim Tyson, Barbara Welke, Bill Welke, and Wilder Welke. My parents, Nancy and Jurgen Fischer, demonstrated interest in my projects and confidence in my abilities for as long as I can remember. They modeled generosity of spirit and open-minded engagement with new ideas. Eric, Simone, Niko, and Monique Fischer have cheered me on this whole time, and the Denver Rosses are a blast. For many years, Lois Ross and I enjoyed sharing our different understanding of the material world. My love and thanks to each and every one of you.

Best of all, I get to be a family with Drew and Ava. When she was five, Ava composed this joke: "*Knock, knock.* Who's there? *Eli.* Eli who? *Elihu Palmer!*" Now she is old enough to read the book which, she has long said with convincing enthusiasm, she can hardly wait to do. Ava is a shining light of compassion, courage, and joy. Drew's deep kindness and generosity are matched by his wide-ranging intellectual curiosity. As my life partner and co-parent, Drew enabled the uncountable hours of work this project required. Drew and Ava have championed the book for a long time, engaged in plentiful conversations about an obscure freethinker, and nurtured me with loving good cheer. They are my great good fortune, and to them I am deeply grateful.

www.ingramcontent.com/pod-product-compliance
Lightning Source LLC
Chambersburg PA
CBHW021849230426
43671CB00006B/327